The
North
American
City

The North American City

FOURTH EDITION

Maurice Yeates

Queen's University
The Ontario Council on Graduate Studies
Canada

 HARPER & ROW, PUBLISHERS, New York
Grand Rapids, Philadelphia, St. Louis, San Francisco,
London, Singapore, Sydney, Tokyo

Project Editor: David Nickol
Cover Design: Wanda Lubelska Design
Art Direction: Heather A. Ziegler
Production Manager: Jeanie Berke
Production Assistant: Paula Roppolo
Compositor: ComCom Division of Haddon Craftsmen, Inc.
Printer and Binder: R. R. Donnelley & Sons, Co.
Cover Printer: Lehigh Press

The North American City, Fourth Edition
Copyright © 1990 by Harper & Row, Publishers, Inc.

Library of Congress Cataloging-in-Publication Data
Yeates, Maurice.
    The North American city. — 4th ed. / Maurice Yeates.
        p.   cm.
    Bibliography: p.
    Includes index.
    ISBN 0-06-047337-1
    1. Cities and towns—North America.   I. Title.
HT122.Y4   1989
307.76'097—dc20   89-33009
                                                          CIP

89 90 91 92 9 8 7 6 5 4 3 2 1

Acknowledgments

Since nearly all of the material cited below is also listed alphabetically by author in the reference section at the back of the book, the reader may find it easier to consult that section for further information about particular source materials used in the text.

The author and publisher wish to express their thanks for permission to reprint or modify material from copyrighted works:

Academic Press, Inc., New York, and the authors for Fig. 1, p. 375, from the *Journal of Urban Economics,* vol. 2 (paper by M. Edel and E. Sclar).

The American Academy of Political and Social Science for Figs. 1-4 and 5, pp. 8–9 and 11, from *The Annals of the American Academy of Political Science,* vol. 242, 1945 (paper by C. D. Harris and E. L. Ullman).

The editors of *Antipode* for Fig. 1, p. 26, and Tables 2(i) and 2(ii), pp. 27 and 28, vol. 6(1), 1974 (paper by D. Harvey and L. Chatterjee).

The Association of American Geographers, Washington, D.C., for the following from the *Annals of the Association of American Geographers:* data on pp. 558–559, vol. 69, 1979 (with special thanks to the author of the paper, S. H. Olson); Table 1, p. 332, vol. 76, 1986 (paper by R. A. Erickson). Also, the following from R. Abler, and J. S. Adams (eds.), *A Comparative Atlas of America's Great Cities: Twenty Metropolitan Regions,* p. 151 (map of Detroit SMSA house prices), p. 162 (map of female concentration in Minneapolis–St. Paul), and p. 22 (map of housing in Los Angeles).

The Advisory Commission on Intergovernmental Relations for the following from *Fiscal Disparities Between Central Cities and Suburbs, 1984:* extracts from Tables 1, 2, 3, 5, A-2, A-7, A-8, and A-33.

American Demographics, Inc., for the table on p. 13 of *American Demographics Magazine,* September 1981 (paper by L. H. Long and D. DeAre).

The Ballinger Publishing Company, Cambridge, Mass., for the diagram on p. 91 from J. S. Adams (ed.), *Urban Policy-Making and Metropolitan Dynamics: A Comparative Geographical Analysis, 1976* (paper by M. J. Dear).

The Brookings Institution, Washington, D.C., for Table 16, p. 243 from

The Metropolitan Transportation Problem, by W. Owen, 1966 (revised edition).

John Borchert for the diagram on p. 4 (modified and redrawn) from *Trade Centers and Trade Areas of the Upper Midwest,* by J. R. Borchert and R. B. Adams, 1963, printed by the Upper Midwest Economic Study, University of Minnesota, Minneapolis.

Irwin Clark, Publishers, for maps of land use (modified and redrawn) on Toronto on pp. 31 and 34 in *Toronto: An Urban Study,* by R. P. Baine and A. L. McMurray, 1977.

The editor and authors of the following from *Economic Geography:* Figure on p. 223, vol. 60, 1984, redrawn and modified (paper by C. L. Moore and M. Jacobson); Figures 1 and 2, vol. 41, 1965 (paper by M. Yeates); Figure on p. 324, vol. 58, 1982 (paper by A. C. Kantor and J. D. Nystuen); Figures on pp. 357, 359, 361, vol. 59, 1983 (paper by A. J. Scott); and extracts from Table 5, p. 360, vol. 61, 1985 (paper by E. J. Malecki).

The publisher of *The Economist* for the diagrams (redrawn) on p. 74, Aug. 24, 1985, and p. 72, Dec. 21, 1985.

Edward Arnold Ltd., London, for table on p. 80 from vol. 10, 1986 *International Journal of Urban and Regional Research* (paper by R. Harris).

Irene Fabbro for permission to redraw maps 4, 5, and 6 from her research paper "The Social Geography of Metropolitan Toronto: A Factorial Ecology Approach," 1986, Department of Geography, York University.

Peter Gordon for the table on p. 12 of "The Distribution of Population and Employment in a Policentric City," by P. Gordon, H. W. Richardson, and H. L. Wong (*Environment and Planning,* 1986, Vol. 18, pp. 161–173).

The editor of *Growth and Change* for Tables 2 and 3, pp. 47 and 48, vol. 13, 1982 (paper by R. L. Morrill).

Harvard University Press, Cambridge, Mass., for extracts from the table on p. 131 of B. Chinitz *Freight and the Metropolis,* 1960.

Graham Humphrys for Figure 4.9, p. 322, from "Power and Industrial Structure," in J. W. House (ed.), *The U.K. Space: Resources, Environment and the Future,* 1986 (paper by G. Humphrys).

The Geographical Society of Chicago for Figure 7.2 (redrawn and updated) from I. Cutler, *Chicago: Metropolis of the Mid-Continent,* 1976.

D. L. Huff for the diagrammatic model of factors affecting consumer space preferences and behavior on pp. 159–173, vol. 6 of *Papers and Proceedings of the Regional Science Association,* 1960 (paper by D. L. Huff).

The authors and l'Institut National de la Recherche Scientifique: Urbanisation, Montreal, for extracts from Tables 2, 3, and 4 from *La Geographic Sociale de Montreal en 1971,* by P. Foggin and M. Polese, 1976.

The editor of the *Journal of Regional Science* for the diagram on p. 418 from vol. 25, 1985 (paper by J. E. Anderson), and Table 2, p. 230 from vol. 27, 1987 (paper by J. C. Stabler).

Kendall-Hunt Publishing Co., Dubuque, Iowa, to redraw and update Fig.

10, p. 143 from *Chicago: Metropolis of the Mid-Continent,* by I. Cutler, 1976, and the author for the diagram on p. 201 in *The Los Angeles Metropolis,* by H. J. Nelson, 1983.

The Longman Group Ltd., Harlow, England, for: Fig. 22, p. 25, from *Shopping Centre Development,* by J. A. Dawson, 1983; and from *Urban Studies:* Table 1 and extracts from Table 6, pp. 209–217, vol. 22, 1985 (paper by B. Edmonston, M. A. Goldberg, and J. Mercer), and Figure 1, p. 356, vol. 14, 1977 (paper by C. E. Reid).

James Lorimer and Co., Ltd., Publishers, Toronto, for Figure 4 (modified and redrawn) from *A Citizen's Guide to City Politics,* by J. Lorimer, 1972.

McGraw-Hill Book Co., New York, for Fig. 2, p. 34, from *The Black Ghetto: A Spatial Behavioral Perspective,* by H. M. Rose, 1971, which has been updated.

Methuen and Co., Ltd., London, for table on p. 223 from *Service Industries,* by R. W. Daniels, 1985.

The Population Reference Bureau Inc., Washington, D.C., for Table 1, p. 9, from *Population Redistribution in the U.S.: Issues for the 1980s,* Population Trends and Public Policy Report, no. 3, March 1983.

R. B. Potter for Fig. 5.9, p. 159, from *The Urban Retailing System,* printed by the Gower Publishing Co., Aldershot (Eng.), 1982.

P. H. Rees for Fig. 4, p. 47, from *The Factorial Ecology of Metropolitan Chicago,* unpublished M.A. thesis, Department of Geography, University of Chicago, 1960.

The Regional Science Association for extracts from Table 2, pp. 55–80, vol. 37, 1976, in *Papers of the Regional Science Association* (paper by K. F. McCarthy).

The editor and the authors for the following from *Research Papers,* Department of Geography, University of Chicago: Table 1 from no. 85, 1963 (paper by B. J. L. Berry, R. J. Tennant, B. J. Garner, and J. W. Simmons).

Sage Publications Inc., Beverly Hills, Calif., for Fig. 1, p. 68, from *Urbanization, Planning and National Development,* by J. Friedmann, 1973; and the compilation of a table by the author from pp. 182–194 from *Small and Large Together: Governing the Metropolis,* by H. W. Hallman, 1977.

James W. Simmons for extracts from the figure on p. 64 from *Systems of Cities: Readings on Structure, Growth and Policy,* edited by L. S. Bourne and J. W. Simmons, 1978, and published by the Oxford University Press, New York.

Stanford University Press, Stanford, Calif., and the Board of Trustees of the Leland Stanford Junior University, for Figure V.14, pp. 42–43, and Table II.1, p. 4, from *Social Area Analysis: Theory, Illustrative Applications and Computational Procedures,* by E. Shevky and W. Bell, 1955.

The Minister of Supply and Services, Ottawa, Canada, for Figure 2a, p. 7, from *Land in Canada's Urban Heartland,* by M. Yeates, 1985.

The editor for Fig. 2 (redrawn with modifications), p. 301, vol. 67, from *Tijdschrift voor Economische en Sociale Geografie* (paper by H. Popp).

The University of Chicago Press for charts I and II (redrawn) from *The City,* by R. E. Park, E. W. Burgess, and R. D. McKenzie, 1925.

John Wiley and Sons, Inc., New York, for Fig. 2.1, p. 12, from *Telecommunications-Transportation Trade-Offs: Options for Tomorrow,* edited by J. M. Nilles, 1976.

V. H. Winston and Sons, Inc., for the following from *Urban Geography:* the figure on p. 135 (redrawn), vol. 6, 1985 (paper by T. C. Archer and E. R. White); modification of the table on pp. 109–110 in vol. 8, 1987 (paper by R. C. Morrill); and Fig. 4.9, p. 89, from *The Geography of Housing,* by L. S. Bourne, 1981.

Contents

Preface   *xi*

1   Cities: The Spatial View   1

Spatial Structure and Aspatial Processes   2
The Components of Urban Analysis   5
Scales of Analysis   14

2   North American Urban Development   27

Urbanization   27
Eras of Development and Waves of Accumulation   30
Urban System Development in the United States   35
The Evolution of the Canadian Urban System   60

3   Cities as Centers of Manufacturing   68

The Importance and Location of Manufacturing   68
Regional Changes in the Location of Manufacturing   73
Least-Cost Theory and the Location of Manufacturing   78
Industrial Restructuring   88

**4   Historical Perspectives on the Internal Structure and
       Growth of Urban Areas**   98

Urban Land Use   98
Historical Perspectives on Spatial Growth and Internal
Structure   100

5   **Models of Urban Land Use and Population**   **127**

Economic Rent, Land Use, and Land Values   127
Models of Urban Population Redistribution   136
Public Policy and Land-Use Change   143

6   **The Social Structure of Cities**   **148**

The Classic Ecological Model of Urban Social Space   149
Behavioral Perspectives Relating to the Analysis of
Social Structure and Change   161
Political Economy Perspectives on the Analysis of
Social Structure and Change   174
Women and Social Space   179

7   **Housing and Society**   **185**

Macro Influences on the Demand for and Supply of Housing   185
Market-Oriented Perspectives on Housing Choice and
Location   189
Behavioral Perspectives on Housing Location   195
Filtering and Public Policy   200

8   **Housing Submarkets and Urban Revitalization**   **203**

Housing Submarkets   203
Urban Revitalization   218

9   **The Location of Employment Opportunities**   **226**

The Location of Manufacturing Employment   227
The Location of Employment in Retail and Service Activities   239
The Location of Office Employment   254

10   **Managing Cities**   **261**

Disparities between Inner and Outer Cities   262
Metropolitan Finance   263
Local Government Fragmentation   272
Issues Facing Local Government   274
Toward Solutions   280

Bibliography   *289*
Index   *309*

Preface

The fourth edition of *The North American City*, like its predecessors, is intended primarily as a textbook for undergraduates, principally at universities and colleges in the United States and Canada. The aim is to provide an overview of the broad scope and increasingly diversified nature of the geographer's interests in, and contributions to, the study of cities. This overview therefore lays the foundations for more advanced study in the field relating to the book's three main themes: the organization of the city system, the internal structure of the city, and public policy relating to urban issues.

FOURTH EDITION REVISIONS

In the almost two decades since the first edition of this book appeared, urban geography has continued to evolve as an important field within the discipline. The number of courses in urban geography has proliferated, and many specialties (or subfields) such as urban social geography, urban systems, retail structure and location, and urban industrial geography have emerged as significant bodies of knowledge. Furthermore, the theoretical approaches to urban analysis have become quite diverse, often giving rise to quite different approaches to the study of urban issues.

The fourth edition of *The North American City* has been pruned and rewritten to reflect these ever-expanding urban interests and the variety of fruitful theoretical approaches that are being applied to the study of urban questions. It is perhaps impossible for any one person to address completely and with full insight the variety of perspectives utilized in modern urban geography. Nevertheless, an attempt has been made to develop a distinct and cohesive argument that reflects the image of current interests.

As a first step, a decision was made to reduce the length of the book to make it more suitable for semester- and quarter-length courses, and focus less on the organization of the urban system, and more on the internal structure of the city. To foster cohesiveness and provide a framework that embraces different theoretical perspectives, a more historical approach has been incorporated. This historical approach is rooted in major eras of economic development, and it permits the incorporation of ideas relating to waves of capital accumulation and the growth of cities at both the urban system and internal structure levels of analysis. This focus on waves, or cycles, of urban development also allows the incorporation of theoretical ideas from such diverse modes of analysis as social ecology, neoclassical economics, and political economy.

This use of a more historical approach led to the exclusion of whole chapters on topics such as central place theory, the classification of cities, economic base theory, interaction, and urban transportation, since many of the ideas that were in these chapters in previous editions could be incorporated into the historical discussion. These aspects of urban geography have been excluded as whole chapters not because they are unimportant, but because they have either become too technical and abstract (as with central place theory), boring and uninteresting (as with economic base theory and interaction), or, as with public mass transit, intriguingly irrelevant to most readers.

Just as the more historical approach has permitted the inclusion of ideas related to central place theory, interaction, economic base, and urban transportation in a more concise framework, so has it permitted the inclusion of other topics of current interest. These topics include women in the city, industrial restructuring and global change, public policy and urban taxation, the analysis of urban conflicts, housing issues and racial questions, and the consequences of the transformation of cities to multinucleated forms.

Apart from a more historical approach, the reader will notice a far greater emphasis on social issues. Almost one-third of the text concerns the social structure of cities, housing and society, and housing submarkets and urban revitalization. In this latter regard, special attention is devoted to public policy issues in the housing sector, and various approaches to urban revitalization, such as redevelopment, gentrification, and incumbent upgrading. The final chapter on managing cities provides a logical conclusion to this framework, for it is evident that a major determinant of the liveability of cities is competent and honest local government.

Finally, all readers will note that in various sections particular attention is devoted to differences in urban outcomes between Canada and the United States. These Canada/U.S. contrasts are highlighted not because they are the only regional differences in the urban experience in North America, but because the sources of the differences, though complex, are quite easy to identify.

ACKNOWLEDGMENTS

Users of the previous three editions will note the absence of Barry Garner as coauthor. During the past decade, he has been Professor of Geography at the University of New South Wales, Australia, and though his interest remains urban geography, his current work has a more antipodean focus. His presence, however, can still be sensed in many chapters.

Another significant change relates to the fact that one of the author's own children participated in an urban geography course at a university that made use of the third edition. This, as many instructors must know, is a testing experience for both parent and offspring, and is probably the reason for the reduction in length of the book. It is also the reason for one or two "editorial" comments and the inclusion of photographs!

In acknowledging the help of the many people who contributed to the success of previous editions, and, I hope, the fourth edition, I would like to thank my colleagues at Queen's University. They, and many friends in the profession, have continued to offer excellent advice, and I wish all their suggestions could have been incorporated. I would like to thank the following reviewers for their advice and suggestions in the preparation of the fourth edition: Martin Cadwallader, University of Wisconsin, Madison; Shayne Davies, University of Texas, Austin; Thomas Reiner, University of Pennsylvania; Charles Sargent, Arizona State University; Keith Semple, University of Saskatchewan. I would also like to thank all the instructors who have used the book and provided the feedback so essential in undertaking this revision. The indefatigable Helen Phelan typed the manuscript, and the secretarial staff at the Ontario Council on Graduate Studies typed the index. Ross Hough, of the Queen's Cartographic Laboratory, undertook the art work for the illustrations. Finally, I would like to thank my family, who have grown used to the cycle of text writing and revisions for this book and its previous editions over the past twenty years. The book, like the cat, is part of the family.

Maurice Yeates
Queen's University, Kingston

The
North
American
City

Chapter

1

Cities: The Spatial View

*T*his book is concerned with urban development in North America, a region defined for our purposes as including the United States and Canada, but excluding Mexico. The United States and Canada are considered together not because the urban experience in the United States is exactly the same as that in Canada, but because urban areas in the two countries share a number of common urban attributes and problems. On the other hand, it is evident that the Mexican urban experience is quite different from that of the United States and Canada. This is the result of a vast number of differences including income, income distribution, culture, historical experiences, population growth rates, demographic change, and economic base.

In this chapter the discussion focuses on some of the background and concepts that are needed to understand the organization and structure of the text. The material is designed to answer the colloquial questions: "Where is this text coming from?" and "Why is the material organized the way that it is?" These questions are answered through a presentation of (1) what is meant by the terms *spatial* and *aspatial,* (2) the methodological components of urban analysis, and (3) the notions of scale and interdependence.

SPATIAL STRUCTURE AND ASPATIAL PROCESSES

At the outset it is crucial to recognize that the spatial arrangement of human activity, as shown in Figure 1.1, is a reflection of the aspatial processes operating in society (Massey, 1984b, p. 3). Consequently, the patterns, distributions, and matters of concern to individuals involved with the spatial aspects of urban issues are, for the most part, an outcome of the many and complex processes inherent in the way North American society is organized. There are very few, if any, spatial processes *per se* (migration and diffusion have been suggested as two), for most are the outcome of aspatial processes (such as those generating employment, unemployment, technological change, and so forth) that operate in space.

The interrelationship between the aspatial and spatial dimensions in Figure 1.1 is indicated as being one-way, but although this is usual, it need not always be the case. Spatial patterns and variations do influence economic, social, and governmental actions, which in turn rebound to influence spatial patterns. For example, in the United States, spatial concentrations of blacks in the inner cities, and inequalities in the provision of educational opportunities, have led to governmental programs to reduce inequalities and promote more equal access to employment—although none of these programs appear to have been successful at solving the horrendous problems facing the black populations of many inner cities. In Canada, regional differences have had a profound effect on various aspects of the revised Canadian constitution that address provincial rights in the social and economic spheres.

Thus, it is important to note that although the aspatial/spatial reflection is

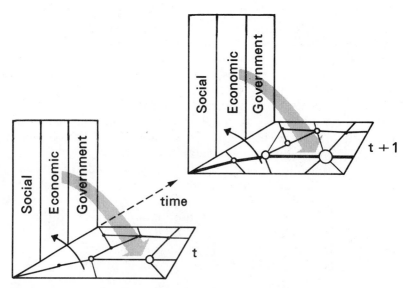

Figure 1.1 Spatial organization is a reflection of the nonspatial organization of society.

considered the primary direction of influence, spatial/aspatial impacts can occur. Furthermore, these interactions occur cumulatively through time, so that an element of a pattern at time $t + 1$ is more likely to be the product of forces that were greater in strength in some previous era *(t)* than those existent at $t + 1$ (Fig. 1.1). This *lagged* nature of spatial patterns means that cities cannot be examined without taking historical context into account. As a consequence, the historical context is emphasized in almost every part of this book.

An Example

Recent developments in urban Canada provide an example that can be simplified to demonstrate the relationship between aspatial processes and spatial patterns (Bourne, 1984). It is possible to identify three general patterns of change that occurred within Canada between 1981 and 1986 at different geographical scales (Tables 1.1 and 1.2). At the national level is concentration, as exemplified by a rising percentage of the population of the country locating in its core (central Canada), and by population increases among the largest cities in western Canada (Webster, 1985). At the regional level, there has been a concentration of population into certain metropolitan regions. Examples of this are the concentration of population into the Calgary–Edmonton corridor (Smith and Johnson, 1978), the Strait of Georgia (Vancouver–Victoria) Urban Region (Gibson, 1976), and southern Ontario (Yeates, 1984) around Toronto. At the local level—that is, within urban regions—there has been a continuing deconcentration of population (Gertler, 1985), as exemplified by central-city

Table 1.1 EXAMPLES OF THE LINK BETWEEN ASPATIAL PROCESSES AND SPATIAL STRUCTURE

Aspatial processes	Spatial structures

Social/cultural processes
  Declining birthrates
  French-language affirmation
  Aging population
  Immigration
  Female participation
	National—concentration
	  Core decline
	  Peripheral growth
	  Western growth

Economic processes
  Energy prices
  Financial concentration
  Manufacturing
  Value of dollar
	Regional—concentration
	  Calgary–Edmonton corridor
	  Strait of Georgia Urban
	  Southern Ontario

Government policies
  Equalization payments
  Auto Pact
	Local—deconcentration
	  Central-city population deconcentration
	  Suburban expansion
	  Exurban developments
	  Redevelopment

Table 1.2   POPULATION CHANGE IN CMAs in Canada, 1981–1986

Rank metropolitan area, 1981	Population (in thousands)		Percent change, 1981–1986
	1981[1]	1986	
1. Toronto	3,130	3,427	9.5
2. Montreal	2,862	2,921	2.1
3. Vancouver	1,268	1,381	8.9
4. Ottawa–Hull	744	819	10.1
5. Edmonton	741	781	6.0
6. Calgary	626	671	7.2
7. Winnipeg	592	625	5.6
8. Quebec	584	603	3.3
9. Hamilton	542	557	2.8
10. St. Catherines–Niagara	342	343	0.2
11. London	327	342	4.7
12. Kitchener	288	311	8.1
13. Halifax	278	296	6.6
14. Victoria	241	256	5.8
15. Windsor	251	254	1.2
16. Oshawa	186	204	9.2
17. Saskatoon	175	201	14.6
18. Regina	173	187	7.7
19. St. John's	155	162	4.6
20. Chicoutimi–Jonquiere	158	159	0.2
21. Sudbury	158	149	−4.6
22. Trois-Rivieres	125	129	2.8
23. Thunder Bay	122	122	0.0
24. Saint John	121	121	0.0

[1]Based on 1986 area.

Source: Statistics Canada (1987) "National Package" 6432, Table 1.

population decline coupled with suburban growth, and by exurban developments (Brunet, 1980).

The question now arising concerns the ways these spatial patterns of change are related to various aspatial processes. The types of social/cultural processes that appear to have had an influence on spatial patterns at the different levels are declining birth rates, aging population, migration, and the affirmation of French-language primacy in Quebec. One of the consequences of declining birth rates is that migration has now become a more important determinant of differential urban growth (or decline) than it was twenty to thirty years ago. The petroleum and natural gas industries have helped to sustain employment opportunities in western Canada despite the calamatous economic decline of the 1981–1982 recession. Stable energy prices in the 1980s and the decrease in the value of the Canadian dollar (compared with the United States dollar) have stimulated employment growth in the manufacturing heartland of central Canada. On the governmental side, equalization payments have the effect of dampening the amount of outmigration from the Maritimes (Simmons, 1984), and the Automotive Trade Agreement ("Auto Pact") with the United States has fostered the continuing concentration of manufacturing in southern Ontario.

It should be recognized that the possible array of influences is extremely large. Many of the different aspatial factors work in complicated ways that may either reinforce or offset a trend. Furthermore, forces that appear to be extremely powerful in a region during one period may have a negative effect during the next (for example, energy prices). Spatial patterns are, therefore, in a constant state of flux or "becoming" as the relative strength and influence of these different aspatial processes change through time (Pred, 1985).

THE COMPONENTS OF URBAN ANALYSIS

What is emphasized in a particular field of study relates not only to the general objective, but to the way in which the inquiry is undertaken. In this book, the objective is to understand processes that give rise to the spatial arrangement of urban phenomena. This understanding is shaped by the way in which the objective is pursued, for the methods that are selected influence not only the type of study that is undertaken, but the phenomena that are regarded as of interest or importance.

Patterns

The analysis of the spatial arrangement of urban phenomena involves four elements: patterns, philosophical approach, theory, and technique (Table 1.3). The choices made in each of these determine to a large extent not only the type of work that is done, but the area of interest as well. The central concern of this volume is spatial distributions—the patterns, structure, and organization of space. The phenomena that are selected for study are those that clearly involve a spatial location. This is the basic reason why much of the second part of the text concerns the arrangement of different types of land uses within urban areas. As land use definitely involves space, interest focuses on the geographic location of one use relative to others, and on interactions among the users. In a sense, a land-use approach fixes patterns as the central concern, although the land-use approach is not the only way to do this.

Philosophical Approach

The second element of analysis, the philosophical approach that is utilized, determines the way in which the analysis is undertaken and the type of evidence that is thought to be meaningful. Throughout the 1960s and early 1970s, a *positivist* approach pervaded most studies. The positivist approach regards "sensed" (that is, measured) experiences as the valid type of information about urban patterns because such data is thought to be value-free. Thus, many

Table 1.3 THE COMPONENTS OF URBAN ANALYSIS

Component	Approach (examples)
1. Patterns	Spatial distributions
2. Philosophical Perspective	Positivist
	Logical positivism
	Phenomenological
	Humanism
	Structuralist
3. Theory	Social human ecology
	Neoclassical economics
	Behavioral approaches
	Classical political economy
	Marxist perspectives
4. Techniques	Maps
	Computer mapping
	Information gathering
	Field work
	Surveys
	Census data
	Techniques for analysis
	Statistical models
	Mathematical models

empirical studies use census tract information to test ideas about the patterns and interrelationships that may exist in space. However, when much of this data is examined, it is found not to be value-free. Rather, it expresses the bias of the group collecting the information, and furthermore does not provide the basis for exhaustive analysis.

Nevertheless, the positivist approach, as exemplified in logical positivism, or the scientific method, is used a great deal in urban studies because it provides a way of examining problems that is replicable. Furthermore, the scientific method (theory → hypotheses → test the hypotheses using information → reevaluate the theory) is an analytical mode that is widely used in the scientific community and is surrounded by methods, procedures, forms of presentation, and evaluative designs that are commonly understood across a large number of disciplines. Many examples cited in this text are from studies that are positivist in nature.

The restrictive nature of the positivist approach, however, has led some analysts to apply other philosophical approaches in their work. For example, a number of studies of people's perception of their environment are cast in a *phenomenological* framework, in which information derived from people's experiences is considered a valid source of knowledge. For example, a particular part of an urban area may be thought to be dangerous and threatening, and people may act in particular ways as a result of this perception. Experiential information may, in fact, have a lot to do with the way in which individuals at different stages in the life cycle react with their environment. For example, Golant defines the urban environment of the elderly as experiential; that is, dependent upon an individual's "perceptions, feelings and evaluation" (1984, p. 61).

The application of phenomenology to the study of the ways in which the elderly interact and are influenced by their immediate environment illustrates why this perspective is often considered one of the roots of the *humanistic* approach to spatial inquiry (Ley and Samuels, 1978; Rowles, 1978). Humanistic approaches are committed to understanding how people respond to and create a total way of life (that is, culture) in various urban places. The responses and creative features that people are able to develop are shaped by internal (family, ethnicity) and external (class, history, location) forces that provide constraints of varying magnitude and permanence (Ley, 1983).

Other writers are pursuing *structuralist* approaches to urban inquiry. In the urban context, the structuralist approach can be regarded as involving an assumption that spatial patterns can only be explained by relating them to the social structure of society, and to the processes that give rise to this social structure. Thus, a change in spatial patterns can come about only through a change in the social structure of society. Johnston (1982), for example, argues that the spatial structure of the American urban system can be understood only in the context of the changing social structure of society as it metamorphosed from mercantile capitalism to industrial capitalism and late capitalism. This particular structural approach can be rather confining, however, as it tends to force the substance to fit the particular theory that is adopted. Nevertheless, this is a useful approach that is utilized later in the text to cast some light on the evolution of the North American urban system.

Theoretical Bases

The third component of analysis involves the theoretical base of urban studies. There are many different theories involving economic, social, and political processes, and in this book a wide variety are examined and evaluated. Theories are usually selected according to the subject matter of concern and the opinion of the original researcher as to which provides the most fruitful path to understanding. Just as there has been considerable debate concerning the most useful philosophical basis for research, there has been much controversy over the most appropriate theoretical approaches. With respect to the social structure of the city, the ecological approach pioneered by the Chicago school in the 1920s and 1930s (Park, Burgess, and McKenzie, 1925), which regarded the pattern of social areas in the city as a natural product of change within communities, has been challenged by a view that regards social patterns in the city as the historical product of the capitalist mode of production (Lefebvre, 1972).

Perhaps some of the most vibrant debates have been concerned with economic processes and spatial patterns. Much of the work of the 1960s and 1970s was couched in a positivist framework and made use of neoclassical economic theory (Fig. 1.2). The location of phenomena in space was therefore regarded as the outcome of a market process—land, housing, and resources in general are allocated as a result of prices set in some market framework, with government playing a mediating, lubricating role when necessary. The harmonies of the marketplace outlined in neoclassical theory—with its assumptions of perfect information, perfect competition, a rational economic person, and so forth— have been challenged on the grounds that markets of that type do not really exist. Some possible solutions are either to modify the neoclassical approach, replacing the fully rational economic person with some kind of learning (cognitive) process, as in behavioral studies (Golledge and Rushton, 1976); or to construct different types of markets for different socioeconomic groups, as in the housing submarket approach.

Another outcome has been to reject the theoretical base of neoclassical economics on the grounds that its assumptions (whatever the modifications) are untenable, and that the theory is not relevant to the examination of a number of urban issues relating to the apparent tension among social groups over the

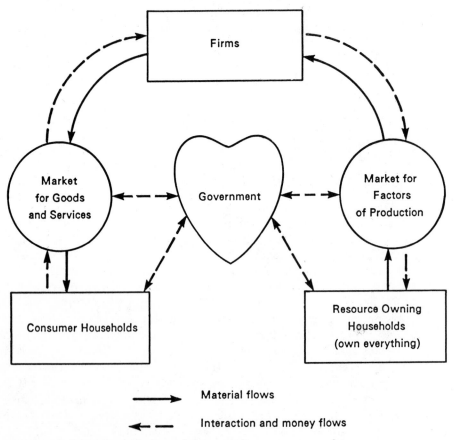

Figure 1.2. A neoclassical view of the way the economy works.

allocation of resources. The result has been a return by some researchers to the basic tenets of nineteenth-century classical political economy (Fig. 1.3). In this approach, the focus is on the major factors of production (land, labor, and capital) and the interactions among them with respect to the allocation of the proceeds from production (Morgan and Sayer, 1985). As used in some urban analyses in the 1970s and 1980s, land tends to play a minor role, but an important new factor of production is introduced in the form of the state. Governments (at the federal, provincial/state, or local level) not only provide the framework within which these groups of players interact, but also acts as a player itself (Simmons and Bourne, 1982). After all, more than 35% of the Gross Domestic Product (GDP) of both the United States and Canada is the product of governmental activities. Of particular interest in parts of this volume, therefore, are the spatial consequences of interactions among labor, capital, and the state.

An alternative approach to analysis within the general classical political

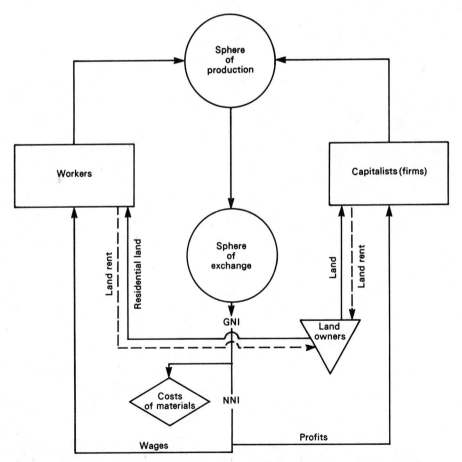

Figure 1.3 A classical political economy view of the way the economy works.

economy framework has been derived from the writings of Marx (Harvey, 1973; 1982; 1985), which focus particularly on the struggle between capital and labor for the wealth created by production. Marxism is, of course, a tremendously powerful force in the world, but not because the theories expounded (such as the labor theory of value and historical materialism) are always particularly tenable (or implementable). Its power derives, instead, from its placement, front and center, of values with universal appeal—the dignity of labor, the sharing of wealth, and the sharing of decision-making. Marx's theories have led, however, to extremely useful analyses on a variety of topics bearing directly on urban development, ranging from the intermetropolitan location of manufacturing to the rise of urban social movements (Fainstein and Fainstein, 1985; Walker and Storper, 1981).

The difficulty with this approach is that in Marxist studies, urban areas themselves do not appear to be the central focus of concern—the concern is really the struggle between capital and labor (the class struggle), which usually takes place in cities only because that is where the majority of the people in North America reside (Castells, 1977). In this text, spatial patterns of urban phenomena are the central issue of concern, although these patterns are considered to be the product of aspatial processes.

Techniques for Analysis

Perhaps one of the major difficulties that students perceive is that frequently the information concerning urban phenomena are examined using techniques that themselves have to be learned if the implications are to be properly appreciated. The simple word *spatial* implies that one way in which information may be presented, and interrelationships examined, is with the use of maps. Maps themselves are perceptions, for they represent choices that have been made by individuals for the presentation of information (Carter, 1984).

For example, Figure 1.4 shows the distribution of urban areas (SMSAs in the United States, CMAs in Canada) in North America that had a population of at least 250,000 in 1980–1981. This map is equal area, that is, the size of a place (for example, a state or province) is drawn directly proportional to its actual size on the surface of the continent. However, the urban areas, since they are minute compared with the continent as a whole, are represented simply as points. The map simply shows the actual geographic position of one large urban place relative to other large places.

Figure 1.5 is not equal area, but equal population, for each SMSA, CMA, and state/province is represented according to the size of its population as a percentage of the population of North America. Thus, New York City's SMSA, with roughly 4% of the population of North America, is represented with 4% of the map's total area. The map has to be distorted from the "reality" of the shape of the continent in Figure 1.4 in order to fit in the differently sized urban areas, and the distances between places are obviously misrepresented. Nevertheless, Figure 1.5 does emphasize why the spatial aspect of urban phenomena is considered an important area of inquiry—about two-thirds of the population of

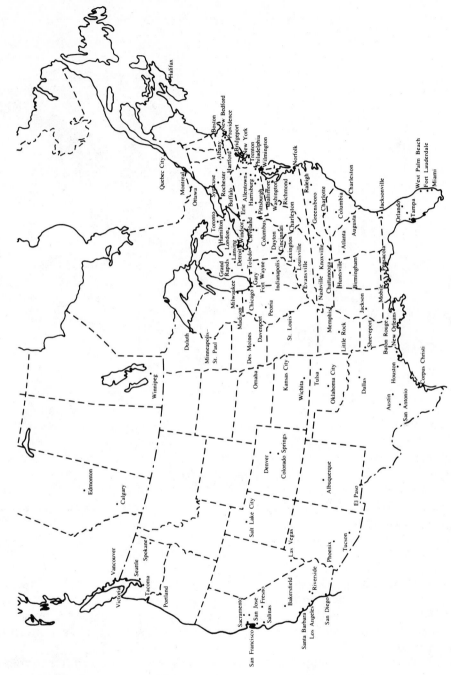

Figure 1.4 The actual location of all SMSAs and CMAs with a population of 250,000 or more in 1980–1981.

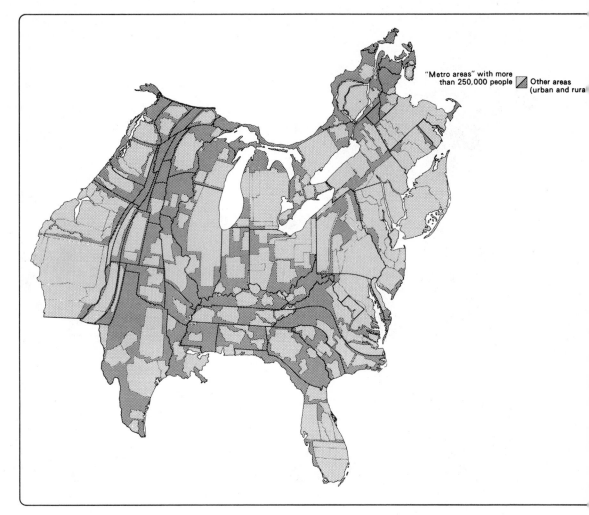

Figure 1.5 An isodemographic map of metropolitan North America, 1980–1981.

North America resides in large urban places, and these are located mainly along the East Coast south to Florida, around the lower Great Lakes, and along the West Coast, particularly in California. In this book, information is presented in map form in a number of different ways for both analytical and interpretive purposes.

Spatially distributed information also has to be related to the various processes that are thought to give rise to these patterns. These relationships are often established through the use of quantitative techniques of different kinds. These quantitative techniques range from those of a statistical nature to more general mathematical modeling. Statistical techniques, which are used to investigate the relationships among sets of sample information, are widely used by researchers (Clark and Hosking, 1986). For example, Scott (1983b) uses logit regression analysis and probability models to examine the relationship between the size and location (spatial aspects) of manufacturing plants and the technical structure of production (an outcome of aspatial processes). It should be noted that recent research has been directed toward establishing procedures to address the idiosyncracies of handling spatially distributed data (Gaile and Willmott, 1984). Although statistical representations are kept to a minimum in this volume, it should always be remembered that many of the results that are discussed have been produced through such analyses.

Mathematical models, ranging from those of the gravity and interaction type to regional input–output analysis (Haynes and Fotheringham, 1984; Hewings, 1986), have been employed by a large number of researchers. These types of models incorporate basic processes. For example, the gravity model postulates that interaction decreases with distance, and this type of simple formulation allows them to be represented in numerical form. Perhaps one of the best known of these is the classic Lowry model (1964), which uses gravity model formulations to link changes in basic employment and the multiplier effect of these changes to the spatial location of households and retail employment. This residential–retail spatial link has been incorporated in many other urban and regional growth models (Fotheringham, 1985).

Although it is true that many of these statistical and mathematical models were introduced into urban analysis during the 1960s, when much research was cast in a positivist mode using neoclassical economic theory, it should be clear that various techniques for analyzing information must be used regardless of the philosophical perspective or theoretical approach that is incorporated. Information of various types, whether it be sensed or experiential, has to be evaluated with respect to the analysis being undertaken. That is not to imply that the techniques used in analysis may be complex—indeed, the techniques that are used should be the simplest possible that cast light on the relationships being investigated.

The Approach of This Book

This chapter demonstrates that there are a variety of approaches that may be used to analyze patterns of urban phenomena. Choosing from among the four major elements of the various approaches is largely a matter of opinion as to which provides the most persuasive line of argument. Consequently, it is necessary to choose which avenue to take, and this choice in effect determines the range of literature that is regarded as pertinent.

This text examines spatial patterns as the outcome of aspatial processes. The outline of the various approaches given earlier should make it clear that any one of a number of avenues may be followed for such an examination. This book is based on the premise that the North American city is primarily the product of economic forces, particularly those that pertain to industrial development in the nineteenth and twentieth centuries. These forces have operated in a capitalist and market (or quasi-market) environment.

SCALES OF ANALYSIS

One question facing any individual concerned with spatially distributed phenomena has to do with the selection of the scale of inquiry. This is obviously true with respect to the mapping of information, but it is also evident in analyses of urban phenomena. The larger the scale of study, the more the personal details become obscured—or to put this in the context of humanism, the larger the scale of the study, the more likely it is that the responses, actions, and aspirations of individuals may be overlooked. However, it is not possible to review the major processes influencing North American urban development from the point of view of many small-scale local studies. As a consequence, a balance has to be achieved in the geographical scale on which the material is presented.

Scale and "Urban" Areas

The issue of scale is illustrated in part by the many different concepts that may be used to define urban areas. Some of these concepts and political definitions are illustrated with respect to Atlanta, Georgia in Table 1.4. The play area of children is quite restricted, so for them Atlanta undoubtedly consists of, at most, the local block (and shopping center). The high school student is aware of his or her own neighborhood (and definitely the local shopping center) as Atlanta.

The political definition of Atlanta is, however, the city of Atlanta, which in 1984 contained a declining population of 420,000, more than one-half of whom were black. Somewhat larger than the city of Atlanta (the inner city), and containing some of the suburbs most heavily dependent on employment opportunities in the central business district (CBD) within the city, is the Metropolitan Atlanta Regional Transit Authority (MARTA), consisting of DeKalb and Fulton counties, which contain a population of 1.1 million, including the city.

MARTA is within the Standard Metropolitan Statistical Area (SMSA) of Atlanta. SMSAs consist of one or more large population nuclei (50,000 or more

Table 1.4 VARIOUS POLITICAL, LEGAL, AND CONCEPTUAL DEFINITIONS OF ATLANTA AT DIFFERENT GEOGRAPHIC SCALES

Criterion	Definition	Estimated population
Financial + business	Atlanta service area	24.3 million
Political	Georgia	5.8 million
Daily urban travel	Urban fields (DUS)	2.8 million
Bureau of Census	SMSA	2.4 million
Public transportation	MARTA	1.1 million
Political	City of Atlanta	425,000
Walking distance	Neighborhood	100–2,000
Play area	Block (or street)	20

Tall buildings demarcate the central business district of most cities. The skyline of San Francisco is particularly dramatic. (*Source:* Geovisuals.)

people) together with adjacent whole counties that have a high degree of economic and social integration with the nucleus (Bureau of the Census, 1984b). Integration is usually defined in terms of commuting (journey to work). It should be noted that whereas Statistics Canada uses a similar procedure to define Census Metropolitan Areas, the CMAs are not aggregations of whole counties, for at the margin of the commuting range only parts of peripheral counties are included. The Canadian definition is then, in a sense, more restricted or precise. The population of the Atlanta SMSA in 1984 was 2.4 million spread over 15 counties.

The *urban field* of Atlanta is more extensive than the SMSA (Friedmann, 1973a), and embraces not only the maximum commuting range to and from the major population nucleus, but also the area used for regular (for example, weekend) recreational activities by the urban population. The modern metropolitan area is, in essence, becoming indistinguishable from the urban field, because "instead of the 1941 compact city surrounded by many dispersed farm households and slow-growing rural service centres, we now have a regional city with a lacerated edge surrounded by dispersed exurbanite households and a few farm households" (Russwurm and Bryant, 1984, p. 133). Exurbanized households are those that have left the metropolitan area to "colonize" the immediate rural environment while maintaining employment in urban-based occupations (Roseman, 1980). The concept of the urban field is therefore now very close to that of the *daily urban system,* which is defined on the basis of the ebb and flow of daily commuting *and* by activity patterns (Berry, 1973). The urban field may, therefore, extend more than 160 kilometers (100 miles) from traditional city centers.

In a more political sense, Atlanta is often used conterminously with Georgia itself, because its SMSA includes more than 40% of the state's population. Thus, many of the actions and policies of the state government are pursued with an eye to their impact on large, urban constituencies. This is true of many state/provincial governments in North America, for in many of these jurisdictions at least 40% of the population is located in a large metropolitan region. Finally, since Atlanta is the financial and wholesale center for a large part of the South (Wheeler and Brown, 1985), its sphere of influence extends over the greater part of seven states and involves an estimated 24.3 million people.

Scale and Interdependence

Whatever the scale of the study, one important characteristic that cannot be ignored is interdependence among cities, among the various parts within cities, and among institutions and people residing in urban and nonurban areas. Interdependence implies a necessity for interaction—the means by which places are organized into a system. Interaction plays a number of crucial roles in shaping the form and structure of the city system, for it fosters cohesion, allows for differentiation, is the medium for spatial organization, and is an agent for bringing about change. Although a number of examples might be used, it is useful to illustrate the notion of interdependence and interaction through a discussion of two important concepts—the multiplier and the hierarchy.

The Multiplier

The idea of the multiplier is used a great deal in the social sciences. It is crucial to economics (the *Keynesian multiplier*) and to planning (the *regional multiplier*). In general, the *multiplier* refers to *the amount of increase in income, jobs, or spending that is associated with a given increase in investment.* The implication is that a given increase in investment in something, let's say a new factory, results not only in the jobs created in the factory, but in jobs elsewhere in the local community as well. The people employed in the new factory purchase local services (such as education and health care); they also have to buy food and other goods, and all this creates more jobs. In turn, income generated by people in these jobs is also spent locally, so through interdependence the jobs in the new factory are multiplied into many other jobs. There are two main ways the multiplier concept has been used in urban studies: A relatively simple way is the economic base multiplier, and a more sophisticated approach is the input/output multiplier.

The Economic Base Approach The economic base approach divides the economy of a city into two parts: The basic (or city-supporting) sector refers to the goods and services produced within a city but sold beyond its borders; the nonbasic (or city-serving) sector refers to the goods and services produced and sold within the city itself. The rationale for the approach is the belief (which seems reasonable) that the existence and growth of a city depends upon the goods and services it produces and sells beyond its borders—the basic component. The size of the nonbasic component is therefore related in some way to the size of the basic component:

$$\text{Total activity in the city (TA)} = \text{Total basic activities (BA)} + \text{Total nonbasic activities (NBA)}$$

For analytical purposes, *activity* should be defined as income (or expenditures), but it is frequently defined in terms of employment. Thus, if total income in a city (TA) = $400 million, and the income from BA = $100 million, then the income from NBA = $300 million. This simple example also suggests that every $1.00 in BA generates $3.00 in NBA. Therefore, if new BA activity is generated, providing an income of $50 million, and the basic-to-nonbasic ratio of 1:3 stays constant, NBA will increase by $150 million, and TA activity will consequently increase by $200 million (200 = 50 + 150). The multiplier, which indicates the growth in TA as a result of an increase in BA, is 4 (or TA ÷ BA).

There are, of course, conceptual and computational difficulties with this approach (Isserman, 1980). The conceptual difficulties relate to the assumption of a BA/NBA split, the primacy given to BA in the growth (or decline) of a city, and problems related to defining the spatial unit involved. The computational difficulties involve how the basic component may be defined, and the fact that employment is often used rather than income because money flows are difficult to obtain.

The basic component, and hence the basic-to-nonbasic ratio, is usually calculated at either the micro level (small scale) for individual cities, or at the macro level (large scale) for a large number of cities. Micro-level studies require detailed analyses of each activity in a city to determine which portions of an activity are basic and nonbasic (Gibson and Worden, 1981). Macro-level studies use some method of determining what might be nonbasic for each sector of activity in any city: a common method of doing this is the minimum requirements approach (Moore and Jacobsen, 1984). These minimum requirements are then summed for each sector to yield the proportion of total employment in a city that can be regarded as nonbasic, or city-serving. These totals can then be plotted on a graph against city size to demonstrate that the nonbasic share of a city's employment increases with city size (Fig. 1.6), which implies that the multiplier (which is scaled at the top of Fig. 1.6) also increases with city size. The multiplier increases with city size because whereas the inhabitants of small cities may have to go to larger places for certain special goods or services, the inhabitants of large places invariably have access to nearly all the goods and services they require within their own metropolis. There is, therefore, a greater leakage of money from small places than from larger cities, and the shift in the plotted lines in Figure 1.6 suggests that this leakage is increasing over time as large cities become more dominant. We will discuss this at greater length in the subsection, The Hierarchy.

The Input/Output Approach   The input/output (I/O) approach does not assume a distinction between basic and nonbasic components of urban economic activities. Instead, the I/O approach recognizes that all aspects of the economy of a nation, region, or urban area are interrelated and interdependent (Cadwallader, 1985; Miller and Blair, 1985). Thus, an increase in the amount of housing

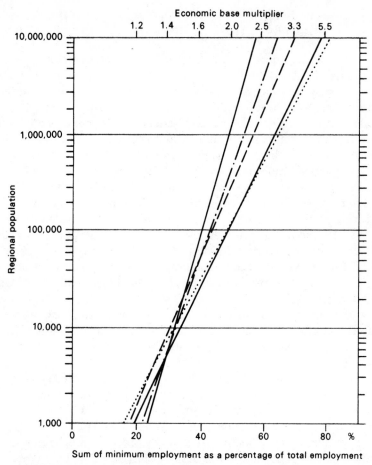

Figure 1.6 The relationship between the proportion of a United States city's employment that is nonbasic (that is, estimated using the minimum requirements approach) and population size. (*Source:* Moore and Jacobsen, 1984, p. 223.)

construction in an urban area generates increases in activity in services of all kinds, not only within the metropolis in which the growth is occurring, but elsewhere in the nation (and world) where activities are linked in some way to those of the housing industry in the growth area. The I/O multiplier for a particular urban area will therefore relate the increase in total output (or income) to an increase in output (or investment) in a particular growth sector (such as housing). In a study of the Los Angeles, California economy, Wolch and Geiger (1986) use I/O multipliers to demonstrate that the not-for-profit sector (such as philanthropic organizations and universities) have an enormous impact on the regional economy.

For example, using interregional, intersectoral I/O tables for the Canadian economy what would be the impact of a $10 million increase in investment in the transportation industry of Montreal (Yeates, 1975)? According to the linkages modeled in the interregional, intersectoral I/O table, the *total* impact on all sectors in Montreal, Quebec, and other regions will be something like this (numbers rounded):

Direct   Indirect

10 + 10 + 10 + 2 + 10 + 0.7 + 15 = $57.7 million
(Montreal) (Quebec) (West) (Ontario) (Maritimes) (Foreign)

The direct investment is $10 million in the transportation industry, which indirectly generates an additional $10 million worth of output over all sectors (housing, services, other manufacturing, etc.) in Montreal. Thus, the multiplier for Montreal is 2.0 (Direct + Indirect ÷ Direct). Parenthetically, it is interesting to note that in a study of the impact of the Boeing Company on the economy of the Puget Sound region, Erickson (1974) calculated that $500 million of new investments by the company from 1963 to 1967 had the effect of raising total income in the region by $950 million—an I/O multiplier of 1.9. The indirect impact elsewhere in Quebec was $10 million; thus, the multiplier for Quebec as a whole is 3.0. The indirect impact on West Canada was $2 million, on Ontario $10 million, on the Maritimes only $.7 million, and in foreign areas (mainly the United States), $15 million. The Canadian multiplier for the investment in Montreal is therefore 4.27, and the total multiplier over all sectors in all regions (including foreign parts) is 5.77.

The Hierarchy

In the previous section it was demonstrated that metropolitan areas have larger economic base multipliers than smaller cities because they are able to provide a wider array of goods and services (Mulligan, 1980). This is why larger cities are invariably higher in the hierarchy of urban places. The concept of the urban hierarchy, which is derived from the pioneering work of Christaller (1933) in central place theory, postulates a ranking of cities into size classes on the basis of their economic, social, and administrative importance. Although there has been much debate about the nature of the central place model and its theoretical base (Eaton and Lipsey, 1982; King, 1984), the concept of the hierarchy is important: Cities not only have a location in space, they have a position at a particular level in the hierarchy as well.

In its structure, the hierarchy of cities can be likened to a pyramid—there are a greater number of smaller cities than larger ones. Conversely, the economic, social, and political importance of cities is akin to an upside-down pyramid, with the few cities at the top exhibiting the largest number of different roles (Fig. 1.7), some of which are quite specialized. Because the notion of the hierarchy was first proposed in the context of service activities, it is with this particular set of characteristics that the concept has been examined most thoroughly.

Perhaps the classic studies in North America involving the establishment

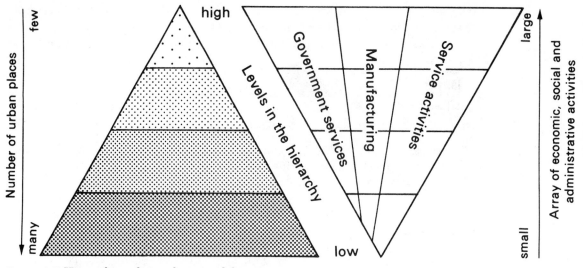

Figure 1.7 Hierarchies of size classes and functions.

of a hierarchy of urban places according to the provision of services are those by Berry and Garrison (1958a, 1958b, 1958c) and Borchert and Adams (1963). For example, Borchert and Adams establish an eight-level hierarchy of urban places in the Upper Midwest, with a highest-order center (Minneapolis–St. Paul, Minnesota) that contains more than 500 convenience, specialty, and wholesale service activities. The lowest-order centers (the hamlets) contain only gasoline and taverns/eating places (Fig. 1.8).

A hierarchy of cities develops as a result of (1) the differently sized markets required for the delivery of different services, and (2) the usefulness of such a system for the diffusion of ideas and innovations—that is, *interaction.* Borchert (1972) demonstrated the nature of interdependence in the hierarchy by examining correspondent banking linkages. This is a revealing measure of the strength of relations among cities, and therefore a good measure of dominance and subdominance. The hierarchical structure postulated in Figure 1.9, which is based on Borchert's analysis, presents the three highest levels and combines a fourth and fifth. The lower levels, which according to the upper Midwest study (Fig. 1.8) could number another five, are not included in the diagram. The highest-order center is the New York metropolitan area, which is the focus of the financial and stock exchange activity on the continent, and is the headquarters location of about 14% of the largest 1,000 United States corporations (Table 1.5). Seven metropolitan areas in the United States are second-order cities, and Toronto and Montreal are competing for that position in Canada. Of particular importance among the second-order cities are Chicago, Illinois (which is in the process of eclipsing Detroit, Michigan) and Los Angeles. Washington, D.C. has achieved its status as a result of its political importance.

Each metropolitan area is, in a sense, the center of a nodal region, the size

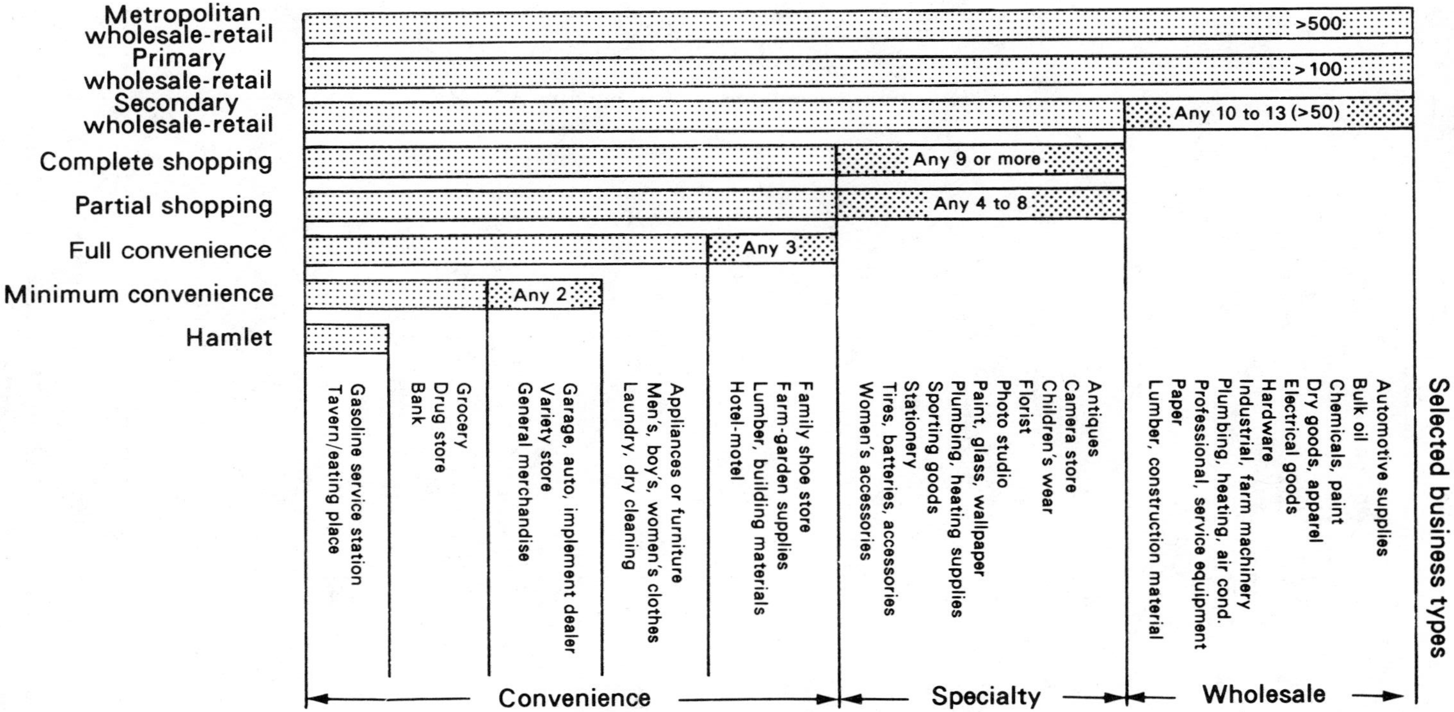
Metropolitan wholesale-retail
Primary wholesale-retail
Secondary wholesale-retail
Complete shopping
Partial shopping
Full convenience
Minimum convenience
Hamlet
>500
>100
Any 10 to 13 (>50)
Any 9 or more
Any 4 to 8
Any 3
Any 2
Selected business types
Automotive supplies
Bulk oil
Chemicals, paint
Dry goods, apparel
Electrical goods
Hardware
Industrial, farm machinery
Plumbing, heating, air cond.
Professional, service equipment
Paper
Lumber, construction material
Antiques
Camera store
Children's wear
Florist
Photo studio
Paint, glass, wallpaper
Plumbing, heating supplies
Sporting goods
Stationery
Tires, batteries, accessories
Women's accessories
Family shoe store
Farm-garden supplies
Lumber, building materials
Hotel-motel
Appliances or furniture
Men's, boy's, women's clothes
Laundry, dry cleaning
Garage, auto, implement dealer
Variety store
General merchandise
Grocery
Drug store
Bank
Gasoline service station
Tavern/eating place
Convenience
Specialty
Wholesale

Figure 1.8 The typical groups of business types found in each order of center in the upper Midwest of the United States. (*Source:* modified from Borchert and Adams, 1963, p. 4.)

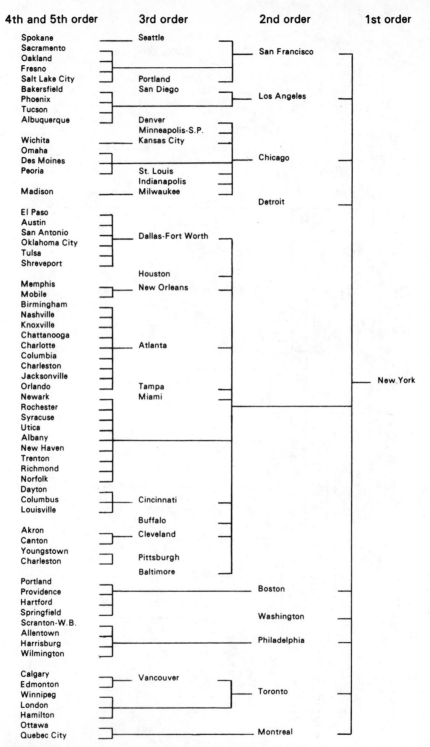

Figure 1.9 The hierarchical structure of the larger metropolises in the North American urban system.

Table 1.5 THE LOCATION OF THE HEADQUARTER OFFICES OF THE 1,000 LARGEST CORPORATIONS IN THE UNITED STATES, 1970–1980; AND POPULATION CHANGE IN SMSAs

Rank	SMSA	Pop. 1980 (thousands)	% Change 1970–1981	Headquarter offices 1970	Headquarter offices 1980	Gain/ Loss
1	New York	9,120	− 8.6	220	140	−80
2	Los Angeles– Long Beach	7,478	6.2	47	46	− 1
3	Chicago	7,104	1.8	73	59	−14
4	Philadelphia	4,717	− 2.2	21	20	− 1
5	Detroit	4,353	− 1.8	19	16	− 3
6	San Francisco– Oakland	3,251	4.5	28	22	− 6
7	Washington	3,061	5.2	2	4	+ 2
8	Dallas–Ft. Worth	2,975	25.1	18	31	+13
9	Houston	2,905	45.3	11	27	+16
10	Boston	2,763	− 4.7	22	32	+10
11	Nassau–Suffolk	2,606	2.0	5	10	+ 5
12	St. Louis	2,356	− 2.3	18	17	− 1
13	Pittsburgh	2,264	− 5.7	27	28	+ 1
14	Baltimore	2,174	5.0	8	5	− 3
15	Minneapolis–St. Paul	2,114	7.5	21	28	+ 7
16	Atlanta	2,030	27.2	6	9	+ 3
17	Newark	1,966	− 4.4	17	15	− 2
18	Cleveland	1,899	− 8.0	33	26	− 7
19	San Diego	1,862	37.1	1	3	+ 2
20	Miami	1,626	28.2	1	5	+ 4
21	Denver–Boulder	1,621	30.8	5	4	− 1
22	Seattle–Everett	1,607	12.8	1	1	0
25	Phoenix	1,509	55.4	3	6	+ 3
26	Cincinnati	1,401	1.0	7	9	+ 2
27	Milwaukee	1,397	− 0.5	17	12	− 5
28	Kansas City	1,327	4.2	6	4	− 2
29	San Jose	1,295	21.6	2	8	+ 6
30	Buffalo	1,243	− 7.9	5	2	− 3
32	Portland	1,243	23.4	8	8	0
39	Rochester	971	1.0	7	6	− 1
54	Hartford	726	0.8	7	7	0
56	Tulsa	689	25.5	2	6	+ 4
63	Richmond	632	15.4	5	6	+ 1
94	Wichita	411	5.6	6	4	− 2
96	Canton	404	2.7	5	3	− 2
98	Bridgeport	395	− 1.6	5	5	0
172	Stamford	199	− 3.4	14	33	+19
	Other urban places			297	333	
	TOTAL			1000	1000	

Sources: Data from the *Statistical Abstract of the United States* and *Fortune 1000*.

of which increases according to its level in the hierarchy. The few high-order centers provide very specialized functions for large regions, whereas the successively greater numbers of smaller cities at successively lower levels provide more general services for hinterlands that are more local. If a metropolitan area of a high order has a limited hinterland (for example Detroit, which dominates only sixth-order centers and lower), then the strength of the center depends disproportionately on its own local economic or political dynamism. Thus, analyzing the urban system in this way gives us some clues as to the relative strength of a metropolis other than that indicated by population size alone.

One important feature of the hierarchy that should be noticed is that it permits specialization—a differentiation of economic activities—and hence a spatial division of labor among cities. A career in corporate law is best pursued in New York City, or in Toronto, Chicago, or some of the other second-order centers. Managers and decision makers are in the headquarter offices of the major centers, not in the smaller towns and cities (the sixth-, seventh-, and eighth-order centers) in which the branch plants for hourly paid workers are located. This hierarchical structure is related to the structure of business and commercial enterprises in North America, for many organizations have developed a size distribution of plants and stores that is hierarchical; for example, national department stores often have class A, B, and so on, stores. This is not at all surprising, for it simply reemphasizes the way in which the aspatial aspects of society are interlinked with the spatial structure of the urban system.

Changes in the Hierarchy   An interesting example of the way in which changes in the aspatial aspects of society are reflected in the changing hierarchy of trade centers in a region is provided by Stabler (1987) with respect to Saskatchewan. On the basis of detailed information pertaining to retail and wholesale activities and services for each urban center, he defines a sixfold hierarchy ranging from "minimum convenience" to "primary wholesale–retail" (see Table 1.6). Then, on the basis of the number of activities and services in each town for 1961 and 1981, he places each of the 598 urban centers in one of the six categories for both time periods. He is therefore able to trace the change in the hierarchy of trade centers in Saskatchewan over a twenty-year time period.

Table 1.6 summarizes these changes and shows the number of urban places in each category in both time periods. In general, it can be observed that the larger places maintained their position at the top of the hierarchy, but the smaller places experienced a decrease in retail and service activities. This is manifested by the fact that whereas 271 of the 598 urban places were classified as "minimum convenience" in 1961, 400 of the 598 were so classified in 1981. The role of communities classified in the lowest four categories has diminished, but that of the ten urban centers in the top two categories has increased.

This change in the hierarchy relates to changes in agricultural production, transportation, and communications technology during the time period 1961–1981. There was a continuation of the consolidation of farm holdings (thus increasing farm size) and of substitution of capital for labor that had com-

Table 1.6   CHANGE IN NUMBER OF COMMUNITIES AT DIFFERENT LEVELS IN THE
HIERARCHY
Saskatchewan 1961–1981

Level of center	Number		Average population		Average number of businesses	
	1961	1981	1961	1981	1961	1981
Primary Wholesale–retail	2	2	103,834	158,379	1,526	3,438
Secondary Wholesale–retail	8	8	14,160	16,713	287	544
Complete shopping	29	22	2,198	3,032	78	134
Partial shopping	99	30	659	1,296	33	57
Full convenience	189	136	296	541	17	21
Minimum convenience	271	400	121	125	6	5

Source: Data extracted from Stabler (1987, Table 2, p. 230).

menced some decades previously. Thus, the agricultural labor force decreased considerably, and the population density (that is, the market potential) in rural areas continued to diminish. The hierarchy was also affected enormously by an extensive upgrading of the provincial road network, which, along with the spread of multiple car ownership that occurred in the 1950s and 1960s, made it easier for people to travel farther for goods and services. These physical improvements facilitated changes in the shopping behavior of rural families which, through advertising (via television and newspapers), became increasingly aware of the greater range of choices in the larger communities.

Conclusion

A discussion of spatially distributed phenomena related to urban areas requires some clear decisions concerning the organization of material. For the sake of clarity, Chapters 2 and 3 are large scale and are concerned with interurban analysis. In these chapters, urban areas are regarded as points (as in Fig. 1.4), and the focus is on why these urban areas are generally located where they are; why they are of different population sizes; and the reasons for differential urban growth. The focus is on the way in which the aspatial processes influence interurban patterns. As a consequence, attention is directed toward analyzing how systems of cities develop (Bourne and Simmons, 1978; Goldberg and Mercer, 1986). The word *system* is used to indicate that the various individual urban places are interdependent—what goes on at one location (or city) has some form of repercussion at other locations.

This idea of interdependence is also crucial to the remaining chapters of the book, which are concerned with smaller-scale geographic inquiries involving intraurban issues. In these chapters, the city is viewed not as a point, but as an area (as in Fig. 1.5), and the concern is with why various phenomena are distributed within urban areas in the way that they are; how the spatial distribution of these phenomena change through time; the aspatial processes that influence change in these interurban patterns; and the social consequences of these changing spatial patterns. The notion of interdependence is again important, for change in one part of the city may well influence phenomena elsewhere within that same city—for example, a new suburban shopping center affects the viability of existing retail outlets in its vicinity and in the older urban nucleation. Interdependence also implies an interest in interaction; that is, the flows of people, messages, and ideas among the constituent parts.

In pursuing the inter- and intralevels of analysis concerning urban areas, it will also be emphasized that the methods used to examine the various questions just outlined helps us to address contemporary urban problems and issues. When we understand how various aspatial processes influence certain spatial patterns, we can develop policies that address related issues of public and private concern; therefore, some chapters will conclude with a discussion of a related public policy issue.

Chapter

2

North American Urban Development

*D*espite the considerable differences in their physical environments and cultural histories, the technically advanced nations of the world have one thing in common—they are all highly urbanized. That is, most of their population resides in urban places. This is a relatively new phenomenon in world history, for prior to 1850 no society could be described as predominantly urbanized, and by 1900 only one—Great Britain—could be so regarded. Yet today, all the industrialized nations are highly urbanized, and urbanization is accelerating rapidly throughout the world, especially among less-developed countries (Fig. 2.1).

URBANIZATION

Urbanization is the process whereby an essentially rural society is transformed into a predominantly urban one. Hence urbanization is usually described as the proportion of the population of an area that resides in urban places above a certain population size. Urbanization curves are generally S-shaped (inset, Fig. 2.1), so the trends depicted for the three continental areas in Figure 2.1 have to be interpreted in the context of their probable position in the general pat-

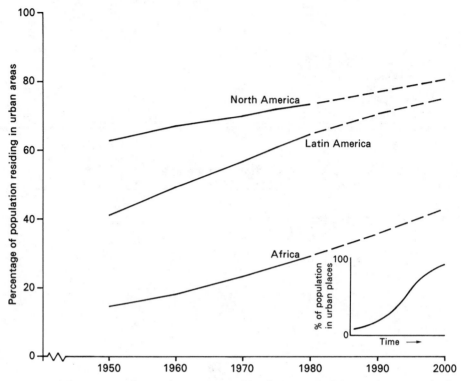

Figure 2.1 Recent trends in urbanization in North America, Latin America, and Africa.

tern. The curve representing North America since 1950 would clearly be the top end of an S-shaped curve, whereas Latin America represents the middle, or steepest part, of the S-curve, and Africa is the lowest segment of the S, which precedes the period of greatest increase in urbanization.

The key question concerns the causes of urbanization. This can be answered in two ways: first, by examining the factors that give rise to cities *per se*; and second, through analyzing the urban dynamic. Cities of various sizes have existed in different places and at different times for more than 5,000 years. They have existed because, as a result of diverse circumstances such as imperial control, priestly power, trade, and so forth, they managed to appropriate part of the surplus product of society at large (particularly the agricultural sector) for the support of the city's inhabitants. *Surplus product* may be defined as the amount of material product in excess of that which is needed to maintain society in its existing state. This surplus can be used in any number of ways, ranging from improvements in human welfare (such as health, education, better diets, etc.) to the construction of monuments and to the manufacture of armaments for defense and the stupidities of war.

The generation of a surplus (through such means as increases in agricultural productivity) and its partial appropriation may result in the formation of cities, but it does not in itself lead to urbanization—something more is required. Urban areas have to match agricultural areas as productive units; that is, urban places have to have a productive dynamic of their own. Thus, whereas urbanization in the late fifteenth and twentieth centuries could not have occurred without the huge increases in food output that commenced with the agricultural revolution of the seventeenth century, the movement of people to urban areas would not have taken place without the industrial revolution of the nineteenth century, which made the cities centers of manufacturing, finance, and large-scale trade.

The growth of urban areas as foci of production, and hence as centers of employment opportunities in the more developed parts of the world, came just at the right time as far as the people were concerned. The agricultural revolution displaced many individuals from rural areas, and the population began to increase as a result of declining death rates. There were, therefore, both push (from rural areas) and pull (employment opportunities in urban areas) factors that led to large-scale rural-to-urban migration: This, coupled with high rates of net natural population increase and foreign immigration, resulted in rapid urbanization in North America over the past 100 years.

North American Urbanization

The determination of what proportion of the total population lives in urban places clearly depends upon the way places are defined as urban in official statistics. Unfortunately, there is no universally accepted definition of urban places, and considerable variation exists from country to country. For example, in Denmark places with 200 inhabitants are called urban, whereas in Korea places with less than 40,000 are not. In Canada, places are designated for census purposes as urban if they have at least 1,000 inhabitants, whereas 2,500 is the critical figure in the United States. In general, most countries use a base figure between 2,000 and 7,500.

The increase in levels of urbanization in North America since the dates of the first census of the United States and Canada is shown in Figure 2.2. For purposes of comparison, and in accordance with the range used among most countries, places are defined as urban if they have at least 5,000 inhabitants. In practically every decade, each census in both countries has reported an increase in the proportion of the total population living in urban places. In the United States, the process of urbanization was quite gradual until about 1920, accelerated through the rest of the nineteenth century and to 1930, slowed during the Depression years of the 1930s and the Second World War in the 1940s, and then increased, but at a decreasing rate, during the 1960s and 1970s. It is interesting to note that it was not until 1930 that more than one-half the population of the United States resided in cities of 5,000 or more.

Although the general trend in the urbanization curve for Canada is similar to that for the United States, there are two main differences. First, until recently, urbanization in Canada lagged about twenty years behind the United States. For example, the population of Canada did not become more

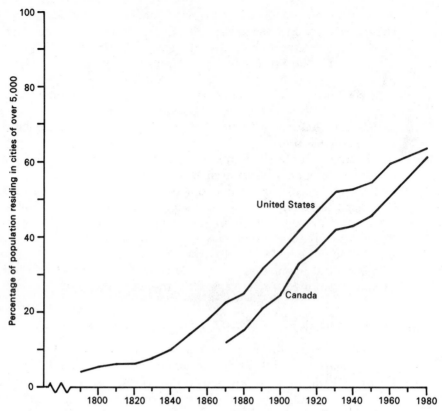

Figure 2.2 Levels of urbanization in the United States since 1790, and in Canada since 1871.

than 50% urban until 1950. As a consequence, although the development of the Canadian urban system can be examined in the context of North American urban development as a whole, there are clearly distinguishing features that require separate attention. Second, the rate of urbanization in Canada since 1950 has been greater than that in the United States, so that by 1980 the proportion of the population in each country residing in places with more than 5,000 people was almost the same—62% versus 63%. Thus, by 1980 the historic twenty-year lag in level of urbanization between the two countries was almost eliminated.

ERAS OF DEVELOPMENT AND WAVES OF ACCUMULATION

Urban development in North America must be examined within the context of economic development and the generation of surpluses from both the rural and urban spheres of production. Although it is not possible to calculate this surplus exactly, it is possible to show how the wealth generated within the region has changed over the past 100 years. Figure 2.3 graphs the changes in the gross

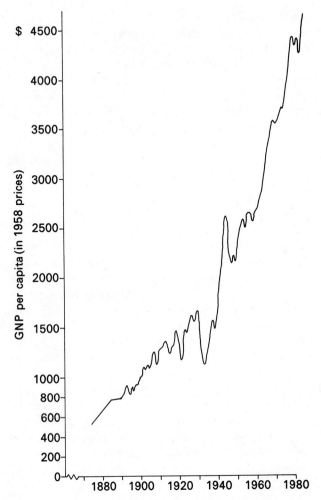

Figure 2.3 One hundred years of change in GNP per capita in the United States, 1884–1984. (*Source:* Compiled from data from the Bureau of the Census, 1984, p. 433; 1975).

national product (GNP, the sum of all goods and services produced) in the United States in 1958 dollars per capita over the past 100 years. Similar information is available for Canada, but only from 1920, and the trend line is about the same as that in Figure 2.3 (Yeates, 1985a, p. 56). In looking at the general change in GNP per capita over the past 100 years, it becomes evident that even though the theoretical amount necessary to maintain society in its existing state obviously increases through time (as a result, primarily, of accumulation), the possibility of a surplus also increases enormously. Society as a whole is six times more wealthy in the 1980s than it was in the 1880s.

The generation of a surplus during a particular time period, which may be appropriated in some way to finance the urban infrastructure (all those physical things that go into urban development: houses, roads, manufacturing plants, services, and so forth), relates quite directly to immediate changes in wealth. If the GNP per capita increases considerably over a few years, then the amount of surplus generated may be comparatively large. On the other hand, if the GNP per capita increases at a decreasing rate (or even decreases), it is quite likely that the surplus will be small or nonexistent, and the money (or capital) available for urban development will likewise be small or nonexistent. It is for this reason that the fluctuations seen in Figure 2.3 are extremely important. These fluctuations have generated considerable interest in the possible existence of economic cycles (Giersch, 1984), and in the relation of these cycles to investment and to urban development (Harvey, 1982, pp. 300–305; 1985, pp. 17–21).

Economic Cycles and Urban Development

Although economic cycles vary enormously in length, and there may be cycles within long-term fluctuations, economic cycles have a similar internal sequence. The bottom of the cycle is the *trough,* where unemployment is high, the rate of return on investments is low, and there is much unused industrial capacity. This is followed by a period of *expansion,* when the rate of unemployment decreases and income, consumer spending, and business investment all increase. The *peak* of the cycle occurs when there is a high use of industrial capacity and labor, and the rate of return on investments in productive capacity and labor begins to level off. There may well be a shift in investments to more speculative, consumption-oriented ventures. As the rate of increase in economic output begins to decelerate and the rate of return on investment decreases, a contraction may occur, leading to a *recession.* When demand and production decrease, the recession may intensify into a deep trough (or depression) if a crisis in confidence occurs as a result of overspeculation. During a recession or depression, unemployment rates become high, and the people become desperate. The period of expansion and the peak are usually (we hope) the longest part of the cycle. Many of the economic policies of government since the 1930s have been directed toward controlling these cycles and attempting to protect people against the worst ravages of downswings.

It has been suggested that there are three different types of fluctuations, or cycles within cycles:

1. Short *inventory cycles,* of one to three years duration, which are related to the immediate adjustments businesses make in response to actual and short-term fluctuations in sales.
2. *Business cycles* of about four to nine years duration are caused by variations in captial investments by business in response to perceived and expected changes in rates of return (profit) on capital investments (Haberler, 1963; Long and Plosser, 1983). These fluctuations have a considerable impact on short-term urban development, as capital investments are often related to the imperatives of immediate changes in the demand for housing, business space, and so forth.

3. *Long swings,* or *long waves,* are variously defined as being of forty to sixty years duration (Kondratieff, 1935) and as being about twenty years (Kuznets, 1961). The Kuznets swings seem to be embedded within the Kondratieff long waves. Rostow (1975) relates these long-term trends to the interplay of: *(a)* the life cycle of major product and technological innovations that give rise to growth or decline in leading sectors of economic activity (Rothwell, 1982); *(b)* changes in the supply and demand (and hence prices) for foodstuffs, raw materials, and energy; and *(c)* changes in population growth rates, household formation rates, and the size of the work force.

Kondratieff Long Waves

The long waves are particularly interesting when they are examined in the context of the growth and spread of urban areas in North America. This is because some of the basic causes of long swings (as listed earlier) are associated with significantly different socioeconomic systems that, in turn, stimulate different patterns of organization and interaction in geographic space. This is a rather complicated statement, and the next part of this chapter will demonstrate what this means in the context of North American urban development.

The basic method used by Kondratieff (1935) to determine the periodicity of the long swings was to transform information related to prices of raw materials and some manufactured products, volumes of trade, and wage rates into deviations from a general trend, and then to use moving averages to estimate the long-term cyclical patterns. The information pertained to France, the United Kingdom, the United States, and to Germany (prior to World War II). A diagram of the time-line of the cycles identified by Kondratieff is presented in Figure 2.4. The fourth Kondratieff cycle since 1930 and the onset of a possible fifth have been included on the basis of information in Kuznets (1961), Rostow (1975), Rothwell (1982), and van Duijn (1983). The waves have been superimposed on a line that indicates the general trend in GNP per capita in the United States since 1800, and the segment for 1975 to 1985 has to be regarded as a fascinating conjecture.

The Major Eras   On the basis of these long swings, which embrace the period from mercantilism to capitalism, it is possible to identify four (and perhaps five) eras. These are:

1. *Frontier mercantile (1790–1840),* in which wealth is created through trade and the accumulation of gold. In this era, profits produced by merchants through trade are used to purchase consumer goods and services and are also reinvested in other trade ventures.
2. *Early, industrial capitalism (1840–1885),* which witnessed the establishment of manufacturing and processing plants by entrepreneurs using capital initially derived from trade (or imported from Europe), but more and more from the profits from the sale of manufactured

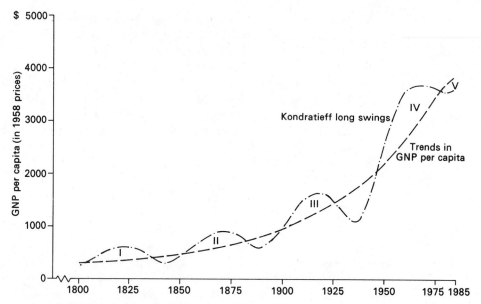

Figure 2.4 Conceptual graph of Kondratieff long waves superimposed on general trend in GPN per capita, 1800–1985.

goods. Most of these plants were relatively small scale and locally owned, and their growth was nurtured behind protectionist trade barriers. Perhaps the most important factors stimulating growth in this period, in terms of Rostow's (1975) three types, are technology in the form of the steam engine and railroad, the availability of cheap immigrant labor in the wake of the famines in Ireland and elsewhere in Europe during the 1840s, and the opening up of the rich agricultural lands of the midwest of the United States and southwest Ontario.

3. *National, industrial capitalism (1885–1935)* is characterized by the emergence of powerful national corporations (Chandler, 1977), large-scale, assembly line manufacturing, and the production of a vast array of consumer items. As national corporations became stronger, the United States moved from a protectionist industrial policy to a free-trade position. Technological change was one of the chief stimulants of the era, with the harnessing of electricity and the invention of the electric motor, the development of fine steels, the telephone, and the invention of the internal combustion engine, which led to the growth of the automobile industry after 1900. Growth was also stimulated by the enormous influx of immigrants between 1885 and 1911 (over 25 million), which both stimulated aggregate demand and held down wages during the early part of the period. There were also great increases in agricultural productivity. Although inequality of income between classes was widening in the United States throughout much of the nineteenth century, particularly from 1880 on, the gap began to

narrow after 1914 as the growth rate of the labor force began to decrease and skilled and semiskilled labor was more in demand. Hence the emergence of the *consumer society*.

4. *Mature industrial capitalism (1935–1975)*, during which time many United States national corporations merged or expanded into large multinational corporations and achieved dominant positions with respect to the North American market and, in some cases, the world market. Two of the prime stimulants for this level of domination were the leading position assumed by the United States following World War II and the number of technological innovations stimulated by the war effort that were transferred to domestic production, particularly those having to do with the aircraft industry. Also, raw materials (particularly oil from the Middle East) were relatively low in price. But growth was also stimulated to an enormous extent by a high rate of population growth (the "baby boom") that lasted for fifteen years (from 1947 to 1962) and by the large-scale migration of blacks (and some whites) to the inner cities of the large metropolitan areas. All these factors combined— greater wealth, a further narrowing of income disparities, technological change, demographic pressures—helped to generate a tremendous demand for services, and consequently for service employment. This period witnessed the emergence of the *service society*.

5. *Global capitalism (1975–)*. It now appears that we have entered into a new era marked by at least three major characteristics (Hall, 1985). First, the dominance of United States multinational corporations is being challenged or replaced in many sectors by Japanese and European (particularly West German) conglomerates. This does not necessarily mean a greater level of competition, for many of the corporations are undertaking joint ventures (Dicken, 1986). Second, of the three stimulants defined by Rostow (1975), technological change in the form of information technologies and biotechnology is particularly important and is generating new products, processes, and forms of industrial organization. Third, there has been a great increase in the number of women in the paid labor force, particularly in the service sector: The participation rate increased from about 40% in 1971 to 60% in 1986. Associated with this shift are social demands related to day care for children, single-parent housing and support services, equal opportunity, and comparable pay for work of comparable value. Also, since the "baby-boomers" have entered the job market, household (particularly one- and two-person households) formation rates have increased.

URBAN SYSTEM DEVELOPMENT IN THE UNITED STATES

Each of the eras just described generated particular forms of urban system organization. One approach to a description of the various forms of urban organization has been provided by Borchert in his classic analyses of the growth of the United States urban system (1967; 1972). In his studies, he defined epochs from the middle (or close to the peak) of each of the long waves defined in Figure 2.4, and focused primarily on one aspect (transportation) of just one stimulant (technological innovation) (Table 2.1). Although this approach enabled him to demonstrate how changes in efficiency of modes of transportation have led to progressively higher levels of integration of the United States urban system, it is somewhat limited in scope.

The evolution of the United States urban system will be examined in this chapter in terms of the eras defined by the long waves (Table 2.1), with the mapped representation of the system occurring just after the peak for each era. Thus, the frontier mercantile era is represented by a map of the size distribution of urban places for 1830–1831, early industrial capitalism by one for 1870–1871, and so forth. The basic theme to be emphasized is the way changes in the structure and organization of the urban system reflect the major socioeconomic forces of each era.

The Frontier Mercantile Era (1790–1840)

The economy of North America throughout the eighteenth and early nineteenth centuries was based almost entirely on agriculture and the export of staple products. Even by 1830, only 9% of the population of the United States resided in places of 5,000 or more, and in the area that became Canada (in 1867), about 3%. The major economic function of most cities was *mercantile*, involving the import of manufactured products from Europe and the export to Europe of fish, furs, timber, and agricultural products. Manufacturing, which until 1775 had essentially been forbidden in the English colonies (and remained discouraged in the Canadas up to 1876), was still very much in its infancy. It was characterized by handicrafts rather than machines, and organized by households and small workshops rather than factories. The major industry was

Table 2.1 GLOSSARY OF TERMINOLOGY RELATED TO THE EVOLUTION OF THE NORTH AMERICAN URBAN SYSTEM

Long waves		Type of city	Borchert (1967; 1972)	
Era	Dates		Era	Dates
Frontier–mercantile	1790–1840	Mercantile	Sail-wagon	–1830
Early industrial capitalism	1840–1885	Classic industrial	Steam/iron rail	1830–1870
National industrial capitalism	1885–1935	Metropolitan	Steam/steel	1870–1920
Mature capitalism	1935–1975	Suburban	Auto, truck, air	1920–1970
Global capitalism	1975–	Galactic	Counterurbanization (Berry, 1976)	1970–

based on cotton textiles, and by 1815 a total of 170 mills were operating in port towns and villages (such as Lowell and New Bedford, Massachusetts) based on hydropower sites in New England (Vance, 1977). The port cities, of course, were also the sites of considerable shipbuilding and repair.

The largest cities during this era, consequently, were found along the Atlantic coast (Figure 2.5), with New York (202,600), Philadelphia, Pennsylvania (161,400), Baltimore, Maryland (80,600), and Boston, Massachusetts (61,400) dominating the trade of the original thirteen colonies and forming the heartland of the developing continent. Each of these cities was competing for the new hinterland opening up west of the Appalachian Mountains. The three next largest cities were located along the routes that traditionally led into the heart of North America. At the Mississippi Delta, New Orleans (46,300) received the produce from the hinterland, but the difficulty of passage upriver impeded the flow of two-way traffic. Quebec City (27,700) and Montreal (27,000), located along the St. Lawrence River, controlled the northern route into the region, but the relative growth of these two cities was already suffering from the loss of hinterland that resulted from the independence of the United States from British colonial rule.

Most of the cities located in the hinterland, which stretched as far west as the Mississippi River, were small in size and served as centers of commerce for

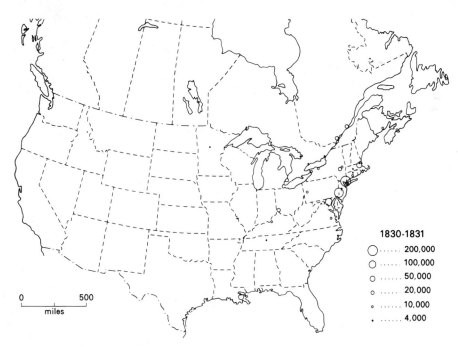

Figure 2.5 The relative size and location of all cities in North America with a population of 4,000 or more in 1830–1831.

the surrounding agricultural settlements. In 1830, Cincinnati, Ohio was the largest of these interior towns (24,800). It acted as a service center for the rich Ohio Valley, with its merchants importing manufactured products and agricultural supplies directly across the Appalachians from the East Coast ports and exporting products down the Ohio and Mississippi rivers via New Orleans to Europe.

Urban System Organization During the Frontier Mercantile Era   A general model of the spatial organization of the urban system in the frontier mercantile era is given in Figure 2.6. A number of port cities along the coast become gateways that serve as intermediary trade centers between the staple- and agricultural producing hinterland and the foreign market to which the area is tied (Johnston, 1982, p. 70). The main flow of information and industrial products is from the foreign market, through the gateway, to the hinterland; only staples and agricultural commodities flow in the reverse direction.

Therefore, particular directions of interaction and spatial arrangements of city sizes develop. The largest and highest-order places are along the coast, with second-order centers farther inland, connecting the ports to the resource towns (or lowest-order centers) of the frontier. Growth is achieved by extending the hinterland into unexploited territory or by capturing part of adjacent areas. In this sense, the Treaty of Paris (1783) was incredibly profitable to United States cities, as the British gave away much of the Great Lakes hinterland of Montreal. The entrepreneurs of New York City then solidified their control of the hinterland with the opening in 1825 of the Erie Canal, which linked the Hudson River to Lake Erie at Buffalo, New York, and hence the whole of the Midwest around the lower Great Lakes.

Early Industrial Capitalism (1840–1885)

Whereas during the frontier mercantile era the cities and towns were directly dependent on the hinterland for their wealth, during the industrial capitalist era towns and cities themselves were the focus of wealth-creating production, although they were still dependent on the agricultural and resource-producing

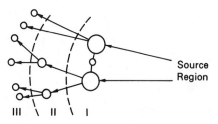 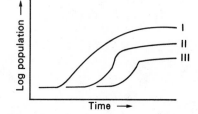

Note: I, II, III refer to level in a size hierarchy

Figure 2.6 The frontier mercantile era: model of urban system organization and paths of growth. (*Source:* Simmons, 1978, p. 64.)

areas for food and materials. Industrial capitalism involves investments by the owners of capital in labor and equipment to produce goods. Market forces also dictate, for the most part, that the goods be produced at competitive prices. There is therefore a continuous drive for greater productivity (that is, output per worker-hour). This was achieved through the development of the factory system (the breaking down of manufacturing into specialized routine tasks) and the realization of economies of scale through increases in factory size.

The era of early industrial capitalism embraces the transformation of the United States economy from one that was based primarily on trade in resources to one that processed resources and, subsequently, manufactured products. The steam engine was undoubtedly the key technological innovation, and its application to production spurred the development of an increasingly varied, although still largely small-scale, manufacturing industry. Whereas in 1850 there were only about 125,000 manufacturing establishments employing 1 million production workers, by 1880 there were more than 250,000 factories and workshops employing almost 3 million workers.

Most important, however, was the use of the steam engine in barges (up the Mississippi and Missouri rivers), ships, and trains. For example, in 1850 there were 9,000 miles of railroad track in the United States, but by 1870 the iron rails covered 53,000 miles. The network linked all the cities of the East Coast, spread inland most extensively through the Midwest around the lower Great Lakes, and by 1869 reached Oakland, California on San Francisco Bay. The building of canals and canalized rivers was also vital to the transport of heavy goods because the iron rail would not support weighty loads. As a consequence of these improvements, the basic framework of the United States transportation system was in place by the end of the era, the gross "friction of distance" between places had been substantially reduced, and a more effective space was emerging within which resources could be mobilized and products distributed.

The Emerging Urban System   Between 1840 and 1885 the population of the United States increased from 17 million to more than 55 million, and the proportion of the population residing in places of 5,000 or more increased from 10% to almost 28% (Table 2.2). The urban population increased, therefore, by about 14 million. By 1870, New York City (Manhattan) had become the dominant place in North America (Fig. 2.7) and, when combined with Brooklyn, had a population in excess of 1.2 million. The cities of the East Coast, and particularly New York City, had built upon their gateway status to become independent financial and commercial centers linking European capital with the high-yielding but often speculative investment opportunities in the United States. These same cities also developed a considerable manufacturing base that was nurtured by protective tariffs, stimulated through the demands of the Civil War, and made competitive in part as a result of the influx of thousands of poor immigrants.

Inland cities in locations convenient to both rail and water transportation also grew phenomenally. St. Louis, Missouri, on the Mississippi River, connected by rail with the east and by steam paddleboat and barge with New

Table 2.2   THE POPULATION OF THE UNITED STATES SINCE 1790 AND CANADA SINCE 1871 AND URBAN DEVELOPMENT

	United States			Canada		
Date	Number of places over 5,000	Total population (millions)	Percent urban	Number of places over 5,000	Total population (millions)	Percent urban
1790	12	3.9	3.4			
1800	21	5.3	5.2			
1810	28	7.2	6.3			
1820	35	9.6	6.2			
1830	56	12.9	7.8			
1840	85	17.0	9.8			
1850	147	23.2	13.9			
1860	229	31.4	17.9			
1870	354	38.6	22.9	21	3.7	12.2
1880	472	50.2	24.9	38	4.3	15.3
1890	694	62.9	31.5	47	4.8	21.0
1900	905	75.9	35.9	63	5.3	24.6
1910	1,202	91.9	41.6	91	7.2	32.6
1920	1,467	105.7	47.1	110	8.8	36.6
1930	1,833	122.7	52.3	137	10.4	41.7
1940	2,042	131.6	52.7	152	11.5	43.0
1950	2,449	150.7	54.5	207	14.0	45.4
1960	3,293	179.3	59.8	259	18.2	50.9
1970	4,140	203.2	61.7	355	21.6	56.2
1980	5,084	226.6	63.4	409	24.3	61.8

Sources: Bureau of the Census (1975, 1984); Leacy (1983); Statistics Canada (1984).

Orleans and the Gulf of Mexico. It grew from a population of 6,000 in 1830 to 311,000 in 1870. Chicago, Illinois became the hub of the midwestern rail system and also had an all-water transport route via the lakes and the Erie Canal to the Atlantic, giving rise to its self-proclaimed status as the "Greatest Primary Grain Port in the World." The population of Chicago grew to almost 300,000 by 1870. Cincinnati, the other big inland city of the Midwest, had grown less dramatically, reaching a population of 216,000 by 1870. Its economy, based on manufacturing (particularly pork meat packing), commerce, and transportation, was more diversified than Chicago's.

Urban System Organization during the Era of Early Industrial Capitalism   When an indigenous manufacturing base developed, it began to change the spatial structure of the urban system quite significantly. Although the economy of many cities was still largely devoted to trade and services, a number were now devoted primarily to manufacturing. A feature of this early industrial era is that cities grew rapidly but tended toward a more hierarchical size distribution. This is shown by the rank-size distributions in Figure 2.8.

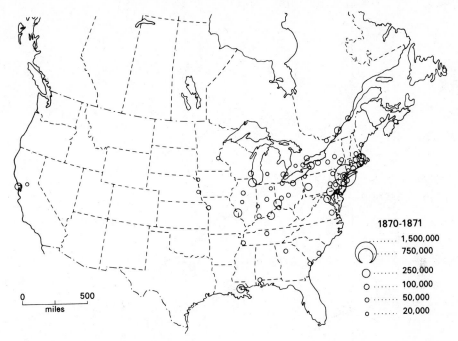

Figure 2.7 The relative size and location of all cities in North America with a population of 20,000 or more in 1870–1871.

Rank-size models can be used to highlight a number of trends related to the populations of cities in a region (Parr and Jones, 1983). The *rank-size rule* says that if cities (defined in some way, such as SMSAs or CMAs) are plotted on double-log paper in descending order according to their population sizes on the vertical axis, and by their corresponding rank on the horizontal axis, the resulting pattern often forms a smooth progression approximating a straight line (Nader, 1984). The largest cities in 1830, 1870, 1920, 1970 (and gross prediction for 2010) are plotted in Figure 2.8, and the simple equation for the rank-size rule is given.

During the mercantile frontier era it was quite possible to have a number of gateway cities of the same size—hence a rank-size distribution for a country could be *stepped,* with one or two large cities, a few regional centers, and many frontier outposts. Or, if there was only one gateway, the rank-size distribution might be *primate,* reflecting the dominance of the highest-order place. In the industrial era, the rank-size distribution was more likely to converge on a straight line as a result of the hierarchical organization of capital flows and the concentration of financial activities in one or two centers. This is beginning to become evident in the plot for 1870 in Figure 2.8.

The spatial patterns of cities and the interactions that develop are also likely to be quite different from those of the previous era (Fig. 2.9). The largest and highest-order places contain a combination of manufacturing and business func-

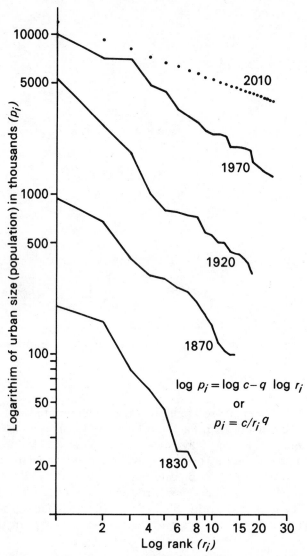

Figure 2.8 Rank-size distribution of major urban areas (by population) in the United States for 1830, 1870, 1920, 1970 (and 2010).

tions, but the smaller places may be either industrial or service centers. The flows of information and goods between these places will, therefore, be quite complex, as each specializes in a different type of production and a different array of activities.

The growth paths of the places indicated in the graph in Figure 2.9 emphasize the differential influences of the business cycle on three different levels in the hierarchy. The largest places, with many different types of economic activi-

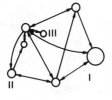 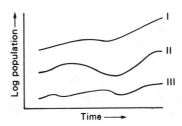

Figure 2.9 The early industrial capitalism era: model of urban system organization and paths of growth. (*Source:* Simmons, 1978, p. 64.)

ties, are influenced by the business cycle, but the effect is dampened because of the large number of possible offsetting growth/decline activities that exist. The smaller places are, however, influenced a great deal by the business cycle, for they have a limited range of activities, and when the demand for the output of the major employment sector decreases, massive local unemployment and great hardship occur.

The Era of National Industrial Capitalism (1885–1935)

The period from 1885 to 1935 was one of full-scale industrialization in which the United States economy completed its transition from an agricultural and mercantile base to an industrial-capitalist one, and in which the urban pattern jelled. Financiers perceived that the greatest return on investments was to be gained from the manufacturing sector, and these investments in turn helped to generate great increases in the wealth of the country. Although the various stimulants that came together at the beginning of the period have been outlined previously, it should be recognized that the First World War, coming in the middle of the cycle, also accelerated the growth of manufacturing, and at the same time weakened the financial strength of Europe while enhancing that of the United States.

One of the chief characteristics of this era were larger and larger units of production. These were made possible by a significant change in the organization of industrial and commercial enterprises that occurred after 1870, when limited liability joint-stock companies were permitted to form. Backed by the finance houses (such as J.P. Morgan), these companies aided the development of market-oriented manufacturing on a scale never before experienced. By 1910, 540 companies employed in excess of 1,000 workers each, and the trend was clearly toward larger units. A brake to this growth came in the form of the Sherman Anti-Trust Act of 1890, but in spite of this law, the increasingly complex system of economic organization allowed functional consolidation to occur, and by the turn of the century a number of gigantic corporations had already come into being. These included Standard Oil (from the J.D. Rockefeller Corporation) and U.S. Steel (from the Carnegie Corporation).

Urban growth based on manufacturing would have been impossible, however, without the extension and consolidation of the railroad network. By 1910 there were some 240,000 miles of track in operation in the United States, and gauges had been standardized. Steel rails replaced iron, permitting the construction of larger locomotives and heavier equipment, and hence longer and cheaper hauls of raw materials, particularly coal. The average freight charge per ton mile was reduced from 3.31 cents in 1865 to 0.70 cents in 1892, and the average length of haul increased from 110 miles per ton in 1882 to 250 miles per ton in 1910 (Pred, 1965). The integration of the United States economy really occurred, therefore, during the third Kondratieff wave.

As a consequence, the number of people living in population centers of 5,000 or more increased by more than 50 million during the era, mostly in cities that contained the new manufacturing plants. The number of production workers in manufacturing increased from about 3 million in 1885 to over 8 million in 1929 (just before the stockmarket crash), and the average number of employees per manufacturing establishment increased from about ten to forty during the same period. There was, therefore, a continuous drive by entrepreneurs to achieve even greater economies of scale.

The big change that became evident during this period was that whereas in the mercantile era profits were generated in the process of trade, through price markups and so forth, in the manufacturing eras the level of profit could be determined at the point of production. The owners of capital therefore tried to select locations that minimized their costs, particularly for labor, raw materials, and transportation; and also to develop methods of production (such as assembly-line manufacturing) that achieve lower costs per unit of output.

Costs with respect to labor involve a number of components, among them wages and the infrastructure of the urban environment within which the factory is located. The drive to keep the cost of labor as low as possible led to enormous poverty and exploitation in industrial cities, which became endemic during the recessionary periods of business cycles. The United States trade union movement consolidated in the 1890s as a reaction to this situation: The unions' goals were higher wage levels, job security, and better working conditions.

Environmental and living conditions in working-class areas of nineteenth-century cities were often quite squalid, for in the drive to keep production costs down and to maximize profits, there was little incentive for the owners of capital to invest in improving conditions in the parts of cities in which they did not live. There has been a continuous series of pressures ever since (in the form of political movements, conflicts, and even riots) to make government at the local, state, and national levels more responsive to the needs for social services and improvements in the infrastructure of cities.

The Urban System during the Era of National Industrial Capitalism   The outcome of this enormous industrial expansion was continued growth in some of the leading cities of the early industrial era, and dramatic growth in cities that specialized in large-scale manufacturing. The urban areas on the East Coast of the United States continued to grow rapidly in population, with the New York metropolitan area quadrupling in size to 5.3 million by 1920, Philadelphia nearly tripling in size to 1.8 million, and Boston and Baltimore maintaining similar rates of growth. In all, 28 cities, extending in a 500-mile arc from Lynn, Massachusetts to Norfolk, Virginia had populations exceeding 100,000 in 1920 (Fig. 2.10).

Even more fascinating is the growth in urban areas in the Midwest and lower Great Lakes area, with Chicago moving from a position of fifth largest city in North America in 1870 to second largest in 1920. Its ninefold increase in urban population (to 2.7 million) was a result of its leading position in transportation, commercial, warehouse, financial, and manufacturing activities. Also notable is the increase in the number of cities along the West Coast with populations in excess of 100,000, led particularly by Los Angeles, California. Finally, there is some development of larger urban areas in the South and in Texas, although this was only in an early stage by 1920.

The growth of industrial cities *per se* was most evident around the lower Great Lakes. Detroit; Cleveland, Ohio; and Pittsburgh, Pennsylvania moved to positions of fourth-, fifth-, and ninth-largest city in the United States by 1920. Detroit, chosen by Ford and Durant (General Motors) as the home of the automobile industry, grew along with the adoption of the automobile. There were 8,000 automobiles registered in the United States in 1900; by 1920 there were 8 million. Cleveland, well served by rail and Great Lakes transportation,

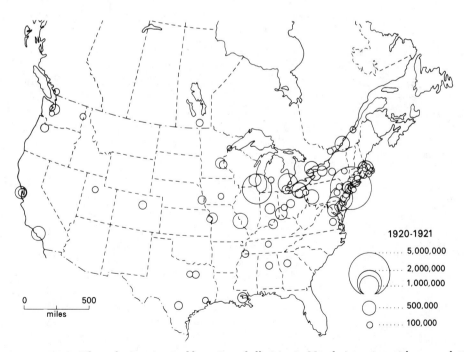

Figure 2.10 The relative size and location of all cities in North America with a population of 100,000 or more in 1920–1921.

developed an iron and steel industry as part of its iron ore transport function, and later became the center of the burgeoning petroleum and petrochemical industry (J.D. Rockefeller). Pittsburgh, located among coalfields, became the center of iron and steel production (Andrew Carnegie).

The Spatial Organization of the Urban System during the Era of National Industrial Capitalism Two main elements of the spatial organization of the urban system under national industrial capitalism became evident by the end of that era. First, the size distribution of the largest urban places became more hierarchical, and second, a highly interconnected manufacturing heartland controlled the economy of the nation (Clapp and Richardson, 1984). The rank-size information in Figure 2.8 demonstrates that the largest places became more dominant, reflecting their status as leaders in the organization and financing of the industrial economy, as well as their significant presence in manufacturing.

This type of situation is presented in diagram form in Figure 2.11, in which the three levels of the size hierarchy of the previous era are replaced by four. The heartland is demarcated by a dashed line, with the hinterland relating to it in a dependent manner. The interurban flows within the heartland are numerous, as the industrial and multifunctional nature of the urban economies generates complex sets of relationships. The interurban flows between the heartland and the regional and small, resource-producing centers of the hinterland are uncomplicated: manufactured goods from the core, raw materials from the hinterland. The growth paths of the variously sized cities are represented as being greatest for cities in the heartland, where profits are generated and reinvested in productive capacity.

Friedmann (1973b) argues that the heartland (core) and the hinterland (periphery) form a spatial system in which innovations (N) diffusing outward from the core are the motor in the growth process (Fig. 2.12). These innovations force the spatial system through successive structural transformations by the processes of innovation diffusion (D), control (C), migration (M), and investment (I). These are indicated by arrows of different width, representing asymmetry in the autonomy/dependency relationship. For example, the volume of control-

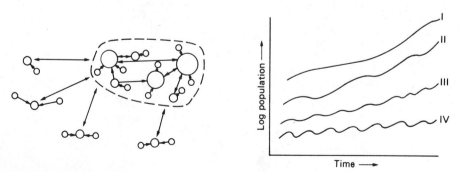

Figure 2.11 The era of national industrial capitalism: model of urban system organization and paths of growth.

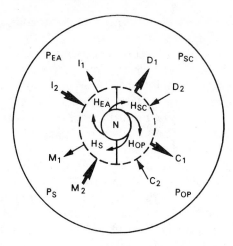

Figure 2.12 A core–periphery model of urban system development. (*Source:* This figure is modified from the original in *Urbanization, Planning, and National Development* by John Friedmann, © 1973, p. 68, by permission of the Publisher, Sage Publications, Inc. [Beverly Hills/London].)

ling decisions emanating from the core may cause a net outflow of capital from the periphery, which in turn intensifies migration from the periphery to the core in response to the changing location of economic and social opportunities. At the same time, however, the continued diffusion of innovations from core to periphery could lead to conditions that demand a partial restructuring of the system's dependency relationships. Continued growth of the system requires that the tensions built up in this way be resolved. Each of the four processes brings about changes in spatial patterns in both heartland (H) and periphery (P). For example, innovation diffusion (D) alters the sociocultural pattern (SC); control (C) processes the pattern of power relationships (OP); migration (M) influences the settlement pattern (S); and investment (I) structures the pattern of economic activities (EA).

The Era of Mature Industrial Capitalism (1935–1975)

Although there was a significant recession following World War I, the Great Depression of the 1930s has been the deepest experienced so far during the capitalist era. It was a terrible time for many people, and a major effort has been made to prevent a similar situation from recurring. Although an economic recovery was underway in the United States by 1935, it was the exigencies of the Second World War that provided much of the technological stimulus to the prolonged period of growth that occurred during the fourth long wave. Governments in both Europe and North America began working closely with private industry and universities in targeted areas of theoretical and applied research and development. These targeted areas included aviation, synthetic materials of all kinds, communications, and the harnessing of nuclear energy.

The result was that the United States emerged from World War II as the most powerful country in the world, and its industrial corporations were in an extraordinarily dominant position with respect not only to products and markets, but to financial and potential governmental support as well. Furthermore, the United States dollar became the preferred medium of international finance. The net result was (1) a shift in the concentration of activity to larger and larger corporations, (2) a tendency for the largest corporations to try to set prices through institutional and organizational arrangements rather than through purely market forces, and (3) the dominance of United States–owned multiple-plant corporations in the world economy. This tendency for concentration in large corporations is illustrated by the fact that in 1973, the 500 largest industrial corporations accounted for over 79% of all corporate profits, and together employed more than 15.5 million individuals.

The fourth Kondratieff long wave is characterized not only by the stimulation of a whole bunch of new technologies and by United States corporate dominance, but also by an increase in the role of government in nearly all aspects of the economy, including defense, trade regulation, and the provision of social services. This feature is easily seen in Figure 2.13, which provides estimates of the proportion of the GNP that emanate from four different, broad sectors of economic activity (the sectors excluded are transportation and construction). Whereas the period from 1885 to 1935 is characterized by limited government influence, government spending in the era of mature industrial

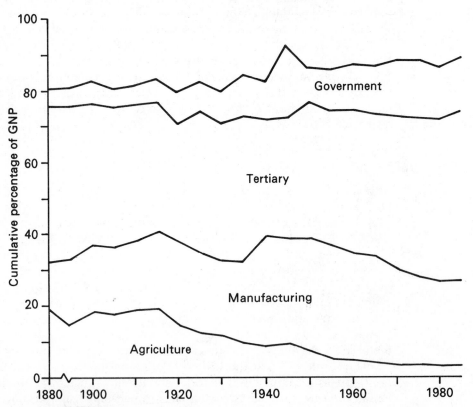

Figure 2.13 The proportion of GNP attributed to four sectors of the United States economy, 1880–1984.

capitalism accounts for a greater share of the GNP than agriculture. Although the percentages for the war years are an aberration, in general the direct role of government in the economy increased threefold throughout the era.

Thus, the geographical direction of government expenditures has an increasingly significant impact on the differential growth among the various regions. Figure 2.14 illustrates the spatial distribution (by state) of federal expenditures per dollar of federal taxes during the middle years of the era. It is quite noticeable that the core, or heartland area, receives far less in federal expenditures than is paid in taxes, whereas the hinterland states receive considerably more. For example, Michigan received $.58 in federal expenditures for every $1.00 in federal taxes in 1965–1967, whereas Georgia received $1.52. There is, therefore, a net drain of monies away from the traditional heartland to the hinterland, that is, from the north to the south and west.

In addition to the increased role of government in the economy, there is a growth in the tertiary sector's contribution to the GNP (Fig. 2.13). Although the tertiary sector (wholesale and retail trade, finance, insurance, and real estate; services, including education and hospitals) has always been a large component of the GNP, during the 1935–1975 era this share grew from about 33% to nearly 45%. This was accompanied by a large increase in employment, particularly among women. For example, whereas manufacturing employment increased by 88% between 1929 and 1970, employment in the tertiary sector increased by 108%.

The stimulation of technological change, the power of large corporations, and the increased role of the government are linked to rapidly rising real per capita incomes and high rates of population growth. The information in Figure 2.3 shows that on a constant-dollar basis, per capita wealth more than doubled during the era. Much of this wealth was devoted to improved living conditions in urban areas. The "baby boom" added an unusual urgency to the need for housing and services within cities, as well as generating a tremendous increase in consumer spending.

The Urban System during the Era of Mature Industrial Capitalism   Figure 2.15 illustrates the relative size and distribution of all SMSAs and CMAs in North America that had a population of 500,000 or more in 1970–1971. The changes in the distribution of population that occurred between the beginning and the end of the fourth long wave can be characterized as relating to:

1. An increase in scale of urbanization, leading to the emergence of super-metropolitan and megalopolitan urban formations.
2. The deconcentration of continental urban growth, resulting in metropolitan urban developments across much of the continent.
3. The spectacular growth of urban areas beyond the old central cities that contained most of the urban population in 1920.

The general deconcentration and metropolitanization of the population between 1920 and 1970 is directly related to the way in which automobile, truck, and air transportation shaped urban development. In particular, the wide-

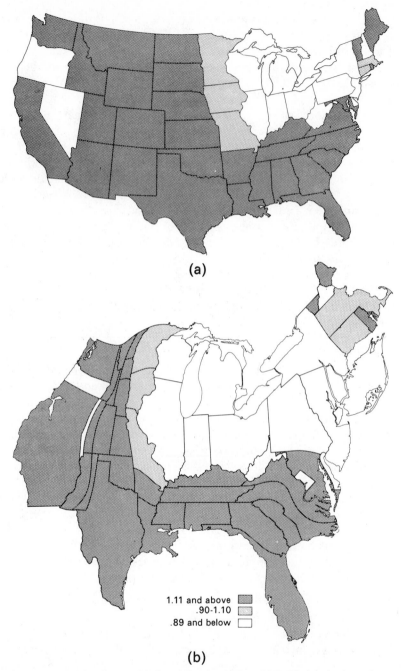

(a)

(b)

1.11 and above
.90–1.10
.89 and below

Figure 2.14 The flows of federal funds, 1965–1967. (Federal expenditures per dollar of federal taxes, by state.)

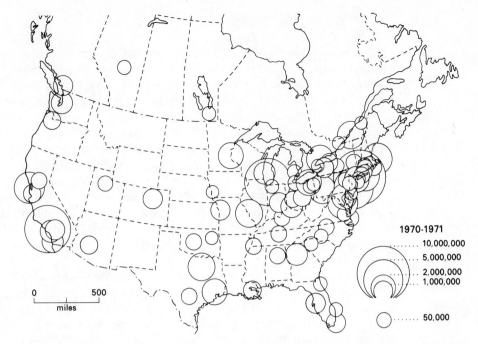

Figure 2.15 The relative size and location of all metropolitan areas (SMSAs and CMAs) in North America with a population of 500,000 or more in 1970–1971.

spread adoption of the automobile (two and three-tenths persons for every automobile in 1970) facilitated the decentralization of population in metropolitan areas. The construction of federally financed highways in the 1930s, the Pennsylvania, Ohio, and Indiana turnpikes in the 1950s, and the high-capacity, limited-access Interstate Highway System in the 1960s and 1970s resulted in a new network of surface transportation that allowed the truck to replace the railroad and created a continental market that could be well served from a number of different locations. At the same time, the rapid growth of air transportation in the 1960s and early 1970s virtually eliminated rail passenger transport and made all metropolitan areas highly accessible to each other.

The most noticeable feature of Figure 2.15 is the extensive concentration of urban population in a 500-mile arc along the East Coast of the United States. This region, which in 1970 contained 43 million people, or one-fifth the population of the United States, has been defined as a *megalopolis* (Gottman, 1961). The metropolises merged into each other, either directly through physical expansion, or indirectly as a result of overlapping commuting fields, creating a continuous urban strip of central cities, suburban tracts, and overgrown dormitory towns. Another supermetropolitan region, a Great Lakes megalopolis is in the process of forming. This megalopolis extends from Milwaukee, Wisconsin and Chicago on the west, through Detroit and Cleveland, to Pittsburgh, Buffalo, and Toronto on the east. In all, it contains an urban population of more than 40 million people.

Probably the most publicized changes in the North American urban system during this era occurred in the South, in Texas, and along the West Coast. Much of this area has been referred to as the "sun belt" (in contrast to the "snow belt" or "rust belt" of the Midwest and Northeast), and there is no doubt that warmth has a certain attraction. Nowhere is this more apparent than in Florida, where four major metropolitan areas grew in response to warmth, recreational facilities and other amenities, and to retirement stimuli. There was also a growth in manufacturing in the South that was associated with the shift from the Northeast of the textile and furniture industries, and with the emergence of Atlanta as a major financial and business center for the region. Urban areas along the Gulf Coast, in Texas, and in Oklahoma grew in population due to the development of oil fields and petrochemicals, and later, because of the electronics and aerospace industries. Dallas, Texas, in particular, emerged as a center of finance for the region.

The rapid growth of Houston, Texas exemplifies quite clearly the importance of entrepreneurial manipulation of federal and local governments, local institutions, and public and private capital as a major cause of growth in sun belt cities. For example, much of the initial economic dynamism in the city during this era is related to the completion of the Houston ship canal by the U.S. Bureau of Public Works and to the decision by NASA to locate the Manned Spacecraft Center in the metropolis.

Even more dramatic was the growth of Los Angeles from a metropolitan area containing nearly 580,000 people in 1920 to the second-largest metropolis on the continent, with a population of over 7 million in 1970. Economic activities deriving from oil, food processing, recreation, the film and television industries, petrochemicals, electronics, and aerospace activities are the underpinnings of a supermetropolitan area that contains 12 million people and extends some 250 miles from Santa Barbara to San Diego, California. A smaller metropolitan area of 4.5 million developed around San Francisco Bay based on a variety of manufacturing, food processing, electronics, finance, commerce, and port-related activities. Farther north along the West Coast, the cities around the Puget Sound developed yet another integrated metropolitan region of 3.5 million that focused on Seattle, Washington and its port and aircraft industries.

One of the significant features of the mature industrial capitalism era is suburbanization. The suburbanization process has been a part of the North American urban scene since the middle of the nineteenth century. Suburban developments can be interpreted as the spatial expression of the class divisions that emerged with the more complex divisions of labor that occurred as the capitalist era evolved and urban areas grew outward (Walker, 1981; Edel, *et al.,* 1984). The period between 1935 and 1975 was one in which the automobile shaped the suburbs, for the automobile provided people with a personal means of transportation, freed the population from reliance on public transportation, and permitted expansion in residential areas with lower density and more rural-seeming environments.

The greatest volume of suburbanization occurred following the Second World War, when the supply of new housing was low due to limited wartime construction, and the demand for housing was high as the population returned to peacetime activities. This need was met by the expansion of federal housing programs to provide low-interest, low downpayment, federally insured mortgages for new housing. As new housing invariably requires the transfer of rural land to urban use at the periphery of cities, the government in effect helped to promote rapid suburbanization and also subsidized middle-class white home-owners.

In consequence, between 1950 and 1970 suburban areas throughout the United States increased in population by 60%, whereas the central cities increased by only 32%. The increase in the population of the central cities was largely attributable to an increase in the nonwhite population, which by 1970 comprised 22.5% of the population of the central cities. Thus, by 1975 the United States was well on its way to a situation in which the great majority of the nonwhite population lived in the central cities and the vast majority of the white population lived in noncentral-city locations. During the 1960s and early 1970s, a number of these central cities became the arena for the expression of much legitimate black rage over a lack of employment opportunities, poor housing, and a wide array of socioeconomic inequalities.

The Spatial Organization of the Urban System during the Era of Mature Industrial Capitalism As the urban system became ever more highly interconnected between 1935 and 1975, the initial, locational advantages of urban growth in the Northeast and lower Great Lakes area became less important. In fact, throughout the entire era the population growth of these large regions was less than that in the rest of the United States (Yeates, 1980). Furthermore, the growth rates of the larger places in the snow belt began to level off (and in a few cases to decline), whereas regional centers in the sun belt gained considerable population. As a result, the rank-size distribution for 1970 begins to become less steep as the regional centers in general, and those in the sun belt in particular, begin to assume greater importance (Fig. 2.8). Given that urban development in North America is related to the outcome of corporate decision making, it is not surprising that there are a number of studies attributing the growth of these regional centers to the corporate headquarters that have been relocated to them (Semple and Phipps, 1982; Stephens and Holly, 1981; Wheeler and Brown, 1985).

The general model of urban system organization that emerges during the 1935–1975 era is thus more complex than one that preceded it (Fig. 2.16). A core/periphery arrangement remains, with the megalopolitan transformations giving rise to corridors of high volume, interurban transportation. The regional centers develop their own strong hinterlands, and in one or two areas "incipient cores" begin to develop due to the concentration of particular local growth

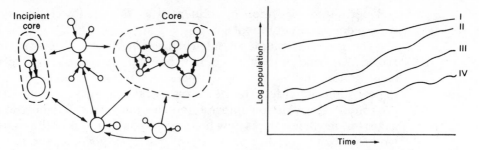

Figure 2.16 The era of mature industrial capitalism: model of urban system organization and paths of growth.

stimuli. The net result is that the population growth rate of the second-level centers (Fig. 2.16)—the regional centers—is far greater than that of the highest level, and the growth rates of the third and fourth levels are also quite large (Davies, 1986).

The Era of Global Capitalism (1975–)

If it is accepted that the era of global capitalism is characterized by both a marked decrease in the international (and national) dominance of United States corporations and by the emergence of new product and process technologies, then it is reasonable to suppose that the urban geography of the fifth Kondratieff may be quite different from that experienced during the fourth long wave (Hall, 1985). Along with these special characteristics, the fifth long wave is marked by a continuation of a number of underlying changes in the structure of the United States economy that were observed toward the end of the 1935– 1975 period.

The information in Figure 2.13 demonstrates that (1) the relative contribution to the GNP of agriculture continues to remain at a low level, (2) the government still plays a large role in the economy, (3) tertiary activities are still increasing, and (4) manufacturing is decreasing. Furthermore, the period from 1975 onward is one in which the population is aging quite significantly. This is important not only because it influences the geographic flow of funds for social services, but also because senior citizens' expenditures directly affect interregional financial transfers. Manson and Groop (1986) estimate that in 1983 one-third of all personal income in the United States was *unrelated* to employment income.

Thus, it is to be expected that during the fifth Kondratieff the urban areas that will incur the greatest growth will be those that have the most diversified economies and many amenities (Keinath, 1985). Furthermore, urban growth will be influenced, according to the Friedmann (1973b) core/periphery model, by the spatial pattern of the sources of the technological innovations that are fundamental to the new era. Also, expenditures by the federal government may well continue to be spatially biased (Lawson, 1985). In this latter regard it is interesting to observe from Figure 2.17 that whereas the discrepancy in the flow of funds was not as great in 1982–1984 as in 1965–1967 (Fig. 2.14), large parts of the snow belt still paid more in federal taxes than they received in federal expenditures.

The Urban System during the Era of Global Capitalism   At this early stage in a new long wave it is wise to be cautious about predicting the expected course of urbanization. Nevertheless, it does appear that a number of significant changes are occurring in the United States urban system that may well continue during the next few decades. These changes can be summarized as (1) macro-level counterurbanization and snow belt/sun belt shifts, (2) regional concentration, and (3) local deconcentration. Thus, the pattern of change is quite similar to that outlined in Chapter 1 as occurring in recent decades with respect to the Canadian urban system.

The term *counterurbanization* was used by Berry (1976) to imply a reversal of a trend that had existed throughout the early 1970s. Whereas urbanization is a process of population concentration, counterurbanization is a process of population deconcentration. Whereas urbanization is a process involving increasing size, density, and heterogeneity (mixing), counterurbanization describes a state of decreasing size of largest places, decreasing densities, and decreasing heterogeneity (that is, more separation). This powerful intuitive statement appears to be substantiated by some, but not all, of the early evidence (Conzen, 1983; Fuguitt, 1985), and is consistent with the major changes that underly the transition to the fifth long wave.

Figure 2.18 shows the changing population growth rates in the aggregate for differently sized groupings of urban places and for types of locations. It is clear that the pattern of population change in the 1970s was quite different from that in the 1960s. The largest SMSAs (3 million or more) actually declined (in the aggregate) in population in the 1970s, and growth rates increased with decreasing SMSA size. Smaller places in nonmetropolitan counties adjacent to metropolitan areas grew faster than the larger places in similar locations. Finally, and probably most indicative of all, nonmetropolitan counties *not* adjacent to metropolitan areas all increased in population a great deal faster in the 1970s than they did in the 1960s. Hence the idea of counterurbanization also includes the notion of *nonmetropolitan growth*. This nonadjacent growth appears to be reversing during the 1980s, however (Fuguitt, 1985).

The fact that metropolitan areas in the sun belt have been increasing in population at a much faster rate than those in the snow belt was a feature that began to emerge during the 1960s, but in the 1970s the trend became even more dramatic (Table 2.3). Many of the snow belt SMSAs actually began to decrease in population size, even when fairly extensive definitions of their area were used. It is interesting to note that some large metropolitan areas in the sun belt are now exhibiting a decrease in the rate of population growth due to the spreading out of population beyond the urban boundaries.

The deconcentration, or spreading out, of population at the local level has

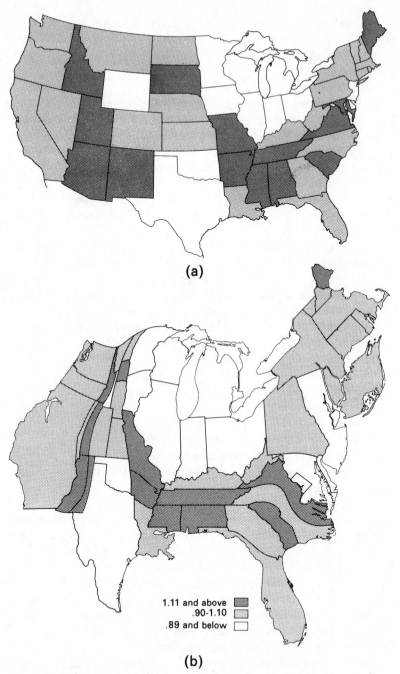

Figure 2.17 The flows of federal funds, 1982–1984. (Federal expenditures per dollar of federal taxes, by state.)

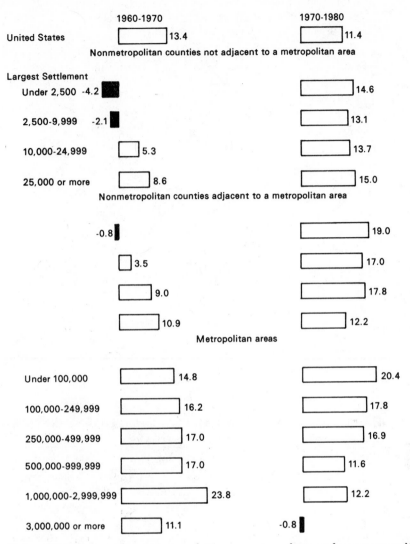

Figure 2.18 Recent change in population in metropolitan and nonmetropolitan areas in the United States, 1960–1970 and 1970–1980.

been occurring over many decades, so the continuation of this trend through the fifth Kondratieff is not unexpected. Table 2.4 shows that the population of the eighty-five largest SMSAs changed from predominantly central-city dwellers to more than 50% suburbanite between 1960 and 1970; in some SMSAs in the East, about two-thirds of the population was located in suburban areas in 1980. Furthermore, a number of people have been relocating from the city to the country, a trend known as *exurbanization.* One important feature underlying central city/suburban disparities of many kinds is that central cities have become *the* location of the urban black population. This is but one mani-

Table 2.3 PERCENT POPULATION CHANGE IN SELECTED
SUN BELT AND SNOW BELT SMSAS
1960–1970 and 1970–1980

Area	1960–1970	1970–1980
United States	13.3	11.4
Sun belt		
Atlanta	36.7	27.4
Dallas–Ft. Worth	39.9	28.3
Denver	32.1	30.7
Houston	40.0	45.3
Los Angeles	16.4	6.2
Miami	35.6	28.3
Phoenix	45.8	55.3
San Antonio	20.6	20.7
San Diego	31.4	37.1
Snow belt		
Chicago	12.2	1.8
Cleveland	8.1	− 8.0
Detroit	11.6	− 1.9
New York	8.2	− 8.6
Philadelphia	10.9	− 2.2
St. Louis	12.3	− 2.3

Source: Long (1983, p. 9).

Table 2.4 PROPORTION OF POPULATION OF SMSAS LOCATED IN CENTRAL CITIES,
1960–1980, AND BLACK HOUSEHOLDS

Area	% in central cities			% Black households	
	1960	1970	1980	1970	1980
United States	51%	49%	44%	17.9%	21.4%
East	41	36	33	17.1	20.3
Midwest	52	48	42	18.8	23.4
South[a]	59	58	54	24.1	28.4
West	49	45	44	8.9	10.5

[a]Excluding Jacksonville, Florida and Baton Rouge, Louisiana.

Source: ACIR (1984, Tables 1 and A.2).

festation of the "decreasing heterogeneity" aspect of the counterurbanization process.

The Spatial Organization of the Urban System during the Era of Global Capitalism
There are, therefore, a number of new features in the spatial organization of the urban system during the era of global capitalism. These are indicated in Figure 2.19.

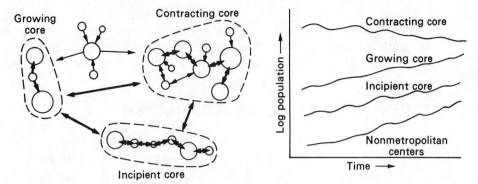

Figure 2.19 The era of global capitalism: model of urban system organization and paths of growth.

1. Certain major metropolitan areas have become transaction centers linking parts of the nation to the network of international capital markets. In the United States, these world cities appear to be New York, Chicago, San Francisco, Los Angeles, Miami, and Dallas–Fort Worth (Friedmann and Wolff, 1982).
2. The old manufacturing heartland appears to be contracting toward the more diversified economies of New York, Boston, and Chicago.
3. The California urban region extending from Los Angeles/San Diego through to San Francisco/Oakland/San Jose has established itself firmly as a core of technological (Silicon Valley) and cultural innovation.
4. An incipient core appears to be developing along the Gulf Coast based on the petrochemical industry and the new information-processing and space technologies (Vining *et al.,* 1982).
5. With the decline in the birth rate, immigration (Maldonado and Moore, 1985) and intercity migration has become a much more important factor in differential urban growth. Whereas in the 1960s internal migration accounted for about 10% of the relative change in population in the United States, in the 1970s it accounted for almost 30%. As a consequence, the growth rate of metropolitan areas can fluctuate quite markedly from year to year according to underlying economic fortunes. For example, with the decrease in oil prices (and consequent investment in related enterprises) in 1985–1986 there was a considerable downturn in the economies of the Gulf cities and a sharp decrease in their rates of growth.

There are, as we have seen, a number of important general features concerning the spatial structure of the United States urban system during the era of global capitalism. First of all, a number of cores (some major, others minor) will be of megalopolitan appearance and will act as conduits to international capital. These supermetropolises will be polycentric in form (Levin, 1978), and the urban areas will blend rather loosely to form galactic arrangements (Lewis, 1983). Within these cores, transport corridors will develop, and the task will be to ensure that interactions among the variety of modes of transportation involved can occur swiftly and relatively cheaply. Given the expected increase in the number and size of core areas, the rank-size distribution of cities toward the end of the fifth long wave will be even flatter than it was at the end of the fourth.

THE EVOLUTION OF THE CANADIAN URBAN SYSTEM

The development of the Canadian urban system should be discussed in the context of United States economic and urban growth as well as its own internal dynamics. Throughout much of the history of the country, either direct connections with Europe and the United States, or, more recently, direct connections with the United States alone, have influenced differential urban growth to a large degree. Furthermore, various national policies implemented by Canada itself—for example, the decision to unite the fledgling nation by railroad (completed in 1885)—have also had a profound effect on national urban development. Some examples of these types of internally generated forces have been discussed in Chapter 1.

In general, it may be useful to divide Canadian urban development into three periods:

1. Frontier–staples (before 1935)
2. Industrial capitalism (1935–1975)
3. Global capitalism (1975–)

This is not to imply that there was no industrial development prior to 1935—indeed there was. Nor are these divisions meant to imply that trade in resources was not important after 1935, for such trade has remained vital. Rather, the 1930s are considered a watershed in capital investment, for prior to that period, a large proportion of the country's capital investment came from the United Kingdom and went primarily into resource development. After the 1930s, much of the investment came from the United States, and a larger share went into industrial development. Since the 1970s, the country has experienced investment from a wider variety of international sources, such as Japan, Hong Kong, and Western Europe, that are directed toward both industrial and resource development. Each of these different investment emphases has had a significant impact upon urban growth.

The Frontier–Staples Era (prior to 1935)

During the nineteenth century, Canada made the transition from an economy that was basically frontier–mercantile at the beginning of the century to one that was staples-oriented with some industrial capacity in Central Canada by the beginning of the twentieth century. In 1831, the largest cities in the area that was to become Canada were Quebec City, Montreal, St. John's (Newfoundland), St. John (New Brunswick), and Halifax—all clearly gateway cities. Gateway cities are also prominent among the ten cities with the largest populations in 1871 (Table 2.5). By 1921, however, the elements of the late twentieth-century urban system were in place (Smith, 1982).

The technological innovations, large-scale immigration, industrial growth in Western Europe, and economic boom of the first few decades of the third Kondratieff long wave combined to shape the urban geography of Canada. These underlying forces are reflected in: (1) the extension and consolidation of the railroad network in the west, (2) the consequent opening of the prairies for wheat production, (3) the exploitation of resources (copper for electric wires, and nickel) on the Shield in northern Quebec and northern Ontario, and (4) the growth of manufacturing in central Canada under the protectionist umbrella of the National Policy. The greatest stimulation to manufacturing came during World War I, however, when Canada was closely involved with the British war effort.

Thus, whereas in 1871 the gateway cities of the east coast and those located on the St. Lawrence River and along Lake Ontario were well-represented among the ten largest places, in 1921 the east coast cities were not represented at all; they were replaced by those of the prairies and west (Table 2.5). Also, Montreal and Toronto had become major metropolises with a wide variety of financial, commercial, and manufacturing activities as their economic bases. Winnipeg had become the hub of rail service for the west, and Edmonton and Calgary had joined it as major regional service centers.

The Spatial Organization of the Urban System During the Frontier–Staples Era
In the frontier–mercantile portion of this long era, the urban system in the part of North America that was to become Canada was organized much as is indicated in Figure 2.6. However, as Canada merged into a staples economy, producing raw materials and agricultural products for export, the urban system be-

Table 2.5   CHANGES IN THE RANK-ORDER OF URBAN PLACES IN CANADA, 1871, 1921, 1971, AND 1981
(Population Figures in Parentheses in Thousands)

1871		1921		1971		1981	
Montreal	(115)	Montreal	(724)	Montreal	(2,743)	Toronto	(2,999)
Quebec City	(60)	Toronto	(611)	Toronto	(2,628)	Montreal	(2,828)
Toronto	(59)	Winnipeg	(228)	Vancouver	(1,082)	Vancouver	(1,268)
St. John	(41)	Vancouver	(223)	Ottawa–Hull	(603)	Ottawa–Hull	(718)
Halifax	(30)	Hamilton	(114)	Winnipeg	(540)	Edmonton	(657)
Hamilton	(27)	Ottawa	(108)	Hamilton	(498)	Calgary	(593)
Ottawa	(24)	Quebec City	(95)	Edmonton	(496)	Winnipeg	(585)
St. John's	(23)	Calgary	(63)	Quebec City	(481)	Quebec City	(576)
London	(18)	London	(61)	Calgary	(403)	Hamilton	(542)
Kingston	(12)	Edmonton	(59)	Windsor	(259)	St. Catharines–Niagara	(304)

Sources: Canada Year Book (1924, Table 37); 1984 (Table 2.10).

came organized in a different fashion. A model of the type of urban system that developed is given in Figure 2.20. Small towns, usually located along railroad branch lines, serve as collecting points for raw materials, which are shipped to the regional centers (level II), and then to the major urban areas for partial processing and export. Information in turn flows back from the largest places to the smallest in a similar hierarchical fashion. The growth paths of the largest places are fairly smooth, but the growth patterns for single-industry resource towns (level III) can be quite uneven, going from boom to bust within a few years. Problems arising from cyclical demand and resource depletion in single-industry towns continue to the current era (Bradbury, 1984; DREE, 1979).

By 1930, the pattern of urban development in Canada conformed quite closely to the model in Figure 2.20. Montreal and Toronto, each reflective of the two different cultural entities (French and English) that were forged in 1867 to produce Canada, served as level I centers. Vancouver, Winnipeg, Calgary, Edmonton, and London are examples of level II centers in such a staples system; Hamilton is the focus of heavy iron, steel, and machinery manufacturing for the country; Ottawa serves as the growing federal capital; and Toronto and Quebec City are the capitals of the two major provinces.

The Era of Industrial Capitalism (1935–1975)

The economy of Canada changed considerably between 1935 and 1975, bringing considerable urban growth. The types of transformations that occurred are summarized briefly in Figure 2.21, which graphs the change in value of output (in constant 1971 Canadian dollars) in tertiary activities, manufacturing, and primary industries (divided into agriculture, forestry, and fishing; and petroleum and mining). Note that the graphs are presented on a semilogarithmic scale, which means that the slopes indicate rates of change at different time periods.

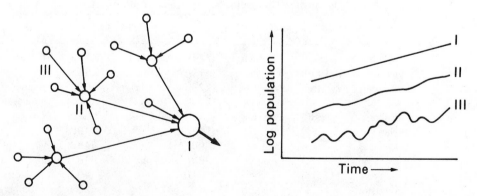

Figure 2.20 The frontier–staples era: model of urban system organization and paths of growth. (*Source:* Simmons, 1978, p. 64.)

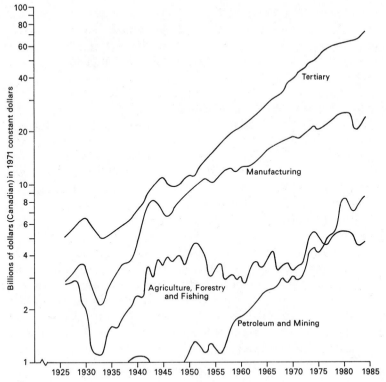

Figure 2.21 The contribution of major sectors of economic activity to GDP, 1926–1984 (in constant 1971 dollars). (*Source:* Data from Leacy, 1983; Statistics Canada, 1984c.)

One basic observation that can be deduced from Figure 2.21 is that the growth rate in GNP per capita in Canada is quite similar to the curve for the United States since 1926 (Fig. 2.3). A major difference is that the depression of the 1930s lasted much longer in Canada than in the United States, and the country did not really recover until the Second World War. Furthermore, the postwar recession was more prolonged in Canada than in the United States, and a sustained period of growth was not really achieved until the 1950s. As a consequence, postwar urban expansion was more advanced in the United States than in Canada. But after 1950, urbanization proceeded at a more rapid rate in Canada than in the United States (Fig. 2.2) as the economy grew apace.

The stimulus for this urban development was the tremendous growth in manufacturing in central Canada. During the 1920s, both agriculture (plus forestry and fishing) and manufacturing accounted for similar amounts of output, but following the exigencies of the war effort, manufacturing embarked upon a period of almost continuous expansion. This was stimulated primarily by investment in branch plant production in Canada by United States–owned corporations. The greatest amount of investment followed the 1965 signing of the Automotive Trades Agreement ("Auto Pact") between Canada and the United States. This agreement resulted in a rationalization of the North American automobile industry and the establishment of a large number of branch plants related to the automobile industry in Ontario, close to United States producers (Holmes, 1983).

Also of significance during this era was the relatively stable contribution of agriculture, forestry, and fishing to the economy as compared with the rapid growth in the value of output in petroleum (plus natural gas) after 1950. Increases in productivity in agriculture and the development of agribusiness further reduced the demand for labor on farms and led to outmigration from agricultural areas (Wallace, 1985), particularly in the provinces of Saskatchewan and Manitoba, and to a concomitant decrease in the population of local service centers. On the other hand, the rapid growth of the petroleum and natural gas industry generated considerable growth in the larger urban centers in Alberta.

The third transformation relates to the tertiary activities, which since 1955 have increased in value of output at a greater rate than manufacturing (the general slope of the line for tertiary activities is steeper than that for manufacturing). Nearly all service activities are located in cities, and those that have contributed the most to the increase, such as health services and governmental activities, are usually oriented toward large cities. As a consequence, the shift to the postindustrial society had a considerable impact on urban growth in the larger places (Bell, 1976).

The Spatial Organization of the Urban System during the Era of Industrial Capitalism
As is indicated in Figure 2.16, during the era of industrial capitalism in Canada a strong core region developed, characterized by a shift of population to the largest urban places. The era was also marked by the continuance of a strong staples economy. As a consequence, the urban system in 1971 reflects these two underlying economic dimensions, along with the dual language/cultural nature of the nation. By 1971, Montreal and Toronto had grown to become the ninth- and twelfth-largest metropolises, respectively, of North America. The growth of Ottawa–Hull reflected the strong role of government in the economy, Edmonton and Calgary were a direct product of the burgeoning petroleum industry, the relative decline of Winnipeg reflected the stagnant agricultural base of the prairies, and the growth of Windsor was symbolic of the strength of the automobile industry.

Perhaps the most significant development in the urban system was the emergence of a strong heartland of almost continuous urban development extending 1,000 kilometers (621 miles) from Windsor to Quebec City (Fig. 2.22). In 1971, this core region encompassed more than 70% of the manufacturing employment in the country and more than 60% of the population. The average inhabitants of the heartland were 25% wealthier than their counterparts in the hinterland. Furthermore, the financial centers of Toronto and Montreal dominated the investment community for the country as a whole and contained nearly all the headquarters offices (Yeates, 1975a; 1985b).

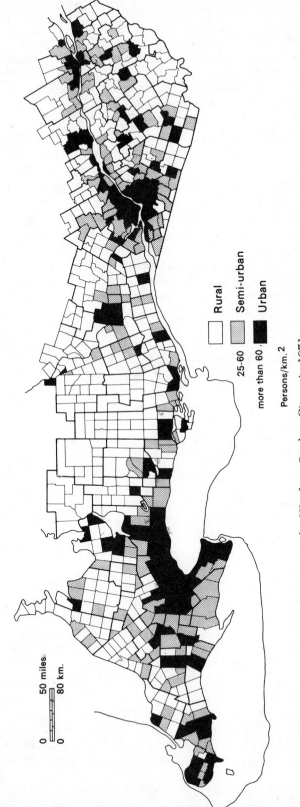

50 miles.
80 km.

0
0

Rural

25-60 Semi-urban

more than 60 Urban

Persons/km.²

Figure 2.22 The extent of urban development in the Windsor–Quebec City axis, 1971.

The Era of Global Capitalism (1975–)

Although it is difficult to predict the particulars of Canadian urban development during the fifth Kondratieff, which is complicated by the continuing staples/industrial nature of the economy, there are some signs as to what is happening. In the first place, it seems clear that global events, with respect to both international finance and trade, will have a great influence on the course of the economy and hence on urban development. Some of these types of events were discussed in Chapter 1, in the example concerning the linkage between the spatial and aspatial aspects of geographic inquiry (pp. 3–5). In that section, the influence of demographic, economic, and governmental factors on the location of economic activities and urban development was outlined.

It is already apparent that a number of significant transformations in the economy are being generated as byproducts of the trends discussed earlier in this chapter. These are summarized in Figure 2.21, in the information for 1970 to 1985. First, the value of petroleum (and mining) in the economy has increased dramatically, in accordance with world prices as modified by national policies. As a consequence, Edmonton and Calgary and other towns and cities in the province of Alberta (such as Red Deer, and Fort MacMurray) achieved the highest rates of growth in the country between 1970 and 1980. The collapse of oil prices in 1986 (not represented in Fig. 2.21) severely dampened growth and caused considerable out-migration. These urban places are, then, very much staple-economy related, and follow boom-and-bust patterns. In a similar vein, agriculturally based Winnipeg, although still increasing slightly in population, continues to grow at a rate below the national average.

The rate of growth of manufacturing in the 1970s, and during the recession years of the early 1980s, also fluctuated quite widely. It is now clear that not only has the relative contribution of manufacturing to GDP been decreasing, but the aggregate rate of growth in manufacturing is low. This has resulted in nonuniform rates of growth among cities that have much of their economic base in manufacturing: Windsor and Hamilton grew quite slowly, for example, whereas Oshawa had a high growth rate during the 1980s.

On the other hand, tertiary activities have continued to be major contributors to the economy, particularly those activities that relate to finance, business services (such as information processing and accounting), and government. These activities are becoming concentrated in the largest metropolises of all— Toronto, Montreal (Slack, 1988), and Vancouver—and many corporate headquarters and international subsidiary offices have relocated from Montreal to Toronto (Semple and Green, 1983). Toronto became the major conduit between the rest of the country and the international capital markets, with Calgary and Edmonton serving as links to the more specialized international petroleum industry.

As a consequence, by the late 1980s the Canadian urban system was exhibiting, in a rather simple manner, the major features of macro-level deconcentration in the era of global capitalism that are suggested in Figure 2.19. Those parts of the hinterland that had staples that were much in demand grew quite rapidly. The core had the appearance, by the mid-1980s, of contracting inward, toward Toronto and southwestern Ontario, which is the home of the United States–linked auto industry and of other associated branch plant activities. In the west, incipient cores may be developing in the form of the Calgary–Edmonton corridor and in the Vancouver–Victoria region, which is also closely linked to the Puget Sound urban region (Smith and Johnson, 1978).

Conclusion

Urban development in North America can be described in the context of major changes in the economy of the region. These major changes can be related fairly conveniently to long waves; that is, to fluctuations in economic growth that are brought about by the convergence of a number of major groups of stimulants—demographic changes (birth rate and foreign immigration), new resources (new lands or new mineral resources), and clusters of enabling technological innovations such as computers which influence production processes in a wide array of activities. The growth of urban places in both the United States and in Canada can be related directly to these Kondratieff long waves; distributional maps are presented for the date nearest the peak of each fluctuation. As the North American urban system is regarded on the whole as being primarily the product of industrialization, and changes during the fifth Kondratieff relate particularly to technological innovation in manufacturing production and processes, the location of manufacturing will be discussed separately, in Chapter 3.

Chapter
3

Cities as Centers of Manufacturing

*T*he relationship between urban growth in North America and manufacturing is extremely important. The rapid growth of cities, which has occurred within an evolving heartland/hinterland framework, is related primarily to industrial development. The intraregional deconcentration of population during the late 1970s and early 1980s was in large part caused by the shift of capital investments away from the industrial core of the Northeast to the South and West (Walker and Storper, 1981). Manufacturing is a vital element in the economic base of most cities, either directly as a basic industry, or indirectly through the multiplier effect and through the interdependencies generated by forward and backward linkages (McDermott and Taylor, 1982).

THE IMPORTANCE AND LOCATION OF MANUFACTURING

Urbanization in North America has been both the product of, and inextricably intertwined with, economic growth. Some time ago, Kaldor (1966) presented a number of propositions concerning economic growth in a country, and these have subsequently been the subject of much debate (Thirwall, 1983). The most basic of Kaldor's propositions is that the faster the rate of growth of manufacturing in a country, the faster the rate of economic growth (as measured, for example, by GDP). This is not just because manufacturing forms a part of GDP, but because the wealth generated by high productivity in manufacturing induces economic activity elsewhere in the economy.

Even in an economy such as Canada's, which is supposedly strongly dependent upon the production of raw materials, the relationship between change in GDP (in constant dollars) from 1951 to 1981 is more strongly related to the growth of manufacturing than it is to the growth of primary and manufacturing industries combined (Fig. 3.1). Manufacturing in North America is, therefore, a most important engine of growth, and consequently, a most important stimulant to urban growth (and, on the downside, to urban decline).

Manufacturing, as an activity may be analyzed in three main ways: with respect to the *components* of the industry, to the *value added,* and to the *stage* of the production process involved. There are two main components to manufacturing—durable and nondurable goods. The durable goods sector (Table 3.1) consists mainly of products that are either not consumed once used, or that do not wear out in the short term. In North America, the urban areas involved in this type of production are located primarily in the traditional Manufacturing Belt that extends from eastern Iowa to southern New England and southern Ontario (Fig. 3.2). In those places in which iron and steel, farm equipment, automobiles, and electrical machinery are produced, there has been considerable instability and some decline as a result of excess capacity, an aging capital stock, and foreign competition (Archer and White, 1985).

The nondurable goods sector consists of those industries that produce manufactured products that are, or may be, consumed rather quickly when used.

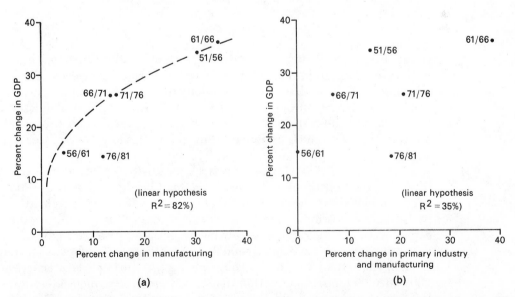

Figure 3.1 The relationship of percentage change in GDP to major sectors of national output in Canada.

Table 3.1   DURABLE AND NONDURABLE GOODS
MANUFACTURING SECTORS
Percent of Total Output, by Sector, 1983

Sector	Percent
Durable goods	57.0 %
Machinery, except electrical	11.0
Electric and electronic equipment	9.8
Fabricated metal products	7.1
Other transportation equipment	5.5
Primary metal industries	5.0
Motor vehicles and equipment	5.9
Investments and related products	3.8
Clay, stone, and glass products	2.9
Lumber and wood products	2.6
Furniture and fixtures	1.6
Nondurable goods	43.0
Food and kindred products	8.1
Chemicals and allied products	7.8
Petroleum and coal products	6.4
Printing and publishing	6.4
Paper and allied products	4.0
Rubber and miscellaneous plastic products	3.3
Apparel and other textile products	3.3
Textile mill products	2.6
Tobacco manufacturers	0.9
Leather and leather products	0.9

Source: Bureau of the Census (1984), *Statistical Abstract of the United States, 1985,* Washington, D.C.: U.S. Department of Commerce, p. 744.

Urban areas specializing in the manufacture of nondurable goods are located in the New England area, the Interstate 95 corridor from New York City to Washington, D.C., and in a broad belt along the southeastern Piedmont plateau, from Virginia to North Carolina and South Carolina (Fig. 3.3). This last area has been growing the fastest in recent years, as the textile and processed foods industries move from the manufacturing belt to this lower-wage area (Johnson, 1985).

A second way of looking at manufacturing is with respect to the value added in the production process. *Value-added* may be defined as the value of the goods produced less the cost of the materials, supplies, fuel, and electricity used in the manufacturing process. Low value-added industries tend to have low capital-to-labor ratios and relatively low wage rates, whereas high value-added industries tend to have high capital: labor ratios and higher wage rates. In Canada, more than 70% of the country's manufacturing is located in southern Ontario and Quebec, and within that area there are distinct differences in the location of high value-added and low value-added industries (Fig. 3.4). High

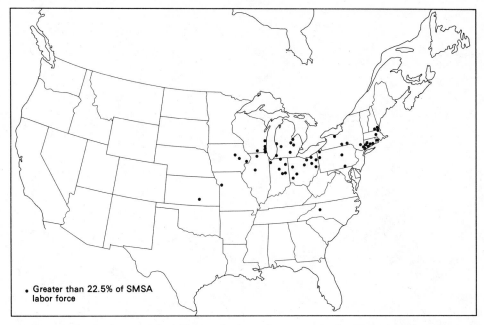

Figure 3.2 The location of durable goods manufacturing in the United States. (*Source:* Archer and White, 1985, p. 134.)

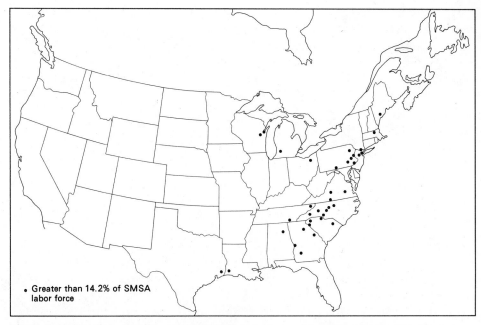

Figure 3.3 The location of nondurable goods manufacturing in the United States. (*Source:* Archer and White, 1985, p. 135.)

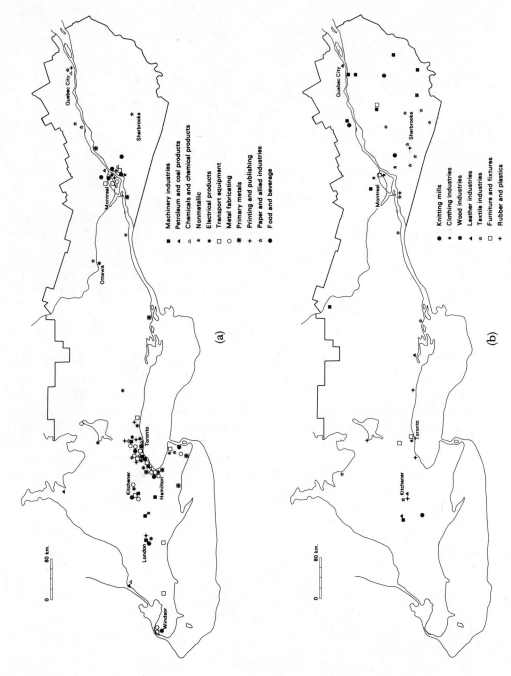

Figure 3.4 The location of (a) high value-added and (b) low value-added industries in central Canada.

value-added industries are located primarily in southern Ontario and Montreal; low value-added industries in southern Quebec. Norcliffe and Stevens (1979) explain the difference in terms of the initial advantage of a wealthier agricultural base in Ontario, and the much higher level of foreign investment in Ontario than in Quebec.

A third way of looking at manufacturing—one that will be used extensively later in this chapter—is with respect to the stage of the production process that is involved. Production can be divided into three main stages. The first is *processing,* which involves the conversion of various types of raw materials into more useful products, such as copper ore into copper ingots or wire. The second stage is that of *fabrication,* which describes the conversion of processed products into a form that can either be used directly, or can be used as part of another product. For example, the copper wire may be fabricated into bunches of wires used for control and information mechanisms in automobiles. The final stage is that of *integration,* which, as the label implies, involves the bringing together of a number of fabricated materials into some finally assembled product. For example, the bunches of electrical wiring may be brought together with the rest of the subassembled pieces for final assembly of an automobile. Some idea of the complexity of this three-stage process in the multinational operations of a major automobile company is illustrated in Figure 3.5, in which the arrows indicate the major directions of flows of the products of the fabrication stage (3 and 4) and the outcome of the integration stage (1 and 2). Note that integration occurs only at one or two locations within each major market, such as New Stanton, Pennsylvania for Volkswagen in the United States.

Thus, manufacturing is extremely important not only for the economic health of the cities in which such activity is dominant, but also for the economies of North America as a whole. But it must be recognized that the changes that have been taking place did not result in increased employment in this type of industrial activity. Even though worker productivity and the number of plants has increased (Table 3.2), the contribution of manufacturing to Total National Income (TNI) has been decreasing since the mid-1960s as a consequence of the emergence of the service society. Though it must be recognized that 1982 was the low-point in the Reagan recession, the actual number of employees in manufacturing has remained fairly constant since the mid-1970s, and the number of production workers has decreased. In fact, part of the increase in productivity that has occurred has undoubtedly been due to production worker layoffs (Clark, 1984a).

REGIONAL CHANGES IN THE LOCATION OF MANUFACTURING

One of the major changes that has occurred in North America since 1971 has been in the regional deconcentration of manufacturing. This type of change has occurred in the United States to a greater degree than in Canada. In Canada, more than 70% of manufacturing employment and value-added created in the process of manufacturing is located in the metropolitan areas and cities of

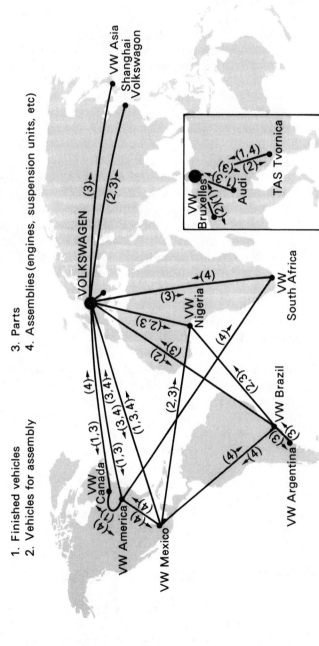

1. Finished vehicles
2. Vehicles for assembly
3. Parts
4. Assemblies (engines, suspension units, etc)

Figure 3.5 The worldwide supply and assembly network for Volkswagen. (*Source: The Economist,* Aug. 24, 1985, p. 74.)

Table 3.2   MANUFACTURING IN THE UNITED STATES
Some Summary Statistics, 1958–1983

Item	1958	1963	1972	1982
% of TNI from manufacturing[a]	29	29	26	22
Number of establishments[b]	95	102	114	123
All employees[c]	16.0	17.0	19.0	19.1
Production workers[c]	11.7	12.2	13.5	12.4
Value-added per production-worker hour[d]	$7.22	$8.35	$9.41	$11.72

[a]TNI = Total National Income

[b]establishments in thousands

[c]employees and production workers expressed as annual average in millions

[d]in 1967 constant dollars (calculated by author)

Source: Bureau of the Census (1984), *Statistical Abstract of the United States, 1985,* Washington, D.C.: U.S. Dept. of Commerce, p. 746.

southern Ontario and Quebec. This is the manufacturing heartland of the country, and there has been little decentralization of manufacturing beyond that region (Yeates, 1986), although there has been some growth of manufacturing in such western cities as Winnipeg, Vancouver, Edmonton, and Calgary.

In the United States, however, there has been considerable deconcentration of industry away from the traditional industrial heartland of North America (that is, the Manufacturing Belt outlined in Fig. 3.6). This has created the problem of deindustrialization in the Manufacturing Belt as a result of the loss of jobs (Bluestone and Harrison, 1982). In the late 1950s, about two-thirds of all employment in manufacturing in the United States was located in the states that formed part of the Manufacturing Belt. The types of manufacturing that predominated at that time involved the production of motor vehicles (automobiles and trucks), chemicals, machinery, primary metals (iron and steel), and textiles and clothing (in New England and New York). This two-thirds share remained fairly steady until 1968, when it began to decrease rather rapidly, so that by 1981 the Manufacturing Belt contained only about 54% of all employees in manufacturing in the country.

Of greater concern than the change in share is the change in actual number of jobs. The information in Table 3.2 emphasizes the fact that *total* employment in manufacturing in the United States has changed little since 1971, apart from fluctuations with the business cycle. There has not been an overall trend for growth, or for decline. As a consequence, manufacturing employment in the towns and cities of the Manufacturing Belt has, on average, been decreasing. In the ten years between 1967 and 1977, the Manufacturing Belt lost 1.6 million jobs in manufacturing, whereas the urban areas outside this area gained 1.8 million jobs. Hence the great interest since the mid-1970s in snow belt–sun belt shifts, and the reasons for them (Sawers and Tabb, 1984).

In fact, in the ten years preceding 1977, the only states that experienced

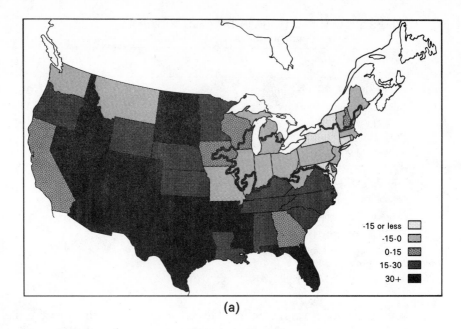

(a)

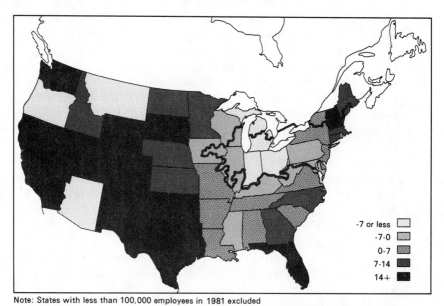

Note: States with less than 100,000 employees in 1981 excluded

(b)

Figure 3.6 Percentage change in manufacturing employment by state (a) 1966–1977 and (b) 1977–1981.

a decrease in manufacturing employment (with the exception of Washington) were in the Manufacturing Belt, and all the states that had a high growth rate (greater than 15%) were located outside the Belt (Fig. 3.6a). The leading state in manufacturing employment in 1977, California, experienced a growth rate of 10%. Thus, the regional concentration of decline was quite remarkable, and it led Norton and Rees (1979) to conclude that the decisive regional distinction that was emerging was in response to significant changes in the traditional core/periphery arrangement of economic activities in the United States.

However, between 1977 and 1981 the rates of change were, in geographical terms, much more variable, although the overall pattern of change continued. During that four-year period, urban areas in the Manufacturing Belt lost 300,000 manufacturing jobs, whereas the rest of the country gained almost 1 million! But not all Manufacturing Belt cities lost, and not all sun belt cities gained (Fig. 3.6b). For example, there was:

1. Significant loss in 1966–1967, but significant gain in 1977–1981 in Connecticut, Massachusetts, Maine, and Washington.
2. Continuing loss during both time periods in Illinois, West Virginia, Ohio, Indiana, and Michigan.
3. Significant gain in 1966–1977, but loss in 1977–1981 in Iowa, Kentucky, and Mississippi.
4. Significant gain during both time periods in California, Georgia, Minnesota, Florida, Texas, and some other states in the West and Southwest.

Thus, although the sun belt/snow belt contrast continues, there are significant subtleties in the overall pattern of change.

The decreased concentration of manufacturing in the Manufacturing Belt is related to (1) the changing nature of the relationship between the core and the periphery, and (2) the dispersal of innovative growth industries (Norton and Rees, 1979). In the traditional core/periphery model, described previously, the core is the location of industrial innovation and the focus of all kinds of fabricating activities that, in the past, grew much faster than resource-processing industries (e.g., leather and tobacco products). The periphery, on the other hand, is supposed to be the focus of resource-based activities, and generally imports fabricated products. The high productivity levels of the core result in a generally higher standard of living than in the periphery.

But given the generally higher wage levels in the core, it becomes vulnerable, in time, to the flight of labor-intensive industries (that is, mostly nondurable industries) (Casetti, 1984). Thus, the shoe, textile, and clothing industries shifted from New England and New York to parts of the South. Deconcentration of some elements of manufacturing has occurred as a result of differential wage rates and labor control (that is, unionization). The 1977–1981 slowdown in the rate of growth of some areas outside the Manufacturing Belt thus may be due to the equalization of relative real-wage rates and levels of unionization throughout the country.

The second basis for deconcentration is somewhat more complex, as it stems from technological change. Norton and Rees (1979) argue that the strength of the Manufacturing Belt stemmed from its leadership in the machine-tool industry, which was instrumental in the development of assembly-line manufacturing. This technology became fairly universal, and more innovative technologies in manufacturing grew from information processing and biochemical engineering. Industries based on these technologies are both within (Massachusetts and Connecticut) and beyond (California and Texas) the Manufacturing Belt, and are related to concentrations of large, research-oriented universities. Thus, trends in the regional deconcentration of manufacturing employment reflected a change in the leadership role of the Manufacturing Belt as a source of innovation. This change related to a major shift in the basis of technological innovation in manufacturing that, to some extent, is not located in the United States anymore, but in Japan and Western Europe.

LEAST-COST THEORY AND THE LOCATION OF MANUFACTURING

Given the general pattern in the location of manufacturing and some of the broad interregional changes that occurred, it is appropriate to examine some general theories relating to industrial location. The most basic body of theory relating to the geography of manufacturing is *location theory,* which attempts to interrelate the changes that are taking place in the economy to changes in the location of manufacturing. As Webber (1984) emphasizes, there are two main parts to the theory. The first part involves an understanding of the way the economy works; the second attempts to link that understanding to the historical evolution of manufacturing through the mechanisms of least-cost theory.

The Nature of the Economy

An appreciation of the importance of location theory requires some understanding of the way that the economy works in the geographical area in which the theory is to be applied. The most fundamental point to reiterate is that the North American economy is basically capitalist, which in the context of manufacturing means that:

1. Production is organized by the owners of firms. A difference between Canada and the United States and other countries in the world is the higher level of private ownership of the means of production (see Fig. 3.7).
2. The objective of the owners of the means of production is to sell the output at a profit. As a result of this imperative, in a competitive environment there is a continuous need to increase productivity. The corollary to this is that the owners of firms may seek to decrease the level of competitiveness by various means in order to decrease the continuous drive for higher productivity.

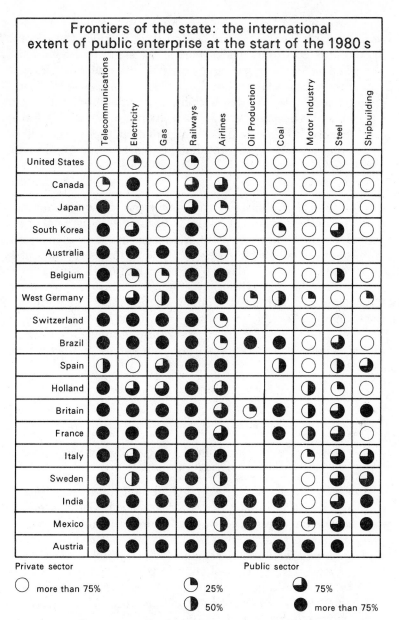

Figure 3.7 The extent of public enterprise in various aspects of industry in selected countries in the early 1980s. (*Source: The Economist,* Dec. 21, 1985, p. 72.)

3. The owners of the firms use capital (that is, money) to buy raw materials, labor, machinery, and so forth to produce the output. This capital is created through household savings and undistributed profits.
4. The allocation of all these resources (capital, labor, raw materials, and products) is achieved through a series of markets that set money prices (or values) for the goods, skills, and production that is being purchased or sold. These markets are usually imperfect; that is, buyers and sellers usually do not have perfect information, there may well be a dominant influence in the market, and there are segmented or discriminatory markets of one kind or another. Nevertheless, there is some kind of market.

In this type of capitalist environment, decisions are not, on the whole, made by some central organization on the basis of certain national or regional objectives and put into effect by planners. Decisions, and in this context, location decisions to purchase or build new manufacturing establishments, are made by the owners of firms on the basis of the information they have at that time. The location decisions may, therefore, be reasonably sensible (that is, close to profit-maximizing) at the time they were made, but as conditions change they may become less sensible (or, on the other hand, even more appropriate). The location of a plant must therefore be examined not only in the context of its appropriateness in its current environment, but also in the context of its historical situation.

Least-Cost Theory

The first person to attempt a general theory of manufacturing location was Alfred Weber (1929). Weber defined locational factors in economic terms, and they are classified in his analysis in a number of ways.

1. *General and special factors:* General factors are applicable to all industry, such as capital costs, whereas special factors are those pertaining to a given industry, such as perishability. General and special factors are excluded from the theory.
2. *Regional factors:* The regional factors, which establish the fundamental locational framework of an industry over a broad area, are transportation costs and labor costs. Weber regarded transportation costs as the prime determinant of interregional location, and labor costs as a secondary determinant.

Weber's location theory therefore focuses on factors that impact at the regional level, and he gives prime importance to transportation costs and labor costs. His method of analysis was to isolate what he regarded as the basic causative factors, examine the impact of these, and then relax the assumptions progressively to introduce other locational factors.

Following this method, it is assumed that the owners of firms are seeking locations for production that will incur the least cost. There are three components of costs to the firm: (1) the costs of inputs, whether these be in the form of raw materials or partially fabricated goods; (2) costs of processing, such as labor and energy, which are called production costs; and (3) costs of delivery of goods. As a consequence, least-cost theory (following Weber, 1929) involves analyzing the influence of transportation costs ([1] and [3]) and production costs (2) on location.

Minimizing Transportation Costs

To begin, we examine what is known about the nature of transportation costs. First, transportation costs for freight increase with distance, but at a decreasing rate, since rate structures are usually set by zones. A certain amount is paid for the first few miles, an additional amount for the next few, and so on, with the width of each zone increasing with its distance from the point of shipment (Fig. 3.8). Second, there are considerable fixed charges; that is, charges that do not vary with distance and have to be paid regardless of trip length. These include the costs of loading and unloading, and are usually referred to as *terminal charges.* A third characteristic of transportation costs is that the magnitude of the terminal charges and the steepness of the cost curves are related to the means of transportation that is used. The differences between truck, rail, and water transport for bulky goods are generally as is shown in the inset in Figure 3.8—water transport (if available) is generally more cost-efficient for long hauls, rail for medium-length hauls, and trucks for shorter distances.

Now that we know the facts about transportation cost curves, we can apply them to a simple situation involving a firm that wishes to build a plant to (1) manufacture a product that requires one material input from one source (SR) and (2) sells its output in one marketplace (MP) (e.g., a given city). (3) The

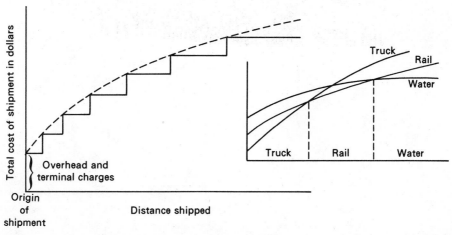

Figure 3.8 The relationship between transportation costs and distance, for selected modes of transportation.

material source (SR) and the market (MP) are separated in space but connected by one means of transport, and (4) there is no weight loss incurred in the raw material in the process of manufacture (that is, 100 units of the raw material will yield 100 units of the finished product). In situations of this type there are two possible least-cost locations—SR and MP. All other sites between these two locations are more expensive because they incur an additional set of terminal charges as well as the disadvantages of two shorter hauls, rather than one that is longer. Thus, in Figure 3.9 the total transportation cost (TTC) of manufacturing at SR and sending the finished product to MP is cost *a,* and sending the raw material from SR to MP for manufacture is also cost *a.* However, if the firm were to manufacture its product at place K, it would also have to pay to ship the raw material and to unload it (cost *y*), and would incur more costs to ship the finished product from K to MP (cost *x*).

In addition, transportation costs are usually higher per unit weight for finished products than for raw materials. One important reason for this difference is that as manufactured goods increase in value through the process of manufacture, transportation costs constitute a lower proportion of the total value of the shipment than they did for the raw materials. Manufactured goods thus are said to be capable of bearing higher transportation charges. Also, it is often the policy of national governments to subsidize transportation charges for

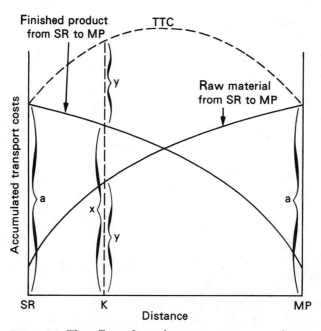

Figure 3.9 The effect of equal transportation costs for raw materials and finished products, assuming a curvilinear relationship between transportation costs and distance.

raw materials produced some distance from ports, in order to promote access to foreign markets (for example, the Crow Rate in Canada, which is being phased out). As a result, the transportation cost curve for finished products is steeper than that for raw materials, and the least-cost location for manufacture will be at the marketplace (Fig. 3.10). Thus, if a given quantity of raw material yields the same quantity of finished product, the industry will locate at the marketplace, where the total cost of transportation will be lowest.

The Effect of Variations in Weight Loss   A given quantity of raw material does not usually yield the same quantity (by weight) of finished product. There is, invariably, a great deal of weight loss in manufacturing, and this has to be taken into account in the simple locational model being discussed. We know that the location of manufacturing will either be at SR or MP, so assume that the freight rates for manufactured product (P) average $20.00 per kilogram per kilometer for the total distance between SR and MP, and that the freight rates for the raw material (R) average $15.00 per kilogram per kilometer for the same distance. Also assume that 1,000 kilograms of R are to be processed into P.

If the manufacturing plant is located at MP, it will always have to transport 1,000 kilograms of materials to MP. Thus, the total transportation cost will be $15,000 per kilometer. If the weight loss is 20% and the firm locates at SR, 1,000 kilograms of raw material will yield 800 kilograms of finished product, and the total cost of shipping this will be $16,000 per kilometer. Thus, with a weight

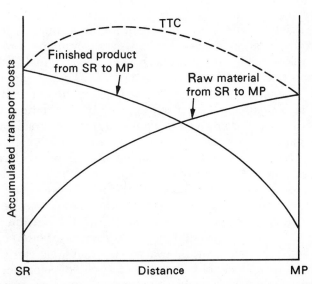

Figure 3.10 The effect of higher transportation costs for finished products than for raw materials, assuming a curvilinear relationship between transport costs and distance. Compare this diagram with Figure 3.9.

loss of 20%, the firm will gain an advantage of $1,000 per kilometer by locating at the marketplace.

However, with a weight loss of 40%, 1,000 kilograms of R yield 600 kilograms of P. Because the cost of transporting this amount at the manufactured-product rate is $12,000 per kilometer, the firm will gain an advantage of $3,000 per kilometer if it locates at the raw-material site. Consequently, given the transportation cost structure for finished products and raw materials, the higher the weight loss the more likely it is that a firm will locate at the source of inputs, if only transportation costs and weight loss are considered.

Hence the importance of the distinction among the processing, fabrication, and integration stages of manufacturing. Processing plants are quite likely to be found at raw-material locations—particularly those involved with the concentration of ores or the manufacture of ingots of various kinds, whereas fabrication and integration is more likely to occur where the major markets are located. For example, INCO (International Nickel Company) a multinational firm headquartered in Toronto with $1.5 billion (Canadian) in annual sales and 22,000 employees in twenty countries worldwide (Bradbury, 1985), distributes its manufacturing enterprises in North America very much according to this model. Nickel and copper are mined and smelted (that is, processed) in Sudbury, Ontario and Thompson, Manitoba. The metals are then sent to plants at Huntington, West Virginia or Burrough, Kentucky, at the edge of the major market. There, high-performance alloys are fabricated, and blades, rings, and discs are produced for integration into aero- and gas-turbine engines that are used elsewhere in the Manufacturing Belt.

Transshipment Points   Thus far we have considered a situation in which only one mode of transportation is used. It is, however, common for more than one mode to be employed, and when this occurs the goods or materials have to be transferred from one type to another, as at a port. Transshipment points are also break-of-bulk points, because the goods being shipped usually have to be broken down into smaller units for subsequent transportation; for example, the contents of an ocean-going vessel would fill many railroad cars or trucks. Transshipment and break-of-bulk points also incur additional costs, such as extra terminal charges for loading and unloading. Therefore, transshipment points (which in North America were often gateway ports) attract manufacturers because some additional costs can be avoided even though the freight rate in shipping the manufactured product to the market may be higher. The attraction of these locations is particularly strong for those manufacturers that use raw materials with a high weight loss. Moreover, firms often choose break-of-bulk sites, and especially ports, because raw materials can easily be collected there from many locations. In fact, before the development of the railroad, inland cities could not grow very large because transportation costs were too high.

The widespread use of containers for the transportation of fabricated products has resulted in significant shifts in the location of plants involved with the final integration of goods. Containers greatly facilitate loading and unloading; thus they reduce the costs of transshipment enormously. As a consequence, break-of-bulk considerations have become less relevant for material at a late stage in the production sequence, and plants involved with the integration of products are more likely to be located within the major markets. An example of this is the location of a new Chrysler/Mitsubishi assembly plant in Lexington, Kentucky that ships engines and electrical components from Japan, and chassis, bodies, and other parts from North American plants.

The Decreasing Influence of Transportation Costs One of the major features of transportation costs is that since 1950 they have been declining steadily in importance as a component of total manufacturing costs. Norcliffe (1975) attributes this decrease to several developments:

1. Over the past few decades the "heavy" industries (iron and steel, metal fabrication, etc.) have declined relative to the rapid growth of the "light" industries (electronics, home appliances, etc.). The heavy industries tend to be more sensitive to transportation cost variations than the light industries.
2. Raw-material locations have become less important as a location factor because fewer raw materials are now needed per unit of output. "At the turn of the nineteenth century, six tons of coal were needed to smelt one ton of iron, whereas today about one-and-a-quarter tons of coal are needed or, in the case of electric furnaces, no coal at all at the

Oakland has become a major container port serving not only the San Francisco Bay area but also a large part of the western United States as well. (*Source:* Geovisuals.)

place of manufacture" (Norcliffe, 1975, p. 22). Furthermore, low-grade ore may be upgraded by beneficating or pelletization, or other substitutes for the raw materials may be used.

3. Many new techniques, such as containers, piggy-back railroad cars and trucks, telecommunications, long-distance transmission lines, and welded pipelines, have made it easier to transport goods, energy, and information a great deal more cheaply than before.

Thus, even though energy costs have risen quite considerably since 1975, the effect on the transportation costs of firms has not been as great as one might have thought.

Production Costs

Given the declining relative importance of transportation costs in the location decision of a firm, the importance in least-cost theory of spatial variations in production costs, and the way in which these production costs may be influenced by agglomeration, has risen accordingly. There are two types of production costs: labor and nonlabor. Nonlabor costs, which involve such things as geographic variations in the price of land, taxes, and heating and air-conditioning costs, do not vary much throughout North America, and they are not a large enough proportion of the costs of the firm to have much influence on location decisions. Webber (1984) estimates that all nonlabor costs comprise only about 2% of total value-added in manufacturing. The availability of national and local government incentives may serve to lower nonlabor production costs at certain locations, but in the medium-term (from four to eight years) a location has to be viable, for governmental subsidies cannot be provided indefinitely.

Variations in Labor Costs   With labor costs (wages or salaries plus fringe benefits) accounting for almost 54% of total value-added in manufacturing in the North American region, it is variations in the costs of management, wage rates (and the structure of union agreements), and the availability of different types of labor that are the most important factors influencing location decisions. Wage-rate variations are quite significant, because wages vary not only geographically, but according to type of industry (high-wage versus low-wage industry), and within an industry. For example, average hourly earnings by production workers in manufacturing in North Carolina in 1983 were 25% less than the national average ($8.83), whereas those in Ohio were 20% above; workers in textile mill production earned 32% less than the national average, whereas those in the aircraft industry received 40% more; and workers in clothing industries in Massachusetts earned over $1.00 per hour more than those in the same industry in Alabama.

These variations in hourly earnings are related to many factors. The most important influence on average hourly earnings is productivity (operationally defined in Table 3.2 as value-added per production-worker hour), which is determined by level of skills, education, and the efficiency of the productive capital (including machinery) available to the worker. Some industries, such as aircraft manufacturing, demand a high level of skills and education, whereas others, such as textiles, can use less-skilled labor. It is often argued that amenities such as a nice climate affect wage levels, in that people are prepared to work for lower wage rates in more attractive or warm locations (wage rates in Florida are, for example, 20% less than the national average). It is also claimed that wage-rate differences are related to levels of unionization (wages are high in states and industries with strong union representation), although it would seem a limited argument in that wage rates, even in unionized industries, have to be related to productivity and industry competitiveness.

The basic point, however, is that given these types of regional, industry, and within-industry variations in wage rates (which change over time) and the profit imperative that exists in the North American economy, manufacturing firms will tend to seek locations for new plants in lower labor-cost areas (providing that productivity is satisfactory). They will also tend to expand production in existing plants in low labor-cost areas, providing that the differences in productivity are not too great. Hence the greater growth of manufacturing industries, particularly those that are labor-intensive, in the generally lower-wage sun belt states.

The Influence of Agglomeration and Concentration   Economies of *agglomeration* are savings in per unit production costs through large-scale production or better management organization. Economies of *concentration* are savings in per unit production costs that can be made by operating a large group of economic activities in a relatively compact geographic area, such as a city. Concentration economies vary more according to geography than do agglomeration economies.

Concentration economies consist of two types: localization economies and urbanization economies. Localization economies arise when firms in the same industry, or in closely related industries, concentrate at the same place because they can take advantage of forward-and-backward linkages and pools of labor that have similar, easily transferable skills. An example of such a situation is the semiconductor industry in "Silicon Valley," Santa Clara County, California, where the leaders of the industry (Hewlett-Packard and National Semiconductor Corp.) are surrounded by a "dense concentration of smaller electronics related suppliers and producers" (Saxenian, 1984, p. 164). All these industries take advantage of the highly trained, research-oriented labor force that focuses around the major universities in the area, and the abundant supply of labor (chiefly new immigrants) for low-wage assembly tasks.

Urbanization economies consist of a number of features in cities that together act to create a situation that may facilitate lower business costs (Mooman, 1986):

1. *Social fixed-overhead capital.* The availability of existing infrastructure in larger cities is a particularly important influence on the location of small and medium-sized plants. Infrastructure involves all those aspects of the physical environment that facilitate the operation of a plant, such as the availability of roads (particularly limited-access highways), waste-disposal facilities, water, power, freight depots, airports, and housing. It should be recognized that society as a whole must pay for the establishment and maintenance of social fixed-overhead capital, so that no one element (for example, manufacturing firms fleeing the inner-city) should be allowed to opt out of paying its share (such as for education).
2. *Economies realized from better information and face-to-face contact.* Norcliffe (1975) argues that large urban areas provide an enhanced information environment that is particularly attractive for the headquarters office, planning, financial, and research and development (R&D) activities of large corporations.
3. *Economies of supply and distribution.* Firms that locate in large urban areas are able to realize economies through the availability of such services as freight-forwarders and large transportation agencies, wholesale suppliers, warehousing, and storage facilities, accounting, advertising, marketing, and financial agencies, and the sheer size of local markets.

Concentration economies may turn into diseconomies in the largest cities as costs rise and efficiency is reduced. Transportation, congestion, pollution, lack of reinvestment in infrastructure, and crime may begin to raise costs to a level sufficient to encourage firms to move from the urban region altogether. Carlino (1982) demonstrates that productive efficiency in large metropolitan areas in the United States has been declining as a result of the combined effect of urbanization diseconomies. His estimates indicate that optimal metropolitan size in this regard has declined from about 3.6 million in the 1960s to 3.4 million in the 1970s, which suggests that the recent decrease in population of some large metropolitan areas in the United States may be related to diseconomies of concentration.

INDUSTRIAL RESTRUCTURING

Although the basic principles of least-cost theory are important, they must be viewed within the context of the tremendous changes that have been occurring in manufacturing in North America during the 1980s. Modern manufacturing has been greatly affected by two fundamental events (United Nations, 1983). First, an increasing concentration of ownership among highly competitive national and multinational corporations means that the location of a particular manufacturing plant must be viewed in the context of the structure and decision-making processes of large organizations.

Second, rapid product and process innovation, stimulated primarily by a new generation of enabling technologies (such as the microchip for information processing and recombinant DNA technology in biochemical engineering), are having as fundamental an impact on manufacturing and manufacturing location as the steam engine and the evolution of industrial capitalism in the late eighteenth century, or the harnessing of electricity and the maturing of capital markets at the end of the nineteenth century. Manufacturing is, as a consequence, undergoing a restructuring characterized by a drive for quantum leaps in the quality and productivity of existing production, and the "development and introduction of radically new products and processes" (NAS/NRC, 1982, p. 9). The growth of manufacturing in California and Texas, along with the resurgence of industrial activity in parts of New England, suggests that the newer industries have greater locational flexibility than the older ones.

Manufacturing's New Era

Just as in our discussion of location theory it was essential to sketch out the nature of the national economy in which location decisions are made, so in the case of fundamental restructuring is it necessary to outline the global context of some elements of the transition. The discussion will be couched in the context of political economy; that is, it will involve the changing relationships among capital (the "business" community), labor, and (instead of land) the state (or national, state/provincial, and local governments). The transition relates to the shift from the era of monopoly capitalism (1935–1975) to the era of global capitalism, from (roughly) 1975 onward (Trachte and Ross, 1985). Given our limited experience with the era of global capitalism, it is likely that some of the statements may be overdrawn (or just plain wrong).

Changing Capital-to-Capital Relations

In the context of manufacturing firms and the relationships among them, the era of mature industrial capitalism may be defined as one in which manufacturing was dominated worldwide by a number of large leading firms, predominantly (although not by any means entirely) headquartered in the United States. These companies had, over a number of decades, reached a *modus operandi* that reduced price competition to the minimum by focusing instead on product differentiation and marketing. In the short term (from three to five years), this kept market shares stable among the major producers of goods. Productivity throughout the era increased considerably as a result of a movement to larger and larger plants that produced larger and larger quantities of standardized consumer products. A large proportion of these products was absorbed by the internal domestic market, but during the 1960s markets for the escalating volumes of output were increasingly sought beyond the national borders. This situation is described by Holmes (1986; 1987) with respect to the automobile industry in North America.

The search for new markets occurred at the time that major European Economic Community and Japanese producers began to move from domestic markets and, in the case of Japan, from the nurturing influence of Pentagon purchases during the Korean war (and later, the war in Vietnam), to the rich North American market (Schoenberger, 1985). Hence during the mid-1960s and 1970s, when United States manufacturing corporations were looking for new markets, Japanese and European producers moved more strongly than before into the North American market (OhUallachain, 1984). They did this through price competition, new products (such as VCRs), and a differentiation of product in style and quality. One element of this differentiation is a greater variety of some products, which was achieved through smaller production runs; this implies decreasing plant size and greater output flexibility within plants. The net result in the era of global capitalism is highly unstable market shares among the major manufacturing corporations that operate, either directly or through wholly or partially owned subsidiaries, in many different countries.

An example of the changing form of business organization that results from greater competition can be seen in the evolving structure of the motion-picture industry in Los Angeles (Christopherson and Storper, 1986; Storper and Christopherson, 1987). The industry originally developed around major companies (MGM, Twentieth-Century Fox, and others) that integrated all aspects of production and distribution within their own organization. Since the mid-1970s, the industry has been developing new modes of production in which many functions are subcontracted to smaller independent organizations in Los Angeles and elsewhere in order to control costs. This has resulted in a re-agglomeration of activities serving the motion-picture, television, and videocassette industries in Los Angeles. A similar rise in importance of subcontracting is occurring in the motor vehicle industry (Holmes, 1986). This increase in the importance of subcontracting implies greater flexibility in plant location.

Changing Capital-to-Labor Relations

Although it should be clear that one way in which this greater competition has come about is through imaginative innovations in production processes that have increased productivity (output per worker-hour), prices have also been reduced in part through major efforts to control the cost of labor and of material inputs. During the era of mature industrial capitalism, the manufacturing labor force became split into two basic components. One set of productive workers became highly unionized, and the other remained unorganized.

The consequence of this was that over the years, and particularly during the long post–World War II growth period, many of the larger corporations and unions created what amounted to highly favorable (when compared with the nonunion sector) working conditions. In return for increases in productivity through scale economies, the work force in these privileged industries (such as iron and steel, transportation and transport equipment, and petrochemical industries) achieved large increases in wage rates, reductions in the length of the work week, good fringe benefits, and a level of job security through complex job demarcation and seniority preference ("last hired, first fired"). On the other hand, about one-half of all manufacturing production workers in the United

States are not members of unions affiliated with the AFL/CIO, and in many cases their wage rates, fringe benefits, job security, and so forth are a great deal less than those in most elements of the unionized industries.

During the 1970s, greater worldwide competition among major companies and the restructuring of manufacturing in general (Monden, 1983) led to an effort by corporations in North America to control labor costs, improve within-plant job flexibility, and limit the extent of company involvement in fringe benefits. All this was in the name of improving productivity, for, as may be discerned from Table 3.3, productivity in manufacturing did not increase as rapidly in North America during the 1970s and early 1980s as in Japan and West Germany, although compensation per hour did, and more. Thus, capital–labor relations in North America in the era of global capitalism will be quite different from those in the era of mature industrial capitalism. These differences are being reflected in those collective agreements that reduce (or hold the line) on benefits, wage increases, and job demarcation.

Changing Capital-to-State Relations

During the period between 1935 and 1975, the role of the state in North American society increased enormously. In terms of capital (and labor), this role can be interpreted as involving three elements. First, with the support of the business community, the state has provided (or organized) ways of delivering increasing levels of benefits and security to labor through such means as Social Security, Medicare, and the whole group of programs collectively referred to as the "social safety net." Second, through regulation and directed government expenditures, the state effectively ensured minimum market shares for the largest companies. We have seen in Chapter 2 how federal expenditures since the 1950s have influenced the growth of different regions in the United States.

Table 3.3 CHANGE (AVERAGE ANNUAL PERCENT) IN PRODUCTIVITY AND COMPENSATION, 1970–1975 TO 1980–1985
United States, Canada, West Germany, Japan, United Kingdom

Index and year	United States	Canada	West Germany	Japan	United Kingdom
Output per hour					
1970–1975	3.4	3.4	5.1	6.8	4.0
1975–1980	1.7	2.7	3.9	8.6	1.4
1980–1985	3.7	2.8	3.5	5.9	5.7
Compensation per hour					
1970–1975	8.2	10.9	12.3	20.3	19.5
1975–1980	9.2	10.8	8.1	7.2	16.3
1980–1985	5.9	8.3	5.3	4.7	9.2

Source: Bureau of the Census (1987), *Statistical Abstract of the United States, 1988,* Washington, D.C.: U.S. Department of Commerce, p. 813.

Finally, there has been a considerable direct involvement by the state in the research and development departments of high-technology industries, through increased expenditures for "defense," medical research, and so forth.

In the transition to global capitalism, some of these relationships are changing quite considerably. First, greater international competition from large multinational corporations is leading to a drive for deregulation as the underwriting of market shares by the state crumbles. Quantum increases in the mobility of capital, particularly in its search for lower labor-cost locations for some aspects of its production, and the search by companies for the control of strategic raw materials (Chapman, 1985), has led to a lessening of business support for the state's provision of social services. Finally, because of the particularly concentrated nature of product and process innovation in the 1970s and 1980s and the depreciation of existing plants and infrastructure (Varaiya and Wiseman, 1981), there has been an excessive need for new capital that has given larger, cash-rich companies the whip-hand in negotiations concerning the location of new plants. Local, state/provincial, and federal governments are now involved in zero-sum game (and sometimes less than zero-sum game) attempts to lure industry to particular locations.

The Location of Multiple-Plant Manufacturing Firms

As manufacturing firms become larger, they evolve more complex forms of organization. In small, single-plant firms, the management function may take place within the manufacturing plant or in the same town, but as the firm gets larger and establishes other plants, various functional specialties emerge, each of these with different locational characteristics. Humphrys (1982) has proposed a fairly simple model that captures the nature of this complexity and emphasizes the different locational forces that are generally involved with each element (Fig. 3.11). The model has three main components: the organizational structure of firms, the general nature of associate labor markets, and the locational attributes of the various parts of the firm. The model emphasizes that the organizational structure of the firm creates a spatial division of labor (Walker, 1985), with managers and white-collar workers concentrating in certain areas and blue-collar workers in others.

The Location of Headquarters Offices and Research and Development

The central position of the headquarters office or management function of the firm is indicated by Figure 3.11. Decisions emanate from this office to both the research and development and the production functions of the firm, which, in turn, provide feedback that is integrated, to a greater or lesser degree, into the decision making apparatus. The headquarters office is involved with the financial, legal, policy making, and strategic decisions, and the personnel involved are the salaried and managerial staff. This managerial force is supported by a wide array of specialists (lawyers, accountants, and so forth) and by general support staff (such as secretaries). The basic locational principle for this aspect

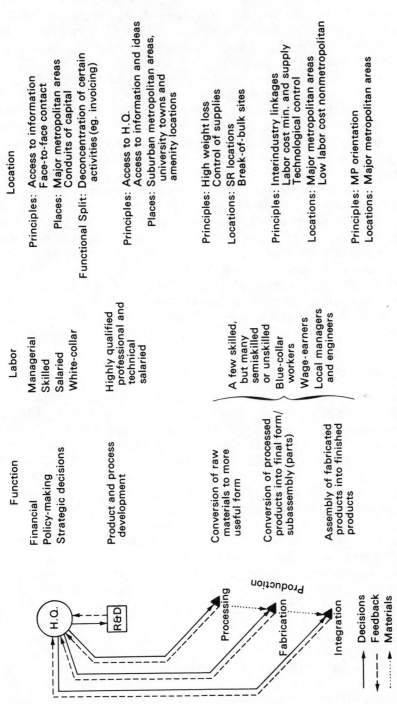

Figure 3.11 The interrelationships among multiple-plant functions, type of labor market, and location. (*Source:* Humphrys, 1982, Fig. 4.9, p. 322.)

of the firm is the necessity for good access to all types of information and finance, which is facilitated by situations that promote face-to-face contact among executives of different companies. The headquarters function is therefore invariably located in a leading metropolis, in a downtown site close to or within the financial community.

Of course, some management functions may be decentralized to suburban locations within the field of the major metropolis, particularly those that are of a routine nature (such as invoicing) and are not too sensitive within the power structure of the firm. One function that is of crucial importance to the modern firm but has its own particular locational imperatives, is research and development. Research and development activities involve highly qualified professional and technical staff and, although the headquarters office requires considerable control over their activities and enormous feedback from them, the most efficient location for research and development is in an environment that fosters creativity and is attractive to well-trained, high-energy individuals. Suburban research parks and small town locations within the vicinity of one or more research-oriented universities appear to be the preferred locations. Also, there must be a high level of accessibility to transportation (airports) for the high-priced staff! It is important to be aware that the research and development and the headquarters functions are closely entwined and, as a consequence, research and development activity invariably is concentrated in the same country as the headquarters office.

The Location of Production Facilities

The Humphrys (1982) model clearly identifies the range of types of production with which a multiple-plant firm may be involved: processing, fabrication, and integration. It is envisaged that, on the whole, materials flow from processing to fabrication to integration, although plants in all stages require machinery as well as material inputs. Each of the three types of production involves both technically skilled and unskilled blue-collar workers, nearly all of whom are paid on an hourly basis. There are also usually local managers and plant engineers who are salaried workers.

Processing Plants   Plants involved in processing invariably deal with materials that incur considerable weight loss in manufacturing. The locations that are selected are therefore always raw-material locations or break-of-bulk sites. Chapman (1985) indicates that there is also a tendency for large multinational corporations to place processing facilities within the vicinity of raw-material locations in order to secure control of supplies. Dome Petroleum, Nova Corporation, and Dow Chemical established polyethylene, ethylene oxide, and vinyl acetate plants (respectively) in Alberta in the late 1970s and early 1980s to this end (Chapman, 1985).

Fabricating Plants   Plants involved in fabrication deal with inputs that incur minimal weight loss during manufacture but that do create bulk. Consequently, a number of other locational forces come into consideration: interindustry linkages, labor costs and supplies, and technological control.

1. *Interindustry linkages.* The traditional argument is that as the output of plants involved in fabrication is directed toward plants involved in final assembly (integration), they will tend to locate within the proximity of the final markets. However, transportation costs have become less of a constraint, so such locations are no longer determinate. However, there may be a number of complex interindustry linkages that occur within the transport-manufacturing area embracing Michigan, Ohio, Indiana, and Ontario.

2. *Labor costs and supplies.* There are three aspects of labor to be taken into account—cost, quality, and the way it is organized. For those plants that require unskilled or semiskilled labor, the firm will invariably search for low-wage locations. Suarez-Villa (1984) demonstrates that many fabricating plants seeking low-wage, nonunionized labor have located along the United States–Mexico border (the so-called sweatshops of the Rio Grande). Some fabricating industries require skilled labor, and these tend to be more constrained in location; for example, metal products are fabricated in Pittsburgh and in Hamilton (Ontario).

3. *Technological control.* Many aspects of fabrication involve the production of materials that are the outcome of much research and development. The components have been patented, but even with this protection companies may be loath to have the producing plant move to a site that could be beyond the control of the head office. These types of plants may well be located, not necessarily in low labor-cost areas, but within the vicinity of the headquarters office. This occurs often in the pharmaceutical drug industry, where firms like to maintain secrecy and control over the development of new drugs.

Plants Involved with Integration The third aspect of production, the integration of fabricated products into finished products for the consumer market, is very much market-oriented in location. The output is bulky, often fragile, and therefore reasonably expensive to ship. As a result, integrated assembly plants are usually found within the major urban regions that have been developing in North America since the 1940s (see Chapter 2). It is significant that all the major automobile companies in the world have located final-assembly plants within these regions.

The Surgical and Medical Instruments Industry

Some aspects of this general framework can be discerned within the surgical and medical instruments industry. This industry doubled in number of establishments and tripled in total employment between 1973 and 1983 (Malecki, 1985). Furthermore, it has one of the highest rates of expenditure on research and development as a percentage of sales of any sector of manufacturing. In

Table 3.4   REGION AND HEADQUARTERS REGION OF BRANCHES AND SUBSIDIARIES IN THE SURGICAL AND MEDICAL INSTRUMENTS INDUSTRY, 1983

Headquarters region	Branch region			
	Northeast	North Central	South	West
Northeast	55	9	13	28
North Central	13	40	11	19
South	6	3	8	3
West	3	2	3	16
TOTAL	77	54	35	66

Source: Malecki (1985, Table 8).

consequence, a little over one-half of the manufacturing plants are concentrated within the same region as their headquarters offices (as is indicated by the numbers on the diagonals in Table 3.4). Those that are dispersed beyond that region are generally found in the lower-wage areas of the South and West, or in proximity to the major conglomerations of research facilities in California and Washington.

The location of plants in this industry, therefore, is strongly influenced by the need for continuous research and development that requires close company control and well-established contacts with users; that is, the hospitals, particularly those that are research-oriented. On the other hand, once a product is developed, it can be manufactured using relatively unskilled labor because the production process is routine and highly mechanized.

Conclusion

The distribution of manufacturing among urban areas in North America is therefore the result of many interacting forces that have operated in different ways over the past 200 years. The real growth in manufacturing occurred after about 1830, and for much of the time the locational factors that had the greatest influence were those that are considered to be in the realm of least-cost theory (that is, transportation costs, weight loss, and labor costs). Even though there were periods of industrial change, these locational factors remained reasonably important. For example, during one period of change at the turn of the century, the implementation of assembly-type factory production which involved scale economies, can also be analyzed using least-cost theory.

The most recent era has witnessed another wave of technological and process innovation which, though diminishing the use of least-cost theory, still emphasizes the importance of assembly at market locations. The phrase *global capitalism* describes a situation in which large multiple-plant corporations, headquartered in different countries, have many aspects of their production located beyond their home base—either in low-wage areas (such as South Korea or Taiwan) or close to major markets (such as Michigan or Ontario). But the type of activities such corporations locate beyond their home base are usually of the processing, fabrication, or integration variety. Thus, the home territory retains the creative and innovative aspects of the enterprise, whereas the other territory receives jobs for its "blue-collar" workers (Massey, 1984a).

This type of division of labor may be acceptable in countries that are reasonably well developed, with a number of strong sectors of industry, because the labor characteristics of a domestic multinational firm may well offset those of a foreign-owned firm operating in its territory. It does create difficulties in less-developed countries, however, because they are receiving only those aspects of production that are low-wage, labor-intensive and, perhaps, environmentally hazardous.

Historical Perspectives on the Internal Structure and Growth of Urban Areas

*I*n this and the next few chapters our concern is with why things are located where they are within cities. The "things" are the various land uses and activities that are characteristic of the North American city. Chapter 4 presents a brief review of the various land uses and provides a historical perspective on the accumulation of urban infrastructure. The emphasis of the discussion is on the patterns of land use and social structure that have occurred during different eras.

URBAN LAND USE

The land uses of urban areas can be divided into six major categories: residential, industrial, commercial, roads and highways, public and quasi-public land, and vacant land. For cities in the 250,000–1.5 million population range in Canada and the United States, the typical land-use structure is about 30% residential, 9% general manufacturing, 4% commercial, 20% roads and highways, 15% publicly used government buildings and parks, and 20% either vacant or being held in some form for later development.

A major concern in some parts of North America (for example, California,

Urban encroachment on prime fruitlands on the rural/urban fringe of metropolitan Hamilton. (*Source:* Geovisuals.)

Florida, and southwestern Ontario) is the amount of highly productive agricultural land being consumed for urban uses (Furuseth and Pierce, 1982; Krueger, 1982; Platt, 1985). The general reason for this concern can be demonstrated using land-consumption rates (LCRs), which measure the amount of urban land being consumed for urban purposes at a particular date. Figure 4.1 shows the change in the general relationship between land-consumption rates and city size for forty urban agglomerations in central Canada, and the hypothetical relationship for United States cities. The graph emphasizes three major points.

First, land-consumption rates are increasing through time. As the population becomes wealthier, transportation improves, and techniques of production and styles of consumption change, more land (space) is consumed by each

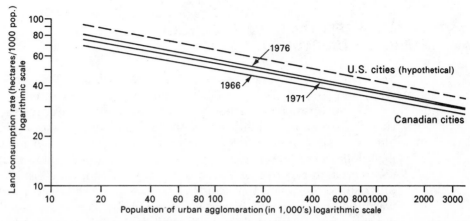

Figure 4.1 The relationship between land consumption rates and city size, in Canada and the United States. (*Source:* Yeates, 1985a, p. 7.)

individual. A corollary to this is that cities that have grown the most in recent decades will tend to have higher average land-consumption rates than those that grew most in earlier epochs.

Second, land-consumption rates tend to decrease with city size. In other words, large cities tend to be more efficient users of land than smaller cities. This is because the greater competition for locations in larger cities forces up land prices and hence intensity of use.

Third, United States cities tend, on the average, to have larger land-consumption rates than Canadian cities—the inhabitants of United States cities consume more land per person than those in Canadian cities. Although there are undoubtedly a large number of interlocking reasons for this difference, there does seem to be some evidence to indicate that public attempts to shape development increase land prices in Canadian cities to a higher general level than those in the United States and, therefore, development generally occurs on smaller lots. For example, in a comparative study of four rapid-growth cities—Phoenix (Arizona), Houston, Calgary, and Edmonton—Sands (1982) demonstrates that local governments in Calgary and Edmonton limit development to areas served by public water and sewer systems and require developers to pay most of these facility costs up-front, whereas development in Houston and Phoenix is allowed to occur in privately established utility districts that are financed by tax-free bonds repaid by user fees. The net result is that Canadian suburban developments tend to be more compact than those in the United States.

These trends in urban land use, which are crystallized in the land-consumption rates, raise an enormous number of questions. In particular, the tendency for land-consumption rates to increase each year is obviously rooted in changes in the structure of urban areas that have taken place over the past 200 years. In the following sections we will examine the historical context for these changes, and in Chapter 5 we will learn about some theoretical models that can be used to analyze the trends.

HISTORICAL PERSPECTIVES ON SPATIAL GROWTH AND INTERNAL STRUCTURE

The spatial growth of cities occurs in surges (Olson, 1979)—there are times when the pace of development is rapid, and there are times that it is less rapid, or even stagnant. These surges occur in about twenty-year cycles (the shorter Kuznet, or building cycles) that are embedded within the Kondratieff long waves. There appear to be two peaks (on average) per long wave: One peak follows the onset of growth in a new era and is followed in turn by a contraction in accordance with a business recession, which is followed by another surge of growth that can lead to overspeculation and overbuilding toward the end of the era. This is indicated in the data on the number of housing starts for Baltimore since 1775 and for the United States as a whole since 1885 (see Fig. 4.2).

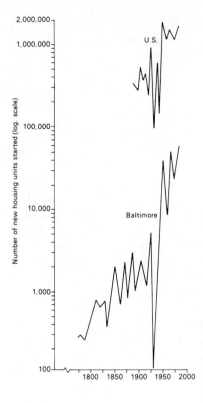

Figure 4.2 Number of new housing units started: United States 1885–1985 and Baltimore 1775–1980. (*Sources:* Data from the Bureau of the Census, 1975; 1984a, p. 724; and Olson, 1979, pp. 558–559.)

The information on housing starts for Baltimore is particularly interesting because of the period of time that is covered by the data. In terms of volume of housing starts, and hence pace of growth, the five eras identified in Figure 2.4 (p. 34) and Table 2.1 (p. 36) are quite discernible in Baltimore:

1. The *mercantile city* existed until 1840; it is characterized by fewer than 800 housing starts per year.
2. Baltimore was a *classic industrial city* from 1840 to 1885; during this period housing starts varied between 1,000 and 2,000 per year.
3. The *metropolitan era* extended from 1885 to 1935; housing starts ranged from 2,000 to 5,000 per year.
4. During the era of greatest *suburban growth*—1935–1975—annual housing starts were generally in the 10,000–50,000 range in Baltimore.
5. During the era of the *galactic city,* from 1975 on, annual housing starts average 25,000 per year.

The important feature of the information in Figure 4.2 is the difference in magnitude in the numbers of housing starts between the eras.

Furthermore, as each era is influenced by a different combination of social, economic, governmental, and cultural (style, design, etc.) forces, the city in effect becomes an accretion that reflects the various strengths of these factors at different times. Also, as new construction usually (but not always) takes place on new land, these reflections can be seen most clearly at the fringe of the city. Baltimore, of course, is not a "typical" North American city, for many have grown in only the most recent time periods.

The Mercantile City (prior to 1840)

During the frontier–mercantile era, cities were, on the whole, quite small and compact. Only toward the end of the era, when industrialization became more prevalent, did some cities grow large. New York City reached a population of 100,000 by 1820, Philadelphia by 1830, and Baltimore and New Orleans by 1840. The internal structure of most cities reflected the dominant mercantile basis. In gateway cities the port, ship-building and repair yards, and places of business of the financial institutions, merchants, and shopkeepers, were all clustered close together. The inland cities, which existed to link with the agricultural and resource-based hinterland, had a similar nucleation of service activities around which residences clustered in a compact fashion.

The reason for this compactness was that the costs of transportation for people and goods were very high—the only sources of power for transportation were either people or horses. Thus, prior to the 1840s, the geographic extent of the North American city was controlled primarily by the distance people could walk to work, shops, and social–recreational activities. In consequence, most people tended to live either close to or within the same building as their place of work and they did not move around the city nearly as much as people do today.

Warner notes that in Boston in 1850 (when it reached 100,000 population) "streets of the well-to-do lay hard by workers' barracks and tenements of the poor; many artisans kept shop and home in the same building or street; and factories, wharves, and offices were but a few blocks from middle-class homes" (1962, p. 19). Some spatial separation of classes did, of course, exist, for the wealthy were able to afford carriages and reside in more solubrious surroundings farther away from the sounds and smells of commerce and the workshops. For nearly everybody, however, a lack of cheap intraurban transport bound the city together in a compact unit, and because very few people traveled frequently between districts within larger urban areas, each district was able to form its own identity.

The Classic Industrial City (1840–1885)

During the era of early industrial capitalism, the classic industrial city was characteristic of North America. What were the main characteristics of the industrial city and its internal spatial structure? The industrial city, as its name implies, was based primarily (though by no means completely) on manufacturing. The rhythm of the city, therefore, was determined by the location of the factory, the organization of the workday, and the social relations that developed as society became influenced by the distinctions among owners, managers, professionals, and workers that became more prominent with increased specialization. The internal structure of the industrial city reflects the imperatives and outcomes of these rhythms and social relations through: (1) the need to provide more space for the population and the economic activities of the rapidly growing cities, (2) the spatial separation of economic activities, and (3) the spatial separation of social classes.

Transport Innovations

The imperative to provide more urban space was not met that well during the period from 1840 to 1885. The only way in which the city could be made less compact was to improve intraurban transportation—movement within cities had to be easier, cheaper, and more accessible. Unfortunately, the chief mode of intraurban transportation that was available—the horse-drawn omnibus on rail lines—was not terribly satisfactory.

The horse-drawn omnibus was first used in North America in New York City, about 1830, and the first system on street rail lines began regular operation in 1831. By 1860, the economic success of this system led to the use of the horse-car in New Orleans, Chicago, Baltimore, St. Louis, Cincinnati, Pittsburgh, and Newark, New Jersey. By 1885, 593 horse-cars were licensed to operate over twenty-seven routes in New York City. Although the average speed of a horse-car (5 miles per hour) was not greatly in excess of normal walking speed, the innovation saved human energy and provided a way for those who could afford the fares to live farther away from their place of work. Cities were able to expand, but not by much, as can be seen from the case of Chicago in Figure 4.3. The mercantile city of Chicago in 1850 had a population of about 30,000, but in 1880 the population was more than 500,000; the urbanized area was extremely congested.

There were attempts to apply the steam engine to intraurban transportation, but it proved inappropriate. It was cumbersome, noisy, and dirty, and above all it tended to frighten horses, emitting blasts of steam that caused pandemonium and panic. But the steam engine did have a considerable influence on the form and growth of the city because lands along the city rail lines and classification yards were developed by railroad companies as industrial sites. Furthermore, the rail lines were used for commuter railroads for those who could afford this mode of transportation on a daily basis. For example, the prosperous merchants and newly wealthy industrialists of Boston generated sufficient commuter traffic to warrant 118 daily commuter trains by 1848. These commuters lived in *exurbs,* or dormitory settlements beyond and distinct from the immediate environs of the urban area but tied to it like beads on a string by the railroad line (see Fig. 4.3).

The Spatial Separation of Economic Activities

One of the outcomes of the greater specialization of economic activities that occurred with industrialization is a clearer spatial distinction of land uses within North American cities. There were, perhaps, two main reasons for this: trans-

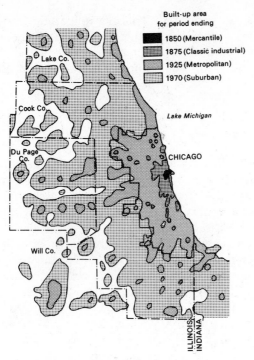

Figure 4.3 The spread of urban development in the Chicago region since 1850. (*Source:* Modified from Cutler, 1976, Fig. 7.2.)

portation improvements and the gradual shift from small workshops to larger-scale factory operations. Manufacturing industries congregated along transportation routes—first along the waterways and later along the side of the railroad tracks.

For example, in 1865 a consortium of nine railroad companies and a number of meat-packing companies (such as Armour and Swift) consolidated numerous small stockyards that were distributed around Chicago into one huge operation—the Union Stock Yards—which eventually occupied 1 square mile south of 39th Street and west of Halsted Street. This consolidation spawned a vast number of other industries at the periphery of the Yards that used as inputs byproducts of the meat-packing industry. At its peak in the early 1920s, the Yards employed over 30,000 people, and had given rise to large working-class districts that were often stench-filled and horrifyingly unsanitary. These conditions were epitomized by the neighborhood known and immortalized as the "Back of the Yards" (Sinclair, 1906).

With manufacturing becoming increasingly concentrated alongside transportation facilities, the commercial, retail, and financial center of the city gradually became more focused on service activities. Retail, financial, wholesale trade, and entertainment facilities concentrated in a central business district

(CBD), and began to cluster in sub-areas within that district. Also, as cities increased in population, neighborhoods of different social classes and ethnicity became much more noticeable.

The Spatial Separation of Social Classes

The innovations of the horse-car and the horse-drawn omnibus, the growing population, the increase in the number of people in different occupations and with quite different levels of income, and the establishment of distinct commercial and industrial areas, gave rise to a more distinct spatial separation of social classes in industrial cities. Low-income groups tended to locate (or be located by industrialists) close to their place of work or in environmentally unattractive, cheap, and shoddy housing. In contrast, the middle-class and upper-income groups began to seek more attractive locations away from the muck, dirt, and squalor of the industrial districts and the noise of commercial areas. The class divisions of society became replicated quite clearly in a spatial separation of social groups.

This is illustrated in a generalized diagram of land uses for Toronto in 1885, when the city had reached a population of about 150,000 (Fig. 4.4). The first-class residences of the upper-income groups are located at the periphery of the city, and the fourth-class residences of the lowest-income workers are located in the center of the city, around the business, warehouse, and industrial districts. This concentric pattern of the location of classes and income groups is a

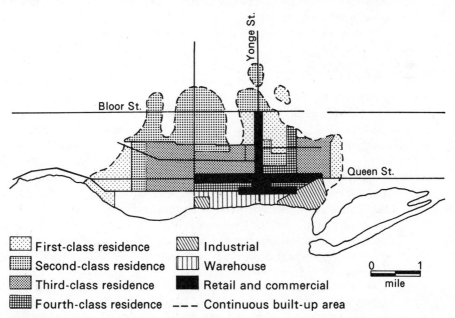

Figure 4.4 A generalized diagram of land uses in Toronto in 1885. (*Source:* Redrawn from Baine and McMurray, 1977, p. 31.)

classic form for industrial cities. Furthermore, it is noticeable that the first- and second-class residences, although on the periphery, are also adjacent to each other in a wedge, or sector, pattern.

One feature of these neighborhoods that is particularly important in North American cities is that class distinctions are frequently mixed in with ethnic, racial, and/or linguistic differences as well (Ward, 1971). For example, in the case of Toronto, the area of fourth-class residences in Figure 4.4 was predominantly Irish and Catholic, whereas the first- and second-class residential areas were predominantly English and Protestant. The area around the Union Stock Yards in Chicago, and particularly the Back of the Yards, consisted of thousands of recent immigrants from Eastern Europe; often, each group of immigrants formed its own local cultural and religious community.

Metropolitanism (1885–1935)

The era from 1885 to 1935 was one in which a number of large metropolises emerged and became the dominant form of urban organization in North America. During the period, the spatial separation of economic activities and socioeconomic groups becomes more distinct and more complex, cities become more spread out (Fig. 4.3), and suburbanization becomes more pervasive (Gordon, 1984). By 1880, twenty-one cities in North America had a population in excess of 100,000: New York City (2 million), Philadelphia (850,000), and Chicago (500,000) were the largest. However, the major cities of North America were becoming appallingly congested and overcrowded, and rapid industrialization had exacerbated inequalities and spatial differentiation as well as creating generally higher average levels of prosperity.

Population Decentralization

Adna Weber (1899), writing in the last decade of the nineteenth century, noted with alarm the high levels of population and congestion in the cities of the Western world, and particularly New York City. Seven wards in that city had population densities in excess of 250 persons per acre in 1880 (downtown areas today average about 30 persons per acre), housed in walk-up tenements (Weber, 1899, p. 460). For most people it was still impossible to live too far away from their places of work, so most people resided in close proximity to the economic activities in and around the central business district and around other major industrial centers. Weber's solution to this unhealthy congestion was to advocate decongestion, but this was not feasible until the advent of means of intraurban transportation that were faster and cheaper than the horse-car and omnibus—the electric streetcar and rapid transit.

The Streetcar   The electric streetcar (or trolley) was first used successfully on the Richmond Union Passenger Railway in Virginia in 1888, and was subsequently adapted by Whitney in Boston in 1889. The immensely superior and efficient operation of the streetcar in Boston resulted in the building or ordering of more than 200 systems in North American cities in the following three years. In 1901 there were 15,000 miles of electric streetcars/railways in the United States. Although the systems required considerable capital outlays, they were relatively easy to construct as the rail lines were laid on the ground surface and the electric wires could be slung overhead—there were no environmental impact studies required in those *laissez-faire* days! Thus, it is not surprising that the trolley became the first form of public transportation to be used on a large scale by employees going to and from work, and the patterns that developed became major traits of North American cities in the twentieth century.

The electric streetcar consequently made it possible for the middle-class population to spread out along major radials from the center of the city, and for residential densities to decrease. The spread that occurred was quite dramatic, as can be seen for Chicago between 1875 and 1925, when its population surpassed 3 million. For the population to spread out, however, land had to be provided and serviced, and homes had to be built. Because the population of most urban areas in North America was increasing rapidly as a result of rural out-migration, high birth rates, and massive immigration in the decades around the turn of the century, the innovation of the trolley is associated with great increases in land sales, values, and speculation.

Warner's (1962) seminal analysis of the effect of the spread of the electric streetcar on the then-suburban developments of Roxbury, West Roxbury, and Dorchester, Massachusetts (in the southern sector of, and immediately adjacent to, the old central city of Boston) provides a detailed discussion of this innovation. Most of the land in these three independent towns, which became suburbs in the late nineteenth century, was beyond the zone of dense settlement in the city of Boston prior to 1850. The horse-car prompted a tentative beginning of

Old streetcar on a "streetcar suburb boulevard," St. Charles Street, in New Orleans. (*Source:* Geovisuals.)

suburbanization in these towns, and in 1870 their population stood at 60,000. By 1900 their combined population had boomed to 227,000. This increase in population was housed in 22,500 new buildings, of which 53.3% were single-family homes, 26.6% were two-family homes, and the remainder were multiple-family dwellings. Such developments could take place only through the expansion of streetcar lines and land development.

Thus, throughout much of North America the expansion of "streetcar suburbs" involved close cooperation between the developer–speculator and the transit companies, and lines were strategically placed and threaded through preplanned subdivisions (Nelson, 1983, pp. 261–273). It was the developer, therefore, who determined the land use. If the developer thought an area of land was capable of supporting high-value housing, then the land was planned accordingly, with large lots.

Although the streetcar systems played an important role in facilitating suburbanization, the streetcar did not initiate the growth. Rather, the speculator and the investor began the process, and the streetcar network in the cities usually reinforced the patterns of growth. Furthermore, transit companies and land-developers could cloak themselves with an aura of moral purpose as they argued that they were assisting in the removal of people from unhealthy, high-density environments to low-density "garden" suburbs (Whitt and Yago, 1985).

Rapid Transit   Rapid transit is a cross between the streetcar and the railroad, involving the application of the electric motor to a system involving rail lines placed in isolated structures on the surface, subsurface (subways), or above the ground (elevated). Thus, rapid-transit facilities proceed at a faster pace (25 to 35 miles per hour) than streetcars (15–18 miles per hour), and can carry many more passengers. Because both the streetcar and rapid transit involve use of the electric motor, both modes were applied to urban transport at about the same time during the 1890s. However, as rapid transit involves much greater fixed costs in construction, its application was slower and more deliberate than the streetcar. Nevertheless, the development of rapid transit had a great impact on the form and structure of the city—particularly with respect to radial (or sectoral) growth and through the creation of centers of economic activity around local transit stations.

Rapid transit is efficient only when it is moving large numbers of people daily. Consequently, rapid-transit systems were constructed to connect the central business district, the chief place of employment and commercial activity, with the principal areas of urban population. In most cases the direction of growth had already been defined by the horse-car, the horse-omnibus, and the streetcar. For example, in Chicago rapid-transit routes on elevated lines (the "El") followed routes originally established by horse-drawn omnibuses and extended by the streetcar system. The expense of the system was (and still is) such that only the most traveled routes in certain sectors could be served. Hence, rapid transit accentuated the radial growth and fingerlike spread of the city (Fig. 4.3).

Apart from further accentuating sectoral growth, rapid transit also added a new dimension to urban structure through its need for discrete passenger loading and unloading points spaced farther apart than ordinary streetcar stops. Thus, each station on a rapid-transit facility has a unique tributary area from which it draws passengers, and some of these areas are larger than others. Street transportation in the larger areas focuses on the rapid-transit stations. The coalescence of transportation and people generates business activity around rapid-transit stations, and those stations with the largest tributaries may have very high densities of business and residential activity in their immediate vicinity.

One interesting aspect of rapid-transit and streetcar systems is that after the great surge in construction of either type of system (or both types, in combination, in most large North American cities—including Los Angeles!) in the early part of the twentieth century, investments in the systems virtually ceased toward the end of the 1920s, and many of them collapsed. There has been a resurgence of interest in rapid-transit systems in recent years, led by the construction of new Toronto and Montreal systems in the 1960s. A 71-mile Bay Area Rapid Transit (BART) system opened in the mid-1970s, connecting San Francisco to the other cities around the Bay; the Washington, D.C. subway is proving quite popular; a 53-mile light-rail rapid-transit system has been built to connect downtown Atlanta with its suburbs; an elevated system has been opened in Miami; and extensions have been added to other systems, such as the 1.3-mile addition to the Broad Street line in Philadelphia. Light-rail lines in Vancouver, Edmonton, and Calgary demonstrate that such systems are feasible in smaller metropolises. The impact of rapid transit on sectoral growth, and the higher densities of development that spring up around the stations are the same in these urban areas as in those whose systems were established at the turn of the century.

A subway station on the new Washington, D.C. Metro rapid-transit system. (*Source:* Geovisuals.)

A light-rail transit (LRT) line and station in downtown Calgary.

Spatial Differentiation within the Metropolis

The structure of the metropolitan industrial city that emerged by the end of that era (the early 1930s) is well summarized in two classical descriptive models. The first of these is Burgess's concentric zone model, which was formulated in the early 1920s and emphasizes the annular growth of cities (Park, Burgess, and McKenzie, 1925). The second is Hoyt's sector model, published in 1939, which focuses on radial aspects of city growth. Both models describe different processes and relate to different types of data. A third model, the Harris–Ullman multiple-nuclei diagram, combines the concentric and sector models (Harris and Ullman, 1945).

The Concentric Zone Model   The Burgess concentric zone model is based directly on the era of massive immigration and migration to North American cities and demonstrates the geographical outcome of assimilation into an urban and American way of life. It envisages a scenario in which the newcomers go first to the center of the city, where there are cheap apartments and many low-paying job opportunities. These people become settled, gain in economic wealth, and a few begin to move upward through the social strata. This upward mobility is accompanied by a move outward, into higher-income neighborhoods. The result is a city consisting of six concentric zones (Fig. 4.5a):

1. The central business district is considered to be the focus of commercial, social, and civic life, and of transportation. This area contains the department stores, shops, tall office buildings, clubs, banks, hotels, theaters, and museums that are of importance to the whole urban area.
2. The second zone surrounds the central business district and is an area of wholesaling, truck, and railroad depots. It is called the *fringe* of the central business district.

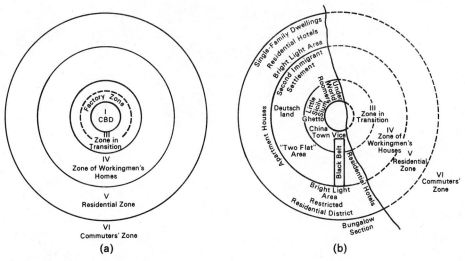

Figure 4.5 (a) The Burgess concentric-zone diagram of urban structure; and (b) its practical application in the Chicago of the 1920s. (*Source:* After Park, Burgess, and McKenzie, 1925, Charts I and II.)

3. The zone *in transition* is a zone that used to contain some of the homes of the wealthy, but as the city expanded and immigration occurred from rural areas and overseas, the wealthy have been replaced with low-income families and individuals. Consequently, it contains the slums and rooming houses common to the peripheral areas of the central business district. Business and light manufacturing encroach into this area because of the intensive demand for services and the supply of cheap labor.

4. The zone of *independent workers' homes* consists primarily of industrial workers who have escaped from the zone of transition. It might be regarded, therefore, as an area of second-generation immigrants and other families who have accumulated sufficient wealth to purchase their own homes.

5. *High-class residences* is a zone of better residences containing single-family dwellings, exclusive restricted districts, and a few high-income apartment buildings.

6. The outermost zone is the *commuters' zone*. It encompasses a broad commuting area of suburban areas containing satellite cities and middle- and upper-class residences along rail or rapid-transit lines.

The details of the practical application of this model to Chicago in 1920 are indicated in Figure 4.5b.

The Sector Model   Hoyt (1939) based his sector model on an intensive study of the internal residential structure of 142 North American cities. From an analysis of the average value of residences (by block) in each city, Hoyt presents a number of specific conclusions, among which the most important are (Fig. 4.6a):

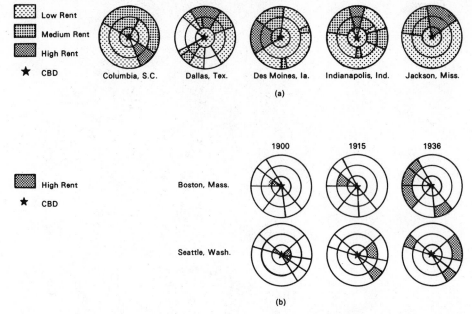

Figure 4.6 The Hoyt sector model of urban structure: (a) idealized pattern of rental districts in 1930 in five sample cities; and (b) generalized change in location of high-rent districts in Boston and Seattle, 1900–1936. (*Source:* H. Hoyt, 1939, Chapters I and II.)

1. The highest rental (or price) area is located in one or more specific sectors on one side of the city. These high-rent areas are generally in peripheral locations, although some high-rent sectors extend continuously from the center of the city.
2. High-rent areas often take the form of wedges, extending in certain sectors along radial lines leading outward from the center to the periphery of the city.
3. Middle-range rental areas tend to be located on either side of the highest rental areas.
4. Some cities contain large areas of middle-range rental units, which tend to be found on the peripheries of low- and high-rent areas.
5. All cities have low-rent areas, frequently found opposite high-rent areas and usually in the more central locations.

Thus, as a city grows, the high-rent (or price) areas follow definite sectoral paths outward from the center of the city (Fig. 4.6b), as do the middle- and low-rent areas. Each sector of the city, therefore, retains its character over fairly long distances once the initial rent differentiation is established.

The Multiple-Nuclei Model   Harris and Ullman (1945) recognized the shortcomings of the concentric zone and sector models and proposed a descriptive model of the North American metropolis as it had emerged by the end of the era of national industrial capitalism that takes into account both concentric and sectoral features *and* the growth of outlying business and commercial districts in suburban locations (Fig. 4.7). Called the *multiple-nuclei model,* this concept suggests that the city has developed a number of areas that group around separate nuclei. These nuclei include the central business district, outlying business areas, and industrial districts around which the various parts of the city tend to be organized for their daily activities.

An Example Land-use information for Toronto in 1940 (Fig. 4.8), when it had a population of about 900,000, provides some illustration of these general observations in the descriptive models. First, it is clear that industrial activities are transportation-oriented (that is, railroad-oriented). Second, the fourth-class residences of the poor are centrally located around the central business district and the industrial areas. Third, the first-class residences are located in the northern sector, whereas the second- and third-class residences of the middle class are in peripheral locations served by streetcars, commuter railroads, and other types of public transit. Fourth, outlying commercial (retail) areas have emerged at major intersections to serve the suburbanized population, and there are also some outlying industrial districts around classification yards.

Suburbanism

The era of the fourth Kondratieff, from 1935 to 1975, and particularly the post–World War II years, was the period of greatest suburbanization of the North American urban population. In examining the underlying bases for the massive deconcentration that occurred, we can discern the effects of: (1) high

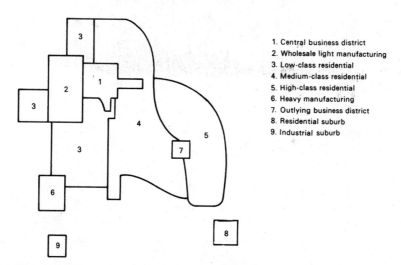

1. Central business district
2. Wholesale light manufacturing
3. Low-class residential
4. Medium-class residential
5. High-class residential
6. Heavy manufacturing
7. Outlying business district
8. Residential suburb
9. Industrial suburb

Figure 4.7 The Harris–Ullman multiple-nuclei diagram of the structure of American cities. (*Source:* Harris and Ullman, 1945, Fig. 5, p. 11.)

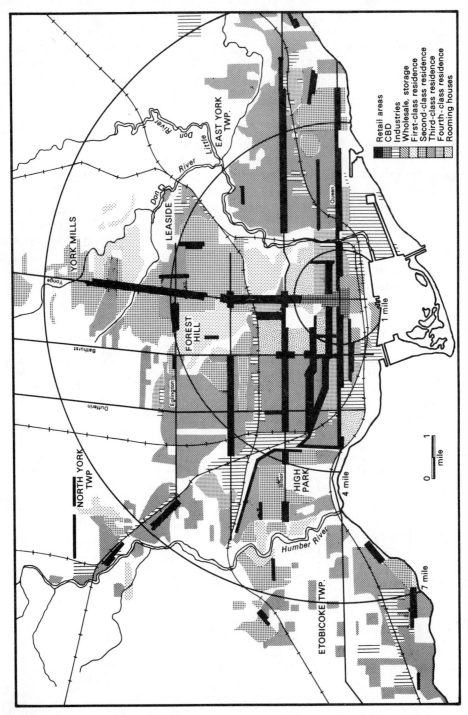

Figure 4.8 A generalized diagram of land uses in Toronto in 1940. (*Source:* Redrawn from Baine and McMurray, 1977, p. 34.)

rates of population growth and family formation; (2) higher levels of per capita wealth and hence consumption, which was partly translated into demands for more and better quality housing space; (3) technological innovations that facilitated decentralization; (4) governmental programs; and (5) development and financial institutions. These forces acted in concert to turn the North American metropolis inside out.

Population Growth, Wealth, and Family Formation

Between 1945 and 1975, the urban population (in places of more than 5,000 people) of North America increased by about 70 million, the per capita income more than doubled, and the rate of family formation was extraordinarily high. In consequence, the demand for housing, and hence the number of new housing units started, was in general about three times that of the average level in the previous era (Fig. 4.2). Furthermore, because of changing income and tasks, the housing units that were built were generally larger, with more rooms and bathrooms per unit. The volume of units built, and the increase in the average size of these units meant that urban areas expanded outward considerably during this era (Fig. 4.3).

Technological Innovation

The technological innovation that had the greatest impact on shaping cities after 1935 was the automobile. In 1903, when Henry Ford sought $100,000 to establish a motor company, he was able to raise only $28,000. Five years later, when W. C. Durant, the founder of General Motors, told an investment banker that eventually a half-million automobiles would be produced per year, the banker was incredulous and showed Durant to the door of his office. The application of the streetcar to intraurban traffic, its extension into interurban traffic, and the use of rapid transit and the commuter railroad, led many persons to believe that the automobile had a limited future. However, the forces that these innovations had set in motion in reshaping and restructuring the city proved ideally suited to the internal combustion engine as applied to the automobile. All the facets of urban life that came to the fore along with the innovation of the streetcar—the suburbanization of the middle class, the desire for travel and recreation beyond the city, the emphasis on individual and family group activities, the beginning of the outward migration of employment opportunities and crosstown commuting—could be developed a great deal further with the use of the automobile.

The Impact of the Automobile on Public Transit Until the mid-1930s, although the increase in automobile ownership was quite dramatic (Table 4.1), the automobile was really used more for social and recreational purposes than for the journey to work. After 1945, when the ownership ratio dropped below four persons per automobile, automobiles were used more and more for commuting purposes and, by 1970, more than three-quarters of all workers living in SMSAs used them for the journey to work.

Table 4.1 AUTOMOBILE OWNERSHIP IN THE UNITED
STATES, 1910–1980

Year	Auto registrations (in thousands)	Auto ownership ratio
1900	8	9,511.3
1910	458	196.6
1920	8,131	13.1
1930	23,035	5.3
1940	27,466	4.8
1950	40,339	3.8
1960	61,682	2.9
1970	89,230	2.3
1980	121,600	1.8

Source: U.S. Bureau of the Census, *Statistical Abstract of the United States,*
1973, pp. 5, 547 (Washington, D.C.: U.S. Government Printing Office,
1973), and, Bureau of the Census (1982), p. 579.

The impact of this high level of automobile use for the journey to work
not only permitted the spread of urban areas into fringe zones far from the
old city core, it also led to the demise of public transportation. In the 1940s
and 1950s, the bus began to replace the relatively inflexible electric streetcar,
and by 1970 the automobile had replaced the bus (Table 4.2). There is some

Table 4.2 PASSENGER TRAFFIC BY STREETCAR,
TROLLEY COACH, AND MOTOR BUS IN
URBAN AREAS IN THE UNITED STATES
1905–1970
In Billions of Total Passengers

Year	Streetcar and trolley coach	Motor bus
1905	5.0	—
1920	13.7	—
1925	12.9	1.5
1930	10.5	2.5
1935	7.4	2.6
1940	6.4	4.2
1945	10.6	9.9
1950	5.6	9.4
1955	2.4	7.3
1960	1.2	6.4
1970	0.4	5.0

Sources: Owen (1966), Table 16; 1970 data from American Transit Association, *Transit Fact Book, 1970–1971,* Table 2.2.

debate as to whether this occurred as a result of user choice—people prefer to travel to work in their own vehicle—or whether the decline in availability and quality of public transportation left commuters with little choice. Whitt and Yago (1985) argue that the automobile industry helped to destroy a number of streetcar and bus systems (for example, in Los Angeles) by purchasing and liquidating them.

Whatever the reason, and one suspects that both individual consumer choice and a lack of alternatives had an effect, the end result is that in the United States in 1980 only 12% of all workers in SMSAs of 1 million or more used public transportation for the journey to work, and only the New York SMSA had a relatively large proportion (45%) (Fulton, 1983). In Canada the proportion of total commuters using public transit in the three metropolises of 1 million or more is much higher (about 30%), due to greater public investment in such systems in recent years.

The Impact of the Truck   People are not the only things requiring mobility within an urban area. The inputs and outputs of industry require shipment, and these multitudes of goods and services have to be transported to all parts of the urban area. Some commodities, such as water, gas, and electricity, can be provided with their own specific transportation networks, but others are not suitable for pipe or wire dispersion. Before the development of the internal combustion engine, very little commodity movement within cities was undertaken by anything other than horse-drawn vehicles. Horses were superseded by 1900 for the movement of people, but they remained in service much longer for the movement of goods. The number of truck registrations increased more than tenfold between 1930 (3 million) and 1970 (30 million), and the flexibility of these vehicles contributed to the decentralization of commercial and industrial activities.

The Influence of Government on Decentralization

A number of policies at the local, state/provincial, and federal levels heavily influenced the suburbanization of population and of economic activities. Perhaps two examples will suffice to illustrate, although there are many that could be cited, some general across the United States and Canada, and some quite specific to individual urban places. The two examples relate to housing and transportation policies at the federal level.

Housing Policies   The tremendous increase in volume of post–World War II housing was made possible by the greater accessibility of new housing. Families could afford new homes in the United States because of policies put in place through various revisions to the Federal Housing Act (FHA). The Housing Act set mortgage guidelines and provided a mechanism for insuring mortgages that were made available through private-sector financial institutions. For example, in 1963 it was possible to obtain a twenty-five- (or even thirty-) year amortized FHA-insured mortgage at 6% interest with $1,000 down payment for a new, single-family detached home ($20,000, the average cost, was almost $60,000 in 1986 dollars). A veteran could obtain a similar loan with no downpayment under a Veterans' Administration (VA) plan.

These government-insured mortgages were for purchasing homes only, not for renovating them. As a result, there was an enormous expansion of housing subdivisions on new land at the periphery of cities. The Canadian situation after World War II was similar but not quite as dramatic because the Central Mortgage and Housing Corporation (CMHC) established by the federal government did not establish such universal schemes with similar low downpayments. Thus the comparative rate of new construction, and of outward expansion, was less than that in the United States.

The amount of suburbanization is reflected in the case of the Los Angeles SMSA: That most "twentieth century" of twentieth-century North American cities reached a population of 7 million by 1970 (Marchand, 1986). One-half of the housing stock in the Los Angeles SMSA in 1970 was built between 1960 and 1970 (Abler and Adams, 1976, p. 223), and the greatest concentration of this new housing was in suburban tracts at the periphery of the sprawling city (Fig. 4.9). The older housing, constructed prior to 1940, was mostly within the older

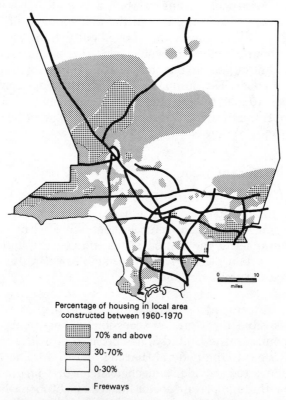

Percentage of housing in local area
constructed between 1960-1970

70% and above

30-70%

0-30%

Freeways

Figure 4.9 Housing built between 1960 and 1970 and freeways in Los Angeles. (*Source:* Housing data from Abler and Adams, 1976, p. 22.)

city, the central business district of which is now demarcated by a circle formed by the intersection of freeways.

Transportation Policies The movement to the suburbs was also accelerated by the construction of urban freeways (or expressways) through and around most large North American metropolises. Although some parkways (such as those in New York City) and limited-access superhighways (such as a few in Los Angeles) had been built before 1940, the tremendous construction of limited-access freeways occurred in the 1950s and 1960s. The impetus was the 1956 Interstate Highway Act, through which the federal government created a trust fund that paid 90% of local construction costs if an urban expressway were tied into the national interstate system. Of the 42,000 miles comprising the planned interstate system, 5,000 miles have been located in metropolitan areas, and those roads have consumed about 90% of the trust fund budget.

These governmental programs have thus been partly responsible for the departure of the middle- and lower-middle-class white population, and of many types of commercial and industrial activities, from central cities in the post–World War II years. Large amounts of land as far as 50 to 75 miles from the old central business district were opened up for urban use. The suburbs are now served by their own system of circumferential, or beltline, freeways, and the intersection of these freeways with the radial freeways has created locations that have great accessibility to the central city, the suburbs, and the continent. They have, as a consequence, become the locations of new manufacturing activity and of extensive regional shopping centers. The freeways make it easy for all circumferential locations to be serviced by trucks, and they facilitate an increase in size, carrying capacity, and power of those vehicles. Consequently, in many large metropolises, crosstown circumferential commuting became more prevalent than suburban-to-central city journeys to work by the mid-1970s.

The Impact of Developers and
Financial Institutions on Decentralization

One of the major features of urban growth since 1945 has been the growing dominance of large corporate developers who work closely with financial institutions during the development process (Lorimer, 1978). These two groups have been able to take advantage of federal housing programs and the demand for housing and office, industrial, and commercial space to completely reshape the North American city between 1935 and 1975. Prior to 1935, most urban development was undertaken by relatively small construction companies. After 1945, the scale of building that was required made it possible for large corporations to develop factory-assembly–type methods of construction for housing, shopping centers, and all types of commercial and industrial buildings.

Levittown Probably the most dramatic example of this type of production was provided by Levitt and Sons on Long Island, New York (Checkoway, 1984). The firm had gained experience with prefabricated building during World War II, and between 1947 and 1950 they used assembly-line and single-style ("Cape Cod") mass-production techniques to construct 17,000 identical houses on 1,400 acres for over 70,000 people, at a uniform price of $7,990. Each house came with all basic facilities (equipped kitchens, bathrooms, and central heating), buyers knew what they were getting in advance from the displayed "model" home, and the purchase could be made easily, in two half-hour steps— one to purchase and the other to clear title. This method of construction and marketing became, in effect, the model that was used across North America for most suburban tract new-home sales after that time. The system also had the beneficial effect of making resales relatively simple as well.

Characteristics of the Postwar Suburbs   There are, perhaps, six main characteristics of postwar suburbs that distinguish them from the streetcar suburbs and those built prior to 1935:

1. The postwar suburbs were built on the assumption that every family owns an automobile, so little thought is given to access to, or servicing by, public transit.
2. The standard prewar house was land-conserving, for most were two-stories high and were built semidetached, or as part of row housing. The standard postwar house is a detached single-story bungalow or split-level.
3. The postwar suburbs were usually built by fairly large development corporations on large, preassembled tracts of land. Frequently, these developments included housing *and* commercial activities. In consequence, many large metropolises became ringed with corporate-held "land banks" awaiting the appropriate financial and demand conditions for development.
4. Although suburbs prior to 1935 were built mainly for the growing middle class, after 1945 nearly all suburban tracts became income-stratified because (like Levittown) they tended to be price-stratified. The labeling of the subdivisions—Golf Course Estates, Pine Ridge Estates, Chateau on the Green—reflects the shades of subtle pretensions.
5. For the most part, the development companies ignored the needs for redevelopment in the old central cities unless governmental programs came along (such as the War on Poverty during the 1960s). The chief types of downtown rebuilding were public–private partnerships for the construction of office, hotel, and convention facilities in the central business districts of the largest metropolises.
6. The development companies and financial institutions reinforced existing underlying racial prejudices that (whether people like to admit it or not) exist throughout much of North American society (Jackson, 1985). Hence by 1970, a ring of virtually all-white suburbs surrounded the inner cities in which the black population was heavily concentrated (Johnston, 1984).

City Structure during the Suburban Era

By taking all the changes in internal structure into consideration it might be possible, albeit complicated, to develop a descriptive diagram of the internal structure of a typical North American metropolis by the mid-1970s (Fig. 4.10). The first zone is the central business district, which is the area of maximum vertical development of office buildings, the largest department stores, and numerous recreational, financial, and entertainment facilities. The second area is the fringe of the central business district, which contains elements of a sector pattern radiating out from the city center. It contains blighted residences, wholesale districts, and industrial sectors. The third area is the inner city, which consists primarily of lower-income people but also contains very definite nucleations of middle- and higher-income groups in well-defined areas.

Farther out beyond these areas are the older, inner-suburban rings, the vestiges of some of the streetcar suburbs and communities developed around rapid-transit stations. This area can also be divided into different income-level residential areas, is served by older regional shopping centers, and contains a number of planned industrial parks. The fourth and fifth zones are the middle-

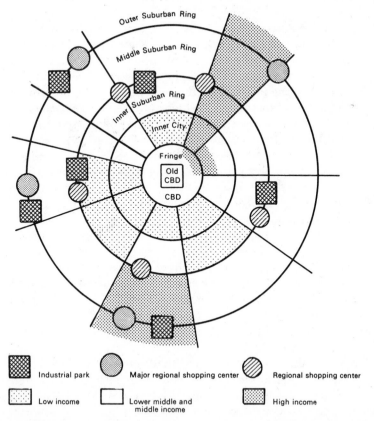

Figure 4.10 A possible configuration of a North American metropolis in the mid-1970s.

and outer-suburban rings, the latter consisting of those suburbs built since 1965 and largely influenced by the outer circumferential freeways. Between the middle- and outer-suburban rings, modern indoor shopping centers and industrial and business parks are located. The middle and outer rings are also subdivided into many income-differentiated communities that often occupy the same or similar sectors as their counterparts in the inner-suburban ring and the inner city (Brown, 1981).

The Galactic City

Most of the trends in, and influences on, the internal structure of urban areas during the period of greatest suburbanization (1935–1975) may well continue through the current era. There are, however, a number of features that might generate distinguishing features that could provide special characteristics to urban areas during the last part of the twentieth century. These distinguishing spatial features could arise from (1) changes in aggregate levels of wealth and income distribution, (2) changes in the size of households and the role of women in the labor force, (3) greater levels of nonmetropolitan growth and the dispersion of manufacturing and office activities.

Distinguishing Features   There is every reason to believe that per capita real wealth will not increase as quickly during the current era as it did in the 1950s and 1960s. There will therefore be less money available at the margin in both the public and private sector to support massive investments in urban infrastructure. In fact, the investment that will occur will increasingly involve public–private partnerships, which means public–developer partnerships. Of equal interest is the changing distribution of income: Whereas in the 1950s and 1960s family incomes tended to converge, at the beginning of the fifth Kondratieff long wave it appears that there is a divergence of income as new kinds of jobs come into existence and some old skills and jobs are less in demand (Berry, 1986).

This divergence of income, along with the aging of the "baby-boomers" and reduced household size, is influencing many women to remain in or reenter the labor force. Also, a large proportion of households now consist of one or two individuals, or single-parent families, the traditional two parents-plus-two children family of the 1950s and 1960s now being a thing of the past (only 4% of households in 1985). The net result is a demand for a variety of housing types in locations that will meet, in part, the individual and/or joint needs of a great variety of different households. For example, if there are two persons with careers in a household unit, the location of the residence has to take into account both journeys to work.

The third element has to do with dispersion within large metropolitan regions, which will undoubtedly continue; and perhaps nonmetropolitan growth, which may have been an aberration of the 1970s. Since 1979, the population has grown more quickly in extended metropolitan areas than in nonmetropolitan areas in the United States (Garnick, 1984). Concentration economies continue to exert a powerful attraction for the location of economic activities, even though these activities are now spread over large urban regions and into the rural/urban fringe. There will, therefore, be a continuous spreading out of population and employment into the outer-suburban ring and the rural/urban fringe, and increasing disparities in economic health among suburban areas (Getis, 1986) as well as inner cities.

With this continuing deconcentration expected within large metropolitan regions, an important question concerns the fate of the old central cities. Canadian central cities remain, by comparison with those in the United States, reasonably healthy, perhaps because of the greater toleration in Canada for controls and governmental involvement, or because Canadian society is not dominated by racial differences and is more prepared to "make do" with such things as older housing (Lemon, 1985). Many United States central cities are, by comparison, in a desperate state.

One of the most desperate, for example, is the city of Newark (58% black in 1980), which declined in population from 382,000 in 1970 to 314,000 in 1984, and is surrounded by middle- and upper-income white suburbs and a few black and partly integrated ones. One-half the residents of Newark in 1984 lived in households headed by single women, and one-third of the residents in the city were on welfare. Unemployment was generally twice the average for the state of New Jersey, and among young black males the rate was usually close to 70%. Since 1973 the city has lost about one-fifth of its property tax base and the number of stores has decreased by one-half. There is only one supermarket in the city, and that is on the boundary with the more prosperous, gentrified suburb of Elizabeth.

Given this level of desperation, where does this extreme case, and others that are approaching it, have to go—farther down or back up? There are signs in the 1980s that the situation may be bottoming out because some companies are relocating part of their office and manufacturing functions from Manhattan and elsewhere in the New York SMSA. They have realized that Newark has land and property that is now cheap, and that it is also well connected by transportation facilities to the rest of the New York–New Jersey metropolitan area and the world. The poor and unemployed of Newark have, however, become marginalized, and a number of issues, such as education and retraining, will have to be addressed if the local inhabitants are to have access to some of the new job opportunities.

A Galactic Arrangement   The outcome of this dispersal is that metropolises are becoming increasingly polynucleated, with many centers of commercial and economic activity. In a few large metropolises, downtown office activities and associated commercial business functions remain significant (for example, New York; Chicago; Toronto; Dallas; San Francisco; Minneapolis, and Tulsa, Oklahoma) but in most metropolitan areas the old downtown is one of many foci of activity, and in some the old central business district is irrelevant. In large metropolitan areas most employment is now located in controlled-climate suburban shopping centers and planned offices or industrial parks (Erickson, 1986).

Figure 4.11 The "night time" population of the northeastern seaboard and the lower Great Lakes. (Source: Bureau of the Census, United States Maps, GE-70 No. 4.)

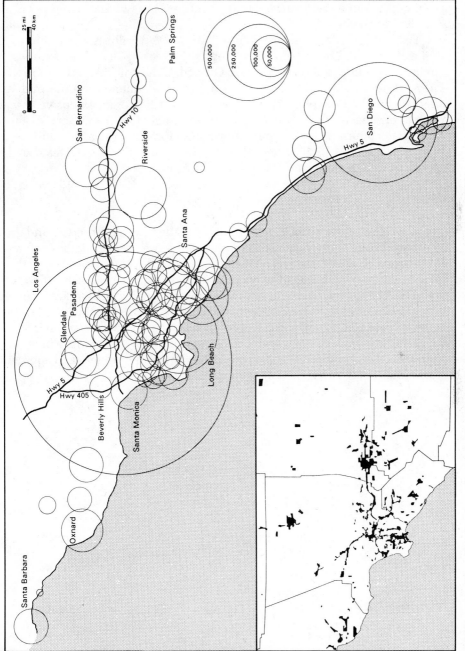

Figure 4.12 The distribution of population in the Los Angeles–San Diego region, 1980, and the distribution of industrial land. (*Sources:* Bureau of the Census, "Summary Characteristics for Governmental Units, 1980"; and H. J. Nelson, 1983, p. 201.)

Urban regions have become a galaxy of clusters of economic activities organized primarily around freeway systems (Fig. 4.11). Crosstown commuting is far more voluminous than central city–suburb commuting (Muller, 1981), and people are living in a wide variety of types of housing, within income- and race-stratified enclaves.

This type of galactic arrangement (Lewis, 1983) is illustrated in Figure 4.12 in the case of the Los Angeles–San Diego supermetropolis, which extends in an almost continuous built-up area from Oxnard, California 200 miles south to San Diego and the United States–Mexico border. It contained, by the mid-1980s, almost 14 million people. The map (Fig. 4.12) indicates an extensive spread of population and municipalities throughout this region of southern California. Industrial, commercial, and recreational activities are spread (in clusters) over this entire area, as is witnessed from the inset map that illustrates the spatial spread of one type of land use—industrial land.

Conclusion

This overview of the historic development of the internal structure and growth of cities in North America has reemphasized a number of themes referred to in previous chapters with respect to interurban development. The first is decentralization, which is leading to polynucleation in metropolises. The second is the effect of a large number of aspatial factors, such as technology, demography, the economy, and government, on spatial patterns within cities. The third is the wavelike impact of these factors on the accumulation of urban infrastructure, and the consequent identification of a number of eras in which certain spatial features predominated. These eras have been defined as mercantile, classic industrial, metropolitan, suburban, and galactic.

Chapter
5

Models of Urban Land Use and Population

The deconcentration and dispersal of people and economic activities within urban areas described in Chapter 4 can be represented by two types of models. One relates to the value of urban land and the location of land uses, and the other relates to the change in distribution of population as measured by population densities. The change in utility of the interpretive power of these models in the different eras will be discussed, and alternative approaches will be suggested.

ECONOMIC RENT, LAND USE, AND LAND VALUES

The work of von Thünen (1793–1850) represents the first serious attempt to provide a theoretical understanding of the location of land uses in geographic space (Hall, 1966). Von Thünen envisaged a country with no connections to the outside world. A metropolis (or marketplace) is located within an unbounded plain over which uniform soil and climatic characteristics prevail. Prices for agricultural goods are set externally at the marketplace; the price of labor and its productivity is uniform—hence market prices can be quoted *per unit area of production.* All producers have exactly the same production and living costs and the same size farms (that is, they have the same costs of being in business). The *only* variable is the transportation costs that are borne by the producers, for although the possibilities are equal in any direction over the plain (homogeneous transportation costs), the costs increase in a linear fashion with distance and vary among commodities.

Economic Rent

Assume that the price at the marketplace per unit area of production (for example, 1 acre) for wheat is $4.00. There are farmers at locations of A, B, and C miles from the marketplace (Fig. 5.1a). The transportation cost for shipping one unit area of wheat from location A to the marketplace (MP) is $0.40, from B to MP is $1.20, and from C to MP is $2.00. The production and living costs for each farmer is $2.00 per unit area of production. With this scenario, the farmer at location A will earn $1.60 more per unit area than basic production and living costs, the producer at B $0.80 more, and the one at C will exactly equal production and living costs—that is, will receive just enough income to remain in business.

With all farmers having equal standards of living, putting in the same effort, and having the same costs of production, they will all wish to locate at A or even closer to MP than A. For example, the farmers at C who are located at the margin of production for wheat (that is, where production and living costs per unit area equal net returns) will perceive that they can make $1.60 more for exactly the same effort at A than at C. This difference, in effect, represents the economic rent at A with respect to C. In general terms, *economic rent* can be defined as *the difference in return received for the use of a unit of land com-*

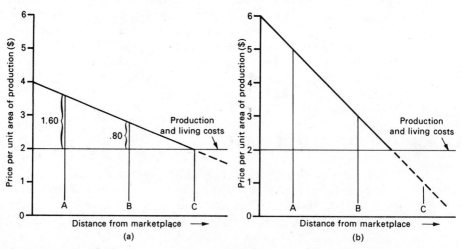

Figure 5.1 Von Thünen's concept of economic rent. (a) Wheat: The economic rent at location A is $1.60; (b) Vegetables: The economic rent at location A is $3.00.

pared with that received at the margin of production. In this particular case, the difference is due solely to variations in transportation costs for wheat, which are directly related to distance.

Assume now the existence of a second commodity, vegetables. Vegetables can be produced more intensively than wheat, but they are bulky and perishable, hence difficult to transport. Consequently, the transportation costs for the output of a unit of land in vegetables is higher than that for wheat—say, $1.00 for A to MP, $3.00 from B to MP, and $5.00 from C to MP. However, the price for the output of one unit of land in vegetables is higher than that for wheat—$6.00. This situation is depicted in Figure 5.1b. In effect, the economic rent curve for vegetables is much steeper than that for wheat because of the difference in the transportation costs. Also note that there is no way that farmers at C can produce vegetables because the transportation costs they would have to bear would not permit production and living costs to be met.

Land-Use Zones

Von Thünen envisaged a market for land that is structured in the following way: A landowner owns all the land and places it to auction for rent each year. Under this situation, it is evident that the farmer practicing the type of production that is yielding the highest net return per unit of land at a particular location will be able to make the highest bid at that site. For example, in Figure 5.1 it is clear that a farmer choosing to produce vegetables at A can outbid a person wishing to produce wheat by up to $1.40 per unit of land. Also, a farmer choosing to produce vegetables at B can just outbid one producing wheat. But at C, a farmer has to produce only wheat in order to survive.

Thus the "highest" (meaning highest price) and "best" (meaning the type of land use that is able to take the best economic advantage of a particular location) use of the land at A and B is vegetables, and at C is wheat. This results in concentric zones of land use around the marketplace, with the inner ring growing vegetables and the outer ring growing wheat (Fig. 5.2). With many more crops and types of animal husbandry there will be many more rings.

The Political Economy of Economic Rent An important question in political economy arises concerning who gets the economic rent, or the surplus above the basic production and living costs for the farmer. In this case, the competition for the surplus is between the landowner and the farmer. For example, farmers at A who produce vegetables can afford to bid up to, but not exceed, $3.00 per unit of land, and the actual contract rent (that is the amount of rent paid to the landowner) will depend on the availability of land (supply) and the number of farmers competing for locations (demand). This kind of bidding process depends, of course, on the existence of a "market"—it could be that the landowner exerts monopoly power and sets the contract rent equal to the economic rent or, alternatively, the landowner may be benevolent and charge somewhat less.

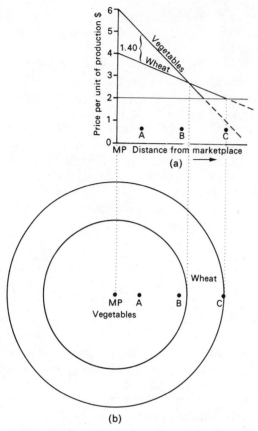

Figure 5.2 Von Thünen's concept of economic rent—the zonation of land uses.

Economic Rent and Land-Use Zones in the Urban Environment

The von Thünen concept of economic rent and land-use zones can be applied to the urban scene with a few modifications to the assumptions (Alonso, 1964). The flat, featureless plain with a homogeneous transportation-cost surface and a central marketplace is replaced in the urban case by a *monocentric* (or single-centered) city on a flat plain over which transportation costs are uniform in any direction. A bidding process is implied, along with the absence of monopoly power. The users of land are assumed to have equal access to the land market and to be equal in tastes and so forth. All employment opportunities and the buying and selling of goods occur at the center of the city, so that people have to go there for economic purposes. Transportation costs increase with distance, so *aggregate transportation costs* (that is, the total cost of getting to a place from all other places in the city) are lowest at the center of the city.

Imagine that there are only three types of land use in the city: central

Examples of the transition from rural to urban land uses: (left) Regina (Saskatchewan), a clear-cut rural/urban zonation; and (right) Montreal, farmland abandoned in anticipation of urban development in the Longueuil district. (*Source:* Geovisuals.)

business district functions—commercial, finance, retail, and wholesale—manufacturing, and residential. Central business district activities must be central to their market and labor force (the rest of the city), so their general economic rent curve is the steepest (Fig. 5.3a). Manufacturers also wish to have maximum access to labor, so they require centrality, but the general economic rent curve for manufacturing is not as steep as that for central business district activities, because the utility (or revenue received per unit of land) at central locations is greater for central business district activities than for manufacturing. Finally, residential activities have the shallowest economic rent curve because individual households cannot generate as much economic rent (or utility) at central locations as central business district and manufacturing activities. In such a situation the zonation of land uses will be as represented in Figure 5.3a.

Land-Use Zones in a Multicentered City   The type of city described in the previous section probably existed in general form only until about 1935, since at that time it was evident that a multinucleated arrangement of land uses had emerged. The multicentered or *polynucleated* form is not that much different conceptually from the monocentric city, just more complicated. The central business district may remain the locus of minimum aggregate travel costs for the entire urban region, or it may be just one among a number. The net result is that the arrangement in our model of three land uses is similar to that presented in Figure 5.3b. Each of the outlying centers, which in the 1980s are invariably located around major freeway intersections, serve as regional centers for the city as a whole, and a pattern of land uses becomes distributed around them in much the same way as around the central business area.

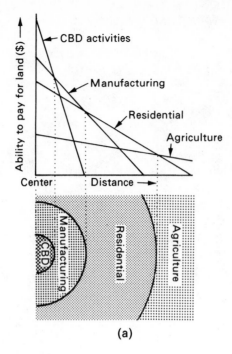

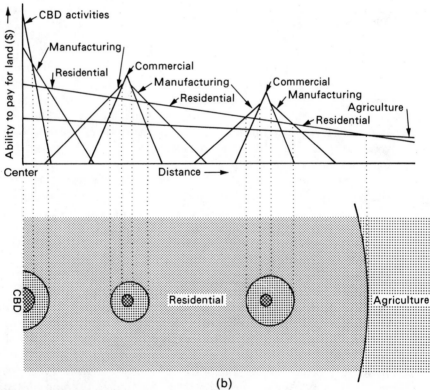

Figure 5.3 Hypothetical land-use zones in (a) a monocentric, and (b) a multicentered city.

Empirical Examinations of the Changing Patterns of Economic Rent

The changing pattern of economic rent in a city can be examined through land values, for these are the outcome of the bidding process for sites. Of course, the bidding process is not perfect, for a particular site comes up for sale infrequently, but tax assessment offices and real estate appraisers do make estimates of the value of sites on the basis of sales of adjacent or similar lots elsewhere in the city. Thus, it is assessed land values (which are used for property-tax purposes), that are frequently used as surrogates for the theoretical economic rent at particular locations.

The change in the average land value in the city of Chicago from 1910 to 1960 (Fig. 5.4) replicates the cyclical trend expressed in housing starts. Maps of the spatial distribution of the land values for 1910, 1930 (at the peak of land speculation prior to the 1930s crash), and in 1960 (Fig. 5.5) demonstrate the effect of access to the central business district (around the intersection of State Street and Madison Avenue), the emergence of outlying centers, and the attraction of Lake Michigan as an amenity. The land-value maps for Chicago in 1910 and 1930 demonstrate that values decline with distance from the central business district (the peak-value intersection—PVI—is at State Street and Madison Avenue), with a zone of higher values tonguing north and south along the lakeshore, reflecting amenity values. The PVI is, theoretically, the locus of minimum aggregate travel costs for the entire metropolis. It would not have this predominant value if it were not the most centrally located piece of land. Foci of higher values around major outlying shopping nucleations become apparent by 1930, for these areas are also essential collecting points in the network of public transportation facilities.

By 1960, however, this simple structure is replaced by one that is more

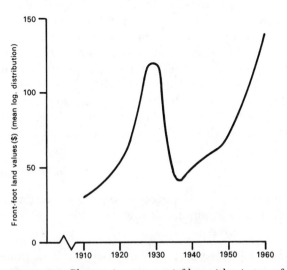

Figure 5.4 Change in average (of logarithmic transformation) of land values in Chicago, 1910–1960.

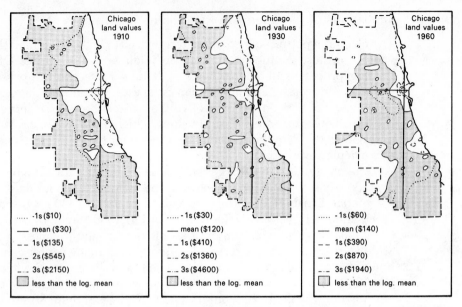

Figure 5.5 Land-value surfaces for the city of Chicago in 1910, 1930, and 1960. (*Source:* Yeates, 1965, Figs. 1 and 2.)

complex. Land values are still highest within the central business district and the ridge northwards along the lakeshore, but they drop off rapidly in the middle part of the city and then rise again toward the periphery. The distribution of land values looks much like one-half a sombrero with a high core in the middle and a rim around the outside encircling a trough within.

Two recent studies suggest that this "sombrero" pattern of land values has strengthened since 1960. Edel and Sclar (1975) demonstrate that whereas residential real estate values declined with distance from the center of Boston until 1940, by 1970 real estate values increased with distance from the center of the city (Fig. 5.6). Similarly, McDonald (1981) shows that the business and commercial land values (his study excludes residential values) in Chicago for 1960 and 1970 (bracketing the opening of the freeway system) was essentially unchanged, since the advantages of access to the central business district were essentially offset by access to the suburban circumferential highway pattern.

Sources of Economic Rent

In our theoretical and empirical discussions of economic rent and land values we have, in fact, referred to a number of sources of rent and/or value. These may be summarized as follows:

1. *Differential rent.* There are, perhaps, two kinds of differential rent (Edel, 1976). Differential Rent I arises as a result of the differential amounts produced in von Thünen–type conditions—varying location.

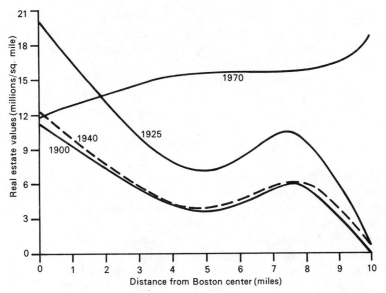

Figure 5.6 The relationship between land values and distance from the center of Boston in 1900, 1925, 1940, and 1970. (*Source:* Edel and Sclar, 1975, p. 375.)

Differential Rent II comes about as a result of varying amounts of capital investment being applied to lots at essentially similar locations within the city.

2. *Monopoly rent* occurs whenever a monopoly comes into being in any part of production or consumption and the value of land is determined only by the price that the monopoly producer is willing to sell at, or the price a monopoly consumer is willing to pay (Scott, 1980). For example, Lorimer claims that suburban land developers were able to add from 20% to 30% to the price of new homes in many Canadian metropolises in the 1970s due to monopoly control of land (1978, p. 100).

3. *Publicly induced rent* refers to land values in particular parts of metropolises that are influenced by public spending—for example, a new bridge across a river that changes the pattern of accessibility. This is evident with expressway interchanges and with many other types of government investments in transportation systems and office establishments. For example, the location of the LBJ Space Center south of Houston has drawn growth in the city in that direction and has also acted as an enormous stimulant to land values.

4. *Amenity rent* is the term used to describe the high values some locations attain by virtue of their physical characteristics (e.g., on hills with views), or their location next to social and recreational amenities. The high land values along waterfronts in many North American cities are good examples.

5. *Social, or class, rent.* Values in many parts of North American cities are greatly affected by the choice of elite households to locate in certain parts of the city, and to exclude less elite households from these areas (Gruen, 1984). For example, some areas are high-rent areas because of the social cachet that is associated with them, such as Nob Hill, San Francisco.

MODELS OF URBAN POPULATION REDISTRIBUTION

The distribution of population densities in urban areas has been of interest to students of urbanism for a long time. Much of the literature is based on research undertaken in the 1950s and 1960s, as North American cities were in the middle of the period of greatest suburbanization. At that time it appeared that in most cities population density was greatest at the center of the city and diminished toward the periphery, and that density was higher in the ring immediately adjacent to the central business district than in the central business district itself. There was also some ridging of population densities along major radials leading from the center of the city.

Population Densities in a Monocentric City

This decrease in population density with distance from the center of the city was not only observed empirically, but can be predicted from von Thünen–type arguments pertaining to economic rent. If it is assumed that the center of the city is the primary focus of employment and economic activities and that locations close to the center are more expensive (high land values) than those at the periphery of the city, then the population will have to trade off space costs and transportation costs (to work) at any particular location. If a household wishes to minimize both space and transportation costs (including the cost of time spent commuting), it will have to live at higher densities close to the center of the city. If a household wishes to have more space, it will invariably have to move to cheaper locations farther from the center of the city and thus incur higher transportation costs. This individual household space cost versus transportation cost trade-off is central to population-density models.

The Clark Model

The relationship between population densities and distance from the center of the city was modeled by Clark (1951) and modified slightly by Newling (1966). Clark collected data pertaining to many urban areas around the world and concluded that population densities were related systematically to distance from, or accessibility to, the center of the city. Specifically, he suggests that urban population densities decrease in a negative exponential fashion (that is, decrease at a decreasing rate) with distance from the central business district. The formulation of this model is:

$$D_d = D_o e^{-bd}$$

where D_d = population density at distance d from the CBD

D_o = a constant indicating the population density at the center of the city, that is, the *central density*

$-b$ = a parameter indicating the rate of decrease of population with distance; that is, the *density gradient*

d = the variable distance

e = base of the natural logarithms.

In general, all that such an equation indicates is that population densities decrease rapidly at first with distance from the central business district and then tend to flatten out. This situation is expressed in Figure 5.7a, and the straightline logarithmic transformation of the model is presented in Figure 5.7b.

One feature that the Clark model (1951) does not incorporate relates to densities at the center of the city. We noted that densities tend to be lower at the center than in the area immediately adjacent to the central business district.

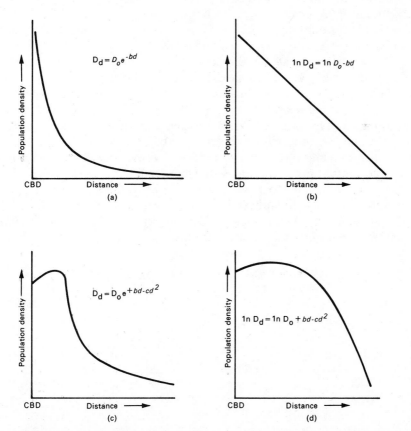

Figure 5.7 (a) Clark's model of urban population densities; and (b) its logarithmic transformation. (c) Newling's modification of Clark's model; and (d) its logarithmic transformation.

This situation occurs because nonresidential land uses, such as commercial, office, and other business activities, tend to preempt other uses in the core. The result is a population "crater" at the center, which Newling (1966) attempted to incorporate in his modification of the Clark model. This crater is presented for comparative purposes as Figure 5.7c, and its logarithmic transformation as Figure 5.7d.

Change in Central Densities and Density Gradients Edmonston, Goldberg, and Mercer (1985) use a particular form of statistical analysis (the two-point method) to estimate the parameters of Clark's model—the *central density* and the *density gradient*—for 204 United States SMSAs and 20 Canadian CMAs from 1950 to 1975. The results of the analysis are presented in Table 5.1, along with a graphic representation for United States cities in 1950 and 1975, and for Canadian cities in 1951 and 1976 (Fig. 5.8). The results demonstrate quite clearly that on a highly aggregated scale the Clark model is tenable for recent time periods, but that central densities, and density gradients, have been continually decreasing; that is, the population-density curves are becoming flatter (Fig. 5.8). Also it is evident, as we indicated earlier, that Canadian cities have higher densities than United States cities (p. 100).

The information in Table 5.2 shows how central densities and density gradients change with city size. It appears that in both countries central densities increase with city size, but the density gradient decreases with city size. Hence, large metropolitan areas have higher land-consumption rates than smaller urban areas not because the density gradient is steeper, but because the central densities are higher. When central densities collapse, as they have done in the United States for large cities, the population literally floods outward to consume vast quantities of space on the rural/urban fringe.

This flooding outward, or tidal wave of metropolitan expansion, is evident in information presented by Anderson (1985) for Detroit. He uses a Newling-type model in order to capture not only the density crater at the center of the city, but other peaks and craters. The curves for 1960, 1970, and 1980 (Fig. 5.9) demonstrate quite clearly the depopulation of the central city of Detroit that has occurred since the early 1960s: In this case the general density gradient is

Table 5.1 DENSITY GRADIENTS AND CENTRAL DENSITIES IN CANADIAN
AND AMERICAN METROPOLITAN AREAS, 1950–1951 TO
1975–1976
(CMAs and SMSAs)

Year	Density gradients		Mean central densities	
	Canada	U.S.	Canada	U.S.
1950–1951	0.93	0.76	50,000	24,000
1960–1961	0.67	0.60	33,000	17,000
1970–1971	0.45	0.50	22,000	13,000
1975–1976	0.42	0.45	20,000	11,000

Source: Edmonston, Goldberg, and Mercer (1985), Table 1.

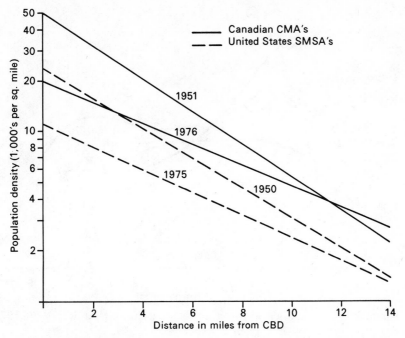

Figure 5.8 The relationship between population density and distance from the center of the city, for United States and Canadian metropolitan areas, 1950–1951 and 1975–1976.

now almost flat. It must be recognized, however, that Detroit is one of North America's more extreme cases of depopulation and abandonment in an old central city.

Population Densities in a Multicentered City

It is clear from our historical discussion of the changing internal structure of North American cities and the information in Table 5.1, that by 1960 the monocentric model was a poor representation of metropolitan areas in North

Table 5.2 DENSITY GRADIENTS AND CENTRAL DENSITIES IN CANADIAN AND AMERICAN METROPOLITAN AREAS, BY POPULATION SIZE, IN 1975–1976

Population size of the central city	Central density		Density gradient	
	Canada	U.S.	Canada	U.S.
100,000–500,000	18,000	10,000	0.43	0.48
500,000–1,000,000	36,000	10,000	0.43	0.26
1,000,000 +	40,000	16,000	0.30	0.19

Source: Edmonston, Goldberg, and Mercer (1985), extracted from Table 6.

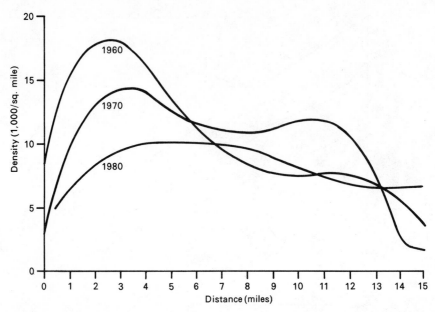

Figure 5.9 Changing density–distance relationships in Detroit in 1960, 1970, and 1980. (*Source:* After Anderson, 1985, p. 418.)

America, and that commuting behavior cannot be described as central-city–oriented. Crosstown commuting and highly dispersed employment opportunities, with many peaks in population and employment, are the facts of life in the polycentric galactic metropolis of the 1980s (Griffith, 1981). For example, in the 11.5 million population five-county area around Los Angeles (Los Angeles, Orange, San Bernardino, Riverside, and Ventura counties) Gordon, Richardson, and Wong (1984) identify the existence of forty-five population peaks in 1970 and fifty-eight such peaks in 1980.

The complex model used for the five-county Los Angeles region, therefore, examines population densities with respect to the peaks existing in both 1970 and 1980. Table 5.3 lists the results for the twenty-six peaks that existed in both 1970 and 1980 in Los Angeles County *only*. The feature to notice from Table 5.3 is that there is no general tendency for the peak densities and gradients to change in the same way—some areas are increasing in density while others are decreasing, and they can be adjacent to each other geographically. Thus, whereas the monocentric model has central densities and density gradients that are becoming flatter over time, the multicentered model demonstrates a far more complex pattern of change.

Monocentric Patterns, Polycentric Patterns, and Race

Although changes in the availability of transportation, government programs in housing and transportation, and the "baby-boomers'" need for housing have been primary influences on decentralization and the shift from the monocen-

Table 5.3   LOS ANGELES COUNTY PEAK DENSITIES AND ASSOCIATED DENSITY
GRADIENTS, 1970 AND 1980

Peak ref. number	1970		1980	
	Peak density	Gradient	Peak density	Gradient
1	19,300	−1.06	21,800	− 1.05
2	5,800	−0.11	4,500	− 0.42
7	9,860	−1.77	8,630	− 1.48
8	7,640	−0.46	8,610	− 0.55
9	13,000	−1.55	14,800	− 1.11
11	5,930	−0.71	5,390	− 1.89
14	15,500	−1.90	11,400	− 1.08
15	11,100	−1.22	13,300	− 1.63
16	13,300	−0.96	14,100	− 1.72
17	17,500	−1.42	15,900	− 1.44
18	22,300	−1.89	24,100	− 1.70
19	31,000	−1.70	33,400	− 2.10
20	11,500	−3.88	20,000	−10.50
21	6,410	−0.26	7,240	− 0.48
22	6,310	−0.95	7,560	− 0.90
23	23,700	−1.94	23,400	− 1.56
24	14,600	−4.64	16,700	− 4.85
25	19,000	−1.85	30,000	− 2.10
26	9,450	−1.05	14,600	− 1.49
27	21,600	−1.13	32,900	− 1.10
28	11,200	−0.63	36,300	− 1.66
29	20,800	−2.17	36,300	− 1.66
30	6,070	−0.03	9,150	− 2.73
31	20,500	−1.48	21,700	− 1.72
33	5,300	−1.18	10,500	− 0.61
34	5,140	−0.22	12,900	− 1.86

Source: Gordon, Richardson, and Wong (1984, p. 12).

tric to the multicentered city, there is no doubt that racial differences have also played an important part in the growth of the polynucleated metropolis. We have previously commented on the flight of the white population in the United States to the suburbs in the post–World War II period. This is documented quite clearly in population-density curves calculated by Reid (1977) for the black and white populations in a sample of thirty-three SMSAs for 1960 and 1970 in the United States (Fig. 5.10). Whereas both the black and white population-density curves in 1960 were of the monocentric city, or Clark-type, by 1970 the white population-density curve had reversed, with white population densities actually increasing toward the periphery of the cities. The black population lives in the old monocentric city, whereas the white population resides in a developing polynucleated galactic city.

Although some of the distinctions between the location of black and white households have something to do with income and affordability, a large part of

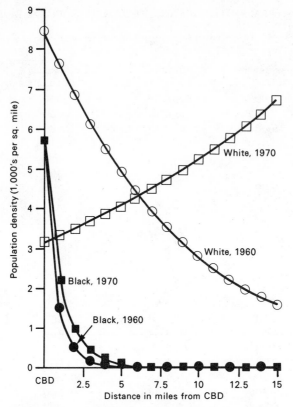

Figure 5.10 The generalized population-density distribution of the black and white population in a sample of thirty-three SMSAs, for 1960 and 1970. (*Source:* Reid, 1977, p. 356.)

the spatial separation is related to prejudice-induced discrimination. As a consequence, toward the end of the 1960s the federal government increased its attempt to prevent discrimination in housing (such as through Title VIII of the Federal Fair Housing Act of 1968). The highly aggregated information in Table 5.4 suggests that although the suburbanization of "other races" (mainly whites) continued between 1970 and 1980, there was also greater suburbanization of blacks.

However, although it may appear that on the central city–suburban geographic scale of analysis segregation may have decreased in the 1970s (Jakubs, 1986), it appears that within suburban areas segregation is continuing. For example in St. Louis, where 50% of the SMSA black population resides in suburbs beyond the central city, segregation in the city is being perpetuated by segregation within and among suburban areas (Farley, 1986). Thus, as the trend of black suburbanization and white exurbanization into fringe areas continues through the 1980s, segregation is remaining just as prevalent as it was in the 1960s. This situation, and the processes involved, will be discussed in greater detail in the chapters that follow.

Table 5.4   THE CHANGING RACIAL COMPOSITION OF SMSA CENTRAL CITIES AND
SUBURBS
United States, 1960–1980

	SMSA total population	Percent		
		Central city	Suburbs	Fringe[a]
Black				
1960	13,063	75.9	21.6	2.5
1970	17,095	76.9	21.2	1.9
1980	20,521	71.9	26.4	1.7
Other races				
1960	109,746	45.6	51.8	2.6
1970	126,277	40.1	57.0	2.9
1980	136,670	35.4	61.0	3.6

[a]The fringe population is the population of counties to the 1970 SMSA definitions added between 1970 and 1980.

Source: Data from Long and DeAre (1981, Table 1). Calculations by author.

PUBLIC POLICY AND LAND-USE CHANGE

There is a market for urban land in North America in which people and business activities compete for certain locations. In the market, "prices" of various kinds are established that, in effect, allocate land among the various types of uses. This market is not, however, allowed to run unfettered, for if it did the negative effects on society would be far greater than any positive effects that might be enumerated (such as land being in its "highest and best use"). For example, in a free and unfettered land market it is highly unlikely that parks would be available for public use in prime locations such as on waterfront land or in high-density areas. Government, and particularly local government, has to intervene in some way to influence the allocation of land to certain uses to achieve social objectives. In this section the discussion will focus on two ways in which local governments usually intervene in North America: One direct method of intervention is through zoning, and an indirect method is through the property tax.

Zoning

One of the most general measures used in North America metropolises to control densities and the use to which land is put is through zoning. Comprehensive zoning first appeared in New York City in 1916 as an outgrowth of the common law of nuisances, which has, as its central principle, the tenet that one must use his or her own rights so as not to infringe upon the rights of others. This idea is interpreted in the land-use situation as meaning that you should not use your own property in such a manner so as to interfere with your neighbors' use of their properties. The concept has been extended over the years to include not only property but also the protection of life, health, comfort, and peace in the community.

It is therefore important to recognize that zoning was devised not as a planning tool for regulating the use or density of occupancy of land, but as an extension of the common law of nuisances (Hason, 1977). This extension achieved a high level of legal validity as a result of a number of appeals of zoning decisions through the courts, the most celebrated case being a decision by the United States Supreme Court in favor of the enactment of a zoning bylaw by the suburb of Euclid, Cleveland in 1926 (Weaver and Babcock, 1979).

The need for zoning arose because the real estate industry and property owners perceived that the value of urban land and property could be seriously affected by what use was made of adjacent properties, or of other properties in the general vicinity. Thus, an expensive upper-middle-class house or row of housing would be affected negatively in value and marketability by the sudden establishment of an incongruent economic activity within the vicinity. Examples include the establishment of sleazy bars in residential communities and the location of noisy, noxious industries within the confines of a quiet neighborhood.

Therefore, the basic premise for zoning, as perceived by the owners of property and the real estate industry, was that the private land market could not be left to operate in an unrestricted manner. What the property industry had realized was that *externalities* (that is, factors not derived from the site itself) profoundly influence the market value of a property, and what they wished to do was to have some level of control over these externalities in order to protect (and even enhance) values.

Types of Zoning

Zoning, as it has developed over the years, has become an exceedingly complex business in part because it involves decisions at the local level, made by locally elected officials, that impinge directly on individual households and businesses. Three types of zoning (which tend to overlap) will be examined: general zoning for the separation of uses, zoning for planning purposes, and zoning desired to achieve performance standards.

Zoning for the Separation of Uses   Much of the zoning that we see in cities is designed to designate certain parcels of land or whole parts of cities for particular uses, often with designated household-unit densities. There are two types of zoning for the separation of uses—*hierarchical zoning* and *specific zoning.* Hierarchical zoning, which still exists in many smaller communities, in effect ranks land uses according to their need for protection. In general, land for housing is at the top, commercial in the middle, and manufacturing at the bottom. Anything can be built on land zoned for manufacturing, only commercial and residential uses on land zoned commercial, and only residential on land zoned residential. Specific zoning, on the other hand, designates land for one use (and stated maximum coverage) and one use only—that is, manufacturing land can only be used by manufacturing industries. Most communities have discovered hierarchical zoning to be dangerous in times of rapid growth, and specific zoning is used most often.

Zoning and Planning   City planners in North America are in a frustrating position—they may go through long procedures with local communities to develop goals and plans, but they find they have little power to actually implement much since it is the developers who actually build things. As a consequence, planners have devised many ways of trying to influence the course of events through zoning. The course of growth of a city may be influenced by zoning land in advance of development: this is called *impact zoning.* Historic sites may be preserved by allowing the use (or density of use) that a developer wishes for that site to be transferred somewhere else: this is known as *transfer zoning.* In fact, transfer zoning for all types of objectives, not just historic preservation, has become the biggest money-making game in many metropolises today. *Percentage zoning* is often used by planners to encourage a mix of land-use types—for example, high-, middle-, and low-income housing plus commercial uses in an area that is being redeveloped. Also, the outward spread of urban development at the urban/rural fringe may be controlled through the use of designated greenbelts involving agriculture and forest uses.

Zoning and Performance Standards   Zoning to achieve certain performance standards, such as the same type of industrial activity (as in industrial parks), or to achieve similar types of housing units (such as bungalow and/or split-level detached houses in one area separate from low-rises), is common in many North American metropolises—particularly in recently developed suburban areas. Unfortunately, this performance standard aspect of zoning has often been used for (or perverted into) *exclusionary zoning,* in which certain income groups are excluded from certain areas by the regulation of lot sizes, minimum floor space for housing, and even the facilities within the house. It is a short step, of course, from this income discrimination to race and class segregation.

Administrative Structures Related to Zoning   Zoning activity in many communities is exceedingly complex and may involve any mix of planning offices, planning boards, zoning commissions, appeal boards, zoning officers, building inspectors, environmental protection agencies, and the local council itself. Given the complexity of the process and the specific interests that are usually involved in any one case, it is not surprising that the process is dominated by the groups whose interests are most affected—the real estate industry, developers, and lawyers. It is an important administrative arena that shapes to a large extent the environment of the community in which we live; therefore the decision-making process must not be the exclusive preserve of those with a direct financial stake.

Zoning and Land-Use Change

In a broad survey of land-use change in metropolitan areas, Wilder (1985) concludes that on the whole:

1. Land tends to remain in the same type of use even though there may be changes made to the buildings on the land.
2. Any change that occurs usually results in more intense use of the land;
3. Certain uses never follow one another—for example, industrial and residential uses rarely follow one another.
4. Land-use change seems to vary by location—succession within the same use is common toward the center of cities, whereas conversion of land use from one type to another is more common at the periphery of cities.

Given these general types of change, it is clear that zoning and its attendant constraints play an important role in influencing the types of changes that occur. The lesson from this is that if a situation demands an orderly land market with fairly predictable succession and land-use change, then strict specific zoning is desirable. If, however, conversion is necessary to promote more radical change, then zoning will have to be less rigid and more flexible. However, major zoning changes significantly affect prices (Chressanthis, 1986), thus providing gains for the owners of the rezoned properties. There should be some mechanism that enables society to recoup all or part of the gains made by individuals or corporations through the act of rezoning. Such recoupment would maintain credibility in the zoning process and for those involved with it. One way of recouping such gains is through the property tax.

The Property Tax and Land Development

The property tax, which will be discussed in greater detail in Chapter 10, is one of the chief ways that local governments raise revenues. In 1980 in Canada, one-third of all municipal revenues came from taxes on property. In the United States, the comparable figure is 54% of all tax revenue raised by local governments. The property tax *(T)* is generated on the basis of assessed property values *(B)* and the local millage rate *(t),* which is the amount to be collected for each dollar of assessed valuation: that is, $T = t \times B$. The mill rate is set locally and varies among municipalities. It also varies within each municipality according to type of land use. Some land uses (for example, office and commercial activities) frequently have a higher mill rate than residential uses. Also, the assessed valuation is often not the current market value of the property, but a value estimated at some time in the past, although there is an attempt in many municipalities to assess the property at some proportion of current market values (Barlowe, 1986, p. 446).

The assessed property value *(B)* is made up of two components: the value of the land (site value), known as the unimproved capital value (UCV); and the value of the improvements to the land (such as the buildings placed on the land), known as the improved capital value (ICV). In North American cities, the assessed property value is made up largely of the improved capital value (Bird and Slack, 1983, p. 73). The question therefore arises, What would be the effect on urban land use and change if the property-tax system were based on site values rather than improvements on the land?

In general, it would seem that property taxes based on improved capital values make the holding cost of land itself too low (Ohta, 1984). If land is not improved; that is, if it is without buildings, the property taxes are low, and this creates a low cost for merely holding the land (other than the cost of foregone revenue that might be realized from the improvements). On the other hand, basing property taxes on improved values may well, in some cases, discourage owners from making additional improvements because of the fear of higher property taxes. Thus, it can be argued that a taxation system based on unimproved capital values (that is, land values) (1) promotes rapid land-use change because it discourages people from holding either unimproved land or improved land that is generating little revenue (or satisfaction), (2) generates improvements closer to the highest and best use at particular locations, and (3) helps to reduce the extent of sprawl at the rural/urban fringe through the promotion of more efficient land use in general.

Conclusion

Our brief overviews of zoning and the property tax emphasize once again that the internal structure of North American cities is the product of a variety of forces that operate in different ways at different times. Undoubtedly, cyclical forces play a powerful role, although it must be recognized that the responses of various urban areas to expansion or contraction varies according to the economic structure, location, and entrepreneurial dynamism of the city at that particular time period (Bergman and Goldstein, 1983). The general theme of deconcentration that pervades the discussion of the historical evolution of cities can be represented reasonably adequately in monocentric and polycentric models of urban land use and population densities. These models in effect crystallize the historic discussion of change and dispersal and also provide a basis for some preliminary discussions of issues of public policy and land use—particularly with respect to zoning and the taxation of property.

Chapter

6

The Social Structure
of Cities

A quick inspection of the streets in any North American city reveals a variety of social, economic, and ethnic characteristics. In some areas the houses are new, large, and obviously occupied by upper-income families. Other areas have older housing that may consist of walk-up apartments. In these areas children are playing in the streets or at the basketball courts, and the small, local stores are owned by people with German, Spanish, Chinese, Korean, or other ethnic-sounding names. The differences among these areas are based on a large number of criteria, such as housing, density, ethnicity, size of families, income, religion, and social organization. Furthermore, all these areas are in a continuous state of change, and any one neighborhood may contain vestiges of previous inhabitants as well as the characteristics of the most recent inhabitants. For example, a neighborhood that is currently predominantly Chinese may contain within it a Polish community center.

The objective of this chapter is to gain some understanding of the general kinds of socioeconomic patterns that exist within cities, and to appreciate the many different types of forces that may bring these spatial patterns into existence and cause them to change. As the kinds of social patterns that are identified are related directly to the aspatial forces believed to bring them into existence, the discussion will focus on some of the major theories related to the differentiation of socioeconomic groups. These theories are: the classical ecological concept, the behavioral approach, a political economy–based perspective, and, finally, gender theory.

THE CLASSIC ECOLOGICAL MODEL OF URBAN SOCIAL SPACE

The concentric zone model of city growth, which emphasizes how waves of immigration and a few general societal forces such as innovations in transportation can continuously alter the internal structure of urban areas, was discussed in Chapter 4. This zonal model was a product of the Chicago school of human ecology of the 1920s (Park, Burgess, and McKenzie, 1925). In this section we will examine the wider manifestations of this approach as it pertains directly to change, and then proceed to a discussion of a derivative of this approach—social area analysis.

The Ecological Concept of Social Space

The basic assumption of the ecological approach to the study of urban social space is that the processes recognized by plant and animal ecologists as operating in the natural environment can be translated to the urban social sphere. Thus, the ecological approach developed in the 1920s as a social science that is "fundamentally interested in the effect of position, in both time and space, upon human institutions and human behavior" (Park, Burgess, and McKenzie, 1925, p. 64). The immediate utility of this approach was twofold. First, it focused on the characteristics of people in certain places and the tensions that occurred at the boundaries separating people of different characteristics. In this way the ecological approach provided a conceptual structure and an array of processes that are intrinsically spatial.

Second, the ecological approach applies to processes that relate to *groups* rather than to individuals and can, therefore, be applied to aggregations of people and households that are collected by the census and published in census units (such as census tracts, blocks, and enumeration areas) of one kind or another. In fact, the ecological approach, with its emphasis on the definition of communities of between 3,000 and 9,000 people, gave rise to the use of census tracts within cities. These units are supposed to represent collections of people and households of roughly similar characteristics. The ease of obtaining and using census tract data may well explain the continued relative popularity of the ecological approach in urban studies.

Invasion–Succession–Dominance

The ecological model postulates an initial stage in which a particular group of people, or a particular land use, occupies a given space or territory. These people or that land use have sufficient characteristics in common to appear relatively homogeneous. Then, an incursion of another group with different characteristics occurs. This new group may be assimilated into the original resident group and adopt its characteristics, it may be repulsed, or it may prove stronger and more able to live in that particular environment than the original resident group. In the last case, the new group may succeed the older group and, as in plant ecology, a new climax stage is reached in which the new species replaces the one that had occupied that niche before it. There is, therefore, an inherent assumption that stable homogeneous social groups and/or land uses are the norm, and that the invasion–succession stages will lead to a new norm.

It is not at all clear that stability is the norm, for most parts of cities are changing continuously. Furthermore, there is also an underlying supposition in the invasion–succession–dominance model that homogeneity is the natural end product, and that heterogeneity (the mixing of different types of peoples, households, and land uses) is a transition state. Thus the ecological model may unfortunately provide subliminal support for preexisting racial and class prejudices in some people. We will observe in Chapters 6 and 7 that although there may be groupings of people in parts of urban areas that exhibit fairly similar characteristics, this cannot of itself be assumed to be a "natural" outcome, for it is invariably created by public and private actions in some way.

Social Distance

One of the private ways in which homogeneity is created is illustrated through the concept of social distance, which in fact indicates the extent of prejudice among groups of people. Social distance indicates the degree of social separation between individuals, families, ethnic groups, neighborhoods, occupations, or any other grouping of individuals. As a social concept, it may be measured behaviorally in terms of who marries whom, residential proximity, and degree of mixing; or it may be measured psychologically by asking individuals to rank others according to a scale of hypothetical social relationships.

For example, Bogardus (1926) measured how native-born, white Americans perceived other groups by asking whether they would (1) admit ethnic group X to a close kinship by marriage, (2) have X as friends, (3) have X as neighbors on the same street, (4) have X in the same part of the city, (5) have X in the same city, and (6) have X in the same country! Numerous studies have demonstrated that "the less social distance there is between individuals, the greater the probability of interaction of some kind" (Knox, 1982, p. 41). The corollary to this idea is that the greater the social distance between individuals or groups, the greater the likelihood of a large physical distance between them as well.

The effect of the rather high level of social distance between much of the black and white population in Chicago is well documented by Berry *et al.* (1976). From a number of case studies involving the movement of blacks into areas occupied previously by whites, they demonstrate that "regardless of socioeconomic characteristics, a concentration of black families is perceived negatively by whites" (Berry *et al.*, 1976, p. 251). The degree of social distance is measured by the way the white population reacted in the face of an immigration of blacks to their neighborhood. The various responses of the Illinois neighborhoods studied included violence in West Englewood, defensive barriers in Garfield Ridge, and quiet white flight in Evanston. In South Shore and Oak Park, the black population was steered into more acceptable locations, and there was a low level of managed integration with higher-income blacks. Park Forest publicly declared its commitment to unrestricted open housing. Berry *et al.* conclude that integration between blacks and whites is unlikely to emerge as long as race remains a status-determining trait. In a more recent study of the same area, Winsberg (1986) concludes that with suburbanization the social distance among groups generally has increased, although within higher-income suburbs social distance between black and white families may be decreasing.

The Social Area Concept and Social Space

One of the questions faced by the human ecologists' approach is the definition of social space. It can be defined many ways and may involve many different criteria. What is needed is some theoretical understanding of the impact of urban development upon the formation of social groups in the city. Such an understanding can lead to the enumeration of criteria that may be used to establish the socioeconomic structure of the city within an ecological framework. A technique called *social area analysis* has been developed for doing this, based on the classical theoretical work of Wirth (1938).

Wirth's View of the Effect of Urbanization on Social Relationships

During the 1930s, American society was changing from one that was predominantly rural to one that was urban. Many people at that time thought that this was unfortunate, as urban areas were regarded as generally iniquitous, if not downright sinful. This attitude underlies Wirth's (1938) analysis of the impact of society's transformation from a rural to an urban state. His interpretation is based on three indisputable characteristics of urban areas: they are generally large in size, have a reasonably high density of population and economic activities, and are reasonably heterogeneous in terms of people and occupations. Wirth hypothesized that size created a large number of possible interactions and, as a result, that most interpersonal contacts were impersonal and secondary and there were few close interrelationships. On the one hand, the individual has more freedom and is less subject to personal and emotional control from others; on the other hand, unsatisfying, transitory contacts lead to a lack of meaningful interaction and consequently to feelings of alienation (Fig. 6.1).

Density reinforces the effect of size, for it results in differentiation and in specialization with respect to economic activities and home and work places. The complexity of society is thus increased, and people are compartmentalized into specialized roles that predominate in particular sub-areas of the city. The result is the segregation of the city into a mosaic of social and economic worlds that are too numerous and complex for anyone to fully comprehend. Finally, cities are the product of immigration of people of diverse origin. They are

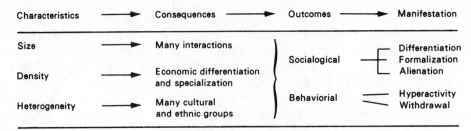

Figure 6.1 Wirth's (1938) view of the outcome of increasing urbanization.

socially heterogeneous, and this characteristic is compounded by the differentiation and specialization of occupations. This heterogeneity results in no common set of ethical values, and thus money becomes the measure of all things, with certain objects, such as a house or automobile, providing external status symbols.

There are, according to Wirth (1938), two main outcomes (Fig. 6.1) of increasing size, density, and heterogeneity as society shifts from a rural to an urban state—one sociological, the other behavioral (Berry, 1981). On the sociological level, urbanization is thought to lead to differentiation, formalization, and alienation. The differentiation effect can be both spatial and aspatial, for economic activities and people become highly specialized in function and role, and both types of specialization can occur in particular locations. The development of a large number of formal institutions is largely the result of excessive differentiation and the need for a means of communication. Alienation can be expressed by withdrawal. At the behavioral level, the stresses of urbanism, from such factors as high urban densities or excessive stimulation, result in a variety of "abnormal" behaviors, such as excessive action. The hypothesized result is that urbanism leads inevitably to social disorientation and a breakdown of family life.

Wirth's (1938) negative view of the outcome of urbanization on family life and social relationships is overdrawn. There is no doubt that as size, density, and heterogeneity increase, people are faced with excessive stimuli and develop a constant preoccupation with surviving the rat race of corporate competitiveness, commuting, and cacophonic environments. Cases of people exhibiting conditions of alienation, or some form of social deviation, do exist in cities, but they also exist in smaller towns and rural areas. However, do these conditions become more numerous in cities because of increasing scale, density, and heterogeneity?

Abundant evidence suggests that when these conditions exist, they invariably occur for other reasons; little evidence suggests that urbanization itself creates social disorientation and a breakdown of family life. In fact, it appears that people are able to live in a world of work *and* have close contacts in their residential neighborhood. Certainly many contacts are ephemeral and family size has decreased, but most people still have a number of close contacts. Furthermore, the stimulation of a large urban area can have positive effects in encouraging new ideas and the communication of innovations (Gans, 1962). Thus, urban areas may be regarded as having a positive effect on creativity, and a wide variety of contacts may prevent people from becoming too insular.

Social Area Analysis

Although Wirth's model may be criticized on the grounds that it is too negative, his view of the effect of urbanization on people has stimulated an enormous number of questions. One question concerns how the change from a rural to an urban state was manifested with respect to the social structure of the city. Shevky, Bell, and Williams (Shevky and Bell, 1955; Shevky and Williams, 1949) hypothesized that the changes Wirth discussed could be related to ecological groups, which are defined statistically and geographically by census tracts. Furthermore, they suggested that the changes could be summarized in terms of three constructs relating to the groups: social rank, family status, and segregation. The last construct, segregation, may relate to the formation of distinct groups by characteristics other than race, such as age and language.

The first construct, social rank, relates to the effect of population size on the range and intensity of relations among families and individuals (Fig. 6.2). It is hypothesized that whereas in the country individuals have a fairly wide range of contacts, in the city most contacts are focused on the particular occupational group with which a person is involved. Consequently, the indicators relating to this trend are those that define the different occupations, and data indicating the changing proportion of employment in the occupations will demonstrate the importance of the social rank construct as urbanization proceeds. The particular statistics that can be used to derive the construct are the proportion of people employed in higher status, white-collar occupations, years of education, and various measures indicating the wealth of the group. Thus, urbanization is hypothesized to result in a clear differentiation of groups by social class, which is measured primarily by occupational status.

The second postulate can be inferred to be an outcome of increasing density

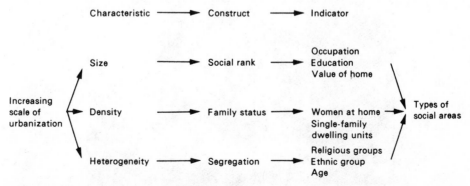

Figure 6.2 Steps in the development of social area constructs and indices. (*Source:* Based on Shevky and Bell, 1955, p. 4.)

which, it is hypothesized, reinforces the effect of size by diversifying economic roles (Fig. 6.2). In the rural state, the entire family is involved in a production process that is agricentric. The urban-industrial family is less unitary, and its members may be concerned with a number of totally unrelated occupations and may be employed in different parts of the city. This diversification of occupations within the family unit can be examined most clearly with respect to the employment of women and the movement of women into urban occupations. Thus, the construct of family status can be measured by the proportion of women in a census tract that are employed outside the home, the size of the family, and the proportion of single-family dwelling units in a census tract. Using these measures, census tracts that are defined as *high family status* contain relatively large families with few women at work and many single-family homes, whereas those areas that are *low family status* contain many women at work, small families, and few single-family homes.

The third construct of the social area analysts, segregation, results from the larger variety of ethnic backgrounds that are encountered as society changes from a rural to an urban state. This diversity is reinforced by the great mobility and redistribution of urban populations that occurs with urban expansion. There is, therefore, a tendency for a sorting of population to occur in terms of age, sex, and ethnic background (Fig. 6.2). A census tract is considered highly segregated if a high proportion of its population consists of individuals of a particular ethnic background, color, age, or gender. It should be noted that the social area analysts have a mechanistic use of the word *segregation,* which they define purely statistically. Later in this chapter the meaning of segregation will be discussed in terms of process.

Empirical Applications of Social Area Analysis in 1950 and 1981   Examples of the use of social area analysis for defining social space in terms of social rank, family status, and segregation are discussed for the city of San Francisco in 1950 and

A segregated social area in San Francisco: Chinatown. (*Source:* Geovisuals.)

the Calgary CMA in 1981. Following a 22% increase in growth in the 1940s, San Francisco reached a population of 775,000 in 1950. Calgary experienced a period of enormous growth (47%) in the 1970s, and had a population of 593,000 by 1981.

Using the same indicators as Figure 6.2, Figure 6.3a shows that the census tracts with the highest social rankings are on the western and northern parts of San Francisco, whereas the lower-ranked tracts are generally on the east, facing the Bay. The family status map (Fig. 6.3b) shows that the higher family status tracts are in the southern part of San Francisco, whereas the lower family status areas are in the central and northern parts of the city, around the historic core. Finally, the most segregated tracts contain concentrations of blacks and Chinese-Americans (Fig. 6.3c) and are generally in lower-income eastern sections and close to the downtown area in the northeast. A composite of these three constructs (Fig. 6.3d) indicates the existence of a high social rank–low family status quadrant in the southwest; a high family status–low social rank area with some segregated sub-areas in the east and south; a high social rank–low family status area with a number of tracts exhibiting segregation in the central and old northern parts of the city; and a small area of low family status–low social rank tracts with some segregation in the old wharf area of the city and out along Mission Street.

The second example, relating to the Calgary CMA, demonstrates similar types of consistency in the spatial distribution of the constructs. The social rank construct has been defined in terms of the three variables listed in Figure 6.2, with the value of homes in a census tract represented by the market value of privately owned dwellings and the monthly gross rent for one-family

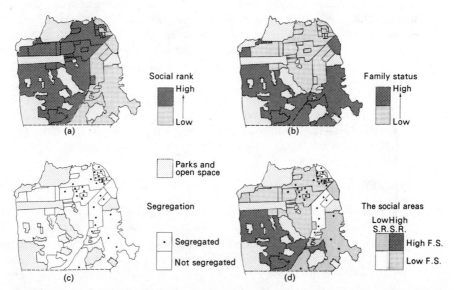

Figure 6.3 The social areas of San Francisco, 1950. (*Source:* After Shevky and Bell, 1955, Fig. V14.)

households. The census tracts are ranked according to the data, the ranks are then summed, and the tracts are resorted according to the sum of the ranks; then they are divided into two groups, labeled *high* and *low*.

The higher social rank areas (Fig. 6.4a) are in the northwest, around the University of Calgary, the southwest close to the Canyon Meadows Golf and Country Club, and a few tracts close to the downtown. The lower social rank areas are adjacent to the industrial parks south and east of the airport, and on the lower-lying areas east of the downtown and within the right-angle bend of the Bow River.

The west/east distinction of the social rank pattern is matched by an inner/ outer pattern of the family status construct. This construct is comprised of two of the variables described in Figure 6.2: Family size is represented by the proportion of households with 3 to 5 persons; and single-family dwelling units are represented by the proportion of private dwellings that are owner-occupied in a census tract. The variable "women at home" is not included because by 1981 the vast majority of women of employment age were at work whether they were members of one-person households or not, and the female labor participation rate in most census tracts is from 50% to 65%. Thus by 1981 this construct was only meaningful if the assumptions related to women in the paid work force were excluded.

The third construct, segregation, is represented not by ethnic groups but by concentrations of older persons. In Calgary, just over 6% of the population in 1981 was over the age of 65, so 15% is more than twice the average proportion for the city as a whole. Older persons are concentrated in census tracts close to the downtown area where there is a better supply of lower-cost rental accommodation.

Generalizing from these three constructs, one finds, as with San Francisco, that there are some remarkably clear contiguous patterns of social space. The northwest and southwest are high social rank–high family status areas. The east side of the city is a low social rank–high family status area. Around the downtown and in a wedge along two limited-access highways are high social rank–low family status census tracts consisting of young, reasonably affluent, childless single persons. The low social rank–low family status areas are in the central part of the city, and it is within these areas that concentrations of older persons are located—the younger and older persons living in the same type of residential accommodation.

Factorial Urban Ecology

The human ecology approach to the definition of social space within urban areas can be criticized not only because of the weak "rural-to-urban" theoretical base, but because of the methodology used to define the constructs and social areas. The methodological objections pertain to the use of census tracts and the subjective selection of measures to define the constructs. The use of census tracts is based on the false assumption that they represent fairly homogeneous groups of population. This gives rise to the "ecological fallacy" in urban

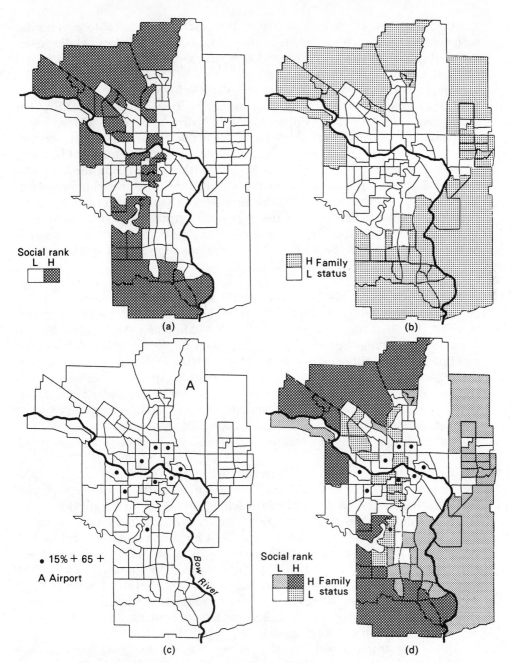

Figure 6.4 The social areas of Calgary, 1981.

analysis, for it is wrong to assume that census tracts contain people with similar socioeconomic characteristics. An additional aspect of this fallacy relates to the fact that all census tracts are treated as if they were equal in population and physical size, whereas they are not.

The second methodological objection, that the indicators are chosen subjectively to support the constructs, also cannot be denied. Consequently, it is interesting to know if the constructs are basic patterns of social structure that can be produced if all the variables that are available pertaining to metropolitan areas are used. The factor-analysis model tries to answer this question by using all the information pertaining to census tracts within cities (Cadwallader, 1985, pp. 124–142). Factor analysis involves a set of procedures that can be used to summarize in a few dimensions a vast number of characteristics that describe particular items. In this case, if the items are census tracts, the number of variables pertaining to census tracts is usually in the hundreds. Factor analysis helps, in effect, to find the underlying dimensions represented by these many variables (Davies, 1984).

Factor Analysis and Social Area Constructs A great wave of factorial urban ecology studies were made during the latter half of the 1960s and the first few years of the 1970s (for example, Rees, 1970). Most of these studies defined social spaces in cities by using census tract data for 1960 or 1961—that is, for one time period—although a few involved analyses of similar sets of data pertaining to the same city during two time periods. In the majority of these studies, one usually finds that dimensions relating to socioeconomic status, family status, and segregation predominate. Thus, objective analyses of a large number of variables relating to social, economic, housing, religious, ethnic, and racial characteristics of census tracts support the constructs defined by the social area analysts.

Two interesting studies of Montreal, one by Greer-Wootten (1972) for 1951 and 1961 and the other by Foggin and Polese (1976) for 1971, provide examples of the application of the factorial urban ecology approach to the study of social space. The study by Greer-Wootten used twenty-seven socioeconomic variables for the census tracts within the Montreal CMA for the two periods, and that by Foggin and Polese used sixty-three variables. Both studies revealed that the variables could, for the most part, be summarized by the three underlying dimensions defined by the social area analysts. Social rank factors contrast high- and low-income groups, family status factors contrast larger family households with smaller family households, and ethnic factors contrast the French-speaking population with the English-speaking population.

But, whereas in many studies the social status and family status factors are of primary importance, in Montreal's case the French/English dimension is central to the differentiation of that city's social space. For example, the social rank dimension contains ethnic overtones because the higher-income groups tend to be concentrated in the English-speaking community and the lower economic status groups in the French-speaking community (Table 6.1). The

Table 6.1   VARIABLES CONSTITUTING THE SIX BASIC UNDERLYING
DIMENSIONS OF SOCIAL SPACE IN MONTREAL

Social rank factors (48% of variance)

High income Managers and professionals University level education English	(1) ⟷	Middle income Construction & transport Secondary education French
Middle income Office worker Secondary education	(2) ⟷	Low income Service activities Secondary and primary

Family status factors (37% of variance)

Family size (4 or more) Young children Home owners	(3) ⟷	Family size (2 or less) No children Renters
Younger household heads	(4) ⟷	Older household heads

Ethnic status factors (15% of variance)

Italian Recent immigration	(5) ⟷	French Nonimmigrants
British	(6) ⟷	French

Source: Foggin and Polese (1976).

Foggin and Polese study also demonstrates that by 1971 the ethnic factor had become more complex, with the English/French contrast being joined by an Italian/French dimension. Similar results were obtained by Le Bourdais and Beaudry (1988) in their study of the residential structure of Montreal in 1981.

Basic Patterns of Social Space

Studies by the social area analysts and by those using the procedures of factorial urban ecology led Berry (1965) to hypothesize that three general patterns of social space had developed in North American cities. The first is the axial, or sectoral, variation of neighborhoods by social status, the second is the concentric variation of neighborhoods according to family status, and the third is the localized concentration of particular ethnic groups in pockets. These hypothetical spatial patterns are presented in Figure 6.5. The social rank diagram obviously echoes Hoyt (1939). The concentric distribution of family status is the product of the availability of new single-family homes at the periphery of cities. Minority groups, whether black, Puerto Rican, Mexican-American, Oriental, or

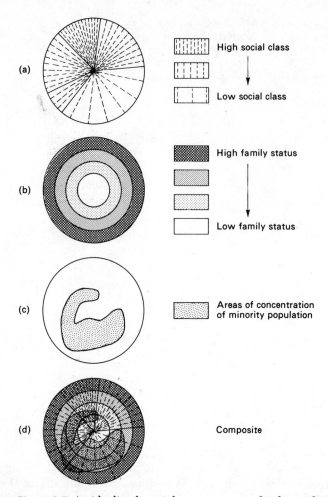

Figure 6.5 An idealized spatial arrangement of indices of (a) social rank, (b) family status, (c) segregation, and (d) a composite view of the spatial variation of social structure, in 1963.

recent immigrants from Italy, usually concentrate in distinct parts of the city for a variety of reasons.

One of the most comprehensive analyses of urban social space using the procedures of factorial urban ecology was undertaken by Murdie (1969) for metropolitan Toronto in 1951 and 1961. Murdie attempted to determine objectively whether (1) the constructs recognized by the social area analysts could be defined for Toronto and (2) if they could be defined, whether they were distributed spatially in the manner hypothesized by Berry (1965). The study involved a factor analysis of eighty-six variables concerning occupation, income, dwelling units, ethnicity, language, religion, sex, and education of the populations of census tracts. For both periods, the results again emphasized the underlying importance of the basic social area constructs: social status, family status, and ethnicity. (However, in 1961 the ethnic status component separated into two independent factors involving Italian and Jewish groups.) In the second part of the study, Murdie demonstrated that these main components were, in fact, distributed as Berry had hypothesized—that is, social rank was distributed sectorally, family status concentrically, and certain religious, national, and linguistic groups were located in distinct clusters.

More recent studies of metropolitan Toronto emphasize a remarkable consistency in the constructs and patterns since the 1950s (Fabbro, 1986; Murdie, 1987). For example, Fabbro (1986) establishes the existence of a social status construct based on education, occupation, and house values that is sectorally distributed; a family status construct based on age of homeowner, residence in owner-occupied dwellings, and an absence of young, nonfamily persons and childless couples that appears to be concentrically distributed; and an ethnic status factor that identifies those parts of the metropolis with a concentration of individuals and families that may be defined generally as non–Anglo-Saxon (Fig. 6.6). These include recent immigrants from Italy, Portugal, and the West Indies, as well as Chinese and Jewish families.

BEHAVIORAL PERSPECTIVES RELATING TO THE ANALYSIS OF SOCIAL STRUCTURE AND CHANGE

Whereas the ecological approach deals with aggregates and is essentially static (describing things as they have become) the behavioral perspective is concerned with individual decision making and is dynamic because it involves the movement of household units within cities. North American society is highly mobile, and the spatial social structure of cities is much influenced by this high level of mobility. In an international study of residential mobility, Long and Boertlein (1977) conclude that the United States, Canada, and Australia have the highest rates of residential mobility of eight countries for which such data are available. In North America, about one-fifth of the population changes residence annually, which implies an average of thirteen moves in a person's lifetime, of which about ten usually occur after an individual's seventeenth birthday. These are, of course, averages, since some people are more mobile than others (Moore, 1986)!

There appears to be little difference in mobility among residents of metropolitan areas versus residents of nonmetropolitan areas in the United States, but there are considerable differences among metropolitan regions. Table 6.2 lists mobility rates for twenty large metropolitan regions, indicating a variation from a low of 11.6% of the population changing residence in any one year for the Pittsburgh SMSA to a high of 29.3% for Dallas. It appears that the SMSAs with the lowest rates are the older metropolitan regions, where the growth rate is minimal, whereas the highest rates are in the newer cities, which are growing more rapidly. In some cases, there are also considerable differences in mobility between the central cities and the suburban regions. For example, in Cleveland

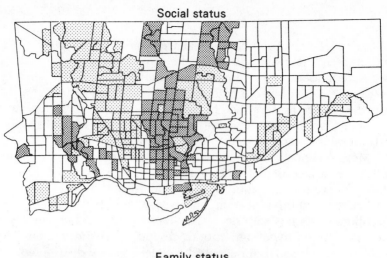

Social status

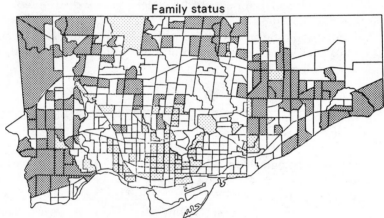

Family status

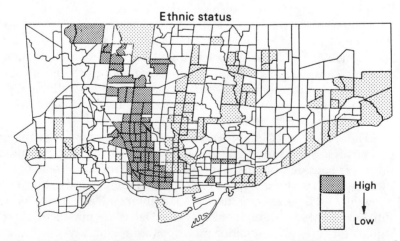

Ethnic status

High

Low

Figure 6.6 The social space of metropolitan Toronto, 1981. (*Source:* Redrawn from Fabbro, 1986, Maps 4, 5, 6.)

Table 6.2   ONE-YEAR RATES OF RESIDENTIAL MOBILITY IN LARGE METROPOLITAN
AREAS OF THE UNITED STATES

Metropolitan region	Percent changing residence in one year		
	Entire region	Central city	Remainder
New York[a]	13.3	13.7	12.8
Chicago[a]	17.5	17.6	17.3
Los Angeles–Long Beach	22.4	22.5	22.4
Philadelphia	13.6	13.2	13.9
Detroit	17.3	19.5	15.8
San Francisco–Oakland	23.3	23.3	23.3
Boston	15.0	15.4	14.9
Pittsburgh	11.6	12.3	11.4
St. Louis	18.4	22.4	17.1
Washington, D.C.	21.4	24.8	20.1
Cleveland	14.3	20.2	11.4
Baltimore	18.9	18.7	19.0
Newark	14.9	17.8	14.2
Minneapolis–St. Paul	19.6	22.5	17.7
Buffalo	14.4	16.3	13.5
Houston	25.1	23.9	28.5
Milwaukee	14.5	17.4	11.2
Paterson–Clifton–Passaic	13.4	13.7	13.3
Cincinnati	18.7	22.3	15.8
Dallas	29.3	34.2	23.5

[a]Standard Consolidated Areas (combinations of SMSAs). All the others are SMSAs.

Source: Long and Boertlein (1977, Table 3).

the central-city mobility rate is 20.2%, compared with 11.4% for the noncentral-city area. Similar differences in magnitude exist in Dallas and Cincinnati. The reasons for these differences must relate to factors specific to the particular cities involved, such as the mobility of minority populations, abnormally high central-city vacancy rates, and differences in levels of ownership.

Mobility and Life-Cycle/Lifestyle Considerations

If it is accepted that the average person changes residence thirteen times in a lifetime, then the causes of these moves must be examined. Once the causes are known, they may cast some light on the location that the person or family selects. Because the thirteen moves include those undertaken within cities; those between cities, rural, and urban regions; and even those from outside North America, the reasons for moving are quite diverse. Just over one-third— or four or five—of a person's lifetime moves are interurban and are related to job opportunities, differences in income levels among cities, and various amenity factors (Clark, 1982). The remaining two-thirds of the moves are intraurban, and can be related to life-cycle and lifestyle considerations. The issue is not, however, just *why households move, but why households choose to move where they do* (Rossi and Shlay, 1982). Thus, in examining the reasons for changes in location we must also examine the factors influencing residential location. The second half of this issue is discussed in Chapter 7.

Life-Cycle Locational Considerations

In a classic study related to family mobility, Rossi (1980) in effect challenged Wirth's (1938) negative views on the effects of residential mobility. He provided evidence to show that the relatively high rates of mobility that were occurring among a rapidly urbanizing population were not due to rootlessness and aberrant social behavior, but to changing housing needs that accompanied life-cycle changes. This new paradigm, after some years in gestation, gave birth to a whole new approach to analyses of residential mobility and public policy (Clark and Moore, 1982). Rossi demonstrated that the majority of intraurban moves are related to changing requirements for living space as the family changes in size, age, and income.

Individuals pass through many stages in their lives, which can be categorized as infancy, early childhood, play age, school age, adolescence, young adulthood, adulthood, late adulthood, and old age. About three of the thirteen lifetime moves made by average North Americans occur before their seventeenth birthday, and probably two of these are life-cycle moves relating to the changing composition of the individual's family. Of the ten moves made by an individual after the age of seventeen, six or seven were probably life-cycle oriented (McCarthy, 1976, p. 73). Although the reasons for moving may differ, the life cycle is important to residential location in at least three ways.

The Life Cycle and Social Space   First, as an individual passes through the life cycle, the type of house and the physical location that is optimally required varies. Second, most of the residential location decisions are made by the heads of the family, in accordance with their perceptions of the family's requirements. These requirements may be difficult to reconcile or compromise because of the stage within the life cycle in which the family members find themselves. For example, the location and space requirements of a teenager differ considerably from those of a child. Third, the length of each stage varies—five stages are crammed into the first twenty years of life, and four throughout the next fifty. As a result, the decision makers in the family may become less responsive to life-cycle changes. This pattern is frequently evidenced by a resistance to residential adjustment in later years due to sentimental attachment to a house and location that are no longer congruent with the family's requirements.

A scenario of the effect of life-cycle changes for a white, middle-class family (the moves of black families are usually more constrained [Lake, 1981]) can show their impact upon locational decisions. During the early years of a person's life, the locational decision is made by the parents, who are the heads of the family. The two (on average) life-cycle moves that occur at this stage, however, are made in response to the requirements of the children, and is often repeated by their own children when they become parents. The third life-cycle move, which generally occurs during the period of maturity, is frequently associated with the gaining of independence, either as a result of leaving school and getting a job, or of going to college. This move is the first one shown in Table 6.3, which presents an idealized distribution of moves related to the adult life cycle. McCarthy (1976) defines this stage as "young single head, no children," and in his study of 42,000 households in Brown County, Wisconsin, the average age of household heads in this group was a little over twenty-five years, and the average size of the household was about one and one-half persons. The next move comes with marriage ("young couple, no children"), and at this stage the young couple may have a large joint income if both partners have jobs, and their locational decision may be determined by a desire for proximity to good and varied recreational facilities. Thus, the couple may well locate in a downtown area or other accessible location, where they can afford a reasonably expensive apartment because of their joint incomes.

This conditional wealth and its concomitant desire for a broad range of recreational and social amenties is usually altered a few years later by the arrival of children. At this stage, the young couple may be about thirty-one to thirty-two years of age and have three or more persons in the family. Thus, other factors now enter the locational decision. In particular, the need for a larger home with more bedrooms, play areas, and proximity to good schools becomes important. In North America these needs are generally met by single-family dwelling units or duplexes, and a young couple is most able to afford such space in new housing in the suburbs, where initial downpayments are low compared with the listed price. The young couple, previously renters in the city, become

Table 6.3 CHANGES IN RESIDENCE RELATED TO CHANGES IN THE ADULT LIFE CYCLE

Age of head	Stage	Household definition of stage	Average age of head	Average size of household	Moves
20	Young adulthood	Young single head, no children	25.4	1.65	1
		Young couple, no children	26.4	2.00	1
30	Adulthood	Young couple, young children	31.5	4.53	1
		Young couple, older children	38.9	5.16	1
50	Late adulthood	Older couple, older children	51.8	5.46	1
		Older couple, no children	62.8	2.27	1
65	Retirement	Older single head, no children	67.1	1.23	1

Source: Data from McCarthy 1976, Table 2, and Long and Boertlein (1977, p. 15).

holders of large mortgages in the suburbs. Hence life-cycle considerations underlie the spatial pattern envisaged in the family status construct.

The next two life-cycle moves are related to the changing size and age of the family and the increased ability of the heads of the household to afford better-quality housing in a "higher class" environment. These moves also involve residential locations in suburban areas, but are usually moves to more established communities where the recreational and social amenities for the entire family are more diverse than those found in new suburban tracts. The last two moves occur when the children leave home. At this time, a large house is not needed, and the older couple may no longer want to undertake the necessary maintenance of a house and yard. Another move often occurs following the death of one of the partners, when the surviving partner seeks less space, cheaper space, or a location near basic services and/or good transportation (Golant, 1984).

The Life-Cycle Model and Household Size The empirical information presented in Table 6.3 and the scenario just outlined requires some modification with respect to the expected situation during the rest of this century (Moore and Clark, 1986). First, it is clear that the magnitude of household sizes, as listed in Table 6.3, are no longer applicable. The averages shown in Table 6.3 relate to the situation during and immediately after the baby-boom years. The most likely average household size for the 1980s and 1990s will be about three, but this does not seem to have affected the demand for single-family residential units, nor the associated locational attributes.

Second, the life-cycle model envisages households with two parents. An increasingly large share of households are single-parent units. The locational choices of households in this group are quite constrained by the availability of rental accommodation, the location of employment opportunities, and by school and day-care facilities. The availability of transportation is an important factor in the choice of location for working women, particularly in single-parent households (Fox, 1983).

The Life-Cycle Model, Age, and Income Intercorrelated with the life cycle are age and income. McCarthy (1976) recognizes that income has an important constraining effect on the ability of the household to respond to changes in space requirements. It is not that higher-income households relocate more often than lower-income households, it is that they have a wider range of choice of locations. Furthermore, the likelihood of moving is much higher among younger groups than older groups. Mobility diminishes as the life cycle progresses, probably as a result of inertia (Davies and Pickles, 1985).

As a consequence, the life-cycle model itself is much too simple. Households do tend to relocate as a result of changing space requirements as they move through the life cycle, but the rate, extent, and geographical range of adjustment varies enormously according to a number of associated characteristics. These associated features relate to type of household, size of household, income, and age.

Lifestyle Locational Considerations

Intermingled with life-cycle changes, which often involve sharp changes in the ways an individual or couple can conduct their lives, are lifestyle considerations. Decreases in family size in North America are accentuating the importance of lifestyle preferences in the creation of social spaces within metropolitan areas. *Lifestyle* refers to the way people want to live, and the people with whom they wish to associate.

One general way of illustrating the effect of lifestyle on location is in the context of the values an individual or family may choose to emphasize. In an urban context, four values that are of interest may be defined as familism, careerism, localism, and cosmopolitanism. *Familism* describes a situation in which an individual places a high value on the unity of the family and its function as a mechanism for propagation and socialization of the young. *Careerism* is strongly developed in North America, and emphasizes upward mobility, the gaining of material benefits, consumerism, desire for responsibility, and a need to be noticed. *Localism* describes a situation in which one's interests are limited to people residing in a well-defined local area, and one's attitudes and behaviors are, in many respects, subservient to the norm accepted within the neighborhood. *Cosmopolitanism,* the opposite of localism, implies a value system that emphasizes the absence of control and the freedom to experience ideas and behaviors from anywhere.

These different values may result in quite different decisions concerning where to locate in a metropolis, and even in which metropolis to locate. Familism is widely accepted by the North American middle class, and the suburb appears to be a creation particularly suited to this lifestyle (Castells, 1977, p. 109). Careerism is strongly followed in the exclusive suburbs and affluent apartment complexes where social interaction is fostered in private schools, business clubs, and a variety of formal social arrangements. Working-class neighborhoods and various ethnic areas seem to place a high value on localism in the form of neighborhood shopping areas and, more dramatically, in local gangs and boss-dominated precincts. Localism is emphasized out of a need to stress the identity of a place and to differentiate it from others. Cosmopolitan lifestyles are prevalent in large metropolitan areas, particularly downtown areas, as they involve people who place a high value on particular cultural experiences and/ or international contacts. To an extent, possibilities for the realization of certain of these values are directly related to income. Many people may want to follow an international, cosmopolitan lifestyle, but they can't afford it!

A good example of the way in which a certain lifestyle can create social space and influence urban growth and redevelopment relates to the creation of gay communities in a number of large metropolitan areas. Gay communities form for a number of reasons ranging from the need by individuals for support to the exclusionary (or oppressive) response of a nonunderstanding and often antagonistic society at large. Such communities are invariably found in parts of downtown areas that were originally low-cost, but the vibrancy of the communities have frequently led to redevelopment (Lauria and Knopp, 1985). In effect, the struggle by gay communities for the right to express themselves in social space is similar to the struggles made by ethnic minorities in previous decades for parts of the metropolitan turf.

Ethnicity and Race

Our examination of the social space of North American cities indicates quite clearly that race and ethnicity in general are profound factors in shaping cities in this part of the world (Castells, 1983). This is because the North American urban experience is the product of mobility, with people coming from many different parts of the world and bringing with them a variety of cultural backgrounds. This is as true at the end of the twentieth century as it was at the end of the nineteenth century. For example, Los Angeles in the 1980s has been referred to as a city of over 100 minorities (Dembart, 1981), with the largest Hispanic-American minority (over 2 million) in the country (Garcia, 1985). If one also takes lifestyle considerations into account, the heterogeneous nature of the modern metropolis becomes even more evident.

Segregated areas are, perhaps, the single most obvious geographical illustration of cleavage in North American society (Bourne *et al.*, 1986). The extent of residential segregation remains extraordinarily high. Winsborough, Taeuber, and Sorensen (1975) calculate the residential segregation index for whites and nonwhites in 109 cities to be about eight on a scale of zero to ten, with ten indicating complete separation between whites and nonwhites and zero indicating complete integration of the two groups. An index of eight implies that the level of segregation is such that 80% of the nonwhite population in these 109 large United States cities would have to be redistributed to white areas to achieve complete residential integration. The important question concerns how these segregated areas come about. Are they the unintended result of self-interested individual behavior or are they the consequence of premeditated actions by particular groups and individuals?

Self-Interested Behavior

There have been two main approaches to an understanding of segregated patterns as an unintended outcome of self-interested behavior. One of these involves the neoclassical approach to residential site selection, and the other involves cultural preferences. The first approach is based on the assumption that the choice of location for a family or individual in a city is related primarily to income—or the proportion of that income that is available for housing. The second argues that the choice of location may be influenced strongly by a need for association with other individuals or for access to certain institutions in the urban environment.

If the distribution of housing prices and of rental prices for residential units is taken as a given, then the first approach argues that location is determined by income. In Figure 6.7, for example, the high-priced areas of Detroit are in suburban locations and along parts of the lakeshore within the city. Thus, the

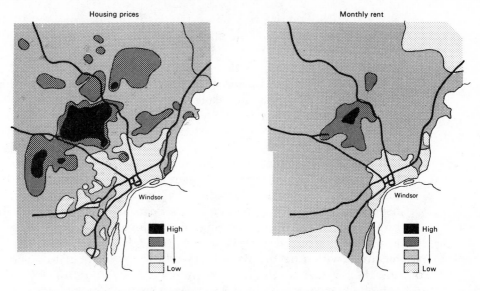

Figure 6.7 The distribution of house prices and monthly rent values for census tracts in Detroit SMSA. (*Source:* Redrawn from Abler and Adams, 1976, p. 151.)

choice of location for low-income families and individuals is restricted by the places that low-priced accommodation may be found. Now, if certain racial and ethnic groups are concentrated at the lower level of the income spectrum, then these groups will most likely dominate within the lower-priced residential areas. Thus, segregated patterns may form as the unintended outcome of individual residential location decisions. Note that in this argument the location of areas of differently priced housing is taken as a given.

In a classic article on the location of ethnic groups in cities, Firey (1945) suggests that sentiment and symbolism may act as culturally based factors leading to the clustering of particular ethnic or social groups in certain areas. Some ethnic and religious groups may well concentrate in certain parts of cities because of the religious, shopping, recreational, and other attributes that may be available to serve the local community. These may be Mexican-American families in Los Angeles, Italian-Americans in Boston's North End, or recent immigrants from Cambodia in Toronto. The attachments of sentiment may also be reinforced by certain physical symbols, such as churches, which relate directly to the life of particular groups.

Nonwhite Ghettos

Ghettos, which are created by the premeditated actions of others, are common features of American urban life for a vast majority of the 24 million urban blacks, 12 million Mexican-Americans, and 3 million Puerto Ricans who are forced by a variety of pressures to live in restricted areas. Almost every urban area in North America that has a significant number of nonwhite inhabitants also has at least one nonwhite ghetto. The term *ghetto* originally referred to the Jewish enclaves in the cities of Eastern and Southern Europe, but is here used to describe areas in which a particular religious, ethnic, or even deviate group is contained. In Eastern Europe the Jewish area was not only distinct from the rest of the city, but was physically bounded by a wall beyond which the residents were not allowed to encroach without a pass.

In North America, a ghetto is a spatially contiguous area of the urban landscape in which the inhabitants have particular social, economic, ethnic, cultural, or linguistic attributes that distinguish them from the majority of the inhabitants of the metropolitan region in which they reside. Because of these differentiating characteristics, the inhabitants are, by and large, not welcome beyond this well-defined area unless they can change sufficiently to be accepted by the mainstream. Such a change would involve the adoption of the culture and values of the majority, and even though all minorities tend to become bicultural with time, the majority population sees no need to become bicultural, and their values act as a barrier to integration. When differences in cultural values are accentuated by differences in color, language, or religion, then the majority's containment of the minority becomes fairly easy to implement. The ghetto is thus a result of external pressure.

One of the major distinguishing features of United States cities relates to the phenomenal growth of black ghettos that occurred between 1910 and 1970 in metropolitan areas outside the South. Rose (1971) indicates that whereas in 1910 twelve of eighteen urban places in the United States with a black population of 25,000 or more were in the South, by 1970 more than one-half of the seventy or more urban places that had at least 25,000 blacks were outside the

A general view (left) and a more detailed picture (right) of the low-rise apartment housing in part of the extensive area occupied by black households in Boston. (*Source:* Geovisuals.)

South. This shift in the relative location and composition of the black urban population is important because in the South the form and structure of the urban ghetto differs quite widely from that in urban centers elsewhere. Southern black urban ghettos are located in parts of the city that have been set aside by the whites as black areas for generations. Blacks in the southern urban ghetto, then, have a clearly prescribed territory in which they have developed their own institutions and stratified residential structure. There is no question as to which race lives where, who is serviced where, and the location of the black/white boundary. This spatially segregated society is almost as strong today as it was in the 1930s.

Although a number of urban black ghettos outside the South have been in existence for a century or more, they have been growing in numbers and size since the 1940s. Blacks came to northern cities to find a situation quite different from that in the South. Although there was no clearly prescribed territory, whites would not accept blacks into their neighborhoods, schools, or community facilities. As a result, the blacks occupied the most deteriorated or undesirable part of the urban area. As in-migration and growth caused pressure on land and housing, the ghetto expanded outward at the periphery, following the lines of least resistance.

The Expansion of the Milwaukee Ghetto   The pattern of growth of a black ghetto in an American city is well illustrated by the case of Milwaukee (Fig. 6.8). The number of blacks in the city of Milwaukee increased quite rapidly, from 20,000 in 1950 to 150,000 in 1980. During this time, nearly all blacks located in one of the three parts of the contiguous ghetto demarcated in Figure 6.8. In 1980, for example, 84% of all blacks in the city of Milwaukee and 82% of all blacks in the SMSA were located within the ghetto area, and nearly all the black population in the SMSA is located within the city (Table 6.4).

The black ghetto was established immediately northwest of the downtown area and to the north of the original location of much of Milwaukee's industrial activity, at the junction of the Milwaukee River and Lake Michigan. Rose (1971) defines a number of territories within the ghetto as follows: There is a core area in which the population is almost completely black (75% or more of the census tract population block in the maps), a fringe area in which the population is at least one-half black; and a zone in transition in which 30–49% of the population is black. The interesting features demonstrated in Figure 6.8 are that the black population is highly clustered, and that an area changes in just a few years from one with few or no blacks (less than 10%) to one almost completely occupied by blacks. The zone in transition is seldom "in transition" for more than two or three years! Furthermore, although the number of blacks located in the SMSA beyond the city more than doubled between 1970 and 1980, the numbers involved are quite small (Table 6.4).

The maps tell us two main things. First, there must be powerful external forces in both the public and private sectors that act to constrain the location of the black population. Second, when the demand for housing becomes high within the black community and growth beyond the core becomes vital, there

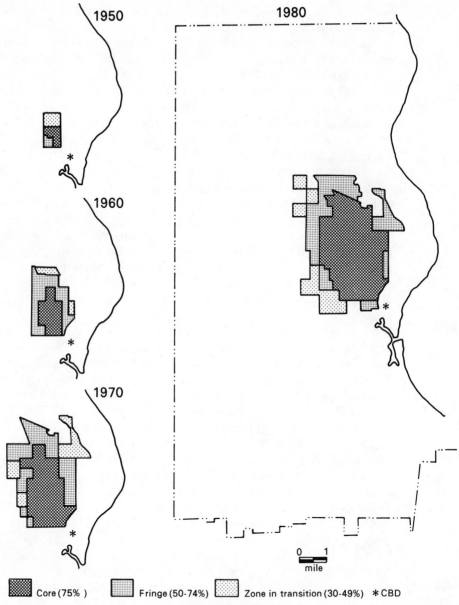

Figure 6.8 The spatial spread of the black ghetto of Milwaukee, 1950–1980. (*Source:* 1950, 1960, and 1970 maps redrawn from Rose, 1971, p. 34; 1980 map prepared by author.)

Table 6.4 POPULATION DATA CONCERNING MILWAUKEE
(Figures in Thousands)

	1970			1980		
	Population	Blacks	% Blacks	Population	Blacks	% Blacks
City of Milwaukee	717	105	15%	636	146	23%
Milwaukee SMSA	1,404	107	8	1,397	151	11

Source: Bureau of the Census, Statistical Abstract for the United States (1984a, p. 22).

must be some mechanism that causes the rapid change within the zone in transition from white to black. Clark (1984b) suggests that so-called real estate agents, including bankers, mortgage lenders, savings-and-loan institutions, and real estate brokers, play a powerful facilitating role in maintaining the ghetto and in promoting rapid change in fringe and transition areas.

Poverty and Homicide Risk   Two of the most prevalent issues relating to black ghettos concern poverty and homicide risk. Although the nonwhite inner city is not homogeneous, in 1984 the average per capita income among blacks was one-half that of whites (Bureau of the Census, 1986). In many ghetto areas the per capita income is about one-fifth of that in wealthier, white suburban areas. Poverty and low income are directly related to employment opportunities, for the unemployment rate among blacks in general is two to three times that of whites, and in ghetto areas the rate may be as high as 70% among young people. Part of the employment problem is related to the decentralization of manufacturing and tertiary activity employment, which has decreased accessibility to jobs (Wilson, 1979, p. 137). Thus, in the case of Milwaukee, the black ghetto grew adjacent to the employment opportunities of the central business and manufacturing districts along the Milwaukee River in the 1950s and 1960s, but now a large number of jobs are in suburban areas that are, for most blacks, quite inaccessible. The extent of poverty is particularly high among black women who are heads of single-parent households.

Wacquant and Wilson (1988) graphically describe the effect of deindustrialization on North Lawndale, a black community of 60,000 on Chicago's West Side. In just a few years during the late 1960s, the district lost a Western Electric plant (43,000 jobs) and a Harvester plant (14,000 jobs), along with smaller factories that provided another 10,000 jobs, none of which have been replaced. The result is that one-half the housing stock has disappeared since 1960, and much of the remainder is quite dilapidated. Infant mortality is increasing, and the murder rate is six times the national average. There is now only one bank and one supermarket, but ninety-nine bars to serve the local population.

Poverty is directly related to homicide risk, which is frighteningly high across the United States in general (Harries, 1980), and even higher within black areas in particular (Rose and McClain, 1981). The homicide rate is far higher in the United States than in any other country in the Western world, and in 1980 it hovered around twelve homicides per 100,000 population, a rate twice that of the 1960s. In 1980 the rate for black males was sixty-five per 100,000, and for black females fourteen per 100,000 (McClain, 1984). These extraordinarily high rates for the country in general, and for the black community in particular, are related to the insane availability of hand guns and the social environment of drugs and unemployment, which generate anger, frustration, gang wars, and stress among blacks (Rose and Deskins, 1980).

Black Suburbanization   In terms of numbers, it appears that there has been an increase in the suburbanization of the black population in recent years (Fairchild and Tucker, 1982). Long and DeAre (1981) conclude that the number of blacks in suburban areas (counties beyond central cities within SMSAs) increased by 50%, or almost 2 million, between 1970 and 1980, *and* the proportion of blacks in the United States residing in such defined suburban areas increased from 15% to 20% during the same decade. This is considered important because it may imply that the federal fair housing laws are working, and that at least some blacks are experiencing a wider range of choices in residential location.

More recent information (Lake, 1981; Rose, 1976; Spain and Long, 1981) suggests that there are two aspects to this suburbanization:

1. About 40% of the black suburbanization occurred in white suburban areas, and this involved particularly high socioeconomic status black families. Thus, there has been some integration of blacks with whites.
2. More than one-half of the black suburbanization occurred in inner-suburban areas that already contained a black majority or that became predominantly black during the 1970s.

There is, therefore, a great deal of support for the "spillover hypothesis" with respect to black suburbanization (Rose, 1976). This hypothesis suggests that black suburbanization occurs in inner-suburban areas that are adjacent to the black areas of central cities. Such black suburban areas are therefore an extension of the ghetto areas of the inner city. In consequence, the outer city of many large metropolitan areas is becoming similar in many aspects of socioeconomic structure to the inner city (Brown and Oldakowski, 1986).

POLITICAL ECONOMY PERSPECTIVES ON THE ANALYSIS OF SOCIAL STRUCTURE AND CHANGE

One of the chief difficulties with both the ecological and behavioral approaches to the analysis of social space is that they downplay the roles of politics and conflict in the growth of urban areas. That is not to say that they ignore politics and conflict, but that the paradigms do not put these features front and center. One of the great advantages of a political economy approach is that it places the conflict, tensions, and interactions among the major factors of production—

land, labor, capital, and the state—at the core of urban analysis. For example, Edel Sclar, and Lauria (1984) examine the way in which the owners of capital and some workers have interacted to develop suburban environments in Boston that, although they appear to give more residential choices, simply retain the same type of choices within spatially contiguous environments; and Hirsch (1983) shows how the leading economic and social (e.g., the University of Chicago) institutions in Chicago managed to protect their interests during the great expansion of the black working-class ghetto that occurred between 1940 and 1960. Political economy perspectives on the analysis of social space are to a large extent concerned with class interests and the interplay among the major groups of actors in urban areas.

Class and Social Space

The ecologic and behavioral concepts of social status are very much income-oriented, and it is assumed that if income changes, then the locational choices of families and individuals change accordingly. This is to a certain degree true, and a large part of the "American Dream" relates to the possibility of upward mobility as a consequence of increases in income generated by hard work and thrift. Nevertheless, it is also evident that social space is also structured to a certain degree by class distinctions based on control, which are formed as a consequence of the relations among people in the productive environment (Scott, 1988)

For example, in the preindustrial era society revolved primarily around agricultural production that involved many tenants working on land owned by a few landlords. The two classes, landowners and tenants were based on the social relations of agricultural production, for the many non-landowners depended upon the few landlords for their homes and livelihood. The industrial revolution produced a new set of social relations that developed in response to the new modes of production. A limited number of people acquired ownership and control of the factories and workshops, leaving a vast majority who did not own the means of production and were made to depend upon those who did for their subsistence. The owners of the means of production wish to maximize profits and control and to pay wages that permit only the reproduction of the labor force, whereas the work force wishes to garner a greater share of the profits in order to improve its living conditions. Hence the struggle over the distribution of the surplus depicted in Figure 1.3, p. 9.

Chapter 2 details the way in which the North American economic system has developed well beyond this simple ownership structure to one in which the ownership of the means of production is spread quite widely. This change has occurred through widespread participation in stockholding, mutual funds, trust funds, bank savings, insurance companies, and pension funds. Thus, the base of ownership has widened so much that the number of owners in this sense probably exceeds that of nonowners.

Another significant word that we have been using is *control*, and it is important to realize that ownership is not the same as control. The ownership of a few shares of stock or participation in a pension fund does not imply control of the policies of the firm and the way in which the means of production will be used. Control is in the hands of the most senior managers and the major stockholders, which are often banks and other financial institutions whose policies are also controlled by a few top managers. Thus in terms of control, there are still two classes: those who have effective control of the large corporations and who make decisions concerning company policy, and those who do not. Control is also exercised by individuals within government who are supposed to mediate and protect the interests of the public at large (Fig. 1.2, p. 8) but, depending on the political group in power, more frequently support the interests of business and financial institutions.

This view of the nature of economic and political control in society leads to a somewhat different perspective on social space within the city. To illustrate, let us reformulate the outcome of the factoral ecology approach into a class framework that emphasizes different levels of control. Referring to Table 6.1, it can be argued that in Quebec Factor I contrasts mainly managers and professionals with blue-collar workers, whereas Factor II contrasts white-collar office workers with low-income groups. These four classes, which occupy particular locations within the metropolis of Quebec, may be ranked in terms of level of control over the means of production as follows:

1. Managers and professionals (English emphasis).
2. White collar, mainly office workers (French or English).
3. Blue-collar workers (French-speaking).
4. The poor (mainly French-speaking).

This, in one sense, reveals the irony of the struggle by the French-speaking majority in the province of Quebec for control of the means of production. The struggle, which took place during the 1970s, focused on language, so that what happened was that control over the means of production remained, on the whole, among the same group of people, who simply became somewhat bilingual or who moved both themselves and their corporate headquarters to English-speaking Ontario.

One aspect of social space that is related to class is homeownership. Certain parts of cities are in effect controlled by absentee landlords, whereas other parts of cities consist of homeowners who reside primarily in their own property. Inner cities contain a large amount of rental accommodation, suburban areas contain much less. There are, as a consequence, different sets of interests between areas that have a high proportion of rental accommodation and those that do not. Areas with high levels of homeownership include people who profit from increases in equity due to general economic growth and the resulting appreciation in home values. Renters, on the other hand, do not have the opportunity to accrue wealth in this way; neither do they have security of tenure beyond the agreement of the lease or costs.

Harris's (1986) samples of residential units in Toronto show a considerable variation in homeownership rates among different classes (Table 6.5). Even in a country in which the homeownership ethos is quite strong (except in the province of Quebec) homeownership rates among working-class Torontonians

Table 6.5   HOMEOWNERSHIP RATES BY CLASS
Toronto, 1931 and 1979

Class	Percent homeowners	
	1931	1975
Owners and managers	61%	82%
Middle class	54	65
Working class	42	49
Owners of small businesses	50	49

Source: Selected data from Harris (1986, p. 80).

is only about 50%, whereas the rates among owners and managers and the middle class are quite high, and have increased much faster than that for the working class in recent decades. Thus, about one-half of the working-class population is living in residential units that are owned (controlled) by others.

Class and Conflict

The example of homeownership demonstrates that North American society and its class structure make conflict over the sharing of wealth and resources inevitable (Kemp, 1986; Janelle and Millward, 1976). There are perhaps three types of areas within cities in which spatial conflicts tend to occur (Blowers, 1980; Gresch and Smith, 1985): (1) highly accessible areas in which the land supply cannot satisfy potential demand—for example, in the central parts of urban areas; (2) areas in transition, where existing uses or users are being replaced by others—for example, in the zone in transition at the periphery of black ghettos; (3) areas experiencing growth, such as at the fringe of cities, where speculation is rampant and discontiguous uses (farms and suburbs) exist cheek-by-jowl. In a later section an example of spatial conflict in the central part of an urban area will be examined, but first it may be useful to outline some of the basic themes in urban conflict analysis.

Conceptual Discussion of Themes in Urban Conflict Analysis   Studies of conflict have generally emphasized four themes (Cox, 1986; Cox and Johnston, 1982):

1. Conflict arising from positive or negative externalities that change the value of a location. (An externality is an event beyond the immediate control of an owner or individual.) Highway improvements, for example, may be positive externalities for some by improving accessibility to the urban environment, and negative externalities for others if a freeway cuts through a neighborhood and destroys its cohesion.
2. Conflict arising from monopolistic control. Urban land is not a liquid asset; it is fixed in a particular location and each site is in this sense unique. The trouble is, some sites are more unique than others—for example, sites adjacent to parks, with views, or in waterfront locations.

Conflicts between the public's desire for access to such locations and the "rights" of the property owners to exclusive use is one of the crucial planning issues in market-oriented economies (Dear and Scott, 1981).

3. Conflicts arising with respect to the level of government intervention in the form of planning, zoning, taxation, and licensing. The public may well argue that its interests are best served by increased government intervention to assure more equal distribution of benefits, whereas owners frequently want less government intervention, arguing that the less the intervention, the more rapid the pace of development. There are frequent struggles over the extent of government intervention, and then over the control of the government itself. For example, in 1981 a tenants' movement in Santa Monica (Los Angeles SMSA) obtained a majority on the local town council and subsequently enacted a "people-oriented" program (Shearer, 1982) that emphasized tenants' rights, accessibility to amenity locations, and social programs for the elderly, the unemployed, and the disadvantaged.

4. Conflicts arising as a result of pressure from particular interest groups. Some interest groups, such as chambers of commerce, and real estate boards, have become part of the fabric of local government, and their views are firmly meshed within the decision-making process. Others, such as tenants' associations and neighborhood preservation committees, represent interests that are often not entrenched within most government organizations and decision-making processes. As a result, pressure from the unrepresented groups often has to be public- and media-oriented, whereas influence from the more established groups that are well represented within the political process can be far less visible.

Each of these themes involves interactions among owners, the public, and government.

Conflict over the Redevelopment of Times Square The Times Square Redevelopment project in New York City illustrates the importance of a number of these themes, in particular the consequences of monopolistic control of land, government intervention, and the reaction of particular pressure groups that are not represented within the existing political process, exemplified in this case by the Clinton Coalition of Concern (CCC). But first, some background. Since 1976 New York City (total jobs around 2 million) has lost about 40,000 jobs in manufacturing but gained more than 200,000 jobs in the finance, insurance, and business services sectors. Growth in New York City has been stimulated by growth in those activities that reflect its role as a leading transaction center in the era of global capitalism. The explosive growth of jobs located within the central business district provided more employment for the white professionals and executives who reside in such suburban areas as Westchester, Rockland, Putnam, and Bergen counties and commute to Manhattan than for the city residents themselves. Furthermore, the increase in office activity created a demand for more office space at the fringe of the midtown central business district. Thus, the underlying cause of the conflict relates to the restructuring of the city's economy in response to changes in the world economy at the onset of the fifth Kondratieff.

The conflict arose over a plan for the conversion of the highly mixed-use Times Square area around 42nd Street, to a massive new office, wholesale, and hotel complex, and to renovate nine theaters (Fainstein and Fainstein, 1985). The vast variety of uses that currently exist include rooming houses, tenements, a large number of reputable small retail and commercial businesses, and a comparatively small number of sex-related businesses that provide the image for the area and create a climate that favors redevelopment.

The actors involved are the consortium of developers involved in the New York State Urban Development Corporation, which does not have to follow zoning and citizen participation requirements although the city does, the owners of small businesses who are being driven out, and residents who fear that the project will stimulate apartment and condominium redevelopment, causing rents to increase. The strongest opposition came from the low-income residents of the Clinton neighborhood, who not only attempted to resist the intimidatory tactics of landlords who tried to vacate buildings for redevelopment, but also attempted to negotiate some form of neighborhood compensation.

The result is that the Times Square Redevelopment plan continued—the interests of the developers, the business community, and the government were too much in harmony for the scheme to be stopped or even to be modified very much. However, the CCC did manage to gain $25 million from the NYSUDC project managers for the preservation of space for low-income housing and small-scale businesses. For us, this example demonstrates that a political economy approach that emphasizes the major groups of actors in class and control terms, and also the economics and politics of the situation, can provide a fruitful framework for an analysis of the dynamics of land-use change.

WOMEN AND SOCIAL SPACE

The approaches to the study of social space that have been discussed thus far do not address in any direct way the fact that urban areas are environments for both women and men. This lack of gender awareness is partly explained by the fact that men and women are usually affected similarly by the various processes shaping social space, but this should not be taken to mean that sex differences are not important. Recent studies have emphasized that women have quite different needs with respect to urban space, and that the description and analysis of urban growth and social space provided thus far is essentially male-oriented (Holcomb, 1984a; Mazey and Lee, 1983). We will therefore describe some of the differences in the structure of the types of social space that are most congruent for women in North American cities, examine these differences in the context of various theories relating to gender roles, and discuss some specific social issues that women face in urban life.

Women in the City

Some key differences with respect to the spatial structure of social space for women and men can be presented relating to location, income, and transportation. In the first place, women are more numerous in large central cities than are men. Washington, D.C. probably is the most female-dominant (numerically) of any city in North America, with a "sex ratio" of eighty-seven (or 115 females for every 100 males). The preponderance of females in central cities is illustrated in Figure 6.9 for Minneapolis–St. Paul, where the SMSA as a whole is female dominant (sex ratio, ninety-three) and the twin cities themselves even more female dominant (Minneapolis, eighty-four; St. Paul, eighty-eight). This preponderance of women in central cities is related to an above-average number of household units headed by women, and to the larger numbers of women among the elderly, since women live on average about five or six years longer than men.

A second characteristic of women in urban areas is that they, along with their children, constitute the bulk of the poor (Sidel, 1986). The poverty rate

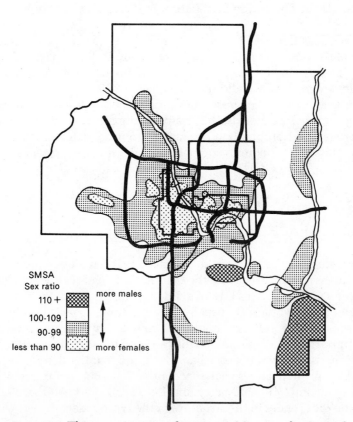

Figure 6.9 The concentration of women in Minneapolis–St. Paul. (*Source:* Redrawn from Abler and Adams, 1976, p. 162.)

for households headed by women was over twice the national average in 1983 (Holcomb, 1984a, p. 247). Pearce estimates that "three-quarters of the poor are women and children" (1983, p. 70). This feminization of poverty is increasing among all races in large measure as a consequence of the unjustly low wage rates, part-time work, and lack of security of employment in many "women's jobs." Other reasons are the shortage of affordable day-care, the failure of the legal and law enforcement systems to ensure that men pay the appropriate share of family support costs following separation and divorce, and the lack of adequate pension and pension transfer rights for older women. Central cities, with their low-cost but often low-quality rental housing units, house the vast majority of poor women (Birch, 1985).

A third spatial characteristic of women in urban areas is that they have shorter journeys to work and rely more heavily upon public transportation than do men (Hanson and Johnston, 1985). The reasons for these differences are partly related to the lower incomes received by women, but are also related to the differences in location of "female jobs" and to the concentration of women in the central cities. Due to their generally lower incomes, women on the whole simply cannot afford to spend as much on travel costs as men. They therefore travel shorter distances, which does not necessarily mean less travel time, and make greater use of public transportation, which in the United States is usually inferior and often dangerous. The concentration of employment of women in certain industries and occupations, such as clerical, sales, service jobs, and nursing, also influences travel distances because these "women's jobs" are spread around metropolitan areas more ubiquitously than "men's jobs," which tend to be concentrated in fewer locations. In this sense, it might well be argued that the more ubiquitous location of "women's jobs" versus the more concentrated location of "men's jobs" helps to maintain the relative inaccessibility of many higher-paid "men's jobs" to a large number of women.

Theories Relating to Gender Roles

Theories relating to gender differences and social space must take into account why the sexual division of labor has occurred, and why the inequities that have been created persist. There are two approaches that may be used to answer these questions: a structural approach that indicates how the sexual division of labor may have been created, and a class approach that explains why the inequities persist. It should be emphasized, however, that these are only two theories selected from a field that is still developing quite rapidly (Lupri, 1983).

Structural Explanations of Gender Roles

The structural approach (Cooke, 1984) argues that differing gender roles developed as a consequence of the changing nature of work as society transformed from preindustrial to industrial, and then to late industrial states. The theory envisages a preindustrial society in which the family was the productive unit and all family members, particularly the spouses, had well-recognized roles.

This continued into the early industrial era, when many families were transformed into domestic industrial units through the system of "putting out," the eighteenth- and nineteenth-century versions of production subcontracting. With the onset of the factory system, the focus of economic production shifted from the family to the factory, child factory labor was eliminated, and women were displaced as the factories became more labor efficient. Hence men became the wage-earners outside the home, and women became responsible for domestic matters. The separation of home and work in the industrial era in effect created a situation in which men created lives in an economic sphere outside the home and women were allocated domestic and supportive roles inside the home. Women in industrial society thus became, in general, economically dependent upon men.

When women did enter the labor force, between leaving school and getting married or, occasionally, as wives, their wages were seen as supplemental to men's wages, and as a result they were paid less than they should have been for the work that they did. With the transformation to a service society and the increase in the number of jobs in the service sector, certain types of employment (particularly the supportive kind) again became labeled female employment, and other kinds male employment, and the male/female wage-rate differentials based on occupation continued accordingly. Only since the 1970s has there been a concerted attempt to eliminate wage differentials between males and females within the same occupation. Wage differentials between male-dominated and female-dominated occupations that require the same general level of skill and training still persist, although are being attacked under pay equity and comparable worth.

Class-Conflict Explanations

The persistence of such inequities may be explained through the application of theories of class conflict arising from political economy approaches. Previously, we have used the idea of classes arising out of the hierarchy of control between capital and labor (see the previous section and Table 6.5). In this context the concept of class control can be translated to the relations between men and women, for men to a large extent control the income and women are dependent upon them. During the late 1970s and 1980s, as women became more prevalent in the work force and began to assume more "male" job positions, a conflict developed because men were in a privileged position. Thus, men may be regarded as a privileged class trying to hold on to the appurtenances of privilege during a time of rapid social and economic change (McDowell, 1983).

One of the ways in which gender conflict in North America may be approaching some resolution in the current era is through the emergence of the *symmetrical family* (Young and Willmot, 1975). The industrial family may be transforming into one in which household roles are becoming more symmetrical, with both partners being involved to greater or lesser degrees in spheres traditionally defined as either women's work (housekeeping, cooking, child care) or men's work (generating wage income). For some classes of domestic activity, external substitutes, such as day care, are also being provided. There is, however, a great deal of skepticism in many circles concerning the extent to which the symmetrical family is emerging (Graff, 1982). More women are at work out of economic necessity, and they are still carrying the burden of work in the home!

Spatial Issues Facing Women in Urban Life

At the outset it should be stated that there are really no "women's issues" with respect to the urban environment as such, for the spatial issues that are raised are issues facing both men and women. However, given the allocation of roles, the resulting inequities, and the persistence of these inequities, there are spatial issues that impinge directly upon women. These issues face women who are living in households with spouses, those living in households without spouses, or those *co-vivant* with another (Table 6.6). Interestingly, women living in households without a spouse now comprise more than one-quarter of all households in the United States. The spatial issues we will address arise from the feminization of poverty and the need for decently paid employment opportunities, and from the male-oriented nature of the structure of North American cities and housing in general.

All individuals should have reasonable access to a range of employment opportunities. Although the types of employment in which most women gain jobs are reasonably well distributed around urban areas, the higher-paying jobs are frequently in downtown locations which require a high level of individual mobility. Unfortunately, many women, particularly those with children, are constrained by the lack of adequate support facilities such as child care outside the home. Ideally, day-care centers should be located close to the home or the

Table 6.6   THE NUMBER OF HOUSEHOLDS IN THE UNITED STATES IN 1975 AND 1984 BY SEX AND RACE

Household head	Number (millions)		% Change	Percent	
	1975	1984		1975	1984
Female[a]					
White	13.7	18.9	38.0%	19.5%	22.6%
Black	2.9	4.2	45.0	4.1	5.1
Male[a]					
White	6.3	9.9	58.0	9.0	11.8
Black	1.0	1.6	56.0	1.4	1.9
Married[b]	46.3	49.0	5.8	66.0	58.6

[a]No spouse present in household.

[b]Spouse in household.

Source: Recompiled from Bureau of the Census, *Statistical Abstracts of the United States* (1986, p. 40).

workplace (preferably within it). This day care has to be of high quality, afford-able, and accessible. Many women find that their spatial range of employment opportunities is limited as a result of the inadequate provision of appropriate child-care facilities within urban areas. There is no way that schemes to reduce the feminization of poverty can be successful unless the community provides the necessary support services.

The second spatial issue relates to the structure of North American metro-politan areas and to the design of housing in general. North American cities are in a very real sense the outcome of male-dominant traits. Suburbs, in particular, reflect a male–paid work and female–home/children ethos. The suburban structure in effect mitigates against women by confining them to a place and role in which there are very few meaningful choices. Likewise, suburban houses are often designed in such a way as to demand almost continuous housekeeping and orderliness, and often have space that is greatly in excess of family require-ments. Holcomb (1984b) argues that women really desire a greater level of accessibility to a variety of conveniences and services, more efficient housing units, and a range of public and private transportation that will assure higher levels of mobility. These requirements imply higher-density urban areas.

Conclusion

The various models and approaches to the analysis of urban social space that have been described and discussed in this chapter illustrate that (1) the types of social space that are defined depend upon the concepts and methods used in their definition, and (2) whatever the theoretical approach used, there are an enormous number of different types of social space that have arisen in North American cities as a result of a complex array of forces. There are, perhaps, two main conclusions, one retrospective and the other prospective in terms of this text.

The retrospective conclusion is that most social spaces within urban areas arise from the wide variety of cultural and economic attributes of individuals and households. In particular, ethnicity, as Castells (1983) has remarked, has been a profound influence in the shaping of North American cities. What this means with respect to the structure of social spaces within the city is that cultural attributes in general have been a profound shaping force. Along with these cultural factors are the equally profound effects of economic and class differences that are expressed primarily in terms of purchasing power and economic control.

The prospective conclusion arises from the observation that it is not why household units choose to move, but where they move that is the most impor-tant issue. It should be evident from the discussion of social spaces within cities that these areas are the product of a multitude of residential location decisions that are mediated in turn through a variety of filters. In Chapters 7 and 8 we will attempt to unravel the various factors that influence residential location decisions and we will again note that the shaping forces are best isolated through the application of a number of different perspectives.

Chapter
7

Housing and Society

The spatial distribution of population and of various social, economic, ethnic, and racial groups within urban areas occur as a result of the location of households in housing units. The factors that influence and shape residential location decisions are therefore of prime importance to urban analysis. Housing is a *complex good* because any given housing unit involves many attributes ranging from space, number of rooms, quality, number of bathrooms, type of house (detached, duplex, row house, low-rise, high-rise), amount of exterior space, and location to such features as atmosphere and design. The basic premise is that households choose different bundles of housing attributes according to their preferences for different types of housing, but that these choices are subject to a range of financial, social, and governmental constraints. In other words, the choice of a residential unit and its location (the spatial decision) is influenced to varying degrees by a host of aspatial factors.

MACRO INFLUENCES ON THE DEMAND FOR AND SUPPLY OF HOUSING

Housing is an extremely important element of urban and human life because it is where most people spend a large portion of their day, and it consumes a large share of their total income. Indeed, for many families the purchase of a house is the largest single investment the family unit ever makes. Thus, for both investment and living reasons, an adequate provision of housing is essential to any society. In North America, the idea of adequate provision of housing is often linked to another idea, that of homeownership, since it is argued that private ownership gives each family a stake in society (Harris, 1986). As a consequence, many national housing programs in both the United States and Canada have been directed toward increasing the general level of homeownership, which itself depends on the demand for, and supply of, housing.

The Demand for Housing

Perhaps the simplest long-run influence on the aggregate demand for housing is the rate of formation of family and nonfamily households (Gober, 1986). The distinction between family and nonfamily households is important: Family households involve children, and nonfamily households do not. During the 1980s, the rate of formation of new family household units has been decreasing, whereas that for nonfamily household units has been increasing. This has changed the demand for different types of housing. There has been a leveling-off in demand for single-family units and an increase in demand for nonfamily-oriented housing such as condominiums. Thus, the demand for housing at some time in the future may be estimated from: (1) the existing number of family and nonfamily household units plus (2) the forecasted increase (or decrease) in the domestically generated demand for family and nonfamily units plus (3) the number of new family and nonfamily units created as a result of immigration minus (4) the number of household units lost as a result of death or alterations in family status.

As long as (1) is known, elements (2), (3) and (4) are influenced by the demographic structure of the population, the propensity for "undoubling," change in family income, number and length of vacancies, replacement demand, and availability of credit. The demographic structure of the population refers to the rate of natural increase, growth from immigration, and the rate of aging, as discussed in Chapter 2, all of which influence the rate of formation of family and nonfamily households. *Undoubling* refers to the rate of reduction of the number of housing units consisting of two or more families, and it is directly related to general levels of income and the supply of housing. The large rise in real incomes that has occurred in North America since World War II is also a very important factor influencing housing demand, although the proportion of a family's income spent on housing tends to decline as income rises. The vacancy rate, which is a composite of the proportion of unoccupied dwelling units and the length of time a vacancy is offered, also influences demand, for it indicates the type and location of housing that is required. The replacement demand can show that even in areas where there is no growth in the number of households, a demand for new housing may arise as a result of changing tastes and rising aspirations.

The availability of credit and of associated interest rates also exert a strong influence on the demand for both rental and individually owned accommodation. Rental prices are influenced to a degree by the availability of credit and interest rates, for both affect the rate of construction and the end costs. Credit and interest rates also have a direct effect on homeownership because the purchase price is probably less important to the purchaser than the size of the downpayment and the monthly carrying charges to retire the principal and pay the interest. For most families, the carrying charges also involve the monthly property taxes and the costs of lighting, heating, and other services.

The mortgage debt of the population of North America has increased at a staggering rate since 1945, when it comprised less than 10% of total North American debt. By the early 1980s, mortgage debt accounted for about 40% of total North American debt. In the United States, the residential (non-farm) mortgage debt in 1985 was an incredible $1.5 trillion, which was greater than the total debt of all levels of government (federal, state, and local). Thus, it is not surprising that individual homeowners are very much interested in interest rates; a rise in rate of 1% results in an increase of about 10% in the total cost of the house over the normal lifetime of a mortgage.

The Supply of Housing

A *housing unit* is defined as a dwelling that has either a separate entry or an individual entry off a hallway or corridor that does not pass through another dwelling. The total housing stock is defined as the volume of existing stock plus new construction, less deletions. Although annual new construction is usually between 2% and 3% of the total housing stock, these relatively few new additions exert a disproportionate effect because they constitute between 30% and 40% of the stock available for purchase or rent at any one time. Furthermore, this new housing stock influences living styles by adopting new designs and fittings, which in turn influences the rate of obsolescence of the existing stock.

One of the most important influences on the number of new housing starts, whether single-family homes or apartments, is the vacancy rate. The vacancy rate provides the most readily available source of information for developers and builders and gives them a good indication of the state of the market and its ability to absorb new units at acceptable prices. Of course, vacancy rates depend on other conditions, such as income levels and the availability of credit, but as a direct yardstick influencing supply, they stand by themselves. From the point of view of households, a vacancy rate of between 3% and 5% is necessary to allow for a reasonable amount of choice and some rent or price stability; from the point of view of the suppliers of housing, vacancy rates should be as low as possible.

Builders and developers are just as influenced in their ability to build by the availability of credit and interest rates as buyers are in their ability to buy. Thus, if a government wishes to induce capital investment into the housing sector, a useful policy has proven to be to provide insurance for institutional investors against loan defaults. This policy was implemented by the United States government after 1945 with its FHA and VA loan programs, which provide an insurance mechanism against default for the *lenders.* This scheme has been severely criticized for leading to a concentration of power among the private lending institutions, which permits them to make decisions concerning who may receive mortgages and the type of housing that would be eligible (Stone, 1978). The policies did result, however, in a tremendous growth of capital available for housing construction. Thus, the lenders (mortgage companies) have an enormous influence on the rate of new construction and, because it is in their interest to support the value of existing mortgages, they control the flow of funds and determine the volume of new construction accordingly. Also, if lenders are unwilling to support and provide loans for remortgaging and improvements in parts of the city, they can halt redevelopment, cause values to fall to almost zero, and create obsolescence.

The Influence of Government on Housing Supply

The supply of housing has been influenced enormously by the governments of the United States and Canada. In the United States, most of the schemes have involved federal initiatives; in Canada, programs have involved the federal and provincial levels of government. Of course, a major indirect influence on construction is the discount rate (in the United States) or the bank rate (Bank of Canada), which determines the rates offered by commercial banks and lenders of mortgages. But governments have also been involved directly in housing through a large number of different programs. In general, these programs can be grouped into four phases in which different types of intervention predominate: (1) the slum clearance and urban renewal phase, (2) the supply subsidies phase, (3) the demand-side subsidies phase, and (4) a back-to-the-market phase.

In the United States before 1960, urban renewal and low-rent public housing were the principal instruments of direct government activity. These programs, such as Title I of the 1949 Federal Housing Act, essentially consisted of subsidies linked to new construction, which in turn was linked to slum clearance. Subsidies were provided by the Department of Housing and Urban Development (HUD) to the suppliers of housing rather than to the consumers, and resulted in the stimulation of new housing construction in the periphery and the demolition of low-income areas in the inner city. In fact, slum clearance and urban renewal under Title I had the effect of actually reducing the total supply of housing generated by the program. Between 1949 and 1968, 439,000 mainly low-income housing units were demolished in inner cities in the United States, and only 124,000 mainly middle-income housing units were constructed under the program. Similar programs in Canada were directed toward renewal in deteriorating parts of downtown areas (Bettison, 1975).

A second phase of direct government intervention in the supply of housing came to the fore in the mid-1960s with the growing disenchantment with urban renewal and public-housing schemes (Bourne, 1981, pp. 191–214). By and large, these new programs were aimed at reducing homeownership costs so that moderate or low-income households could afford to live in new housing of reasonable quality. The FHA and VA schemes are prominent examples of these types of programs in the United States. In Canada, the Central Mortgage and Housing Corporation (CMHC) provided similar lender-insurance schemes, and between 1957 and 1970 roughly one-fifth of new construction in the country was undertaken with CMHC funds. In both countries these programs, which in effect subsidize the cost of supplying homes by providing fully insured mortgages, received widespread support from both the property industry and the purchasing public. However, by the early 1970s it was becoming widely recognized that these supply-side subsidy programs had primarily benefited white families in the middle-income range, and had also helped to promote massive suburbanization and sprawl as a result of the emphasis on new homes.

Thus, during the 1970s there was a gradual shift in emphasis in both Canada and the United States toward demand-side subsidies and the establishment of housing programs for particularly disadvantaged groups, such as poor non-whites and the elderly poor. Demand-side subsidies are designed to raise the purchasing and renting power of low-income families through the disbursement of vouchers that can be used only for that purpose. The assumption is that if the house-purchasing power of low-income households is raised to an adequate level, then the market will respond and supply adequate rental housing. In addition to such demand-side schemes, a plethora of particular supply-side programs exist, usually operated at the local (and/or provincial) level for the provision of housing for the poor, the elderly, and the physically handicapped.

During the 1980s, a conservative political phase in both the United States and Canada led to a reduction in the funds allocated to demand-side subsidies. Despite growing waiting lists, there were severe cutbacks in low-income housing programs. For example, in 1981 the United States federal government allocated $30 billion for low-income housing, but in 1986 President Reagan requested only $500 million, and no new funds were requested for 1987. The major new initiative proposed in recent years in the United States is for the privatization of public housing, a program that appears to be working only for those in single-family housing with adequate household incomes. The result is that local and provincial governments are under pressure to provide the low-income residential accommodation that is so greatly needed.

MARKET-ORIENTED PERSPECTIVES ON HOUSING CHOICE AND LOCATION

A vast body of theory relating to housing consumption and location has stemmed from the neoclassical economic approach, which emphasizes the decision-making processes of individual households in a market framework (Muth, 1961, 1978; Quigley, 1978). In general, the central theme of the theory is the contention that households are seeking to maximize their utility by purchasing the bundle of goods that jointly offers them maximum satisfaction, subject to individual household budget constraints. In terms of location in urban space, this theme can be rephrased: Households seek to maximize their place utility by seeking a location and a housing unit that offers them the greatest satisfaction subject to the constraint of income.

The Simple Residential Location Model

In the simple residential location model, the bundle of goods for which an individual is assumed to be spending income (Y) is housing (H), transportation (T), and all other goods (G), that is: $Y = H + T + G$. The "all other goods" category includes food, clothing, and entertainment, and in the simple model this component is assumed to consume a constant proportion of a household's income regardless of the level of wealth. Under these conditions, the residential location decision for a household is regarded as involving a trade-off between housing costs and transportation costs. The transportation cost component is represented by journey to work costs because work trips account for 40% to 45% of total trips and comprise more than twice as many of any other kind of trips made by a household. The model is, therefore, directly applicable to a monocentric city situation because, in this case, transportation costs are assumed to increase with distance from the central business district; however, it also applies to a polycentric situation, for the journey to work costs can pertain to any set of job locations.

Thus, the location of maximum place utility for a residential household involves a selection between the costs of a house and the costs of traveling to and from work sites in the urban area. The line *H–J* in Figure 7.1 represents the average budget line for an income group and defines the possible combination of purchases of the two goods, housing and commuting. Now, what will be the trade-off location (or maximum place utility) for an individual household? This question is answered by introducing household indifference curves, and sets of indifference curves, for three households A, B, and C that are mapped on Figure 7.1a. These indifference curves represent the consumption of housing and travel costs that give equal satisfaction at particular combinations of expenditures. The highest curves represent the largest combinations of expenditures. Hence, a household will seek to locate where an indifference curve just touches, or is tangential to, the budget line *(H–J)* for the income group. The three sets of indifference curves (A, B, and C) represent the various preferences of households for these particular goods. In other words, household C weights housing costs higher and travel costs lower than the others. The location of an individual household, therefore, depends on the preferences of individual households *vis-à-vis* housing and journey to work costs.

The average budget line of another, perhaps lower, income group may be represented by *R–L* (Fig. 7.1b). A number of low-income households, each with their own preferences indicated by maps of indifference curves, can also be positioned along this line, with perhaps the greatest number coinciding around the indifference map for household X. Likewise, it is assumed that the greatest number of higher-income households have indifference maps that coincide around B. There are cases where lower-income households are prepared to pay more for housing than higher-income households, but their journey to work

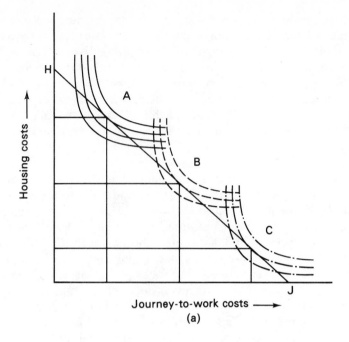

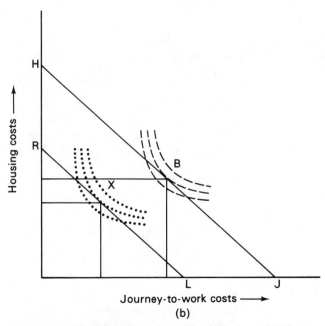

Figure 7.1 (a) Indifference curves for three households in an income group related to an average budget line; and (b) a comparison between the trade-offs of high- and low-income groups.

costs have to be exceedingly low; there are also cases where some lower-income households are willing to pay more than the higher-income households in travel costs, but their housing costs have to be very low. Nevertheless, the lower-income group may be able to exercise some of their preferences in locations that have not been appropriated by the higher-income group. Furthermore, the great heterogeneity of the housing stock in urban areas may make it possible for the different income groups to achieve satisfactory place utility, given the different budget constraints, in quite similar geographic locations within the city.

Application of the Simple Residential Location Model: Pittsburgh   A model based on the central premise of traditional urban residential location theory, which is that households substitute transportation costs for housing prices in choosing residential locations, has been examined by Quigley (1978), using the actual choices made by a sample of 3,000 renter households in the Pittsburgh metropolitan area. The model also assumes that the locating households have known and fixed workplaces in a multicentered metropolitan area. The results indicate that households at different income levels do, in effect, substitute housing costs for transportation costs by consuming different house types and greater or lesser space. As family size increases households are more likely to locate in detached homes or duplexes, and for the same family size high income households occupy considerably more space than low-income households.

Some Criticisms of the Model   An important point to recognize concerning the simple residential location model is that it has provided the basis for the development of an elaborate theory (Wheaton, 1983). This theory has been incredibly influential in the analysis of housing and housing markets. The major criticisms of the approach focus on two basic issues. The first is the assumption that all households do have choices with respect to house type and location within budget constraints. But, it is quite evident that in many situations, particularly those relating to the poor, the elderly, and to racial minorities, the range of choice is limited due to income constraints. Second, the model, however complicated, always assumes a large proportion of a household budget to be fixed in "all other goods." This is not the case, for often families make trade-offs among all aspects of their budget. For example, it has been demonstrated that when poor families receive demand-side housing subsidies, they often allocate their increased income to food and other goods rather than to more housing, because they have already been forced to spend more than they would like on accommodation.

The Ecological Perspective

In Chapter 6 we learned that the ecological perspective involves analyses of social space in terms of groups, or aggregates of people or households. This particular perspective can therefore be regarded as a macro perspective because it differs in scale of aggregation from the discussion in the previous section that involved the individual, or micro, behavior. What is needed, therefore, is an approach that tries to marry the micro-scale behavior of individuals and households with the social structure of the city as defined using the macro, or ecological, perspective. Rees (1970) has attempted to marry the micro and macro scales of analyses, along with the structure of the city as defined from social area analysis and factorial urban ecology, into a residential location model that isolates most of the characteristics considered by individuals or households in their choice of a home and its location.

Rees isolates three elements in an individual's or family's location decision, the first of which defines the position of the decision-making unit in social space. In order to present the model as simply as possible, each element is defined with respect to two dimensions, although each dimension may involve a combination of characteristics. Thus the diagram (Fig. 7.2), which describes the position of the family in social space, is defined in terms of socioeconomic status and stage in the life cycle. Socioeconomic status is regarded as being a composite of three characteristics related to individuals or families: education, occupation, and income. Life cycle is defined very much in terms of the household definition of *stage* outlined in Table 6.3, with the "older single head, no children" being combined with "young single head, no children," and the "older couple, no children" being combined with "young couple, no children." Thus, the stage in the life-cycle scale along the horizontal axis is really ordered in terms of size of family, implying a change in size and structure of a family at different periods. This does not, of course, do justice to the specific residential location needs of the young and the old, which are quite different. It should be noted that this definition of social space in terms of socioeconomic status and stage in the life cycle ignores ethnic or racial differences as well as lifestyle preferences.

The position of a family or nonfamily household in social space in Figure 7.2a can be interpreted with respect to four different cases, A, B, C, and D. A decision-making unit in position A in Figure 7.2a is fairly wealthy, has a college-level education, and is employed in a professional or managerial occupation. The family is small in number, and the ages of the heads of the household are either in the mid-fifties (or older) or in the twenties. The heads of a household located at B have a low income, few years of education, and are employed in a low-status occupation or are unemployed. They consist of small families, and could be young and single or elderly "roomers." A household unit positioned at C is relatively large in size, generally with four or more persons to the family, and the heads of the household are generally between thirty and fifty-five years of age. This household is low income, has few years of education, and the heads of the household are employed in low-status occupations. A household unit located at D in social space is also quite large, and is similar in age to C, but the family is comparatively wealthy, with the heads of the household employed in high-status professional or managerial positions.

The housing-space graph (Fig. 7.2b) also defines individual houses with respect to two dimensions. These dimensions are value and quality on the vertical axis, and type of house on the horizontal axis. Although to measure the quality of a house is quite difficult, this particular aspect of housing has been represented in terms of internal space and internal and external appearance with respect to level of furnishings and interior and exterior finish. Quality is also supposed to be a component of value, although value is also made up of other locational considerations and should, perhaps, be examined separately. The type of home is scaled according to the amount of exterior private space and the accessibility of the unit to the outside, with single-family homes being the most accessible and high-rise apartments the least. Thus, a dwelling unit positioned at M (in Fig. 7.2b) is a luxurious, high-priced, spacious, often high-rise, apartment; whereas N defines a blighted, low-priced, and overcrowded apartment. A dwelling unit positioned at O, on the other hand, is a low-priced, spacious, single-family unit.

Although the first two elements of the Rees model, social space and housing space, are at the micro scale of aggregation, the next two elements are at the macro scale. Community space (Fig. 7.2c) is also, for the sake of simplicity, a two-dimensional categorization, based on the social status and family status constructs of the social area analysts as redefined in more general terms by factor analysis. The first factor, (on the vertical axis) represents the socioeconomic status of groups aggregated into census tracts, and the second factor represents the family status of groups also aggregated into census tracts. Thus, W is a high socioeconomic status but low family status census tract, whereas Y is a low socioeconomic status but high family status census tract, and vice versa for Z and X.

The fourth element, locational or physical space, presents an idealized pattern of socioeconomic status and family status in North American cities. Family status is assumed to be distributed in a primarily concentric manner, with the size of families increasing toward the periphery, and socioeconomic status is assumed to be distributed sectorially, although in the modern United States city the number of higher-status and middle-status wedges in the inner city are diminishing. A census unit positioned at F could consist of high socioeconomic status suburbanites residing in large homes on 2-acre lots, whereas G might represent low socioeconomic status families in small, three-bedroom homes on quarter-acre lots. A unit positioned at J could be a tract containing many poor single or elderly individuals living in rooms, and K could represent middle-class families living in well-established suburban communities.

The components of the residential location decision are, consequently, considered to operate quite simply with respect to the micro and macro elements. A family located at D in social space usually wants to occupy P in housing space, which is found in tract Z in community space, which could be located in F in locational space. Conversely, an individual or elderly couple located at B in social space usually occupies a residential unit at N in housing space, which is positioned in tract X in community space, which is probably located in J in locational space. Likewise, a family located at C in social space is usually able to occupy a house at O in housing space, which is positioned in census tract Y in community space, which is located in G in locational space.

The ecological approach to the choice of a house and its location in the city

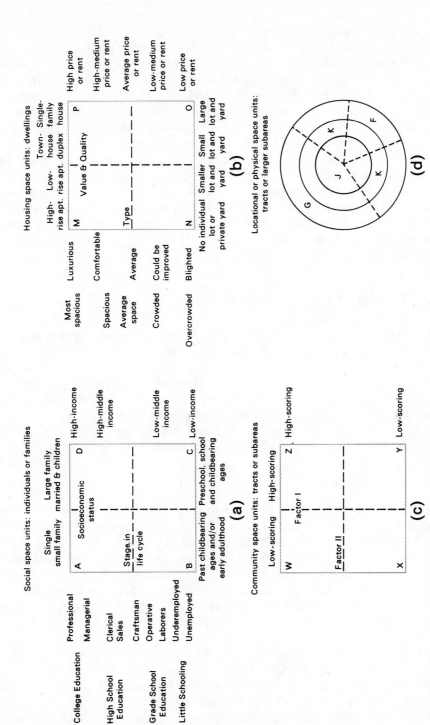

Figure 7.2 The ecological approach to the residential location decision. (*Source:* Rees, 1968, Fig. 4.)

is descriptive. It defines some of the considerations involved and describes the average outcome, but it does not provide a theoretical rationale for the decision making that is involved. It implies, for example, that poor elderly people live in blighted housing in the inner city, which is often the case. This housing condition is not satisfactory for the elderly poor, but it does describe the situation and identify the various variables involved. The Rees model is, of course, incomplete. It does not include the ethnic, racial, and lifestyle components of social space, and it greatly simplifies the characteristics of housing. A more complex descriptive model would include these, but such a model could not be presented in diagrammatic form. The ecological approach does not incorporate the effect of workplace location on the decision-making process, and so it can be regarded as complementary to the traditional approach. The ecological approach is similar to the traditional approach, however, in that it assumes households can make choices in the selection of housing and its location in the city, constrained, of course, by budget size.

BEHAVIORAL PERSPECTIVES ON HOUSING LOCATION

The behavioral approach to residential location decisions focuses on the ways in which individuals and households go about making location decisions, and it emphasizes the roles that various external agencies, such as real estate agents, play in influencing these decisions. The approach accepts the crucial importance of budget constraints and of the trade-offs that households have to make among various components of their budgets, including location decisions. The thrust of the approach is that these locational decisions are mediated in some way by the actual process of making the decision to relocate.

The Brown–Moore Model

The mediation process is explained best in terms of the simple Brown–Moore model (Brown and Moore, 1970), which has had a considerable influence on the development of research in residential location (Huff, 1986; Popp, 1976). The Brown–Moore model focuses on the general way in which a household goes about making a decision to relocate as a consequence of "stress." The model envisages a two-stage decision process, first the decision to move (or not to move), and then the relocation decision itself. The various aspects of these two components are presented in flow-sequence form in Figure 7.3.

The Decision to Move

The decision to move is the end result of internal and external factors that create stress in the household. Internal stress arises from the changing needs of the household for tangible features such as space and facilities, and for less tangible requirements arising from changing expectations. These stresses can

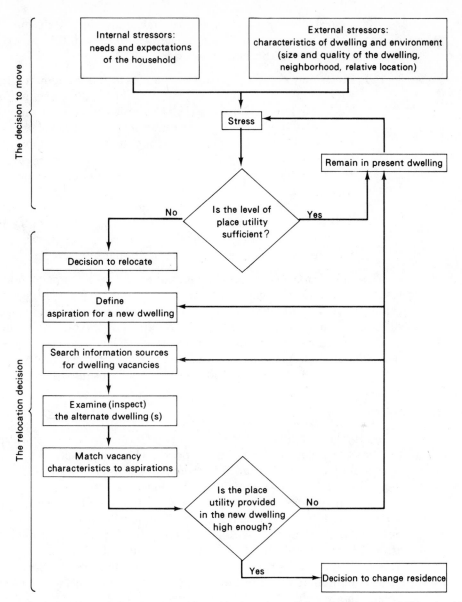

Figure 7.3 A behavioral approach to the residential location decision. (*Source:* After Popp, 1976, p. 301.)

be regarded as resulting for the most part from life-cycle and lifestyle changes among the individuals comprising the household. For example, the addition of children invariably leads to requirements for more space. At the other end of the cycle, the "empty-nest" syndrome frequently leads to a search for a home with less space.

External stress occurs from changes in the dwelling itself, most commonly due to deterioration with age, and in the neighborhood. It is important to note that, with respect to the neighborhood:

1. Stress may occur as a result of changes in the immediate environment, such as with an influx of a different racial or ethnic group. For example, Taub, Taylor, and Durham (1984) examine the way in which homeowners in neighborhoods that are undergoing rapid racial change or incurring increasing rates of crime change their household investment decisions and decide to move elsewhere. This results in *tipping,* or the rapid change in occupancy of an area from one racial or ethnic group to another.

2. Stress may also be a result of changes in what a particular household desires in (and is prepared to put into) the immediate neighborhood. For example, young families make more use of certain features and facilities, such as schools and recreational parks, than older families.

These internal and external factors may give rise in a particular household to a level of stress that causes the household to consider whether the utility of that particular residential unit in that particular location is sufficient. This consideration will, of course, be strongly influenced by the magnitude of the household budget. If the level of utility of a particular place is sufficient, the household will remain in its present dwelling. If the level of place utility is insufficient ("No" in Fig. 7.3), the household will begin to consider relocating.

The Relocation Decision

When the household decides to relocate, it has to define its aspirations; that is, the type of house and neighborhood to which it would like to move. The household has to decide on the amount of space and design characteristics it would like for the dwelling unit, and the locational attributes *vis-á-vis* shopping facilities and employment that are to be emphasized. These are complex decisions because they may involve trade-offs among competing interests if a number of members of the household have jobs and/or educational facilities to attend. Furthermore, the type of housing unit and the most desirable location are also influenced strongly by life-cycle considerations. Elderly and female-headed households seek to satisfy slightly different considerations than jointly headed households (Morrow-Jones, 1986).

Once the aspiration region of the household has been defined, the members of the household then search through the housing market, as expressed in advertisements and retail listings, to identify a short list of possible alternatives. The search is often not thorough, and is mediated strongly by real estate agents, who have a powerful influence on the geographic and social areas in which the household conducts the search (Palm, 1976). White, middle-class families are conditioned by peer-group pressure, as encouraged by real estate agents, to focus their search on particular suburban communities (Cutter, 1982), and particular ethnic groups are also guided by agents to "appropriate" parts of the city (Palm, 1985). The real estate agent plays an extremely important role in mediating the search and, therefore, in determining the social structure of the city.

When a vacancy is found that conforms with the joint aspirations of the household, the question then arises as to whether a level of utility might be realized at that location (in that particular unit) that is sufficient to warrant moving. If the utility is high enough, the household unit will move to the new residence. If it is not high enough, the household unit may decide to remain in its present location, redefine its aspirations, or look for other vacancies.

Case Studies Involving the Brown–Moore Model

Various elements of the Brown–Moore model have been examined empirically in both North America and Europe (Brown and Moore, 1970). A number of studies have investigated the concept of stress as it applies to relocation decisions, and the internal and external factors that give rise to a decision to move. Two of these studies give quite different examples of the type of approaches that can be taken. Long and DeAre (1981) examine a census survey of the reasons reported by household heads for moving between metropolitan and nonmetropolitan areas (Table 7.1). There is one group of reasons that, in effect, is subsumed under the notion of stress. Employment-related factors lie behind two-fifths of the metropolitan to nonmetropolitan moves, but almost one-half of the nonmetropolitan to metropolitan moves. On the other hand, housing and neighborhood considerations are much more important in metropolitan to nonmetropolitan moves than in nonmetropolitan to metropolitan.

At a micro level, Snow and Leahy (1980) examine, in historical context, the process of racial transition in the Hough District of Cleveland during the late 1950s and early 1960s. They were interested in examining whether rapid neighborhood deterioration accompanied racial transition from white to black occupancy, or whether the deterioration had begun prior to the changeover. The researchers concluded that the rapid transition and deterioration occurred as a result of a variety of external factors: (1) obsolete infrastructure—the neigh-

Table 7.1 REASONS REPORTED BY HOUSEHOLD HEADS FOR MOVING
BETWEEN METROPOLITAN AND NONMETROPOLITAN AREAS
(Percent of Responses)

Main type of reason for moving	Metropolitan to nonmetropolitan	Nonmetropolitan to metropolitan
Employment	40.7 %	48.5 %
Family	17.7	18.4
Housing and neighborhood	15.3	7.1
Retirement	5.6	1.8
Other	20.7	24.2

Source: Data from Long and DeAre (1981, p. 13).

borhood was built in the horse-and-buggy days, with narrow streets, and was unsuited to an automobile-oriented middle class; (2) deteriorating housing stock—during the Depression years the white homeowners were generally unable to maintain the housing stock, so deterioration had been occurring for some time; (3) urban renewal programs sponsored by the federal government and the city of Cleveland in the 1950s, which displaced large numbers of blacks from other areas who resettled in the Hough District.

The Mediators   Much of the research into the mediating role of real estate agents and brokers was pioneered by Palm (1976). In a more recent study of the real estate industry in the Denver, Colorado metropolitan area, she demonstrated that the search is strongly constrained by the ethnic backgrounds of both the sellers and the buyers (Palm, 1985). Sellers prefer to list with local real estate agents of the same ethnic background. Real estate agents, particularly black real estate agents, do not feel free to seek new listings in cross-ethnic areas, and buyers tend to go to sellers of the same ethnic background. Finally, the network of real estate agents tends to follow racial and ethnic lines, so information concerning the local market is quite restricted for minority groups.

Evaluation of the Behavioral Approach

The behavioral approach is therefore a useful way of examining housing location decisions. The basic issue with the use of models of this type, however, is that they concentrate exclusively on demand and assume that the consumer is sovereign in making household location decisions. This approach gives us only a partial explanation of the residential location process, for there are many instances in which the consumer is not sovereign and choice is limited by supply. There may, for example, be considerable dissatisfaction in certain areas with multiple-family housing, but the lack of any other choice within the same area severely limits the possibility of alleviating stress. Studies within this perspective may therefore ignore an important restriction on the decision-making process and may conclude that the residential structure of cities is the way it is because that is what people want (Massey *et al.*, 1976).

FILTERING AND PUBLIC POLICY

The moving of a household from one dwelling unit to another involves a *filtering* of dwellings. The filtering process has been of crucial ideological importance to the formulation of housing policies in North America. In general, the filtering process describes the way in which a dwelling unit originally occupied by families or individuals from one income group is later occupied by people from another income group. Thus, it is possible for a house to change in ownership from a lower-income family to a higher-income family, which is described as *upward filtering*. More commonly, as the price of a house relative to all other house prices at a given time decreases due to aging, deterioration, and creeping obsolescence, the house will through time pass to progressively lower-income families or individuals (Fig. 7.4). This is known as *downward filtering*.

Five factors appear to influence the upward or downward filtering of dwelling units: the supply of housing, the rate of household formation, changes in real income levels, changes in housing quality (Myers, 1975), and changes in the lifestyles of households. The first of these has been particularly important with respect to the establishment by governments of housing policies in North America. The filtering concept seems to imply that if the rate of new housing construction is slightly in excess of the rate of new household formation, then it will be possible for the relative value of older housing to be decreased slightly and hence become available to lower-income households. Thus, the filtering concept provides a plausible excuse for a public policy directed at providing well-insured mortgage loans for middle- and upper-income groups, for such policies increase the supply of housing and all income groups could move into better-quality housing as the relative prices of dwelling units decline.

There are, however, at least three objections to policies that have adopted

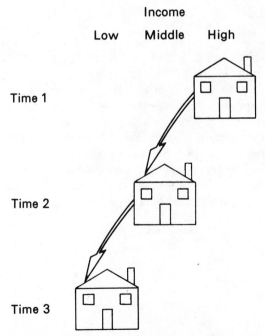

Figure 7.4 Downward filtering: A house passes, through time, from being inhabited by a higher-income household to progressively lower-income households.

the filtering principle. The first is that the policy appears to accept the idea that new housing should be provided, on the whole, for middle- and upper-income groups, and that it is alright for the poorer segments of society to occupy older housing. Since new housing is built on the metropolitan fringe and older housing exists in the inner city, the results with respect to spatial segregation are obvious. Thus, the filtering concept can be used to legitimize inequality (Boddy and Gray, 1979). The second objection relates to the necessity of keeping the supply of housing in excess of demand. If the supply of housing is not kept ahead of demand, upward filtering of dwelling units may occur, and the general level of housing for all but the highest-income groups may deteriorate.

The third objection to acceptance of the filtering principle in housing policies is that it assumes that household units can move freely into dwelling units as they become available. Studies of filtering, however, indicate that different parts of metropolitan areas experience different rates of filtering, and that price levels are affected not only by the supply of dwelling units and the demand in these different areas but also by competition from other land uses (Maher, 1974, p. 121). It is therefore impossible to assume that the increase of housing supplied for one particular income group will affect the supply of dwelling units available for others. The housing market in a metropolitan area is not a single entity, but consists of several submarkets, and although there may be sufficient or excess supply in one submarket, there may be insufficient supply and excess demand in another.

Conclusion

It is clear that although market-oriented perspectives on housing choice and residential location within the city provide a powerful basis for understanding the social structure of the city, these approaches have to be modified in various ways. The behavioral approach demonstrates one form of modification to the market-oriented perspective, and our brief overview of the filtering process shows that the application of a simplistic view of change can have unfortunate applications in public policy. Chapter 8 provides a more detailed discussion of the subtleties of the many different types of housing submarkets within cities, and indicates various ways in which these subtleties may be taken into account in public and private approaches to urban revitalization.

Chapter
8

Housing Submarkets and Urban Revitalization

Many different types of housing submarkets exist within urban areas. Once again, the spatial pattern of housing submarkets is the product of aspatial influences that have compounded in different ways through time. In this chapter the focus is quite specifically on the ways in which submarkets are created, and the ways in which the housing submarket perspective can be used in the analysis of urban revitalization.

HOUSING SUBMARKETS

There are a number of ways to define housing submarkets, so perhaps the best approach is to focus on definitions that are clearly related to our discussions in Chapters 6 and 7. Bourne (1981) suggests three types of definitions based on the human ecology approach—defining the housing submarkets by housing stock, household type, or neighborhood. One way of looking at housing submarkets is according to the stock that is available, and in Figure 8.1a *housing stock* is defined in terms of three factors: type of housing unit (apartments or condominiums, row houses, and single-family detached houses); form of tenancy (owner, rental, public sector); and price or rent (from high to low). In North

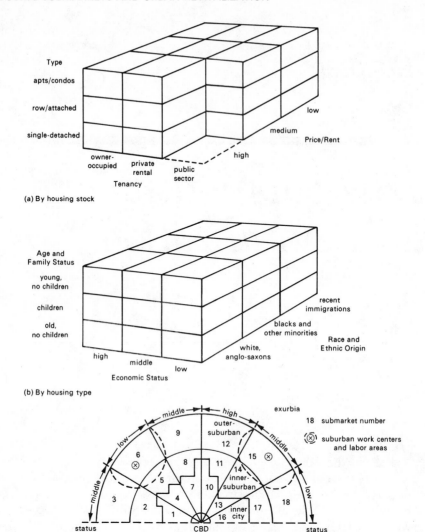

(a) By housing stock

(b) By housing type

(c) By neighborhoods

Figure 8.1 General types of housing submarkets. (*Source:* Redrawn from Bourne, 1981, p. 89.)

America, public-sector housing provides an extremely small share of total housing, but it is concentrated in quite specific parts of the city and, in effect, provides an example of the way in which government investment structures the social space of the city. Furthermore, some of the various types of submarkets in turn affect the political environment. For example, Pratt (1986) demonstrates that housing tenure (owner versus renter) is related to the political outlook of nonmanual workers, but not to that of manual workers, in Vancouver.

Housing submarkets can also be defined in terms of the occupants of the housing; that is, by *household type*. Figure 8.1b presents these submarkets in terms of the interaction of three factors derived from social area analysis: age and family status, economic status, and race or ethnic origin. Perhaps a fourth dimension should be added, although it is difficult to present this in diagrammatic form. This fourth dimension is lifestyle, for it is apparent that certain households form different types of style markets, such as the downtown market and for, high-income households, the country estate or hobby-farm market.

These housing stock and household type submarkets are represented by distinctive patterns of neighborhoods and communities (see Fig. 7.2, p. 193). Figure 8.1c shows a city with a number of suburban work centers and diagrams eighteen of these submarkets, with the exurban fringe representing a nineteenth submarket. The important question, of course, is how these different submarkets are created, for when this is known it may be possible to correct some of the inequalities that occur with respect to housing access.

The Creation of Housing Submarkets

The first important point to understand is that the various factors that contribute to the creation of housing submarkets are interrelated because the whole industry dealing with property is interconnected in one way or another. A model of the property industry, which contains a sketch of some of the more important interconnections, is presented in Figure 8.2. Lorimer's (1972) model of the property industry is divided into two components, the *existing buildings sector* and the *building industry sector*. At the heart of the former are the property investors, or owners, who range from large corporations that may own many multimillion-dollar properties, to the landlord who operates a few apartment buildings, to the individual homeowners whose homes are their only big investment.

Although the existing buildings sector is dominated numerically by the large number of individual homeowners, the dominant voices from the sector influencing the property industry come from the few large property investors. All the property owners are serviced to a greater or lesser degree by property insurance companies, insurance agents, lawyers, real estate agents, mortgage lenders, and the utilities. Thus, the policies and attitudes of these property service industries influence the property investors, and their policies in turn are largely in accordance with the few large property-owning companies that have considerable political and economic clout. On the other hand, the many individual property owners have little impact on the service industries.

The attitudes and policies of the service industries are also influenced by the groups operating in the building industry sector, at the heart of which are the developers. This sector is concerned with adding to the existing stock of buildings in the urban area, and to do so the developers have to obtain funds and insurance, deal with public utilities and local governments to obtain infrastructure and building permits, and operate through the construction companies with the various elements of the construction industry. Although the property industry has traditionally been characterized by a large number of small

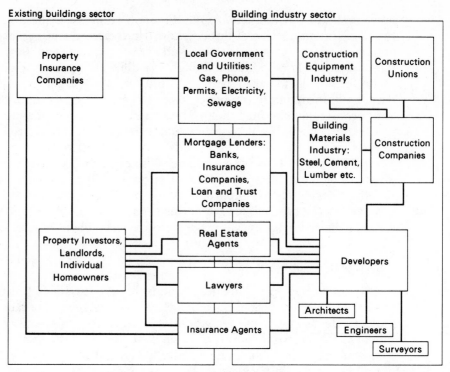

Figure 8.2 A model of the property industry. (*Source:* Lorimer, 1972, p. 19.)

construction companies and individual developers, the complexity of the industry is such that a few large development corporations now dominate most of the new construction that takes place in metropolitan areas. Thus, one of the basic requirements for a free-market system—that is, a large number of independent producers and consumers making decisions in a situation of perfect knowledge—no longer exists. On both the property investor and the development sides, a few large companies have a major influence on the entire industry.

Given that property investment and development has consolidated into the hands of a few large corporations, and that there is a complex, interlocked industry serving them, it is not surprising to note that many of the activities outlined in separate boxes in Figure 8.1 have become integrated both vertically and horizontally. A single firm may assume many different functions. For example, many life insurance companies are now developers, property owners, and mortgage lenders, and many banks have now gone far beyond the business of lending, into property development, sales, and direct ownership. Thus, many large vertically and horizontally integrated organizations are now more concerned with financing their own projects than with funding the small, independent property investors or home builders. Furthermore, the concentration of capital, investment decision making, and property development in the hands of a few large corporations can lead to quite dramatic changes in the location and type of capital investment within urban areas and among North American cities.

Redlining

Redlining, although it is now illegal, is one of the mechanisms that have been used (and probably still is) by mortgage lending institutions to refuse to make loans on residential properties lying within certain parts of a city (Dingemans, 1979). The word *redlining* conjures up an image of a map tacked on a wall in a loan manager's office that has various parts of the city outlined in red, within which mortgage companies, regardless of the credit-worthiness of the applicant, will not make loans. Even though there are few cases where a map has actually been drawn, there is ample evidence to indicate that loan managers do have a mental image of the areas in which credit-worthy persons who wish to purchase property will be denied loans purely because of the location of the property.

In the spring of 1975, the United States Senate Committee on Banking received data that showed a consistent pattern of refusals to make loans to credit-worthy persons who wished to purchase property in the older neighborhoods of Los Angeles, St. Louis, New York City, and Washington, D.C. One particular savings-and-loan association in Chicago had deposits of $10.4 million from residents in redlined neighborhoods but had not made a single loan in these areas. In cases where loans had been made to purchasers within redlined areas, the mortgages often carried interest rates that were much higher than normal and that were to be reassessed at frequent intervals during the amortization period.

Characteristics of Redlined Neighborhoods A neighborhood that is redlined often tends to have one or more of the following characteristics: (1) older housing, (2) blue-collar workers, (3) white-ethnic or black populations, (4) racially integrated, (5) adjacent to low-income neighborhoods, and (6) many poor single individuals residing in rental units. Neighborhoods exhibiting one or more of these characteristics are usually located in the inner city, or central cities, of metropolitan areas, although there are examples of redlining in the downtown sections of commuter railroad exurbs. The result of redlining is that properties become hard to sell, maintenance and rehabilitation are discouraged, and ownership of the various properties falls into the hands of "slum lords," speculators who try to exact as much rent as they can for a minimal investment.

The Financial Institutions' Notion of Risk The reasons given by mortgage lenders for their refusal to make loans in redlined areas generally revolve around the financial institution's notion of risk. The loan manager has a perception of the area as being inhabited by people with unfavorable credit histories, irregular employment, and unstable families. This image is often based on hearsay rather than on substantiated facts, and may frequently be a misinterpretation of the way in which minority groups cope with their situation. Another factor that appears to make the area risky is the fear of vandalism, which is accentuated when the loan manager perceives that the response to impending foreclosure is likely to be vandalism. In some cases there is a real communication problem between the loan managers of the financial institutions and the would-be borrowers, for the managers may never be near the area and have no first-hand knowledge of the condition of the area involved. But whatever the reasons for refusal, it seems clear that when a loan is refused to a credit-worthy person purely on the grounds of the location of the property, some element of class or racial bias may well be involved in the evaluation of the application.

There are, however, many cases in which the financial institution is correct in its high-risk evaluation. Many older parts of inner cities are inappropriately zoned or are deficient in basic urban infrastructure. In these cases property values are likely to decline, and the investment may be quite unsound from the lender's point of view. One principle is, however, quite clear: Loans should be made or not made to people, not areas, and when a loan at normal interest rates is denied to an individual, the reasons for the denial should be made known to the applicant. There is legislation prohibiting discrimination in mortgage lending and interest rates in Canada and the United States, and mortgage companies have to disclose the areas of the metropolis in which they are lending. But some cases of alleged discrimination are difficult to prove because the individual denied has to have knowledge of cases in which people in a similar credit position have been accepted for loans. Furthermore, the individual with limited resources is pitted against a faceless institution that has large resources. Consequently, discriminatory practices and redlining procedures can continue because it is difficult to prove that such practices exist and have negative effects on neighborhoods.

Examples The difficulty of assessing the continuing pervasiveness of redlining is exhibited in two recent studies, one on a Canadian city, and the other on some small Michigan cities. Murdie (1986) demonstrates that as a consequence of government mortgage insurance policies, large financial institutions have tended to concentrate their loans in suburban parts of Toronto. This has tended to work in favor of middle-class Anglo-Saxons. Recent immigrants, mainly from Southern Europe, have had to resort to the private lending market in order to purchase homes in the more central part of the city. As the immigrant community has become more established, the pattern of using private mortgages has continued. There has therefore been a clear tendency for large loan institutions to cater to the new house submarket for which CMHC-insured loans are available.

Kantor and Nystuen (1982) demonstrate that *de facto* redlining—in which a neighborhood deteriorates as a result of a series of individual loan denials that become recursive through time (that is, one loan denial makes it more probable that another loan will be denied in the same area)—has occurred in Flint and Ann Arbor, Michigan. Furthermore, they suggest that these loan denials are a plausible explanation for some of the urban decay that exists. The parts of these cities that have the greatest percentage of loan applications accepted are in the areas of white population, and the parts with the lowest rate of loan acceptances are in the areas of black population. For example, in Figure 8.3 it is evident that the census tracts inhabited primarily by the black population have an extremely low rate of mortgage loan acceptances, whereas the areas of mainly white population have a high rate.

The Role of Financial and Governmental Institutions in the Creation of Housing Submarkets

It is evident that the ability of household units to obtain credit and mortgages determines whether and where they are able to purchase a home. Credit-worthiness is obviously not simply a choice within income constraints, but a decision structured by the loan policies of private lenders and government institutions. There are a wide variety of private lending institutions in both Canada and the United States—commercial banks, trust companies, mortgage banks, and federal and state savings-and-loans—and they tend to have somewhat different policies. We have seen, in the example cited by Murdie (1986), how major commercial financial institutions, which are clearly in the business of lending to generate profits and maintain values for their shareholders, tend to restrict mortgages to household units of middle income or above who are purchasing fairly new properties in acceptable neighborhoods.

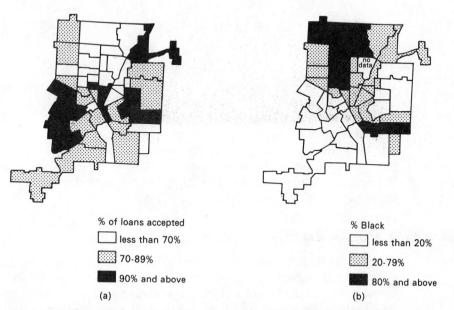

Figure 8.3 Flint, Michigan: (a) the percentage of mortgage loan applications accepted; and (b) the distribution of the black population in 1980, by census tract. (*Source:* Redrawn from Kantor and Nystuen, 1982, p. 324.)

Table 8.1   SUBMARKETS HOUSING FINANCE IN BALTIMORE, 1970

Housing submarket	Total houses sold	Sales per 100 properties	% Transactions by source of funds							
			Cash	Private	Fed S&L	State S&L	Mtge bank	Commercial bank	Savings bank	Other[a]
Inner City	1,199	1.86	65.7%	15.0%	3.0%	12.0%	2.2%	0.5%	0.2%	1.7%
1. East	646	2.33	64.7	15.0	2.2	14.3	2.2	0.5	0.1	1.2
2. West	553	1.51	67.0	15.1	4.0	9.2	2.3	0.4	0.4	2.2
Ethnic	760	3.34	39.9	5.5	6.1	43.2	2.0	0.8	0.9	2.2
1. E. Baltimore	579	3.40	39.7	4.8	5.5	43.7	2.4	1.0	1.2	2.2
2. S. Baltimore	181	3.20	40.3	7.7	7.7	41.4	0.6			
Hampden	99	2.40	40.4	8.1	18.2	26.3	4.0		3.0	
W. Baltimore	497	2.32	30.6	12.5	12.1	11.7	22.3	1.6	3.1	6.0
S. Baltimore	322	3.16	28.3	7.4	22.7	13.4	13.4	1.9	4.0	9.0
High Turnover	2,072	5.28	19.1	6.1	13.6	14.9	32.8	1.2	5.7	6.2
1. Northwest	1,071	5.42	20.0	7.2	9.7	13.8	40.9	1.1	2.9	4.5
2. Northeast	693	5.07	20.6	6.4	14.4	16.5	29.0	1.4	5.6	5.9
3. North	308	5.35	12.7	1.4	25.3	18.1	13.3	0.7	15.9	12.7
Middle income	1,077	3.15	20.8	4.4	29.8	17.0	8.6	1.9	8.7	9.0
1. Southwest	212	3.46	17.0	6.6	29.2	8.5	15.1	1.0	10.8	11.7
2. Northeast	865	3.09	21.7	3.8	30.0	19.2	7.0	2.0	8.2	8.2
Upper income	361	3.84	19.4	6.9	23.5	10.5	8.6	7.2	21.1	2.8

Source: Harvey and Chatterjee (1974, Tables 2[i] and 2[ii]).

In the United States, the federally chartered savings-and-loan associations are required to serve as local mutual thrift institutions in which people can invest their funds to provide a neighborhood credit pool for home finance. Thus, the state savings-and-loan companies tend to provide loans for houses in the lower-priced categories as well as those that are higher-priced. There is a tendency, however, for some savings-and-loan companies to develop a stronger profit orientation, and a large number of cases of neighborhood change have led to some of the institutions financing mortgages in the suburbs for household units migrating from the old neighborhood.

Housing Submarkets in Baltimore

The Harvey–Chatterjee study of the effect of financial and governmental institutions on the creation of housing submarkets in the city of Baltimore is extremely important because it is one of the first to adopt a political economy approach to the analysis of the creation of submarkets (Harvey and Chatterjee, 1974). That is, the study is based on the view that the spatial outcome is not so

% Sales insured		Average sales price[b]	Census tract information					
FHA	VA		Median income[c]	% Black occupied du's	% Units owner-occupied	Mean dollar values owner-occupied	% renter-occupied	Mean monthly rent
2.9%	1.1%	$3,498	$6,259	72.2%	28.5%	$6,259	71.5%	$77.5
3.4	1.4	3,437	6,201	65.1	29.3	6,380	70.7	75.2
2.3	0.6	3,568	6,297	76.9	27.9	6,963	72.1	78.9
2.6	0.7	6,372	8,822	1.0	66.0	8,005	34.0	76.8
3.2	0.7	6,769	8,836	1.2	66.3	8,368	33.7	78.7
0.6	0.6	5,102	8,785	0.2	64.7	6,504	35.3	69.6
14.1	2.0	7,059	8,730	0.3	58.8	7,860	41.2	76.8
_25.8_	4.2	8,664	9,566	84.1	50.0	13,842	50.0	103.7
_22.7_	10.6	8,751	8,941	0.1	56.9	9,741	43.1	82.0
_38.2_	9.5	9,902	10,413	34.3	53.5	11,886	46.5	113.8
_46.8_	7.4	9,312	9,483	55.4	49.3	11,867	50.7	110.6
_34.5_	10.2	9,779	10,753	30.4	58.5	11,533	41.5	111.5
_31.5_	15.5	12,330	11,510	1.3	49.0	12,726	51.0	125.1
17.7	11.1	12,760	10,639	2.8	62.6	13,221	37.5	104.1
_30.2_	17.0	12,848	10,655	4.4	48.8	13,470	51.2	108.1
14.7	9.7	12,751	10,634	2.3	66.2	13,174	33.8	103.0
11.9	3.6	27,413	17,577	1.7	50.8	27,097	49.2	141.4

[a]Assumed mortgages and subject to mortgage.

[b]Ground rent is sometimes included in the sales price and this distorts the averages in certain respects. The relative differentials between the submarkets are of the right order, however.

[c]Weighted average of median incomes for census tracts in submarket.

much a result of market forces, which is assumed in the types of submarkets defined in Figure 8.1, as it is a consequence of the interplay between the state, private capital, and households. In particular, the interplay involves (1) governmental policies as expressed through FHA and VA programs, (2) the actions of private lending institutions that work within a financial environment that is structured in large part by government policies, and (3) the varied socioeconomic characteristics of the households.

Harvey and Chatterjee (1974) demonstrate that the outcome of this interplay is the creation of eight primary submarkets in the city of Baltimore, some of which are further divided, to make thirteen submarkets in all. These submarkets are listed in Table 8.1, along with details concerning the volume of house sales, the sources of funds involved, the average selling prices, and the socioeconomic characteristics of the submarket as indicated by census tract information. The numbers in italics indicate the dominant source of home financing and the extent of government involvement in the form of FHA- and VA-insured loans.

From the information in Table 8.1 it is possible to identify five general submarkets in Baltimore that are distinctly different in the sources of funds that can be obtained for home financing. The locations of these are indicated in Figure 8.4, and can be defined as:

1. The inner city, which consists primarily of blacks living in rental units. In those dwelling units that were sold, cash and other forms of private financing predominate. The purchase price of these homes is by far the lowest in the city, and is far lower than the mean value of owner-occupied homes, according to the census tract information. Note the absence of governmental or institutional financial involvement.

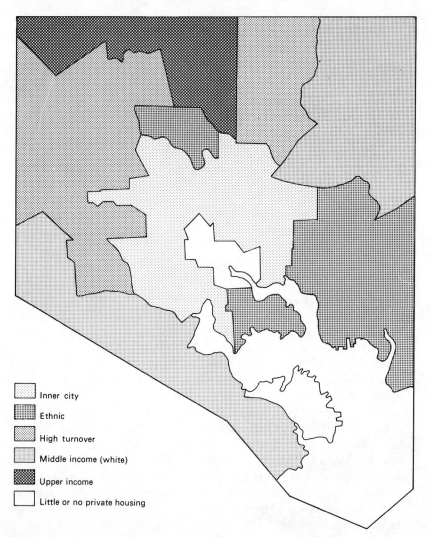

□ Inner city

▨ Ethnic

▨ High turnover

▨ Middle income (white)

▨ Upper income

□ Little or no private housing

Figure 8.4 The location of major housing submarkets by source of finance in the city of Baltimore. (*Source:* Harvey and Chatterjee, 1974, p. 26.)

2. The ethnic areas have a high proportion of dwelling units that are owner-occupied, and a fairly low proportion of rental units. Incomes are below average, but a large proportion of the houses sold in 1970 were financed by local state savings-and-loan companies and by cash transactions.

3. The black areas in which homeownership is relatively high (West Baltimore and the "high turnover" market) are serviced mainly by mortgage banks operating with FHA loan guarantees. The general income level in the area is middle range, and the value of homes is also about the average for the city. These are generally areas of racial change, and the local savings-and-loans companies appear reluctant to get too involved with financing black homeownership.

4. The white middle-income areas of northeast, southwest, and South Baltimore have housing that was financed primarily through the state savings-and-loan companies with FHA mortgage guarantees. More than one-half of the dwelling units are owner-occupied, and the value of the homes is about average for the city.

5. The upper-income area, which lies on the northern periphery of the city, receives loans directly from savings banks and federal savings-and-loan companies and makes relatively little use of FHA guarantees.

An interesting feature of this information is that it illustrates the way in which federally insured loans are used to finance middle-class white and black homeownership but are rarely used to finance housing in low-income black and low-middle-income ethnic areas.

Real Estate Agents and Housing Submarkets

Houses can be sold in two ways, either through real estate agents or by the owners of the property themselves. About 85% of single-family homes are sold with the assistance of real estate agents, and this is normally done on the basis of a commission that is a fixed percentage (about 6%) of the selling price. Thus, although the seller pays the real estate agent, it is the buyer who actually provides the money, and it is clearly to the advantage of the agent to get the highest price possible in a sale, or package of sales. Jud and Frew (1986) demonstrate that real estate agents are the salespersons for the property industry and generate effects similar to that of advertising. That is, they increase the level of demand among buyers and generally stimulate higher prices.

In terms of the creation of housing submarkets, the evidence (Barresi, 1968; Palm, 1985) demonstrates that real estate agents act as:

1. Screening agents who filter would-be buyers and direct them to areas of possible purchase. This screening process is vital, for many movers, as shown in the discussion of the search model, have limited information and may be only marginally interested in relocating.

2. Specialists who frequently have information only about certain types of housing and/or particular parts of urban areas. Thus, if potential buyers feel constrained to use only one or two agents they will automatically be constrained in the range and location of their choices.

3. Supporters of the *status quo,* for as a part of the property industry, the agent is generally conservative in nature and has no intention of fostering social change. Consequently, the policies of many of the agencies support those of the lending institutions, development industry, and so forth. Real estate agents are also in favor of any social trends or policies that promote high rates of homeownership and residential mobility.

Real Estate Agent Practice in Denver

As indicated previously, Palm (1985) has examined the degree to which the real estate industry in Denver is divided into submarkets along racial or ethnic lines. The three hypotheses that she examines are that: (1) the sellers choose real estate agents who are of their own (or similar) ethnic or racial group, (2) the sales area in which an agent operates is influenced by the race or ethnicity of the agent, and (3) the network of business contacts with which the agent works and, therefore, obtains cross-listings and other types of cooperation from, is largely within the same general racial or ethnic group.

Using sample information and personal interviews, Palm demonstrates that each of these hypotheses is tenable. Furthermore, she shows that "sellers are not listing with an agency simply because it is located within the local neighborhood; they are expressing an ethnic preference in their behaviour" (Palm, 1985, p. 64). In the case of sales area limitations, black agents far more than Hispanic agents recognize that their color severely limits the parts of the metropolis in which they may do business. Finally, the contact network within which agents work and receive information is strongly structured in terms of race and ethnic background. Anglo agents deal with other Anglo agents, black agents deal with other blacks, and Hispanics with Hispanics. Given this racially biased and segmented structure, it is no wonder that submarkets remain firm.

Landlords and Submarkets

Landlords seek to obtain the highest returns from their capital investment. Harvey and Chatterjee (1974) have shown how the principle of leverage and the possibility for loans greatly influence the potential rate of return on a landlord's actual monetary investment. If landlords can borrow a large proportion of the needed capital investment, then the leverage on their own investment is great and they can, in effect, charge fairly reasonable rents to receive an acceptable rate of return on their own monetary investment. However, if landlords have to put up a lot of their own money to purchase a property, as in older urban areas, the rate of return on their own investment is quite low, and the landlords will charge higher rents and perhaps skimp on maintenance in order to achieve an acceptable rate of return. Landlords may, consequently, create their own submarket of people, such as the elderly poor who will not complain and have no other choice than to live in highly subdivided multiple-family housing.

Landlords also make decisions as to which market they want to rent to. These decisions are also based on effective rates of return, the amount of maintenance required, and limiting depreciation of the building. For example, some apartment complexes with many amenities are available only for the middle- and upper-income elderly, singles, or couples without children. The creation by landlords of submarkets of this type is obviously based on a perception that increased noise and maintenance problems may occur if they rent to families with children. Furthermore, in such situations the attractive facilities (pools, sauna, and game rooms) are, in effect, rarely used, so depreciation on these lifestyle amenities is quite low. Thus, there may be an abundance of apartments available for the middle- and upper-income elderly or no-children submarkets, but very few rental units available for families with children.

Students frequently ask how it is possible for landlords to discriminate in this way and create submarkets that are favorable to their particular interests. Certainly, a whole host of national and local acts and bylaws are in place to prevent discrimination. But in situations of high demand, landlords can discriminate by judicious use of the filters through which potential tenants have to pass in order to obtain rental accommodation: the application, the building superintendant, and the rental agency itself. For example, one maneuver adopted by landlords is to have standby "renters" (friends) who are willing to testify that they have just rented a unit if the landlord wishes to avoid renting to a particular applicant.

The Abandoned Housing Submarket

The abandoned housing submarket (or nonmarket) consists of housing units that have been withdrawn from the property market permanently because the owner is unable or unwilling to return the units to their former use. In the United States, the problem of abandoned housing and business activities is focused in inner cities located along the northeast coast and the lower Great Lakes area, and it has begun in some areas of the South (such as Dallas, Houston, and New Orleans) and the West Coast (such as Oakland). The magnitude of the problem is greatest in such cities as New York, Baltimore, Boston, Cleveland, St. Louis, Detroit, Newark, Chicago, and Washington, D.C. Although the number of abandoned dwelling units is difficult to measure, it is clear that the level of abandonment in these cities is quite high and is increasing.

One of the spatial characteristics of abandoned housing and business activities is that the vacated properties are found in clusters in particular parts of the central cities. This means that although in a city as a whole the actual number of abandoned properties might be quite low, in certain districts the concentration can be quite high. For example, high concentrations of abandonment occur in the Brownsville–East New York area of Brooklyn, New York (Carey, 1976), the Tioga district of North Philadelphia, and the Montgomery District in St.

Louis, where more than 20% of the residential and commercial units have been left vacant.

The Causes of Abandonment

The question that arises, of course, is how and why abandonment occurs. Dear (1976) presents a most persuasive explanation that incorporates many of the concepts and trends we have discussed or referred to in this and the preceding chapters. The explanation, presented in model form in Figure 8.5, involves a consideration of the driving mechanism behind abandonment; this leads to a discussion of why it is localized in particular neighborhoods, which leads, in turn, to an explanation of the cause of abandonment in these specific neighborhoods and, finally, to an explanation of the dynamics of why, once abandonment occurs, it tends to spread like an uncontrollable cancer.

The forces behind abandonment are the suburbanization of the population and of industrial and service activities, and a decline in the level of in-migration to the inner cities to the point that there is now a net loss of population in the central portion of most large metropolitan areas and an excess supply of housing and other structures in certain areas. There are two elements to the localization of abandonment in specific neighborhoods. First, the abandoned housing may be the lowest-quality housing in the worst part of the urban environment and,

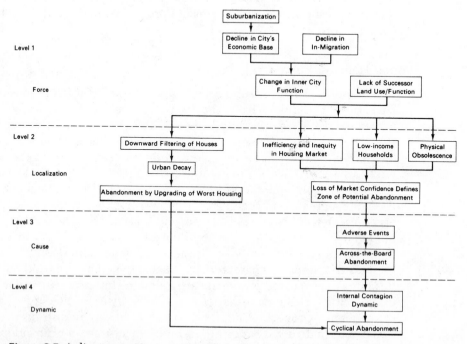

Figure 8.5 A diagrammatic representation of an explanation for abandoned housing and business activities. (*Source:* Dear, 1976, p. 91.)

Abandoned housing awaiting renovation in Boston in 1982. (*Source:* Geovisuals.)

as such, forms the residue of the house-filtering chain. Second, the particular housing submarket for the poor is a factor, for the lowest-income families and individuals can do nothing about purchasing homes, improving them, or preventing the spread of obsolescence. This lack of purchasing power is accentuated by the kind of institutional practices discussed previously, and the consequence is a lack of property resale values. When the values sink low enough, a zone of potential abandonment develops and provides the stage onto which the disease can spread.

The actual cause of abandonment of a specific property is an adverse event occurring within the zone of potential abandonment that leads an individual or corporate owner to cease having any interest in the building even if it is in reasonably good condition. This adverse event could be a fire or vandalism, but such adverse events outside this zone would not lead to abandonment.

Once begun, abandonment proceeds in a contagious manner, and adverse events are no longer required, for the process has developed an internal dynamic of its own. This dynamic involves the property owners' negative perception of the housing market in the area, which is reinforced by the swift manner in which vacant apartments are soon stripped of all saleable items. Thus, the neighborhood slips into a cycle of abandonment that is, in effect, a downward spiral of decay. In many cases, property owners receive some return on their capital investment by maintaining building insurance (the link between property owners and insurers can be seen in Fig. 8.2) and arranging, through intermediaries, for the last rites of an arsonist.

Public Policies Concerning Abandonment

A free-market approach to the solution of the problem of abandonment would be to leave it to the market forces to remedy the situation some time in the future. But for existing or potential abandoned housing stock, the future is now.

No person should be sacrificed to the remedial actions of market forces that may come into play sometime in the future. Apart from our concern for the inhabitants of these areas, there are also secondary concerns relating to public health, to the importance of preserving, renovating, and/or replacing physical structures in some orderly fashion, and to the maintenance of a reasonable tax base. Changes in the tax base often summarize in aggregate form what is happening to a city. For example, in the case of Detroit, the property tax base declined by 32% (in constant dollars) between 1971 and 1976 (Fainstein and Fainstein, 1983, p. 269), and although the decline is not solely the result of abandonment, the percentage does provide a barometer of what is happening in the city as a whole.

Some of the policy approaches recommended by Dear (1976) involve:

1. The establishment of a public or quasi-public corporation that is given the specific task of replacing the vacating landlords and property owners.
2. The provision by government of the necessary level of funds that are required for redevelopment and rehabilitation.
3. The implementation of a scheme of housing allowances for the poor in order to give them some purchasing power in the marketplace for housing.
4. Preventing the spread of abandonment by moving swiftly to prevent the abandonment of additional properties in particular areas (a so-called abandonment watch).
5. The development of community-oriented plans to rehabilitate areas of extensive abandonment, which may well imply a program for changing the economic structure and land use of much of the area.

The underlying premise for these recommendations is that for this type of phenomenon (abandonment) market forces are not working, have become irrelevant, and should be replaced by some form of public action.

URBAN REVITALIZATION

In this section three types of urban revitalization will be defined and examined: redevelopment, incumbent upgrading, and gentrification. We will also examine each in terms of their costs and benefits to society. But as almost any sensible accountant will tell you, it is the method by which these costs and benefits are measured that is important, and the method is determined largely by ideological concerns. What happens in cities is the outcome of the actions of people, whether these people be developers, homeowners, renters, or politicians, so nothing is inevitable; the effects are also experienced by people. Thus, an important way of evaluating the costs and benefits of a particular revitalization project is by its contribution to social justice (Harvey, 1973).

What is meant by social justice? Holcomb and Beauregard enumerate the ultimate characteristics of social justice as: elimination of poverty, acceptable levels of economic security for all, absence of racial and gender discrimination, democratic decision making, an absence of unemployment, reasonable accessibility for all to the resources of the city, and the universal availability of affordable housing (1981, p. 66). Although these characteristics may never be completely attainable, it is important to evaluate revitalization schemes in terms of their incremental contribution to social justice.

Redevelopment

In a classic study of urban development in the New York metropolitan area, Hoover and Vernon (1959) hypothesized the existence of a five-stage evolutionary model of urban redevelopment. This model has proved to be useful for the examination of redevelopment in a number of North American cities (Smith and McCann, 1981). The evolutionary model of redevelopment may be summarized as follows:

> **Stage 1** is *residential development* in single-family houses. . . .
>
> **Stage 2** is a *transition stage* in which there is substantial new construction and population growth . . . but in which a high and increasing proportion of the new housing is in apartments, so that average density is increasing. Much of the apartment construction replaces older single-family houses. . . .
>
> **Stage 3** is a *down-grading stage,* in which old housing (both multi-family and single) is being adapted to greater-density use than it was originally designed for. In this stage, there is usually little actual new construction, but there is some population and density growth through conversion and crowding of existing structures. . . .
>
> **Stage 4,** the *thinning-out stage* . . . is the phase in which density and dwelling occupancy are gradually reduced. Most of the shrinkage comes about through a decline in household size. . . . But the shrinkage may also reflect merging of dwelling units, vacancy, abandonment, and demolition. This stage is characterized by little or no residential construction and by a decline in population. . . .
>
> **Stage 5** is the *renewal stage,* in which obsolete areas of housing . . . are being replaced by new multi-family housing [Hoover and Vernon, 1959, pp. 185–198].

Redevelopment will therefore occur either as a consequence of the pressures of demand (in Stage 2) or as a result of deterioration (in Stage 5).

Redevelopment, as differentiated from incumbent upgrading and gentrification, is frequently characterized by a combination of changes. These changes can include land use, structures, types of residential units, per capita income, social status, and stage in the life cycle of the population. The land use may change from residential units to commercial or multiple-family structures. Areas that were previously commercial or in manufacturing may be converted to higher-density commercial uses or to high-density residential activities. The succeeding population frequently consists of individuals or two-person households in either the young adult or late-mature stages of the life cycle. There is therefore a complete change in the neighborhoods involved, and the original inhabitants are displaced. These previous inhabitants are invariably at the lower end of the income spectrum. The benefits have accrued to the wealthier succeeding populations, and the burdens of finding new locations in which to live and the costs of new housing have fallen on the poorer segments of society. But redevelopment may well have created additional employment opportunities while it was in process.

The sources of capital for the redevelopment usually vary according to the stage in the evolutionary model. In the demand-driven transition stage the investment usually comes from the private sector. A demand-driven land and housing market generates increases in prices and the possibility of profits. As a consequence, the private investment community is extremely active at this stage. A second, intrinsically geographic characteristic of this stage is that the private capital investment is spatially selective, for certain locations that are highly accessible to the rest of the city are the preferred foci of investment. A third feature is that developers try to attain monopoly or quasi-monopoly control of preferred locations. For example, in Houston one developer owns 25% of the downtown area (Holcomb and Beauregard, 1981, p. 55).

In the supply-driven renewal stage, private capital has little interest in redevelopment because the opportunities for profit are limited. Hence public expenditures are made, or there is some form of public–private partnership in which the involvement of public funds is deemed to make investment by the private sector sufficiently profitable. This public–private partnership may take the form of universal schemes or particular projects. Examples of *universal schemes* are the successive Housing Acts in the United States after 1954 that made the redevelopment of decaying parts of cities more attractive to private developers because of the involvement of public funds. The outcome, however, has invariably been displacement of the poor and construction of a few middle- and upper-income housing units and many more sterile civic centers, convention halls, office buildings, and high-priced hotels. Public–private partnerships in specific projects are associated with particular political objectives, for the

Restoration of historic Front Street buildings in Toronto. (*Source:* Geovisuals.)

investment wins votes. A good example of this is investment in sports complexes that add to civic pride—if the local team wins—but have a debatable impact on the local economy while incurring considerable up-front public investments and, often, continuous tax breaks and subsidies. Another example of a particular type of public–private partnership in redevelopment is historic preservation such as Penn's Landing in Philadelphia and Historic Properties in Halifax (Nova Scotia).

The basic issue with redevelopment, therefore, is not so much that it occurs, but who benefits when it does occur. The evidence, as may be witnessed from the numerous case studies in Fainstein *et al.* (1983), is that too often lower-income individuals and families are displaced and have to relocate to housing that represents no improvement on that which they have left, whereas higher-income households and commercial developers benefit. Shill and Nathan (1983 p. 119) in a study of nine revitalizing neighborhoods in five cities, however, contend that, when forced to leave and find new accommodation, lower-income households on the whole improve the quality of their housing. The basic point, therefore, is that although redevelopment is obviously highly necessary in certain parts of most North American cities, it must be undertaken in such a way as to provide benefits for all segments of the urban community, particularly those households that are directly affected.

Gentrification

Although the term *gentrification* seems to have been coined by Glass (1964) with respect to a type of revitalization in London, England involving the upper-income takeover of Victorian mews, it is used to describe a process that has come to public attention with respect to North American cities only during the 1980s. *Gentrification* refers to an influx of upper- and middle-class households into an area of old homes that were previously occupied by lower-middle and low-income individuals and households. The Victorian mews had previously been occupied by horses and stable personnel.

The recent explosion of literature on this phenomenon (e.g., Clark, 1985; Palen and London, 1984; Schaffer and Smith, 1986) emphasizes through a large number of case studies that this type of process generally occurs in a physically small area, usually involves old homes that, when renovated, have charm, happens close to a place of historic (e.g., Society Hill, Philadelphia) or amenity interest, and is usually found within 1 mile of a traditional central business district (Holcomb and Beauregard, 1981, p. 40). The reason why gentrification has attracted a great deal of interest is that many people concerned about the health of the old inner cities are hoping that the small amount that has occurred heralds an impending larger-scale movement of people back to the inner city.

Theoretical Explanations of Gentrification

The many case studies of gentrification emphasize that there may well be a number of different types of explanations of the phenomenon (Ley, 1986). As these explanations once again exemplify a basic underlying theme of this text—the applicability of a variety of approaches to an understanding of spatially distributed phenomenon—it is useful to have a brief discussion of each. These explanations may be grouped into five categories:

1. *Economic causes.* A number of studies have emphasized that the cost of new housing at the periphery of the city is now so high in many North American suburbs that equivalent-space inner-city housing seems cheap by comparison (e.g., James, 1977). Thus a number of middle-income families may simply be responding to this price or rent gap. Actually, this underlies one of the reasons why many Canadian inner cities contain more middle-income families than those in the United States, for the cost of new housing in Canadian suburbs has invariably been higher than similar new housing in United States suburbs.

2. *Demographic explanations.* One observation from a number of case studies is that gentrifiers appear to consist of younger, higher-income professional households with few children. The numbers in this group have swelled as the "baby-boomers" are now reaching middle-age, thus creating a significant demand for well-located residential units.

3. *Economic base explanations.* The cities that have experienced the greatest amount of gentrification appear to be those that have a high percentage of their labor force in financial, business, and associated commercial activities. Such cities invariably have strong financial and commercial cores and a large, well-paid labor force, a proportion of whom may seek downtown residential locations.

4. *Sociocultural explanations.* These are based on Firey's (1945) ideas regarding "sentiment and symbolism." A greater proportion of the population of North America may be becoming prourban, consciously choosing the cultural, social, and recreational amenities of the city over those of the suburb and exurb.

5. *Political economy explanations.* These emphasize the interplay among capital, labor, and the state. Smith (1979) argues that landowners and other financial interests follow a policy of neglecting the inner city (disinvesting) until such time as local governments may change their zoning, housing bylaws, or regulations sufficiently to stimulate reinvestments that yield tremendous profits.

London, Lee, and Lipton (1986) examined these five explanations for gentrification in forty-eight cities in the United States and concluded that they are all, to various degrees, quite tenable. The social movement approach exemplified in the sociocultural explanation is particularly persuasive.

The Impact of Gentrification

The impact of gentrification upon United States cities has not been that great. The few examples that have occurred have created enormous interest, but the numbers of people involved are quite small. The evidence for the 1970s indicates that the back-to-the-city movement had not (in the United States) narrowed in any way the income gap between the suburbs and the old central cities (Long and Dahmann, 1980). Furthermore, many of the examples of gentrification given in the literature appear to involve either redevelopment (the tearing down of housing and the construction of different types of residential units), or incumbent upgrading, which will be discussed in the next section.

The most important issue relates, however, to the benefits and costs of gentrification. An approach that provides a framework that leads automatically into a discussion of benefits and costs with respect to the various groups involved—those coming (the gentrifiers), those displaced, city government, and the building industry—is the political economy approach. The conclusion seems to be, once again, that with gentrification city government may well benefit as a consequence of revitalization and a regeneration of the tax base; the investors and building industry almost always benefit as a consequence of capital gains and tax breaks; the gentrifiers may benefit through capital gains and locational attributes, but also bear financial costs and locational risks; and the displaced bear the burden of seeking new residences that may, in some cases, result in an improvement in housing conditions but in others lead to no improvement, but only to higher rents.

Smith and LeFaivre (1984) contend that one of the additional costs of gentrification is the impact it may have on surrounding, stable lower-middle-income (working-class) neighborhoods. Although gentrification may have resulted, in some cases, in the revitalization of an unstable and declining area, if successful it may generate pressure on housing prices in the immediately adjacent communities. The authors cite sections of South and East Baltimore, and Queen Village and Pennsport next to Society Hill, Philadelphia as places where vital stable communities have been replaced by tarted-up, higher-income enclaves (Smith and LeFaivre, 1984). O'Loughlin and Munski (1979) provide good examples of rapidly increasing housing prices in Lower Marigny, adjacent to the gentrified Vieux Carre in New Orleans, that led to the displacement of the existing population and its replacement by higher-income households.

Incumbent Upgrading

According to Clay (1979), incumbent upgrading occurs in working-class neighborhoods in which considerable renovation is done to the housing stock but the residential units remain occupied by the existing community. There may be some change in the age structure of the neighborhood as younger households replace older ones or families return to the "old neighborhood." The types of neighborhoods in which these occur are those that have a strong cultural and/or ethnic base. As can be seen in Table 8.2, incumbent upgrading does not include the kind of social, income, and residential unit changes that are involved in either gentrification or redevelopment.

One of the major differences between this type of revitalization and the other two discussed in this section is the capital base for the renewal. The big disadvantage faced by lower-income neighborhoods is that capital frequently

Incumbent upgrading by a family of Portuguese origin in Toronto. (*Source:* Geovisuals.)

flows from the area, and new capital often avoids the area. There tends to be disinvestment as the houses and general infrastructure are allowed to deteriorate. The problem, therefore, is to promote the reinvestment that is needed for individual homeowners and renters to upgrade their immediate environment. This can often be achieved only through the lobbying efforts of local groups to persuade local governments to improve public services and to generate a flow of public and private funds for renovations. These districts often face a form of quasi-redlining, so government action is frequently required to ensure a flow of funds (Holcomb and Beauregard, 1981, pp. 46–50). The study by Murdie (1986) demonstrates quite clearly that new immigrants to Toronto have had to use private funds to upgrade the houses in the neighborhoods in which they have settled.

Table 8.2 COMPARISON OF CHANGE CHARACTERISTICS AMONG NEIGHBORHOODS UNDERGOING REDEVELOPMENT, INCUMBENT UPGRADING, AND GENTRIFICATION

Characteristics of change	Redevelopment	Incumbent upgrading	Gentrification
Social status	x		x
Per capita income	x		x
Land use	x		
Structures	x		
Housing type	x		
Population density			x
Persons per room			x
Stage in life cycle	x	x	

Conclusion

Chapter 8 has emphasized that households have access to different and varied numbers of housing submarkets. These submarkets are structured by a variety of different actors that, in effect, limit the range of choice of a household unit at a particular income level. It is only through an understanding of the way in which these constraints operate that individuals and families can begin to work around them and to demand relief from them.

Chapter
9

The Location of
Employment Opportunities

*I*n discussing why certain phenomena, such as land uses or types of residence, are located where they are in cities, we have usually commenced with an examination of theoretical statements that relate the location of these phenomena to employment opportunities. The widespread distribution of geographic sources of employment is illustrated in Table 9.1, which indicates the proportion of total employment (in SMSAs) located in suburban municipalities that have 5,000 or more jobs in manufacturing and tertiary activities. Table 9.1 demonstrates some significant shifts, with a number of metropolitan areas (Newark, Boston, and Detroit) having about one-half of their total MSA employment concentrated in large suburban nucleations. In the cases of Newark and Detroit, suburban employment exceeds total employment in the central city. In other metropolitan areas (such as Chicago, Cleveland, Philadelphia, and San Francisco–Oakland) large suburban employment nucleations provide about one-third of total MSA employment.

Any discussion related to the location of employment opportunities within urban areas must therefore take into account a number of features and trends:

- The location of manufacturing and service employment in a multinucleated context.

Table 9.1   THE CONCENTRATION OF EMPLOYMENT IN LARGE SUBURBAN NUCLEATIONS[a]

	1967		1977	
	Number of suburban nucleations	Percent of MSA employment	Number of suburban nucleations	Percent of MSA employment
Boston	29	45.0%	34	48.0%
Chicago	31	21.6	44	30.2
Cleveland	11	21.7	15	26.8
Detroit	22	38.5	26	45.5
Los Angeles–Long Beach	39	45.0	34	48.0
New York	11	6.5	13	8.4
Newark	21	45.8	25	51.6
Philadelphia	14	16.6	22	28.0
Pittsburgh	5	5.2	8	6.0
San Francisco–Oakland	15	32.9	18	38.7

[a]Suburban employment nucleations are defined as municipalities having 5,000 or more jobs in manufacturing, retail trade, wholesale trade, and selected service industries combined.

Source: Erikson (1986, p. 332).

- The changing pattern of employment opportunities from central city nucleations to suburban nucleations.
- The access various socioeconomic groups have to employment opportunities.

The review will be placed in a theoretical context with empirical examples, and relates first to manufacturing employment, and second to retail and office activities.

THE LOCATION OF MANUFACTURING EMPLOYMENT

Although manufacturing land occupies only about 9% of the developed land in most North American industrial cities, it is an important aspect of the urban economy. Not only do the manufacturing activities on the land provide a large number of jobs, they also contribute a large proportion of the basic activity of the region. In the Pittsburgh metropolitan area, for example, although manufacturing production consumes little land, it provides jobs for about 30% of the labor force, and these jobs contribute 36% of the total earned income of the region. It is therefore extremely important to know something about the historical sequence with respect to industrial development, the major types of locations of manufacturing, the processes influencing growth or decline in employment among these locational types, and policy issues relating to decentralization.

The Historical Sequence

Following the themes developed in Chapters 2, 3, and 4, the historical evolution of manufacturing in urban areas will be discussed in terms of developments in technology and organizational change in manufacturing. These two features are examined historically in terms of (1) the pattern before the industrial revolution, (2) the Early Industrial Revolution waterway era, (3) the Middle Industrial Revolution railway era, (4) the Late Industrial Revolution highway era, and (5) the age of industrial restructuring.

In the preindustrial United States, manufacturing was usually related either to the shipbuilding and repair industry, or to the fabrication of consumables (clothing, leather, or horse-servicing products) for the local domestic market. These activities were located on the waterfront and close to the center of the town, which was also adjacent to the waterfront. Later, during the Early Industrial Revolution era, the waterway became even more important, for it was not only the mode of transportation for raw materials and some of the production, but in the case of rivers, it was also a source of power and a material input into the manufacturing process. This powerful locational force is mediated by a second force, the relative immobility of labor located within the towns and cities. Thus, manufacturers either established both plants and industrial towns at appropriate water locations—for example, Waltham, Massachusetts or Paterson, New Jersey—or located their plants close to the central parts of existing cities.

The Middle Industrial Revolution Railway Era

The rapid development of the North American railroad network in the middle and late nineteenth century reinforced the advantages of central areas in most urban concentrations. This was particularly due to the twin effects of the focusing of lines on the downtown areas and the central concentration of labor. Thus, a melange of wholesale and manufacturing establishments became located on the lands around these rail lines, close to the downtown terminals. Furthermore, in the process of serving each other, they developed a complex network of ancillary industries. This is witnessed in the conglomeration of industries around the Flats of Cleveland and the Union Stockyards in Chicago.

Not only were the lands along the railroad tracks attractive locations for industry, it was in the best interests of the railroad companies to attract manufacturing to them. This was because the railroad companies themselves owned much of the property adjacent to the tracks, an ownership that was invariably the result of government land grants. Thus, right from the outset, the railroad companies were also in the urban land-development business: They used their land grants and purchased rights of way to lure factories to their facilities. This is well illustrated in the case of the belt-line railroad companies that developed in almost every large metropolis during the last quarter of the nineteenth century.

The Belt-Lines and Early Decentralization   Belt-line railroads were constructed to allow interconnections and transfers of rolling stock, and the goods they contained, among the major intercity trunk lines that tended to focus radially on the centers of cities. The Belt Railroad Company (BRC) in Chicago fostered industrial production from the day it was opened for traffic in the 1880s. The inducements were cheap land and direct rail access. However, the BRC inducements were greater than those offered by the major railroad companies because they offered freedom of access to all of Chicago's trunk-line railroads. The plentiful supply of cheap, transportation-serviced land was particularly important for those industries that could not obtain land for new plants or for expansion near the center of the city.

Until the 1880s, manufacturing in Chicago had concentrated around the Chicago River near the present Loop (central business district). Soon this area became overcrowded, and the BRC became active in promoting the mouth of the Calumet River as an alternative industrial site, for the Calumet district was on BRC rails. The largest industrial district promoted and operated by BRC was, however, the Clearing Industrial District, adjacent to the Clearing Yard. This city of factories was developed by a land syndicate organized by BRC in the 1920s and 1930s as a planned industrial community with its own streets, water, and sewage services. Around those industrial areas clustered the homes of the people employed in the factories, the rhythm of the home being tied to the daily rhythm of the factory.

Thus in one sense, the decentralization of manufacturing began during the latter part of the nineteenth century and was directly related to the need for cheap space and the cost advantages that could be derived by manufacturers from more flexible forms of access. Around these new industrial areas

The Scarborough Classification Yard east of Toronto. Note the industrial buildings on the margin of the yard. (*Source:* Geovisuals.)

grew working-class neighborhoods that, because of the limited availability of transportation, were tied to the fortunes of the local factories. The rate of decentralization was, however, limited—for example, as late as 1910, 75% of the manufacturing employment in Manhattan, New York City was in the small area south of 14th Street (Pratt, 1911). This pattern of mainly inner-city manufacturing was not broken until the use of trucks for transportation became widespread.

The Late Industrial Revolution Highway Era

The era of the Late Industrial Revolution, until the 1960s, was characterized by the decentralization of manufacturing activity within metropolitan areas. The decentralization of manufacturing activity on a large scale was made possible by the truck, which allows goods to be moved around cities with ease, and by the growing use of the automobile for commuting to the decentralized workplaces. But decentralization did not occur uniformly in all urban places, for large places experienced decentralization a great deal sooner than middle-sized cities.

One urban area that experienced decentralization at quite an early date is the New York metropolitan area. The proportion of production workers located in Manhattan declined even between 1869 and 1889, although the actual number of workers increased enormously (Table 9.2). Decentralization continued during the first half of the twentieth century, but only since the early 1950s has the actual number of workers in manufacturing decreased as well.

Change in the Location of Manufacturing Plants in Vancouver   The total figures relating to changes in the location of plants and manufacturing in a particular urban region do not reveal the complexity of the change. It is therefore neces-

Table 9.2   ESTIMATES OF THE CHANGING GEOGRAPHICAL DISTRIBUTION OF PRODUCTION WORKERS
New York Metropolitan Region, 1869–1970

Year	Number of employees (thousands)	Number of employees in Manhattan	Manhattan (percent)	Metropolitan region (percent)
1869	240.3	131.4	54.7%	45.3%
1889	683.0	356.5	52.2	47.8
1919	1,158.6	384.7	33.2	66.8
1956	1,483.3	376.8	25.4	74.6
1970	1,889.9	332.6	17.6	82.4

Sources: Chinitz (1960, p. 131); comparative estimates for 1970 calculated from 1970 census, Bureau of the Census [PHC(1)-145] (microfiche).

sary to develop a simple statement of change that incorporates an array of possible causes and shifts. Steed (1973) has developed such an accounting equation, which is of significant use in analyzing plant location dynamics:

$$x_i = b_i - d_i + m_i - e_i$$

where x_i = the net change in the number of plants in region i
   b_i = the number of births
   d_i = the number of plants closing down completely
   m_i = the number of plants migrating to an area
   e_i = the number of plants emigrating from an area.

Steed applied this equation to the change in the distribution of manufacturing in thirteen sub-areas within the greater Vancouver area for the two periods 1954–1957 and 1964–1967. The thirteen sub-areas were chosen so as to isolate the city core from several other foci (e.g., North Vancouver and Burnaby) and suburban areas around the city. Briefly, the innermost and the historic industrial areas exhibited by far the largest decrease in total number of plants between 1955 and 1965, whereas the greatest absolute increases were experienced in the outer zone, particularly along the north area of the Fraser River and in East Vancouver and Burnaby.

An application of Steed's equation indicates that the absolute decline in the central part of the Vancouver region was related to the heavy out-migration of plants during the early part of the 1955–1965 period. During the 1954–1957 period, this sub-area generated one in three of the region's migrant plants, and although a number of plants stayed within the downtown area, a large number moved to other locations within the region. By the end of the period, the situation was more stable, for although the heavy out-migration persisted, it was offset by a high plant birth rate and fewer mortalities. The areas of greatest net increase received their gains primarily through new plant births, and secondarily as a result of plant immigration. On the average, about one-third of the net increase was due to immigrating plants, whereas two-thirds was the result of the establishment of entirely new plants in the region. Most of the immigrating plants were originally from the downtown area.

Thus in Vancouver, the apparent decentralization of industry was primarily the result of the entry of new plants. These new plants located either in the inner industrial core or in the outer growth areas. The plant births in the inner core were offset, however, by a large number of deaths and emigrants, whereas the growth areas did not exhibit these symptoms. The inner core therefore continued in its role as a place in which new plants could experiment and establish themselves with limited capital outlay. The growth areas gained in importance, primarily because it is here that space was available, although in the Vancouver region industrial space was extremely expensive. The application of the equation is therefore quite instructive, even for an area where the total manufacturing picture is one of great absolute growth during the era.

Impact of Restructuring in Manufacturing

From about the mid-1970s on, manufacturing in North America has been subjected to an enormous number of pressures as a result of major changes in technology, international competition, and methods of financing. These have been discussed in some detail in Chapter 3. The consequences of these changes have been felt at the intraurban level as well as the interurban. The decentralization of manufacturing has accelerated, and the most evident spatial outcome has been the establishment of whole new complexes of industrial activity in particular parts of the outer suburban ring.

There are, perhaps, three main features of this economic restructuring that had a major effect on the acceleration of the decentralization process. The first is the simple fact that in order to be competitive, many existing firms have had to reinvest in new means of production. New capital investments invariably mean new plant locations, on newly developed urban land. This is reinforced by the second element, which is that the amount of capital required for investments in new technologies is quite massive, and the machinery is often environmentally sensitive. It pays, therefore, for a manufacturing plant to build new plants, perhaps in a "greenfield" location at the periphery of a city.

The third element relates to the complex arrangements of suppliers and marketing activities in modern manufacturing. Production runs tend to be shorter, and the output has to be marketed quickly. Inventories have to be kept as low as possible because inventories cost money to purchase and store. If they are to keep their inventories low, firms require maximum access to both suppliers and markets. These three features all combine to reinforce the tendency for modern manufacturing plants to seek peripheral locations once their products are well established.

The Major Locational Types

At this juncture it is useful to gather together some of the elements of locational structure into a general description of the intrametropolitan location of manufacturing. An interesting definition of locational types is suggested by Cameron (1973), who defines four major spatial groups of industry in an urban area: (1) central clusters, (2) decentralized clusters, (3) random spreads, and (4) peripheral concentrations. These four groups are defined as an outcome of locational decisions made in the context of land costs (or the price of space) and of accessibility to suppliers and markets.

Central Clusters

In the case of manufacturing firms located in central clusters, which are defined as groups of plants located close to the central business district (Fig. 9.1), most of their market is within the central business district and the metropolis itself. Even though land costs or rent may be comparatively high compared with peripheral locations, the complex array of concentration economies focused in the core area (see Chapter 3) are the main features that attract firms and permit

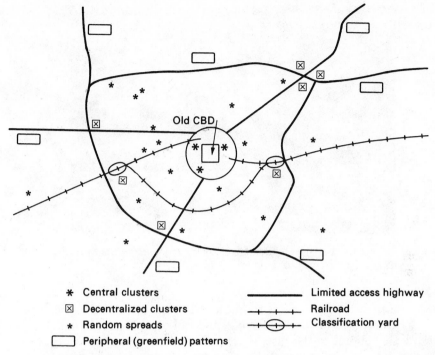

* Central clusters   ——————— Limited access highway
⊠ Decentralized clusters   —+—+—+— Railroad
* Random spreads   —+—⊕—+— Classification yard
▭ Peripheral (greenfield) patterns

Figure 9.1 Location of centralized and decentralized clusters, random spreads, and peripheral plants in a hypothetical city.

them to be competitive enough to remain in business (Scott, 1982a, 1983a). In addition, there is the advantage of face-to-face contact with members of other firms or final purchasers within the cluster, the central business district, and the urban area in general.

Plants in central clusters tend to be characterized by one or more of the following features: they are involved with less-standardized production or they are small in scale; the firm may be developing a new or slightly different product line or it may be producing a very particular product to satisfy a small market niche (Steed, 1976). An industry that exemplifies a number of these characteristics is the high-fashion portion of the garment district of Manhattan. Manufacturing firms focusing on the high-fashion segment of the industry are involved in the production of less-standardized products, the plants are small in scale, the product lines are continually changing in response to innovations in fashion, and the firms cater to a particular market niche.

Decentralized Clusters

Plants locating in decentralized clusters purchase most of their material inputs from, and sell most of their product output to, customers located outside the metropolitan area. In consequence, accessibility to markets and suppliers is greater and easier at locations adjacent to transportation facilities that provide

A large industrial park (decentralized cluster) near a major freeway interchange (QEW–427) west of Toronto. (*Source:* Geovisuals.)

a high level of access to markets beyond the urban area. Today, when truck transportation and both road and rail container terminals are located in areas peripheral to the city, accessibility costs per unit of output will be lowest in these peripheral areas around major transport foci (Fig. 9.1).

Although locations close to transportation facilities are of vital importance in creating the decentralized cluster, some external economy considerations may enhance the advantage of the clustered situations. For example, some plants may share common transportation facilities, warehousing, and business services. Route 128 is a good example of the way in which firms and plants quickly perceived the advantage of a peripheral belt highway that provides a high level of access to areas beyond the metropolis. It is a circumferential expressway located about 12 miles (radial distance) from the center of Boston. Conzen and Lewis (1976) note that by the early 1970s there were about 730 companies with plants located adjacent to the expressway, and that these plants provided more than 66,000 jobs. Among the firms locating in decentralized clusters of this type are those concerned with electronics, the manufacture of computer hardware and the creation of software, and the manufacture and packaging of drugs. By the mid-1970s, Route 128 had become saturated with plants, and Interstate 495, located farther out, about 25 miles distant from the center of Boston, was becoming the next locus for decentralized clusters. Whereas the clustering of plants along Route 128 occurred in an unplanned manner, the clusters close to the interchanges on Interstate 495 are often in privately developed industrial parks.

Industrial Parks   Industrial parks have been in existence in North American cities for many decades and have been an important factor in decentralization. An *industrial park* is a tract of land that is subdivided and developed according to a comprehensive plan for the use of a community of manufacturing plants and/or offices. The basic infrastructure, including streets, water, sewage, transportation facilities, and electrical power, is provided by the company or city building the park. In some cases buildings are provided for rent. These industrial parks can serve an incubator function for new firms and may also be associated with the development of new subdivisions. Although many industrial parks are privately developed, a large number are owned by local governments that use the facilities to attract industry to the local community.

Random Spread

In the case of plants that appear to be located in a random spread fashion within metropolitan areas, one of the most significant influences on location is that their output is directed almost entirely toward the metropolis in which they are situated. The types of plants involved are usually those concerned with the assembly of consumer durables, such as washing machines, television sets and refrigerators. They use prefabricated, nonbulky parts as inputs, and assemble these into relatively bulky, space-consuming final products. Thus, plants in this category require space for assembly and warehousing, and good access to the retail distributors throughout the metropolitan area. The final product is invariably transported by truck and, as a consequence, the plant can locate almost anywhere that is relatively low-cost in the urban region.

Random spreads of manufacturing activity are found most clearly in cities that have grown rapidly since the 1930s, such as Los Angeles, Dallas–Fort Worth, and Denver. Nelson (1983) notes that manufacturing in Los Angeles is distributed in a dispersed fashion throughout the extended megalopolis in much the same way as retailing, thus reinforcing the polycentric nature of the modern city.

Peripheral Patterns

There are two critical characteristics shared by plants that are located in a peripheral pattern within metropolitan areas. The first is that they require large amounts of ground-floor space for production, storage, and parking for their employees. The second is that they comprise industries with nonlocal markets, and are therefore oriented toward regions outside the metropolitan area in which they are located. Firms with these characteristics must establish themselves where there is plenty of land available at a reasonable cost. Locations in peripheral areas adjacent to good highway facilities are preferred (Fig. 9.1).

Examples of industries that are generally found in peripheral locations are those involving the production of aircraft, motor vehicles and parts, and farm machinery. Nelson (1983) has observed that the aircraft industry, which was established fairly early in the growth of Los Angeles, has periodically had to move farther out to obtain more space for larger hangars and longer runways as the metropolis expanded. In some instances, the peripheral location of a new plant has led to the development of a new town on the periphery of a metropolis; a firm that produces transportation equipment stimulated the growth of Glendale, Arizona, for example.

Processes Influencing the Changing Location of Manufacturing within Cities

The basic problem with the discussion in the previous section is that although it provides a useful description of the major locational types of manufacturing within cities, it is not dynamic. That is, the description of locational types does not have those factors that influence change in the structure of manufacturing as a central theoretical concept. It is difficult to use such a descriptive approach to discuss change in the location of manufacturing within the city. Recent research in the intraurban location of manufacturing has utilized two main approaches for the analysis of change: product life cycles, and capital/labor substitution.

Product Life Cycles

The product life-cycle approach relates the stages in the development and marketing of the main output of a plant to the probable location of the production facility within a metropolis. The product cycle, in its simple form, consists of four stages (Fig. 9.2): (1) an *innovation* stage that entails relatively high development costs, short production runs, experimental marketing, and a high level of personal involvement by the developers of the product, (2) a *growth* phase that occurs after the market has been sufficiently developed and the product is found to have market appeal, (3) a *standardization* phase when the

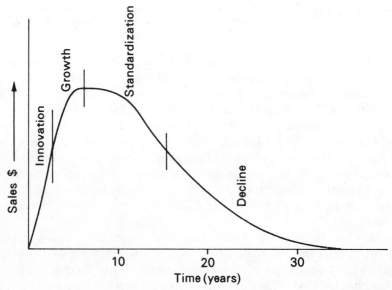

Figure 9.2 The stages in an industrial product life cycle.

market share can be clearly identified and the plant is concerned mainly with volume production, and (4) a final stage of *output decline* characterized by decreased market share followed by a decline in volume produced, and by declining profitability (Malecki, 1981).

The first phase is concerned mainly with product innovation, and the second and third phases usually involve some process innovations. The length of the product cycle varies according to the goods being produced. Oakey (1985) cites the case of medium-technology consumer products such as washing machines and toasters as having, with appropriate face-lifts, a possible cycle of twenty-five to thirty years, whereas modern high-technology computer products have a cycle of about five years. Furthermore, a particular type of product, such as a radio, may be continually updated as new technologies and ideas are generated.

In some instances, the change in location of an industrial plant within a city can be related to changes in the product cycle. It is not unusual for new firms with a new product to be established within central clusters, for the possibility of short-term rentals and the external economies generated by existing plants and the activities of the central business district creates an environment that serves as an incubator for the new plant. An alternative location could well be some new industrial park in the decentralized clusters, where low-cost facilities and other services are provided by the managers of the park.

If the product is accepted and reaches a growth phase, the incubator facilities are no longer congruent with the production requirements. Frequently, a specially constructed plant that has ready access to low-cost but productive labor is required. Such plants may be built in the decentralized clusters, but they are more likely to be established in peripheral locations. Often, plants at this stage seek capital or tax advantages from state/provincial or local governments as part of their profit-maximizing strategy. Older plants involved in commodities that have a long product cycle, such as refrigerators, may be found randomly distributed within the metropolitan area.

The product life-cycle approach, therefore, relates decentralization to the fact that firms are concerned with the development and marketing of a product that at some time or another will be superceded by another product. The various locational types tend to consist of plants at different stages in the life-cycle sequence. Central clusters have an incubation function, but they also have plants at the tail-end of the cycle that exist despite inertia. Decentralized clusters also serve an incubation function, but they also have plants in the growth phase. Peripheral locations invariably have plants in the standardized phase, whereas random spreads frequently consist of plants in the late standardization/decline phase.

Capital/Labor Substitution

In a remarkable series of articles, Scott has utilized some of the more important ideas in political economy relating to capital and labor, and to the general concepts of external, agglomeration, and concentration economies to provide a rich framework for the analysis of change in the intraurban location of manufacturing (1981; 1982a; 1982b; 1983a; 1983b; 1984; 1986). The capital/labor aspect of his work has its roots in an earlier theoretical discussion by Moses and Williamson (1967): their recognition of external, agglomeration, and concentration considerations allows Scott to focus on the degree to which different types of firms are able to integrate the various components of their production process, and the effect that this has upon the creation of spatial clusters of interlinked economic activities (Scott 1983c).

A basic feature of Scott's work is its explicit recognition of spatial differences in the strength of external, agglomeration, and concentration economy effects, and in the availability of land and labor within metropolitan areas. To summarize, he argues that in the aggregate there are significant differences between the center and the periphery of a metropolis among external, agglomeration, and concentration economies, on the one hand, and in the availability of land and labor on the other hand. These differences exist in both monocentric and polynucleated metropolises.

The advantages to be derived from external, agglomeration, and concentration economies are greatest at the center and smallest at the periphery; on the other hand, land and labor costs are highest at the center and lowest at the periphery. For various reasons, such as the drive by firms to lower labor costs or to control labor, firms tend to try to substitute capital for labor. Since land is cheaper and in greater supply at the periphery, and therefore more attractive for capital investments, this invariably implies a decentralization of industry. There is, therefore, a spatial Heckscher–Ohlin effect (Blackley and Greytak, 1986), with plants having a lower capital-to-labor ratio in central locations and a higher capital-to-labor ratio in peripheral locations.

This centrifical pattern is offset to a degree by the desire of some types of manufacturing industries to locate in clusters where they can gain either external economies or concentration advantages with respect to the provision of inputs and the marketing of outputs. This applies particularly to those plants that either choose not to, or cannot, integrate (vertically or horizontally) many aspects of their production and marketing functions. Thus, the integrated plants can locate in free-standing peripheral patterns (or random spreads), whereas those types of manufacturing activities that participate in a great deal of subcontracting or have to be close to their markets tend to locate in decentralized clusters within the vicinity of their associated activities. Scott demonstrates a number of these locational features in detailed case studies of the printed circuits, women's dress, and high-technology industries in the Los Angeles metropolitan area (1983b; 1984).

For example, with respect to the printed circuits industry in the Los Angeles metropolitan area, Scott demonstrates that the smaller, more labor-intensive plants tend to be more clustered than the larger, more integrated plants (1983b). The data for a sample of printed circuits plants indicate that they tend to locate close to their main suppliers (of laminates and chemicals), customers, and subcontractors (Fig. 9.3). Thus, the size of the individual plants and the organization of industry influence the locational pattern of the firms in metropolitan space. In a more general context, Blackley and Greytak (1986) provide

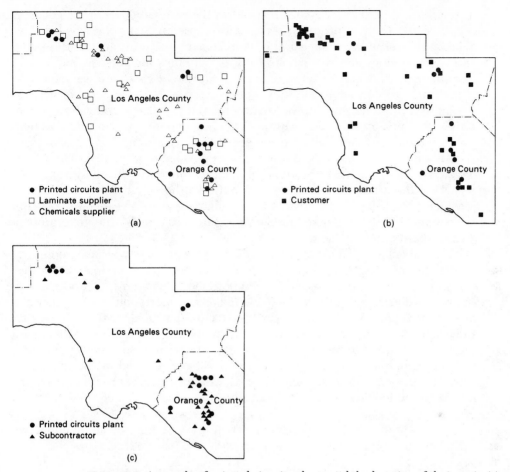

Figure 9.3 A sample of printed circuits plants and the location of their main (a) suppliers, (b) customers, and (c) subcontractors in Los Angeles. (*Source:* Redrawn from Scott, 1983b, pp. 357, 359, 361.)

evidence with respect to Cincinnati that industrial activities tend to be capital intensive in peripheral locations and labor intensive in central locations. Thus, the inexorable substitution of capital for labor is expressed spatially in decentralization.

THE LOCATION OF EMPLOYMENT IN RETAIL AND SERVICE ACTIVITIES

At the outset, it is important that we distinguish between producer and consumer services (Daniels, 1986). In North America, the largest and fastest-growing sector of employment involves these two types of services. Producer services are intermediary activities that aid in the production of other goods or activities. Examples of producer services are those involving the development of computer software, finance and brokerage activities, insurance and reinsurance, wholesaling, and the whole array of activities included in marketing. Consumer services relate to the final consumption of goods and services, and pertain primarily to retail activities. The location of producer services will, for the most part, be covered in the section related to office employment. Retail activities, which provide a large number of employment opportunities, particularly for female workers, are the subject of this discussion.

Although only from 3% to 4% of the developed land in an urban area is devoted to retail activities, these commercial activities are extremely important aspects of the urban environment. Not only are they large generators of employment, they also are the places where a large part of the income (60%) of the residents of the city is spent. Commercial areas are also the generators of a large share of the traffic flow.

Until about 1890, most of the retail activities in a city were located in the central business district, although there were a number of food and other convenience stores servicing local neighborhoods. Between 1890 and 1935, as the population decentralized along the major transportation arteries, so did a number of retail activities that served the day-to-day needs of the increasingly suburban population. This gave rise to unplanned strips of retail activities along the major streets, and to nucleations at major traffic intersections. Since 1935, the automobile and the demand for parking have resulted in the growth of suburban planned shopping centers and in the development of large specialized retail outlets involved with food, furniture, electronics, clothes, and general household goods.

The literature on the geography of retailing (Wilson, 1986) has involved two main components:

1. Spatial aspects of retail location are concerned with where stores or clusters of types of stores are located in a metropolitan area.
2. Spatial aspects of consumer behavior and cognition involve the factors influencing where and how far consumers are prepared to go to shop, and how they learn about the retail system. There is a particular focus on the ways in which different socioeconomic groups learn about the availability of different retail activities, goods, and prices (Potter, 1982).

In the next section, we will focus on the first of these interests, although there will be some discussion of the second.

Urban Retail Location

The typology of urban retail structure is based on three theoretical elements:

1. The idea of hierarchies as derived from central place theory, which in the context of intraurban retail location argues that a hierarchy of retail locations will develop in response to the geographic distribution of

consumers. Some retail locations have a large number of stores or types of retail activities under one roof and serve a large market area, whereas other retail locations consist of a smaller number of stores that serve the daily needs of a local market area.

2. The concept of external economies, which argues that certain advantages of joint attraction can be gained when individual retail outlets are located close together. This gives rise to a clustering of retail activities.

3. Accessibility, as reflected in the land value. Retail activities have to be in accessible locations, and those requiring the largest market area, such as department stores, have to be in the most-accessible locations. Retail activities are therefore found along radial and ring arterial roads and expressways, particularly at intersections. Those retail activities that are intended for the largest market area locate at major expressway interchanges, and those with local markets are established more ubiquitously around the urban area on neighborhood throughstreets.

These ideas—hierarchies, external economies, and accessibility as articulated in land-value theory—form the basis of a typology of urban retail structure that has been demonstrated to exist throughout North America as well as in other parts of the world (Berry, 1967; Jones and Simmons, 1987; Morrill, 1987; Potter, 1982). This urban retail structure is defined geographically in terms of specialized areas, ribbons, and nucleations (Fig. 9.4).

Specialized Areas

Specialized areas are recognizable clusters of commercial activity within cities. Often they are freestanding, although they may be present in the larger outlying shopping centers. They are usually well developed in the central business district, where two types can be identified: (1) local clusters of establishments of the same business type, for example entertainment districts, and (2) functional areas consisting of different commercial activities that are interrelated, for example printing districts.

Many of these specialized areas are so strongly developed that the districts or streets in which they are located have become household names and are known throughout the country. In Manhattan, for example, Wall Street is synonymous with the financial community, Park Avenue with the headquarters offices of many of North America's largest corporations, Madison Avenue with advertising, and Fifth Avenue with high-quality, high-price retailing. In Toronto, Yonge Street is well known for some of the more risque aspects of life's rich pattern.

Outside the central business district, the dominant locational factor for this component of the urban commercial structure is accessibility to the portion of the market served. Hence these areas are typically found on major arterial roads within the urban area or at the foci of public transportation or freeway systems, and they may be planned or unplanned. Clustering occurs because the firms or stores involved find that there are considerable external economies to

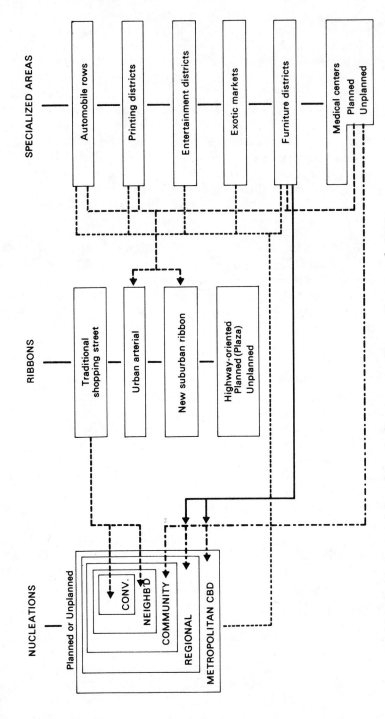

Figure 9.4 Major components of the urban retailing pattern. (*Source:* Berry *et al.*, 1963, Table 1.)

242

be gained by locating close to other, similar activities, or because they want to share some type of common facility or joint power of attraction.

Examples of specialized areas encountered within cities include:

1. "Automobile rows," comprising contiguous strings of establishments selling new and used automobiles and providing facilities for parts, repairs, and servicing. These areas are strung out along the main highways and radial streets.

2. Medical districts, comprising offices of doctors, dentists, and related medical facilities. The older, unplanned medical districts are often located at the upper-floor level within the outlying shopping centers, although more recently the tendency has been for these to be replaced or supplemented by planned office complexes away from shopping centers but at accessible locations near them, particularly in the suburbs.

3. Household-furnishing districts, comprising concentrations of furniture, household appliances, and related stores.

4. Exotic markets, such as Maxwell Street in Chicago, "Chinatown" in San Francisco, and Kensington Market in Toronto.

5. Large, independent discount stores that include many types of retail activities under one roof. These are normally located away from other elements of the business pattern, especially the shopping centers to which they often offer serious competition. They are generally found at arterial locations, for they depend on shoppers who travel by automobile. They are freestanding because the wide range of goods they offer permits one-stop shopping visits and thus does not necessitate linkages with other stores.

Ribbons

Ribbons, the second major component of the commercial structure, are most noticeable in the central city, where their constituents form the backdrop to most well-traveled routes through the urban area. Businesses that have a tendency to locate in one or another of the types of ribbons are those that need a certain minimum degree of accessibility to the market served. They do not, however, require sites of maximum centrality within urban areas, and consequently can survive at locations along major arteries and urban highways (Fig. 9.5). Although several different types of ribbons can be recognized, it is important to remember that the character of these is repeated from one part of the city to another.

Retail activities located on *highway-oriented ribbons* serve demands originating from the traffic on the major highways. This traffic may be both local and nonlocal. Generally, the greater the volume of traffic on the highway, the more important it is as a generator of demand and, consequently, the greater the density of commercial development along it. For the most part, these ribbons are uncontrolled developments, although along some of the newer intraurban

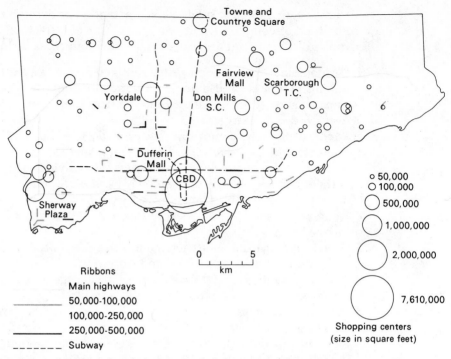

Figure 9.5 Ribbon developments and shopping centers in the Toronto area.

highways, planned service plazas are the rule. Typical businesses on highway-oriented ribbons include gasoline and service stations, chain restaurants and drive-ins, ice-cream parlors, and motels. These are essentially freestanding establishments among which there is very little functional linkage, and which cater, essentially, to one-stop shopping trips originating from the transient market on the highways.

Commercial activities located on *urban-arterial ribbons* serve the demands of the local area and, in general, they are either large consumers of space or services that are needed only occasionally and that therefore involve special-purpose trips. The businesses located in these areas include furniture and appliance stores, office equipment sales, funeral parlors, garden supplies, lumber yards, building and household supplies, and large supermarkets. These types of activities are freestanding, in that they cater to one-stop shopping trips.

Traditional shopping streets are distinctive features of the older parts of North American cities. They should be thought of as ribbon developments only in the sense of being morphologically similar to the other ribbon types. In functional structure, the traditional shopping streets are similar to lower-level, unplanned retail nucleations (Fig. 9.6). Typical businesses in these ribbons would be small groceries, fruit and vegetable stores, drugstores, laundries and laundromats, beauty salons, and barbershops. As such, they constitute small clusters of low-order convenience goods and services that are interjected into the arterial ribbons at minor street intersections. In the older parts of cities,

Figure 9.6 A representative example of retail activities that are typical of different levels in the hierarchy of commercial nucleations.

these traditional shopping streets have undergone considerable change over the years in response to the changing social, economic, and ethnic nature of the local neighborhood. If the general level of purchasing power in a neighborhood decreases, then the shopping street may become a "skid row." On the other hand, with gentrification or redevelopment, an older shopping street may begin to reflect the needs and tastes of the newer, wealthier market.

The Nucleations

The third component of the commercial structure of cities is the nucleated shopping center, various types of which are distributed fairly evenly throughout urban areas (Fig. 9.6). In the older, built-up parts of the central city, shopping centers are usually found at the intersection of two or more ribbon developments, where high vehicular and pedestrian traffic intensity provide the focus for their unplanned growth. Accordingly, they are associated with high degrees of centrality, which is reflected in the locational correlation between their presence and peaks of higher land values at street intersections throughout the urban area. In the postwar period, newer planned centers were added to the pattern of the older centers, and there now exists a hierarchy of planned and unplanned nucleations in which the planned component dominates.

The hierarchy of shopping nucleations usually involves five to seven levels, depending on the size and complexity of the metropolis. A fivefold hierarchy, typical of cities in the .5-million population range, is as follows:

1. Isolated store clusters at street corners.
2. Neighborhood nucleations with 50,000–250,000 square feet of retail space.

3. Community level nucleations containing 250,000–500,000 square feet of space.
4. Regional nucleations containing 500,000–1 million square feet of space.
5. Major regional nucleations containing more than 1 million square feet of commercial space.

In a mononucleated city, the central business district is often the largest shopping nucleation and may form a sixth level, but in a polynucleated city it may be just one of a number of major regional nucleations that cater to a particular geographic sector. In Toronto and San Francisco, the central business districts still contain the largest amounts of retail space of all the nucleations in their respective metropolitan areas; however in Los Angeles, the downtown area is at the regional level in the hierarchy.

It should be reemphasized that the number of levels in the hierarchy that may be present in a particular city depends upon the size of the urban area. A large metropolis will have all the levels in a number of complex forms that reflect the socioeconomic structure of the part of the city to which they relate, whereas a smaller and relatively homogeneous urban area may have only three or four. For example, it is evident in many metropolises that there is a hierarchy of retail locations relating primarily to a black community, and another relating to the white, predominantly suburban, population.

Figure 9.6 shows some of the types of retail activities that enter at different levels in the hierarchy. The higher-order nucleations generally have activities particular to their level and to lower levels in the hierarchy. The *streetcorner* developments constitute the most ubiquitous element in the pattern of nucleated centers; they are scattered throughout residential neighborhoods to ensure maximum accessibility to basic goods for consumers residing within a two- to three-block radius of the cluster. They normally comprise from one to four businesses of the lowest-threshold types, and the grocer–drugstore combination is most common.

Neighborhood centers are characterized by the addition of higher-threshold convenience-type stores that supply the major necessities to consumers living in local areas of the city. Grocery stores, small supermarkets, delicatessens, barbershops and beauty salons, taverns, and perhaps small eating places are the most usual business types represented.

Centers at the higher levels in the hierarchy are distinguished by retail shops that are added to the convenience functions of the lower-level centers. In addition, they provide a range of personal, professional, and business services. *Community centers* provide less-specialized shops, such as variety and clothing stores, small furniture and appliance stores, florists, jewelers, and in many cases, a post office. Supplementing these are a range of more ubiquitous services and entertainment facilities.

The highest-level *regional centers* are set above the community centers by the addition of higher-order functions—for example, a branch of a downtown department store—and by greater duplication of functions typical of the lower-level centers. Increased specialization of business types thus becomes the keynote. In addition, a far greater range of services is provided from offices on the upper floors of centers at this level, including a variety of medical services, professional services (architects, lawyers, and real estate agents), specialized training (dance and language), and business services.

The *superregional* centers are much larger than the regional nucleations, and frequently have a number of department stores that provide a full range of retail and service activities. Also, large planned malls contain numerous specialty stores and some exotic forms of recreation. For example, the West Edmonton Mall has more than 4 million square feet of mall space, contains 827 stores and services, and provides about 15,000 (mostly part-time) jobs. It also has an ice rink, a wave tank for wave-riding all year, carnival-type entertainment facilities, and miniature golf putting!

The Hierarchy of Retail Nucleations in Seattle   Morrill (1987) has shown how a hierarchy of nucleations containing retail and service businesses exists in the Seattle metropolitan area, which has a population about 1.6 million. His study involves an analysis of the number of establishments, the general type of activity, and the sales volume in the thirty-four largest nucleations in the metropolitan area. The study is of particular importance because it covers much of the same geographic territory and research methodology as the earlier, classic work of Berry and Garrison (1958a; 1958b). It is therefore possible to see the effect of suburbanization and the growth of planned shopping centers on the hierarchy of nucleations in this urban area over a thirty-year time period.

Is is important to note that the Seattle metropolitan area is polynucleated, as are most large metropolises. In this case the hierarchical structure is, in part, a complex outcome of the merging of a number of cities. Thus, at the highest level, the structure involves the Seattle central business district (Table 9.3), with the Bellevue central business district at the second level and the Everett central

The West Edmonton Mall is the latest example of the extent to which entertainment is included in a super-regional shopping center.

Table 9.3 THE HIERARCHY OF RETAIL NUCLEATIONS
Seattle Metropolitan Area, 1982

Level	Number of nucleations	Average number of retail establishments per nucleation	Average number of service establishments per nucleation	% High level establishments	Weighted average 1982 retail sales per nucleation (millions)
I	1—Seattle CBD	1,420	2,640	43%	$ 925
II	1—Bellevue CBD	500	615	39	470
III	5—Large regional	363	347	33	316
IV	9—Regional	253	227	30	214
V	18—Community	115	120	30	77
Metropolitan area totals:		12,500	15,100	28%	$ 9,140

Source: Data from Morrill (1987, Table 2, pp. 109–110).

business district among five nucleations at a third level described as "large regional." The information in Table 9.3 demonstrates quite clearly that the higher the level of the nucleation, the greater the average number of retail and service establishments per center, the greater the proportion of those establishments that are high level, and the larger the average volume of retail trade per nucleation. With reference to the number of levels in the hierarchy, it is evident that the Seattle metropolitan area must have at least seven or eight levels, as the data presented by Morrill concerns only the larger nucleations.

The structure of this hierarchy of nucleations has changed considerably since the 1950s. In particular, the nucleations in levels III and IV (see Table 9.3) consist primarily of suburban planned regional shopping malls, and it is these that have been growing the fastest in sales volume. In this case, the impact of newer shopping centers and suburbanization is evidenced most clearly at the regional level in the hierarchy of nucleations, with the Seattle central business district declining in relative importance. For example, downtown Seattle provided over 30% of total metropolitan retail trade in 1954, but only 19% in 1982; whereas the five centers at level III increased their share from 7.2% to 9%, and those at level IV increased theirs from 14% to 17%.

Spatial Aspects of Consumer Behavior and Cognition

The basic concepts underlying the notion of a hierarchy of nucleations are that individuals have perfect information about the alternative shopping facilities available to them in the urban environment, and that they act rationally to minimize the total costs (travel and purchase costs) of buying a bundle of goods. The behavioral approach relaxes these assumptions by recognizing that individuals have different values, desires, levels of mobility, and cultural traits, and that these characteristics also influence the spatial structure of retailing. In particular, individuals have varying degrees of knowledge about the availability of goods and services within urban areas, and these various *cognitive images,* or mental maps of retail structure, change in accordance with external stimuli such as advertising and with events particular to each individual, such as life-cycle changes or changing income levels.

As a result, studies of consumer behavior focus on the external and particular factors that influence the cognitive (learned) images that individuals have about the retail structure of urban areas. These two groups of factors are identified for illustrative purposes in Figure 9.7. In Figure 9.7, the possible geographic range of retail alternatives is influenced by two groups of factors. One group consists of the particular characteristics of the consumer as represented by such factors as ethnicity, income, and age. These factors interact with each other to generate different ranges over which an individual consumer may be willing or able to travel for particular goods. For example, Figure 9.8 demonstrates the interaction between income and stage in the life cycle. The older the person and the lower the income, the more restricted the geographical area over which a person will travel to make purchases.

The second group of characteristics identified in Figure 9.7 is composed of the external factors that influence how much a person knows about the retail structure of an urban area and the possible places in which purchases of particular types of goods may be made. These factors fall into two basic groups: (1) sources of information and (2) available experiential information, which is derived from an evaluation of previous information and practice. Individuals with limited sources of information will tend to have more restricted knowl-

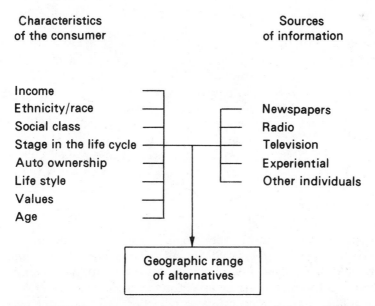

Figure 9.7 The external and particular factors relating to individuals that influence the range of retail alternatives considered by a consumer. (*Source:* Redrawn from Huff, 1960.)

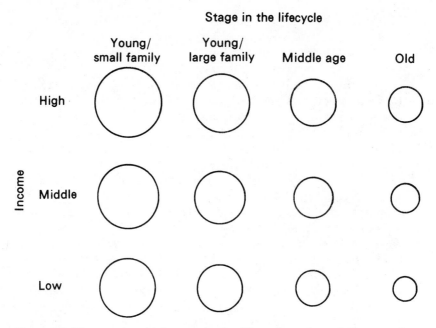

Figure 9.8 The way in which stage in the life cycle and age influences the geographic range of retail activity. (*Source:* Potter, 1982, Fig. 5.9, p. 159.)

edge of the retail opportunities in an urban area. On the other hand, those with a greater variety of information sources will tend to have a much wider range of retail opportunities.

These information factors become particularly important when viewed in the context of the distinctive locations of different racial and income groups in metropolitan areas. The amount of information that people have about different retail opportunities is determined to a large degree by the marketing strategies of stores and shopping centers. Quite often, the retail opportunities in suburban malls are not relayed to those living in the inner city. Likewise, the variety of specialized retail facilities in ethnic areas within the older sections of large metropolises are frequently unknown to those residing in suburban locations.

The Suburbanization of Retailing

As the population of metropolitan areas has decentralized, so has retail trade (Kellerman, 1985; Morrill, 1982). Since 1950, changes in the commercial structure of cities have accelerated (1) in conjunction with suburbanization, and (2) as a result of the increasing polarization of the less wealthy, mainly black and ethnic minority populations, in central cities and the more affluent, mainly white population, in suburban areas. Examples of the phenomenal rate of this decentralization are indicated in Table 9.4. For the largest 159 SMSAs in the

Table 9.4   PERCENT CHANGE IN RETAIL SALES[a]
For Central Cities, Suburbs, and CBDs in the 159 Largest SMSAs, 1972–1977

SMSA group	Whole SMSA	Central city	Suburbs	CBDs
50 largest	7.5 %	− 4.0 %	16%	−22%
Next 72	12.5	3.4	22	−26
Next 37	14.2	10.0	23	−20
All 159	9.0	0.0	19	−23

[a]Calculated from a constant-dollar base.

Source: Morrill (1982, p. 47).

United States, the total volume of retail trade (in constant dollars) that occurred in central cities did not change at all, but suburban retail trade increased by 19%. The amount of retail trade that occurred generally within the central business areas decreased by almost one-quarter in the five-year period that is documented.

There are, however, some significant differences in the rates of change of retail activity in the suburbs and central cities from the largest SMSAs (population greater than 800,000) to the smaller SMSAs. In general, the volume of retail trade in the central cities of the largest of the SMSAs decreased, whereas that of the smaller SMSAs increased. The rate of change in retail trade is therefore related to the size of the metropolis, with the central cities of the largest urban areas experiencing the greatest decreases in volume.

One interesting issue relates to the change in retail trade in central business areas. In a number of large cities—Detroit, Newark, and Oakland being examples of extreme cases—retail activity in the downtown areas has become almost a phenomena of the past. The information in Table 9.5 indicates, however, that in many large metropolitan areas (such as Seattle), the central business district is still the largest focused location of retail activity, although the central business district share of SMSA retail trade volume seldom exceeds 10%. In a number of metropolitan areas (San Jose, Portland, Atlanta, Honolulu, Hawaii, Miami, Buffalo), the largest single focus of retail activity is not the central business district, but a suburban shopping mall. An important feature to note is that the sales volumes of most of the individual central business districts listed in Table 9.5 have been decreasing, whereas those of the suburban malls have been increasing.

The implications of the decentralization documented in this section are important from the point of view of access to services and employment opportunities. Quite obviously, those families and individuals residing in central cities are experiencing a general decrease in accessibility to retail service activities. They are, in effect, becoming disadvantaged with respect to alternatives. For example, in Figure 9.9 it is clear that most of the shopping centers in San Antonio, Texas are located in the wealthier northern sector of the metropolitan

Table 9.5   SALES VOLUMES OF UNITED STATES SHOPPING AREAS, 1977
(In Millions of Dollars)

Rank	City and area	1977 sales	Percent change, 1972–1977	Percent of all SMSA sales
1	New York, Manhattan CBD	$ 2,983	− 29 %	12.0 %
2	Chicago Loop CBD	933	− 22	4.0
3	Philadelphia CBD	838	− 8	6.0
4	San Francisco CBD	831	8	7.0
5	Los Angeles CBD	531	2	2.0
6	Washington CBD	476	− 27	4.0
7	Boston CBD	464	− 24	5.0
8	San Jose, Valley Fair	421	210	8.0
9	Pittsburgh CBD	412	− 13	6.0
10	New Orleans CBD	409	− 16	11.0
11	New York, Brooklyn CBD	361	− 36	1.5
12	Portland, Beaverton	342	300[a]	8.0
13	Minneapolis CBD	325	− 19	5.0
14	Atlanta, Lennox Square	315	128	4.0
15	Cleveland CBD	314	− 19	5.0
16	Honolulu, Waikiki	307	29	12.0
17	Honolulu, Ala Moana	307	1	12.0
18	Los Angeles, Beverly Hills	304	38	1.3
19	Houston CBD	293	− 16	3.0
20	San Jose, Cherry Chase	293	[b]	6.0
21	Seattle CBD	289	2	5.0
22	San Jose, Old Mill	288	235	6.0
23	Atlanta, Cumberland Mall	276	[b]	4.0
24	Chicago, Woodfield Mall	273	34	1.3
25	Atlanta CBD	271	− 40	4.0
26	Louisville CBD	271	− 19	9.0
27	Pittsburgh, Monroeville Mall	262	126	4.0
28	Cincinnati CBD	260	− 21	5.5
29	Santa Ana, South Coast Plaza	252	95	3.0
32	Birmingham CBD	245	− 10	9.0
33	Dallas CBD	243	0	2.0
34	Detroit CBD	242	− 41	1.5
37	San Antonio CBD	231	− 6	7.5
40	Des Moines CBD	228	26	17.0
46	St. Louis CBD	219	− 19	3.0
47	Denver CBD	210	—[c]	4.0
52	Newark CBD	205	− 36	3.0
53	Miami CBD	200	3	4.0
60	Baltimore CBD	194	− 33	3.0
69	Spokane CBD	186	− 4	15.0
75	Indianapolis CBD	181	− 27	4.0
80	Boise CBD	176	3	27.0
84	Milwaukee CBD	176	− 23	4.0

[a]This figure is an estimate.

[b]CBD areas for 1972 and 1977 are not comparable.

[c]No data are available, due to disclosure rule.

Source: Morrill (1982, p. 48).

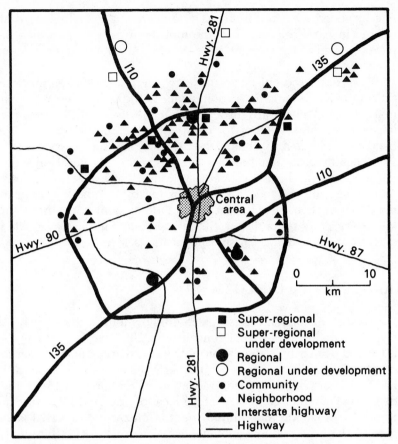

Figure 9.9 The location of planned shopping centers in San Antonio, Texas. (*Source:* Redrawn from Dawson, 1983, Fig. 22, p. 25.)

area, and all the large super-regional malls are arrayed along the belt-line freeway serving the suburban communities. The newer major shopping centers are also in the northern sector. Retail activities are one of the biggest generators of employment in urban areas, particularly for women. It is therefore of particular concern that opportunities for employment in retail activities in central cities are declining, whereas those in the wealthier suburbs are increasing. In effect, it is the access of minority women to retail employment opportunities (albeit part-time) that is decreasing.

The Location of Supermarkets One aspect of retail activity that illustrates not only the effect of the spreading out of the market, but also the effect of the changing corporate structure of retailing, is the supermarket. Lee and McCracken (1982) show that in Denver between 1960 and 1980, supermarkets became more decentralized, in a clustered fashion. They also increased in size but decreased in number. These changing spatial patterns and sizes are related in part to the shift in the industry from one in which independents played a significant role (in 1960) to one in which the chains dominated (in 1980).

The "dispersed-but-in clusters" arrangement is related to the decentralization of the market and to the dominance of the chains. Individual supermarkets in a particular chain are dispersed, but the stores of different chains tend to locate close to each other for competitive reasons. Also, as the industry has become dominated by chains, the range of goods and services sold within the stores has increased and the floor area has become larger. Hence the stores have become more and more concentrated in discrete spatial locations around the metropolis, and the industry is dominated by the marketing strategies of the major national chains. The location of employment opportunities in supermarkets is therefore quite dispersed, but it is becoming less available in the inner city and more available in specific locations within the suburbs.

THE LOCATION OF OFFICE EMPLOYMENT

One of the major features of office employment is that it is heavily concentrated, spatially. This spatial concentration has two features: (1) Employment is located primarily in the major metropolitan areas, and (2) a large part of this employment is located in central business or downtown areas, although there has been considerable decentralization of certain office activities in recent decades. The chief centers of office location, defined by Armstrong (1979) as those places having total employment in office activities that is 25% or more greater than the national average, are New York City, Chicago, Los Angeles, Washington, D.C., Boston, Atlanta, and Toronto. These are the places that provide office activities not only to serve the needs of their own metropolitan areas, but to serve significant parts of the United States, Canada, and the rest of the world as well. The New York SMSA, in particular, has more than 10% of the total United States employment in office activities, although the share has decreased considerably over the past few decades.

The second feature of office location, despite all the discussion of decentralization, is that the largest share of office employment and space remains in central business areas (Code, 1985). For example, Manhattan has about one-half (1.2 million jobs) of the total office employment in the New York SMSA, and over 8.4 million square meters (90 million square feet) of office space (Bateman, 1985; Schwartz, 1979). Furthermore, there has been significant construction of new office space in Manhattan during the 1980s, such as Olympia and York's "World Financial Center," which provides more than .5 million square meters (6 million square feet) of additional space. It must be emphasized, however, that considerable office employment has relocated from the New York area to contiguous counties and states and even farther afield. For example, Westchester County, to the northeast of New York City, has 2.32 million square meters (25 million square feet) of office space and total office employment of more than 400,000.

Principles of Office Location A review of the literature indicates that four basic themes underlie the theory of office location (Clapp, 1980; Goddard, 1975; Lichtenberg, 1960). These principles are: contact intensity, contact variety, employee accessibility, and decentralization. Some of these principles act in concert, whereas others counteract each other to a degree. The first three of these principles help to explain why the central business areas of major metropolises remain a strong foci of office activities, whereas the fourth may at times act together with the third to give rise to the suburbanization of some office functions.

The Principle of Contact Intensity A major theme underlying many office location studies is that certain types of office occupations tend to be attracted to locations that have the greatest accessibility to contacts. This is not meant to imply that all workers in the office need this large number of contacts, but the managers and officers who bring in the business need them. Thus, the greater the contact needs of an occupation, the greater the attraction to centers of intensive contact activity. Gad (1979) demonstrates that the office activities with the greatest need for contacts with others in downtown locations are: law firms, public relations consultants, banks, trust companies, insurance agents, and investment dealers. Most of these activities have to do with financial or securities functions, hence this broad class of activity remains tied to central business district locations because the major players like to meet personally to discuss deals and obtain information.

   The social structure of the central business district has become oriented toward facilitating face-to-face contact, particularly over lunch hour. Mens clubs, sports clubs, and restaurants in downtown areas are geared for this type of social–business activity during the day. Many women quite rightly suggest that in this type of male-structured social–business environment they suffer certain business disadvantages. As a consequence, there has been a strong effort in recent years to change this male business lifestyle to accommodate women business colleagues, and also for women to establish social networks of their own.

The Principle of Contact Variety If the principle of contact intensity is taken as given, then certain occupational groups appear to have a greater need for a wide variety of contacts than others. This is, for example, particularly true of law firms, public relations consultants, real estate developers, and insurance agencies. Lawyers, for example, not only need to meet clients and other lawyers, but also experts such as appraisers and accountants. It is evident that the location with the largest variety of possible contacts is the downtown area.

The Principle of Employee Accessibility A third theme underlying most office location studies is that firms will tend to locate where they have good access to skilled and reasonable-cost labor. In this context, turnover costs are particularly important, and firms try to reduce turnover costs either by good labor policies and/or by having good access to easily substitutable labor. Central locations in urban areas are therefore preferred, particularly if these locations are well served by public transit facilities. A large proportion of the office labor force is female, and women tend to have less access to automobiles than do males. It is therefore not surprising that those urban areas with adequate public transit systems tend to have a large proportion of office employment in central locations.

Nelson (1986) demonstrates that as office activities become functionally more complex and use computer networks, a number of office activities have become decentralized ("back offices") in order to gain access to lower-wage female labor located in the suburbs. Her study pertains to the Walnut Creek–Concord, California area, which is essentially a suburb of San Francisco. A number of functions related to customer accounts and billing are located in office buildings constructed adjacent to freeways in order to gain the advantages of low rents and large supply of well-educated female labor that is located in this rapidly growing outer suburban area.

The Principle of Decentralization   Since 1960 an increasing proportion of new office space and employment in metropolitan areas has been in suburban locations, especially in the smaller SMSAs and CMAs. Suburban Atlanta, for example, had only one suburban office park in 1964; ten years later there were forty suburban office parks, and now there are nearly one hundred. In most urban areas, new office complexes have developed at locations adjacent to airports, regional shopping malls, and at freeway interchanges. Thus, the principle of decentralization states that in those urban areas where there is a highly dispersed population and a well-developed peripheral freeway system, decentralization is fostered and the suburbanization of offices occurs.

There are many reasons why offices are gravitating to the suburbs. Economic forces play an important role. Land is generally cheaper and property taxes lower, resulting in savings in rental costs of as much as 20% at suburban locations as compared with downtown. But although these savings are important, the dominant component in the economics of running an office is the cost of labor. Although wage rates are not significantly different between central city and suburban locations, commuting costs certainly are. Given the overwhelming preference by white-collar employees for commuting by automobile, peripheral locations are more accessible to the suburban labor pool of most cities. Since a high proportion of office workers are women, suburban locations also maximize proximity to the better-educated female labor pool.

As with most situations, the suburbanization of office activities has a number of positive and negative consequences. These are classified in Table 9.6 as economic, social, and environmental. In general, the positive consequences may be presumed to outweigh the negative, for if they did not the suburbanization of office activities would not be so prevalent.

The Impact of New Technologies on Office Location   The recent technological revolution has had a large impact on communication and information flows. Offices are places at which information is produced, channeled, sorted, and processed. Hence it is not surprising that a whole variety of communication technologies are influencing how office activities are accomplished (Goddard

Table 9.6 SOME POSITIVE AND NEGATIVE CONSEQUENCES OF THE SUBURBANIZATION OF OFFICE ACTIVITIES

Economic		Social		Environmental	
Positive	Negative	Positive	Negative	Positive	Negative
Reduces operating overheads (rent, taxes)	Induces lower-density space use, reduces operating savings	Reduces average journey to work times for CBD and inner-city workers	Increases journey to work times of some suburban workers	Improved building design	Extensive unimaginative groundlevel parking lots
Availability of cheaper labor	Increases wage-rates in local labor market	Increases use of private transport for journey to work	Reduces use of public transport for journey to work	Landscaped development	Extensive sprawl of large areas of suburban land at low-use intensity
Stimulates female participation rates	Extends labor market areas	More comfortable and pleasant working conditions	Limited access to other services during working hours	Upgrades existing suburban commercial centers	Increases congestion in established suburban centers
Diversifies suburban business activities	Strengthens differences among development prospects of suburban areas	Increases residential amenities	Raises house prices in accessible suburban residential areas	Reduces pedestrian–transport conflict	Sterility of large parking lots
Increased suburban growth prospects	Mainly routine functions located in suburbs				

Source: From Daniels (1985, p. 223); modified by the author.

and Pye, 1977). The questions invariably boil down to: "Which aspects of office activities are influenced most, locationally?" and "To what extent do the new communications technologies substitute for the face-to-face contact requirements underlying the principles of contact intensity and contact variety?"

There are, perhaps, four stages in the spatial aspects of the evolution of office activities that are heavily information-oriented (Nilles *et al.,* 1976). These stages are presented in diagrammatic form in Figure 9.10:

> **Stage 1** is represented by two corporate headquarters in which information-oriented activities are predominantly centralized. This mode existed until the mid-1960s.

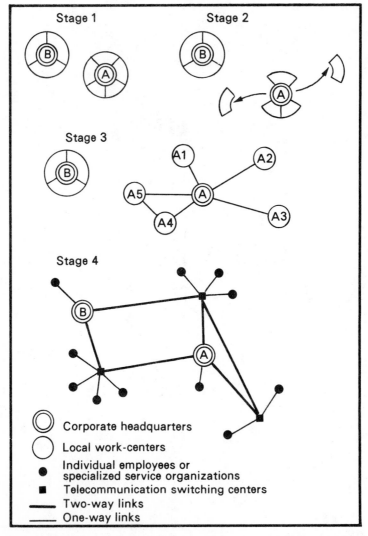

Figure 9.10 The evolution of the spatial structure of an organization utilizing innovations in communications technology. (*Source:* Redrawn from Nilles *et al.,* 1976, Fig. 2.1, p. 12.)

Stage 2 was achieved when one of the two headquarters (A) decided to decentralize some of the functional units of the office, such as accounting. Telecommunications and ground shuttle transportation served to maintain communications links.

Stage 3 commenced in the mid-1970s with the widespread use of computers as well as normal telecommunications technology. The corporate headquarters (A) decentralized more of its functions to "back office" locations but maintained contact through a network that focused primarily on the base. The computer network became the major means of transmitting information, although the shuttles were still necessary.

Stage 4 is predicted by the mid-1980s. Widespread spatial fragmentation of office functions occurrs, with firms cooperating in the maintenance of shared information networks and shuttle services, as well as providing their own network for more confidential flows. In terms of residential locations, employees begin to cluster around the particular facilities in which they are working. In theory, therefore, a system is in place such that the actual physical headquarters office is run by a small group of senior personnel who require face-to-face contact and the associated technical and support staff, while routine office functions are located in suburban areas or other parts of the country.

It should be noted that although this decentralized scenario is possible, it does not appear to be occurring as rapidly as some have predicted. This is because (1) there is a vast physical investment in central-city infrastructure that cannot be discarded, (2) the basic locational principles remain powerful and foster office locations in the central business districts, and (3) the power structure of office management often requires that upper-level management and associated staff be as physically close to the headquarters offices as possible. Thus, the heads of different functional units, such as accounting, invoicing, and marketing, often resist decentralization because it may also mean a loss of personal influence.

Conclusion

The location of employment opportunities in manufacturing, retail activities, and offices has therefore changed considerably over the past few decades. In general, the location of employment in these different types of industries is now reflecting the polynucleated structure of the city. This is particularly true of retail activities, in which consumer demand and purchasing power determine the location of shopping centers and malls. With respect to manufacturing activities, it is evident that this type of employment is located more frequently in decentralized clusters and in peripherally dispersed locations. The only type of employment that remains to a considerable extent in central locations is employment derived from office activities. In this case, there are strong forces fostering both centralization and decentralization.

The modern North American metropolis has therefore become an environment in which employment opportunities are widely dispersed. An important consideration resulting from this employment dispersion has to do with the general spatial distribution of the availability of different types of employment opportunities, and with the general socioeconomic structure of the metropolis. Manufacturing jobs are generally increasing in the suburbs and decreasing in the central city. Jobs in retail activities are increasing in the suburbs and decreasing in the central city. Employment in office activities remains fairly high in the central business areas of most central cities, although there is considerable decentralization. However, many United States cities now have a socioeconomic structure in which a large proportion of the black population resides in the inner city, close to the office jobs for which that population may be largely untrained, and some distance from the suburban jobs in manufacturing and retailing. The net result is a spatial mismatch, known in the literature as the "mismatch hypothesis," with the white population having relatively good access to suburban employment opportunities and downtown office jobs, and the black population having much more limited access to a wide range of employment opportunities (Wilson, 1979).

Chapter
10

Managing Cities

Local government issues impinge directly upon everyone's daily life. In those places where people live in a hostile and dangerous environment, such as in parts of many United States inner cities, the underlying cause of the hostility is the disparity between that community's living conditions and those of the rest of society (Fox, 1986). It is one of the main tasks of urban government to ensure that the services and opportunities over which it has jurisdiction are available to *all* the inhabitants of an urban area.

Much of the discussion in this book has revolved around the broad theme of decentralization. This theme is extremely important, for since 1970 the United States and Canada have become suburbanized to an extent that was rarely thought of even in the mid-1950s. Although it is tempting to consider these suburban areas as outer cities with characteristics somewhat independent from those in the inner city, a corollary to the major theme of decentralization is that the suburbs are linked to the central city and that the future of the North American city depends on a more coordinated management of all its parts, suburbs included.

DISPARITIES BETWEEN INNER AND OUTER CITIES

The chief reason for the confusion between the inner city and the outer city is the lack of any clear definition. *Inner city* has been used throughout this text to mean the area that conforms geographically to the political limits of the old central city at the core of the metropolis. It is apparent, however, that even in spatial terms this definition can be misleading, for older central cities are by no means homogeneous. What is important is whether there are distinct differences between inner cities and outer cities, and whether any disparity that exists is changing.

In Table 10.1 seven measures that illustrate the differences between central cities and suburbs in the largest metropolises in the United States are presented. Although they show that one in five persons in central cities is black and that the concentration of blacks has been increasing, they also show that four out of five persons are not black. Thus, to characterize central cities as consisting predominantly of blacks may be true in a few cases, but not in all. The suburbs, however, are overwhelmingly white!

As far as the young and elderly—the more dependent segments of society—are concerned, it is evident that the suburbs have a greater proportion of households with children than the central cities, and that the central cities have a greater proportion of households that are elderly. However, with respect to these two criteria, central-city and noncentral-city areas are becoming more alike.

The great differences between central cities and suburbs are represented in the financial information. On a per capita basis, suburban areas are 15%

Table 10.1   SELECTED MEASURES OF DISPARITY BETWEEN CENTRAL CITIES AND SUBURBS
United States, 1970–1980

	Central city		Outside central city	
	1970	1980	1970	1980
% population black[a]	17.9	21.4	4.0	5.5
% household with own children (718)[a]	38.5	33.1	49.9	41.3
% households elderly[a]	23.2	22.7	19.3	19.7
Per capita income[a]		$ 6,972		7,989
Average household income[a]		$14,601		20,270
Per capita education expense[b]	$171	408	205	461
Total aid per capita[b]	$149	633	131	442

[a]85 largest SMSAs.

[b]65 largest SMSAs.

Source: Advisory Commission on Intergovernmental Relations (1984), *Fiscal Disparities: Central Cities and Suburbs, 1981.* Washington, D.C.: ACIR, extracted from Tables 1, 2, 3, 5.

wealthier than central cities, and on a household basis they are almost 40% wealthier. This latter disparity is particularly disheartening because households usually include dependents under the age of 18 years, and it is quite evident that the children of the central cities are significantly disadvantaged. The consequences of this disparity in income levels are demonstrated by indicators relating to education and to government aid: Per capita education expenditures are 13% greater in the suburbs, although the gap is decreasing. On the other hand, total aid per capita is 27% greater in the central cities than in the suburbs.

There is, however, considerable variation across the United States in the relative health of particular central cities and suburbs. Although central-city incomes in large metropolises in the East, Midwest, and South tend to be below the national average, those in the Southwest and West tend to be above it (Table 10.2). Furthermore, the central cities of the East, Midwest, and South are continuing to lose jobs, and those in the Southwest and West are gaining them.

METROPOLITAN FINANCE

What is needed to address issues related to or derived from these disparities are governmental policies, whether at the federal, state/provincial, or local level. In some cases, the issues can be tackled by the addition of new rules or the alteration of existing ones, such as those involving building codes and zoning ordinances. Increasingly, however, the issues can be tackled only by larger investments in facilities and services, support for needy people, and the payment of subsidies to achieve specified goals. The extent to which these policies are possible depends not only on the willingness of governments to implement corrective policies, but also on their ability to do so. The problem of providing adequate public services, therefore, depends in part on the political climate of the time, the structure of local government finance, and the increasing demands of local municipalities.

At the outset we must recognize the different constitutional frameworks operating in Canada and the United States. In the Canadian version of federalism, the provincial governments have limited but explicit powers, and Parliament (the federal government) has powers relating to the common interests of the nation as a whole and any residual powers not explicitly granted to the provinces. In the United States, the federal government has quite explicit powers as stated in the Constitution and defined by subsequent amendments and Supreme Court decisions, and the states have general and residual powers relating to their particular geographical jurisdictions. These differences have important repercussions with respect to local government.

In Canada, the British North America Act of 1867 states explicitly that provincial legislatures have sovereignty over municipal institutions, and since the 1950s, as the country has become more urbanized, the provincial governments have been paying more attention to municipalities and their problems. In the United States the Constitution does not mention governments below the

Table 10.2   SOME INDICES OF DISPARITY BETWEEN SELECTED UNITED STATES
CENTRAL CITIES AND SUBURBS, AND UNWEIGHTED AVERAGES,
1970–1980

SMSA and region	% of SMSA pop. in city		Index of income disparity		% Change in city jobs	
	1970	1980	1970	1980	1966–1970	1970–1980
Washington, D.C.	0.26%	0.22%	0.84	0.86	8.2%	− 9.8%
Boston	0.23	0.21	0.79	0.78	− 4.0	− 4.4
Buffalo	0.34	0.28	0.85	0.79	−15.8	−21.6
New York	0.68	0.65	0.84	0.79	− 1.9	− 6.9
Philadelphia	0.40	0.35	0.83	0.72	− 4.1	−17.3
Newark	0.20	0.19	0.56	0.50	−12.5	−26.6
Chicago	0.50	0.42	0.80	0.79	−12.1	−11.5
Columbus	0.59	0.58	0.81	0.88	20.5	23.0
Wichita	0.71	0.68	1.11	1.16	21.2	28.8
Detroit	0.35	0.30	0.80	0.69	−18.8	−30.3
Minneapolis	0.36	0.32	0.92	0.85	−19.0	−13.3
St. Louis	0.26	0.20	0.78	0.74	−14.2	−27.0
Birmingham	0.40	0.35	0.84	0.77	5.7	− 2.8
Miami	0.26	0.21	0.77	0.64	7.4	24.2
Atlanta	0.35	0.25	0.84	0.74	19.5	−20.0
Tulsa	0.65	0.57	1.35	1.54	35.4	32.7
Corpus Christi	0.71	0.71	1.34	1.19	16.0	50.4
Dallas	0.54	0.46	1.09	1.01	41.2	19.7
Phoenix	0.60	0.52	1.00	0.95	51.1	56.6
Los Angeles	0.45	0.44	1.03	1.02	5.4	24.0
San Francisco	0.34	0.31	0.95	0.82	5.6	0.3
Denver	0.41	0.31	1.02	0.90	19.6	4.6
Albuquerque	0.77	0.79	1.44	1.24	25.8	80.1
Seattle	0.41	0.34	1.07	1.03	15.2	12.0

Source: Advisory Commission on Intergovernmental Relations (1984), *Fiscal Disparities: Central Cities and Suburbs, 1981.* Washington, D.C.: ACIR, extracted from Tables A-33, A-7, A-2.

state level; consequently, matters and responsibilities relating to local government have been defined by usage, law, and court decision. One interesting result is that state constitutions are now filled with protective devices for local governments, consisting primarily of protections against excessive interference by state governments into the affairs of local municipalities.

Although these differences may not appear all that significant at this juncture, it will become evident that a major result of the differences is that it is far easier to reform local government in Canada than in the United States. Canadian provincial legislatures can implement new forms of local government and change the functions of local government through the actions of provincial parliaments, and although they might not want to antagonize too many voters in a local area, the majority party is responsible to the province as a whole, not just to a particular municipality. In the United States, such direct action for reform is far more difficult at the state level, for state governments will not act unless they are assured of majority support in the areas to be affected by the proposed governmental restructuring. Thus, changes in the structure and finance of local government in response to the urbanization, metropolitanization, and megalopolitanization of the population are more possible in Canada than in the United States because of the different constitutional frameworks within which both countries operate. Change in local government is not impossible in the United States, however.

The Changing Role of Local Government

One essential feature to understand with respect to the fiscal problems faced by many local governments is that although the responsibilities of municipalities have expanded greatly since the turn of the century, the sources of finance have not widened to a comparable extent. Although the role of the federal and state/provincial governments in alleviating social problems has increased dramatically in the present century, the responsibility of local governments for matters of social concern has increased at least as much. In fact, the relative importance of local governments as providers of services is greater in Canada and the United States than in any other major country.

Local Government at the End of the Nineteenth Century

This situation is in stark contrast to the situation at the turn of the century, when local governments had generally small budgets and played a relatively minor role in the economic, cultural, and social lives of cities. The one exception was in education. School districts were created as independent units because of the conviction that public education should have its own financial base and be independent of the policies and politics of other local government units, such as the municipalities and counties.

At the turn of the century, urban residents generally had little desire to participate in local government. As a result, participation was delegated to those individuals who were prepared to undertake the administration of the developing urban areas. In many instances these individuals undertook the responsibility in order to attain the rewards associated with positions of power. This power was maintained in a comparatively democratic system through the judicious usage of patronage, influence, and bribery. During this period, for example, the leaders of Tammany Hall tended to regard the direction of New York City as a personal commercial venture.

At the time, therefore, it was not considered that local governments should guide and stimulate the development of the city. Although a body of laws had been established concerned with restricting private property rights, particularly those relating to offensive trades and industries in residential areas, these laws were seldom enforced. In fact, the *laissez-faire* doctrine as applied to government of any form was "the less, the better." As enunciated by President

Grover Cleveland in his second inaugural address, this meant that although "the people should patriotically and cheerfully support their government, its functions do not include the support of the people."

A Period of Change

From 1910 to 1935 the responsibilities of local government grew as their service functions expanded and extended into new areas. At the same time, the urban community began to demand more of its local government. Continuing urban expansion, changes in technology, and the growth of the national economy translated themselves into more public expenditures, taxes, and governmental intervention. As a result of the now-widespread use of the automobile, fundamental changes were taking place in the form and structure of cities. Extensive programs were needed to deal with the construction of new streets and roads, street lighting, water lines and sanitary sewers, storm drainage systems, and electrical networks. The responsibility for much of this activity lay with local governments. In addition, the continually rising incomes and expectations resulted in a greater demand for schools, hospitals, and better law enforcement and fire prevention: Local governments were increasingly being forced by the electorate to encourage and promote privately owned and operated facilities in addition to public ones.

A major stimulus to the changing power and responsibility of local government was the Great Depression, which shattered established procedures for government action. The economic collapse increased popular demand for positive action by all levels of government to alleviate the crisis. These pressures were felt most acutely at the local level, and the inherent weaknesses of the administrative and financial structures of local government rapidly became apparent. Most local governments were in a relatively weak financial position because the capital costs incurred in the growth of their service function had largely been financed by borrowing. In fact, between 1913 and the early 1930s, the yearly interest payments alone on loans to local governments in the United States rose from $167 million to a staggering $1.5 billion. The actions of the federal government in Washington, D.C. had to be extended in order to alleviate the ever-increasing problems, for the financial power of most local governments was severely limited.

The Present Situation

Despite considerable spatial variations in the extent of their obligations and responsibilities, particularly between Canada and the United States, local governments have their own corporate powers, including the right to obtain and dispose of property and the authority to provide services and to enforce regulations, especially zoning ordinances and building controls. Local governments have the power to raise revenue by imposing charges or collecting taxes. Many municipalities now function as agents of social change through the enforcement of fair-housing and public-accommodation laws. Today, more than ever before, local governments in both Canada and the United States have a direct effect on people's lives through taxation and the delivery of a wide array of services.

Since World War II, both the financial responsibilities of local government and their number have been increasing at a rapid rate. Since 1950, state and local governments have been the fastest-growing sectors of the national economy. Whereas the United States' GNP is three times larger than it was twenty years ago, state and local government expenditures have increased sixfold in the same period. Today, nearly two-thirds of the total expenditure is made in metropolitan areas. This rise in public expenditure is related to rising price levels and to the increased population of urban areas, but it has occurred mostly because the scope and quality of state and local government services have been greatly expanded. For an increasingly large segment of the urban population, the activities of local governments are decisive factors in determining the quality of life in the city.

The Range of Local Government Responsibilities

The range of administrative, service, and social activities undertaken by municipalities in the North American region is immense. Although large municipalities have assumed a wider range of responsibilities than small ones, a general outline of the activities undertaken by most municipalities is as listed in Table 10.3. This list is not meant to imply that all local governments, particularly those with small populations, undertake all these functions. Moreover, although the allocation of expenditures reflects a changing emphasis on social concerns—as shown by the increase in the share of expenditures allocated to housing versus the large decrease in relative expenditures on highways—the effect of rapidly accumulating deficits and the increased expenditures on utilities demonstrates the pressure being placed on municipal budgets. One feature that should be noted is the increased share devoted to servicing debts.

The Sources of Local Government Revenue

National, state/provincial, and local governments are keen competitors for the tax dollar, and over the years a rough division of revenue sources has developed among the three tiers of government. The federal governments of both the United States and Canada raise the vast bulk of their revenue from personal-income, corporation, payroll, and sales or excise taxes. They are able to impose relatively high rates of taxation because the respective national territories are completely under their jurisdiction. Many of the states, and all of the Canadian provinces, also raise revenue through state/provincial income taxes, sales taxes, and other devices such as lotteries.

Smaller geographical units, such as municipalities, cannot take full advantage of these sources of revenue, either because they are not allowed to do so (such as with income taxes) or because they are afraid to do so in an economic system in which people, businesses, and capital can move relatively freely from one municipality to another. A disproportionate levy of sales taxes among adja-

Table 10.3 EXPENDITURES BY MUNICIPALITIES IN THE UNITED STATES, 1965 AND 1985[a]

Activity	Expenditure (in billions)		Percent		Comparative change, 1965–1985
	1985	1965	1985	1965	
Police protection	$ 12.5	$ 1.7	9.2 %	8.2 %	12.2 %
Fire protection	6.8	1.1	5.0	5.3	− 5.7
Highways	8.7	1.8	6.4	8.7	−26.4
Sewage, etc.	11.4	1.8	8.4	8.7	− 3.4
Public welfare	5.7	0.9	4.2	4.3	− 2.3
Education	11.4	2.5	8.4	12.1	−30.5
Libraries	1.3	0.2	1.0	1.0	0.0
Health and hospitals	6.6	1.1	4.9	5.3	− 7.5
Parks and recreation	5.0	0.8	3.7	3.9	− 5.1
Housing, etc.	5.1	0.7	3.8	3.4	11.7
Airports	1.7	0.2	1.3	1.0	30.0
Utilities	29.5	4.0	21.8	19.3	12.9
Interest	6.8	0.6	5.0	2.9	72.4
Administration	6.1	1.0	4.6	4.8	− 4.1
Other	16.6	2.3	12.3	11.1	10.8
TOTAL	$ 135.2	$ 20.7	100.0 %	100.0 %	

[a]The dollar values do not indicate all the money from all sources that is devoted to a particular activity. Other revenue may be derived for some activities (such as hospitals) from a share of the property tax or state/provincial transfers.

Source: U.S. Bureau of the Census, *City Government Finances,* series GF No. 4, annual.

cent municipalities, for example, could well encourage people and businesses to move to, or shop in, those municipalities in which the tax is lower. Thus, although municipalities do differ in their sales tax levies, the differences are usually not excessive.

Consequently, municipalities raise or receive revenue from a variety of sources (Table 10.4), among which the most important are property taxes and direct transfers from state/provincial governments. In Canada, municipalities receive, on average, between 80% and 85% of their revenue from property taxes and the various provincial governments; in the United States, property and state taxes account for just over one-half of the revenues, excluding utility revenues, which are on a direct-user charge basis. The reason for the lower proportion in the United States is that municipalities there have greater constitutional freedoms than their counterparts in Canada and have implemented a greater variety of local taxes.

The Property Tax

The property tax is essentially agrarian in origin and has been the basis of local government support since municipalities became legally established in both Canada and the United States. It is still the most productive source of revenue

Table 10.4   THE SOURCES OF REVENUE RECEIVED BY MUNICIPALITIES
United States, 1965 and 1985

Source	Amount received ($ billions)		Percent		Comparative change, 1965–1985
	1985	1965	1985	1965	
State governments	$ 23.1	$ 2.8	17.1%	13.8%	23.9%
Local property tax	23.5	6.5	17.4	32.0	−45.6
Local sales taxes	13.9	1.8	10.3	8.9	15.7
Local licenses	10.3	1.0	7.6	4.9	55.0
Local direct charges	31.1	3.1	23.0	15.3	50.3
Utility revenue	26.4	3.9	19.6	19.2	2.0
Other	6.7	1.2	5.0	5.9	−18.0
TOTAL	135.0	20.3	100.0	100.0	

Source: U.S. Bureau of the Census, City Government Finances, series GE No. 4, annual.

in North America after federal income and excise taxes. Although its importance to local governments has declined in recent decades, it nevertheless still accounts for about one-sixth of the income of all municipalities in the United States and over one-third of the income of urban governments in Canada.

The relative importance of the property tax varies markedly from city to city and often varies among municipalities in the same metropolitan area. For example, in New York City, the property tax provided 20% of total revenue in 1985, whereas in Boston property taxes contributed almost 30%. On the West Coast, the city of San Francisco receives 14% of its total revenue from property taxes, whereas the city of Los Angeles gets only 9% of its revenue from that particular source. In Canada, the city of Toronto gains 48% of its revenue from property taxes, whereas Calgary receives less than 30% from this source.

Taxes levied on property are a good and sound measure of taxation as long as the value of the property is fairly assessed and the property itself is a true measure of an individual's or family's wealth. But it has become widely understood that this is not the case, particularly when taxes are also imposed on income at the federal and state/provincial levels. Local property taxes have therefore become decidedly unpopular, and are considered to be the most unfair tax in the fiscal system. The property tax is unpopular because it is imposed at relatively high rates in real money terms. Although property-tax bills average only between 2% and 3% of the market value of the property, this average corresponds to a flat-rate income tax of 10% or more after exemptions, and when applied to commercial property, often to a sales tax of 25% or more.

The property tax is also a regressive tax (Bird and Slack, 1983). The burden, expressed as a percentage of income, is much higher for low-income people than for the wealthy because housing is such a large component of consumer spending for low-income groups. Netzer (1974) estimates that whereas the property tax on owner-occupied, single-family houses averaged 4.9% of family income in the United States, it was twice as high for the lowest-income homeowners (7.3%) as it was for those in the higher-income groups, for whom the tax averaged less than 3.7%. In a detailed study of property tax and household income in Guelph, cited in the 1972 Ontario budget statement, it was determined that whereas low-income families paid 5% or more of their income in property taxes, high-income families paid 3% or less of their income in property taxes. It is therefore not surprising that in many urban areas middle- and low-income homeowners are overwhelmingly supportive of initiatives designed to stabilize or lower the property-tax rate.

Non-Property Taxes

Faced with rising costs and mounting public needs, local governments have been forced to tap sources of revenue other than the property tax. Since World War II, taxes have been levied by local governments on a range of things, including motor vehicles, gasoline, business gross receipts, cigarettes, alcoholic beverages, payrolls, and retail sales. Only the last two have provided a significant source of revenue, and their use has been restricted mainly to the large central cities of metropolitan areas.

The municipal payroll has proven to be a significant source of revenue in those central cities where it has been introduced, including New York City, Philadelphia, St. Louis, and Baltimore. In New York City, receipts from the levy amount to about 10% of the total revenue received. As the system is commonly employed, residents are taxed on income regardless of source, and nonresidents are taxed on that portion of their income earned within the central city levying the tax. The main attraction of the tax for the central cities is that it enables them to exploit a source of extraterritorial revenue. This revenue is from commuters who work in the central city but reside in the suburbs and for whom the central-city government provides services and facilities that they would otherwise enjoy without contributing toward their cost.

The local sales tax is another important source of non–property-tax revenues and is now used by more than 2,000 local governments. As with the municipal payroll tax, it enables municipalities to tap nonresidents for revenue, and it has the additional advantages of revenue productivity and ease of administration. Like the property tax, however, it is decidedly regressive and a general nuisance to the shopper. Moreover, in certain situations it can penalize local merchants, because in a large metropolitan area consumers are often able to avoid the levy by shopping in adjacent territories. For these reasons, the proportionate contribution of sales taxes to total revenues has been declining, and local governments have been attempting to compensate for this loss by raising the charges for business, commercial, and other licenses. The effect of the costs of licenses on prices is not nearly as visible to the consumer as are sales taxes.

Service Charges

A third major source of local government revenue is comprised of the charges levied on the users of public services and utilities. In the case of utilities, including water, electricity, gas, and public transit, the revenues provide about one-fifth of the money received by local governments. The direct-user charges for these utilities do not cover the entire cost of their provision. For example, about 75% of the local government cost of supplying water and 20% of the outlays for refuse collection and transportation (excluding highway construction), is recouped from user charges. Service charges are based on the quantity of service used or the benefits received by urban residents. In one sense they can be thought of as regressive, but so are telephone service charges imposed by the private sector. The charges may be justified, however, when individuals can decide just how much or how little of a particular service they want to use. There is a certain minimum level of service required by all urban residents, regardless of income, so in many cases the consumer is not required to pay for the full cost of the service, such as with public transit.

Service charges cannot be applied to all local public services. They are inappropriate, for example, in the case of *pure public goods;* that is, services that no one can be denied, whether they pay for them or not, and for which the benefits to one person do not in any way preclude enjoyment of the same benefits by others. An example is the visual attractiveness of open space and parks. Service charges are also inappropriate for redistributive activities, and whenever the service provides social rather than private benefits. Thus, although the costs of financing libraries could be defrayed in part by user charges, libraries are financed from taxes because they serve an educational, and hence social, function.

User charges are also difficult to apply when cost–benefit relationships are inexactly specified, as in the case of pollution control. Consequently, opportunities for imposing service charges are considerably more restricted than for levying taxes, and they are best used when private needs are being satisfied (particularly when there would otherwise be significant waste, as with unmetered water). Although there is undoubtedly scope for intensifying the use of service charges, and some public-finance experts argue that there are good grounds for doing so, the very nature of these charges causes them to be a relatively unimportant source of revenue, compared to taxation.

Intergovernmental Transfers

An increasingly large proportion of local government's total revenue is derived from transfers from state/provincial governments, which in turn often receive some of their funds from the federal level. In the United States, direct transfers from state governments now account for almost 23% of total local government revenue, or a little more than the amount received from property taxes. In Canada, an even greater proportion of local government revenues—about 50%—is received from provincial governments. There is a trickle-down effect involving the transfer of funds from the federal level to the state/provincial governments and from the state/provincial governments to the local level. The greater constitutional freedom of the United States allows the federal government to undertake transfers directly to the local government level in some cases.

The only problem with these transfers is that they are usually either for specific purposes or in the form of conditional grants. Most of the transfers are for education, to supplement the revenue generated from local sources. In both Canada and the United States, these intergovernmental transfers now provide more than 50% of the resources needed for primary and secondary education. Other specific services, such as transportation, communications, and welfare, also receive subsidies, but these are smaller by comparison. Many of the transfers are in the form of conditional grants. The higher levels of government will, for example, transfer $1.00 for every $1.00 spent by a local government on a specific objective. These conditional grant schemes often compound the fiscal dilemma of local governments, because they feel forced to distort their local priorities to take advantage of the conditional grant and cost-sharing schemes offered by the higher levels of government.

LOCAL GOVERNMENT FRAGMENTATION

It is estimated that 81,780 different local government units existed in the United States in 1982, and that 29,861 of these local governments existed in the 303 SMSAs that were established at that time. Some of the types of local government in the SMSAs are indicated in Table 10.5, which does not include the many different agencies that are subordinate to local government. This fragmented situation is quite similar to that experienced in Canada: In 1986 there were 4,835 units of general government and special districts existing in the ten provinces, and this figure also does not include the many subordinate agencies of local government that often act as if they were governmental units. It should be noted that the form of local government that appears to be proliferating is the special district.

The extent of fragmentation does vary markedly among metropolitan areas. Table 10.6 lists the number of units of general government, special districts, and school districts in the fifteen largest SMSAs in the United States

Table 10.5   TYPES OF GOVERNMENT UNITS IN SMSAs
United States, 1977 and 1982

| | Number | | % Change |
Type of unit	1982	1977	1977–1982
School districts	5,692	5,751	− 1.0 %
County governments	670	670	0.0
Municipalities	7,018	6,923	1.4
Townships (incl. New England towns)	4,756	4,752	0.1
Special districts	11,725	10,640	10.2
TOTAL	28,861	28,736	3.9

Source: U.S. Bureau of the Census (1982), *Census of Governments: Local Government in Metropolitan Areas,* vol. 5.

Table 10.6 THE NUMBER OF LOCAL GOVERNMENTS IN THE FIFTEEN LARGEST SMSAs, Ranked by Population Size

SMSA	Population (1980)	Local governments
New York	10,803	542
Los Angeles–Long Beach	7,478	276
Chicago	7,103	1,194
Philadelphia	4,708	867
Detroit	4,044	238
Houston	3,385	608
San Francisco–Oakland	3,252	331
Washington, D.C.	2,966	87
Dallas–Fort Worth	2,886	330
Boston	2,603	189
Pittsburgh	2,310	739
St. Louis	2,302	574
Baltimore	2,174	49
Cleveland	1,899	217
Newark	1,763	218

Source: Advisory Commission on Intergovernmental Relations (1984), *Fiscal Disparities: Central Cities and Suburbs, 1981,* Washington, D.C.: ACIR, Tables A-1 and A-8.

in 1981. In general, younger metropolitan areas have fewer units and simpler spatial patterns of local government than older ones. Although the complexity of the local government structure is to a degree related to city size, it is abundantly clear that there is enormous variation in the complexity of governmental jurisdictions among the group of larger metropolises. The most prolific SMSA in this regard is Chicago, with 1,194 local government units, followed by Philadelphia, Pittsburgh, and Houston. The last metropolis celebrated its large population increase in the 1970s (almost 60%) by doubling the number of local governments operating throughout the urban area. But size is only a rough guide, for the SMSA of Los Angeles–Long Beach, with a population of almost 7.5 million, had only 276 local governments; Baltimore had only 49.

The profusion of governmental entities in urban regions is made even more complicated by the many kinds of jurisdictions that occur. First are the elected governments of the municipalities, including villages, incorporated towns, cities, boroughs, townships, and counties. Second is a multiplicity of special districts, involving ad hoc special-purpose bodies such as school, fire, police, health, library, zoning, and housing districts. These districts are by far the most numerous in urban areas today, and despite the trend to consolidation in recent years, the number of special districts has been growing at an alarming rate as the scope of public-service provision has been enlarged. The special districts add to the confusion of urban spatial organization because they typically overlap with each other and with the underlying layer of other political divisions.

Even in areas where metropolitan governments have been amalgamated through one means or another, the profusion of local governments can still be great. For example, although metropolitan Toronto consists of a federation of five municipalities and one central city, there are also ninety-four special-body governments that are variously concerned with providing services, management, regulation, and utilities. The confusing and highly fragmented pattern of local government in North American urban areas can therefore be regarded as a numerical nightmare that is almost impossible to comprehend.

ISSUES FACING LOCAL GOVERNMENT

The shortcomings of the various ways local governments raise funds, even the regressive nature of the property tax itself, would be less pronounced if only the taxes were applied on a uniform basis throughout a metropolitan area. The fact that they are not is due in large part to the proliferation and fragmentation of local government areas. Two main kinds of problems stem from this: (1) fiscal problems related to the existing methods of financing local government activities, and (2) organizational problems arising from the difficulty of coordinating the various local government responsibilities within metropolitan areas. The second group of problems is in fact very much a result of the first since, in order to raise funds, local governments are often forced to pursue conflicting rather than cooperative policies in service provision.

Fiscal Problems

Although the federal governments of both Canada and the United States raise about 60% of their revenues from such progressive means as income taxes and business taxes, they also depend upon more regressive forms of taxation. Local governments are thus left with two disadvantages. The first is the regressive nature of many of the taxes on which local governments depend. The second is that these types of regressive taxes do not keep up with inflation. As a result, municipalities are supported by a tax system that to a large degree is unfair, and that also fails to raise sufficient revenue in times of inflation.

Fiscal Imbalance

The major problem arising from the fragmentation of local government structure is without doubt the tremendous disparity concerning revenue resources and expenditure needs among different units within an urban area. This disparity leads to significant spatial variation in the level and quality of public services provided from place to place within the same city. It also leads to marked differences in the level of tax rates, which can influence the location patterns of economic activity within metropolitan areas in undesirable ways.

The disparity between resources and needs is most pronounced between the central cities and the suburbs, although not all suburban communities enjoy favorable resource bases. The problem of fiscal imbalance involves all units of metropolitan government, for those that are in a reasonably sound financial position today may be in a disadvantageous position in a few years. Nevertheless, the worsening fiscal squeeze is one of the most acute problems facing central cities. It is the result of decentralization and of the fragmented pattern of local government that exists in nearly all metropolitan areas.

Central cities are almost without exception characterized by insufficient funds and resources relative to the demands for services. The building stock is generally old and dilapidated, and the high densities make them a major fire risk, thereby necessitating higher levels of fire protection. High crime rates are translated into higher costs of providing police protection. Median family incomes are appreciably lower than in the suburbs, a situation that is aggravated by higher unemployment rates. The massive concentration of the poor in central cities is, of course, a major source of demand for services. In this regard, it is interesting to note that the high concentration of poverty in the central cities is not unrelated to the difficulties low-income people have in finding low-cost housing in suburban areas, a situation that is made worse by the tendency of many communities to use their powers of zoning to keep low-income groups out. Central cities, then, not only abound with problems, but they are increasingly charged with the responsibility of solving them on behalf of the whole metropolitan area.

The demand for, and costs of, providing health and welfare services, and especially various forms of public assistance, are high. Whereas on average about 10% of local government tax revenues are spent on income-redistributive activities, in the central cities the figure approaches 25% and is steadily rising as prices increase and in-migration from lagging regions continues. At the same time, the opportunities for increasing tax revenues are severely limited, especially since an increasingly large amount of economic activity has decentralized from the core areas. As it is, tax rates in central cities are higher relative to personal income than in the suburbs, and to increase taxes on the poor to give them more services hardly makes sense.

Furthermore, many of the larger central cities have assumed responsibilities that are normally borne by other levels of government. For example, New York City bears the costs of municipal hospitals, large public universities, and a considerable portion of the welfare costs. Other metropolitan areas also assume such responsibilities, but generally not all three. For example, in the city of Chicago the hospital system is financed by the county, postsecondary public education by the state, and welfare largely by the state and federal governments.

To give some idea of the staggering costs facing some central cities, consider the case of Medicaid for the elderly poor in New York City. This vital social service is received by 10% of the city's population. New York City pays one-fourth of all Medicaid costs and is obviously caught in a financial treadmill, for the city contains a disproportionately large share of the region's elderly. It should be remembered that the Medicaid payments go to doctors, pharmacists, nursing homes, and hospitals, not as direct payments to the elderly, and it is the spiraling prices charged by the providers that is yielding these excessive costs.

Despite the constraints on raising revenue, and the ever-increasing needs, local governments exhibit, on the whole, good fiscal responsibility. In the 1970s, and especially during the recession of the early 1980s, a number of local governments were in financial disarray. Debts were mounting, and some metropolises, such as New York City, were in a crisis situation, requesting and receiving considerable additional support from the state and federal governments. Since that time, order has been restored in most jurisdictions on the budgetary side. But order had been restored through severe trimming of many line items related to social concerns, and through delaying maintenance and repair to physical infrastructures. The Williamsburg Bridge (one of the connections between Brooklyn and Manhattan) was closed down due to poor maintenance—this is but the tip of the maintenance iceberg that is about to wash over many municipalities with enormous accumulated foregone expenditures.

Spillovers

Existing arrangements for local government taxation cannot adequately cope with spillovers, the effects of which are accentuated by the proliferation of small geographic entities. *Spillovers,* or externalities, arise because the actions of individuals or groups (e.g., local governments) at one location affect the utility of those at other locations. Thus, they are an expression of interdependencies in spatial organization, and are essentially geographic. Spillovers arise in many ways, can assume many forms, and may be either positive or negative in their effects. For example, high-quality police protection in one jurisdiction is commonly reflected in lower crime rates in neighboring communities, and a well-developed school system in one district enhances the general well-being of the urban complex as a whole.

The problem of spillover is significant whenever the external benefits of providing services are very large in relation to the internal ones, and the services are financed by taxes. This is particularly the case for education, and for those activities whose costs and benefits cannot be confined to small spatial units, such as with pollution control, recreational facilities, and public transportation systems. Under these conditions, it is unreasonable to expect that adequate levels of service will be provided, for voters in a community are unlikely to be willing to pay higher taxes to finance services whose benefits are largely realized by others.

The situation is different, of course, when service charges are employed. These charges overcome some of the problems of geographic spillover because costs can be recouped from users who benefit from a particular service regardless of where they reside. But because most local revenue is raised by taxation, spillover is an important factor contributing to inequalities in the levels of service provided in the different parts of metropolitan areas.

Organizational Problems

The very nature of many urban problems is such that they cannot be handled effectively by a large number of local governments acting in isolation. Although this high degree of political fragmentation may be defended on the grounds of continuing the democratic tradition of home rule, it can also be deplored as being hopelessly unsuited to the realities of modern metropolitan life. From the governmental point of view, the metropolitan whole should be more than the sum of its administrative parts. Because it is not, many urgent problems have remained difficult to solve and will inevitably continue to be so unless existing conditions are radically changed.

Fiscal Zoning

In fact, far from cooperating with each other, many local governments within a metropolitan area compete for acceptable tax-yielding economic activities. The heavy reliance on the property tax forces local governments to meet increased costs, or to hold outlays to a reasonable level, by using their powers of zoning for fiscal ends. Different types of land use demand different services and at the same time are capable of making different-sized contributions to the public purse. Thus, whereas commercial uses and high-income residences often contribute in taxes two or three times the cost of the services they require, residential property of moderate value pays only a fraction of the cost of the public services it requires.

Local governments, therefore, often compete for high-revenue–low service-cost land uses and try to exclude low-revenue–high-cost uses through various zoning mechanisms. A new suburban community may, for example, permit the construction of a large regional shopping center that takes business away from other commercial areas in the metropolis. At the same time, it may institute large-lot zoning for residential construction that effectively limits population densities in its jurisdiction and promotes residential construction for high-income families.

Fiscal zoning is therefore an extremely important instrument of local government. When practiced, it more often than not leads to a conflict of interest between policies aimed at short-term gains for individual communities and the long-term impacts on the urban area as a whole. For in the attempt to speed up the process whereby benefits are derived from the use of land, communities may make decisions that are in their immediate interests but run counter to the proper development of the wider urban environment. It is largely as a result of such decisions that huge shopping centers, for example, are built in the newest suburban communities even though they have an immediate negative impact on the rest of the commercial structure of the metropolis. For example, the West Edmonton Mall virtually killed retail activities in the downtown area.

Conflicting Programs

The problems arising from fragmented local government in metropolitan areas are most clearly revealed in conflicting programs of service provision, especially those administered by the boards of the special districts. *Special districts* are limited-purpose governmental units that exist as corporate entities and have significant fiscal and administrative independence from general-purpose local governments. In fact, about 46% of the 11,725 special districts that existed within SMSAs in the United States in 1982 had their own property-taxing power. The types of functions that they handle are listed in Table 10.7, and they have been established so that the operation of particular activities can gain the advantages of geographic flexibility, technical specialization, and fiscal self-sufficiency. They can, therefore, be established to operate over wide areas, including natural drainage areas or entire metropolises, and can raise their own revenues through a variety of means such as bonds and user charges. Thus,

Table 10.7   THE MAJOR FUNCTIONS OF SPECIAL DISTRICTS IN SMSAs, 1982

Function	Number
Single-function districts	**10,904**
Fire Protection	2,697
Natural Resources	1,876
Drainage	586
Soil conservation	564
Irrigation/water conservation	352
Flood control	216
Other	158
Utilities	1,290
Water supply	1,231
Transit	38
Electric power	18
Gas supply	3
Sewage	1,172
Housing and Urban Renewal	1,055
School Buildings	821
Parks and Recreation	469
Cemeteries	234
Hospitals	226
Highways	219
Libraries	204
Health	128
Other	513
Multiple-function districts	**821**
Sewerage and Water Supply	586
Natural Resources	63
Other	172
TOTAL	11,725

Source: Calculated by the author from U.S. Bureau of the Census (1984), *Census of Governments: Local Governments in Metropolitan Areas,* Table 14.

concentration on a single activity or related activities over a wide area is supposed to yield much greater levels of efficiency in operation.

There are, in general, two kinds of special districts. One group serves an entire metropolitan area, and the other group operates within the confines of local municipalities. Most of the *metropolitan districts* deal with single functions, for example: the Milwaukee Metropolitan Sewer District; the San Diego County Water Authority; the Raleigh–Durham Airport Authority, North Carolina; the Cleveland Metropolitan Park District; and the Golden Gate Bridge and Highway District, San Francisco.

A few of the metropolitan districts are multistate, the largest of which is the New York–New Jersey Port Authority, which operates six airports, the World Trade Center, six interstate bridges and tunnels, and many other activities related to trade and transportation. This particular authority also provides an example of how special-purpose districts can operate in a manner that is contrary to the best interests of the municipalities served. By labeling the twin-tower World Trade Center a port facility, the Port Authority is able to avoid paying property taxes on the towers even though many users of the offices are only remotely concerned with trade and would otherwise have to locate elsewhere, in properties that are not tax exempt.

The most numerous special districts are those that provide *localized services.* They have been formed in many suburban areas to undertake activities that local government could not, either because it was not sufficiently organized or because it lacked the power to undertake the activity. More than 90% of all special districts have been established to provide local services, and most of these deal with single functions. Most of the local services deal with fire protection, water supply, sewage, housing and urban renewal, and school districts. The result of such proliferation of local special-district governments is quite frequently a lack of coordination of policies in matters requiring integration, such as land-use planning, conservation, and the implementation of meaningful building codes.

Public Awareness and Control

In addition to the problems of coordination and economic efficiency, those of public awareness and control of public bodies are vitally significant. There is little doubt that the public is generally not aware of how many different units of local government influence their daily lives. This is evident by the very low voter turnout for local elections for representatives to such boards. This lack of public awareness is quite serious, for the operation of the bodies responsible for the special districts then falls into the hands of those who perceive the concern as being of direct interest to them, and particularly to their business activities. In particular, many special-district boards are dominated by financial, insurance, and real estate interests that view such representation as important for business protection as well as for public relations. The vast bulk of the public is not represented, and is totally ignorant of the fact that it is not represented.

No wonder the property industry and financial institutions control most of the important decision making in local governments.

TOWARD SOLUTIONS

The dilemma of local finance and the fragmentation of local government units is at the heart of problems facing the inner and outer cities. Although many solutions have been suggested, they may be grouped into two categories. First, there are solutions that involve reforms in the fiscal basis and fragmented structure of local government and do not focus on how decisions are made concerning the allocation of capital investments. As these reforms are more likely to be considered and implemented, they will be discussed at greater length than the second type of solution that is being proposed. This second solution says, in effect, that the root cause of the problem is a failure to recognize that the allocation of resources is of fundamental importance, and that what is required is more community ownership and involvement in decision making. Although labels can be quite misleading, the former is referred to as involving structural reforms and the latter as involving more radical solutions.

Structural Reforms

The most widespread method for attempting to resolve some of the fiscal problems and associated issues arising from extensive local government fragmentation involves changes within the existing framework of government. In Canada and, to a lesser degree, the United States, these in effect mean changes from above, or changes implemented by higher levels of government. Earlier in this chapter it was indicated that changes from above are easier to implement in Canada than the United States because the states and the United States federal government are reluctant to implement changes without a clear mandate to do so from all the areas that would be affected. Those reforms that have been undertaken in North America involve both fiscal and governmental reorganization.

Fiscal Reform

The reforms that are being implemented or discussed on the fiscal side involve increasing grants from higher levels of government, the transfer of municipal responsibilities to other levels of government, and the provision of new tax money for municipalities. Each of these involves a variety of measures, and all have political implications. A few of these political implications will be outlined, as it is impossible to cover them all.

Intergovernmental Grants   Probably the most likely procedures to be implemented for ameliorating the fiscal dilemma involve increases in the magnitude of grants received from the federal government (in the United States) and from state/provincial governments. The data in Table 10.4 confirm that these grants have increased in recent years. Unfortunately, most transfers have been conditional; what is required is an increase in the magnitude of unconditional grants. In Canada, the provincial governments provide about 30% of local government revenues, nearly all of which are earmarked for specific purposes.

Transfer of Responsibilities   The second set of proposals involves the transfer of responsibilities to the state/provincial and federal levels. This general proposal is predicated upon the observation that some local governments have accepted social responsibilities that are handled by other levels of government elsewhere, and that many of the social responsibilities yield benefits to the wider area beyond that under the jurisdiction of the local government involved. Good examples of responsibilities that are increasingly being funded by state/provincial or federal government are education, hospitals, and public housing.

New Methods of Raising Revenue   A third set of proposals involves developing additional methods of raising revenue for local governments, or giving municipalities new powers of taxation. If we accept that the current property tax not only is essentially regressive, but it fails to really recoup the land values realized as a result of public investments, then one additional method of raising revenue might be to replace the property tax with a site-value tax based on current market values. The advantages of site-value taxation have been discussed previously, but there is considerable opposition, particularly from homeowners.

Another approach could be to give local governments new powers of taxation. One tax that has been suggested is a municipal income tax, which could be structured to be progressive and sensitive to inflation. For such a tax to be fair, it would have to be levied on a metropolitan-wide basis, which would mean that budgets would have to be established for the metropolis as a whole. This, of course, raises the important issue of the reform of the structure of local government.

Government Area Reform

The large number of local governments is not of itself bad, the problems arise over the confusion and insularity over what these governments do, not the numbers themselves. Ideally, small jurisdictions should do what they do best, and large jurisdictions should deal with those urban functions that they do best. The question that arises, of course, concerns which size unit can perform a given urban function the best. The relationship between the provision of urban functions and services and the size of the jurisdiction concerned has been studied many times, and a number of these studies were conducted in the context of economies of scale. However, it is difficult to determine how any particular economy of scale is related to some procedure for local government reform.

One attempt to resolve this difficulty is made by Hallman (1977). The first step is to define more precisely the types of functions and services that would best be provided at each of three different scales of community size. The communities are considered to involve three sizes: (1) small communities consist of neighborhoods and small municipalities that contain a population up to about 40,000, (2) intermediate communities embrace central cities, some large municipalities, and urban counties and contain populations up to 250,000, and (3) areawide communities include the entire urban region or metropolis and contain a population of up to a few million. Decisions regarding which size community should provide a particular function are made on the basis of economy-of-scale studies and the degree of interaction with the population that is needed. The outcome of Hallman's analysis of the economy-of-scale literature pertaining to particular functions and the need for community interaction is presented in Table 10.8. It should be noted that, in most cases, the revenue required for these functions is assumed to be derived from an area-wide tax base and intergovernmental transfers.

Although it is often possible to be reasonably precise in determining the best-size community to offer a service, in a number of cases extensive coordination among different jurisdictions is required. In these instances, two levels of local government jurisdiction should provide the service, and the higher-level jurisdiction should coordinate the effort. Thus police service, although best provided at the smaller scale to provide greater possibilities for direct contact with the public, is also required to cover the metropolis. Educational services are a little more difficult to allocate in the United States than in Canada, for in the United States questions concerning integration and the best way to achieve equality of opportunity for different racial and ethnic groups often override economy-of-scale considerations. This is not meant to imply that schools organized within large jurisdictions suffer severe diseconomies of scale, for they do not. Table 10.8 is compiled, however, on the basis of the smallest scale that can provide the activity with the highest level of economic efficiency and service sensitivity.

The second step toward resolution of the urban activity–local government question is to examine which form of local government structure is best suited to provide urban functions and services in the manner proposed in Table 10.8. The implication is that some form of two-tier structure of local government would be most appropriate. This has been recognized in many metropolitan areas in Canada and the United States, although the methods used to implement two-tier local government have varied quite significantly. The most common method is to establish either single-function or multifunction special districts to offer a particular service or a related set of services over an entire metropolitan or county area. In our discussion of these special districts we indicated that although they are the most common means of creating two-tier government, they lead to a fragmented and insular approach to urban problems. Two other approaches that attempt to provide a greater level of coordination between municipalities and the various urban functions are unification and federation.

Table 10.8 AN IDEAL ALLOCATION OF URBAN FUNCTIONS AND SERVICES AMONG THREE DIFFERENTLY SIZED COMMUNITIES WITHIN A METROPOLITAN AREA

Activity	Size of community		
	Small	Intermediate	Area-wide
Refuse disposal			x
Refuse collection	x		
Sewage disposal			x
Water treatment and trunk lines			x
Water sales	x		
Airports and ports			x
Bus and truck terminals			x
Railroads and rail yards			x
Mass transit			x
Transport planning			x
Snow removal	x	x	
Street cleaning	x		
Parking lots	x	x	
Cultural facilities			x
Regional parks			x
Community recreational facilities	x		
Planning and land-use control			x
Building codes and regulation			x
Building permits and inspection	x	x	
Housing (low-income, elderly)		x	
Housing redevelopment	x	x	
Police	x		x
Fire protection		x	
Ambulance		x	
Health services	x		x
Hospitals		x	x
Welfare	x		x
Social services	x		
Vocational training		x	x
Elementary education	x		
Secondary education	x	x	

Source: Table compiled by the author from a detailed discussion of the economy of scale for urban functions literature in Hallman (1977, pp. 182–194).

Unification   Unification most frequently involves the reallocation of responsibility for certain functions from all municipalities to a geographically larger jurisdiction, such as a county. A single metropolitan government is created to look after area-wide problems, but local service provision remains in the hands of existing local governments. Thus a certain measure of metropolitan control is obtained without creating yet another unit of government. Although the plan would seem reasonably attractive on paper, such restructuring has usually occurred only in those cases where the metropolitan area lies almost exclusively in a single county. Of the seven metropolitan counties that have approved city–county consolidation—Baton Rouge–East Baton Rouge (Louisiana, 1947), Nashville–Davidson County (Tennessee, 1962), Jacksonville–Duval County (Florida, 1967), Columbus–Muscogee County (Ohio, 1970), Lexington–Fayette County (Kentucky, 1972), Anchorage–Greater Anchorage Borough (Alaska, 1975), and Indianapolis–Marion County (Indiana, 1969)—in only one, Columbus–Muscogee County, does unification extend beyond the core county.

The basic problem with city–county consolidation in the United States is that the constitutional arrangements under which municipalities and counties operate emanate from different bases. Consequently, a state may require a constitutional amendment (to be voted on by all residents) in order to allow the consolidation. The procedure can take years and involve so many groups and hearings that the process itself is the greatest impediment. Nevertheless, the evidence available suggests that such mergers may be worthwhile, for not only are economies of scale in the delivery of certain functions realized, but services are extended to cover all parts of the metropolitan area and a more equitable tax system is developed.

Federation   Federation involves some kind of amalgamation of local government units. One-county unification is in effect one-tier federation. But federation is more flexible in that it allows for the advantages of two- and even three-tiered local government in situations where the metropolitan region spreads over a number of counties as well as municipalities. In a two-tiered federation, a special governmental unit is created to look after areawide functions. Local municipalities may be left alone—small ones may even be amalgamated—to look after local service provision.

The idea of federated metropolitan areas has been an appealing one in the United States and Canada since the establishment of the London County Council in England in 1888 and 1889 (O'Leary, 1987), but in the United States various attempts in Boston (1896), Oakland (1921), and Pittsburgh (1929) all failed. The only example of a near-federated form of municipal government in the United States is Dade County, Miami, where a two-tier form of government for the incorporated municipalities and counties and a one-tier metropolitan government for the unincorporated portions of the county was approved in 1957. The Dade County experience suggests that although reorganization eliminated considerable duplication and generated some economies of scale, the overall costs per capita of local government increased because services were expanded and bureaucrats in the poorer municipalities had their salaries raised to the metropolitan level. A major reason why federation—or any form of local government reform—is difficult to pursue in the United States arises from the constitutional autonomy of the municipalities and the political requirement for widespread support in each jurisdiction involved. Nevertheless, de facto federation has evolved over a number of years in Nassau County, New York and in Minneapolis–St. Paul.

The legal responsibility of provincial governments for the establishment and reorganization of municipalities has made local government reform in Canada far easier to implement. Commencing with the establishment of federated government in metropolitan Toronto in 1954, the province of Ontario undertook widespread local government reform and allocated specific functions to different levels of government. Regional governments were created in eleven other jurisdictions in Ontario between 1969 and 1974. Similar federal reorganization occurred with the establishment of Winnipeg "unicity"—a one-tier form of government—in 1972. The other provinces have generally adopted nonfederal forms of local government reform, such as allocating specific functions to the Montreal Urban Community (which embraces all the municipalities on the island of Montreal) on a metropolitan-wide basis or implementing opt-out schemes for municipalities that do not wish to participate in regional special districts, as in British Columbia (Sancton, 1985).

The Canadian experience with federated metropolitan government has been reasonably encouraging. In Toronto, where the federated government has been established the longest, the government has flourished and there have been major accomplishments. Since metropolitan-wide financing is required and specific functions are allocated to metropolises to coordinate and local municipalities to implement (such as education), many disparities of the kind that occur in United States metropolises have been alleviated. In the areas of education, water supply, and sewage disposal, many of the earlier problems of deteriorating services have been arrested (although not eradicated) over the entire metropolitan area. A metropolitan park district of many thousand acres has been established, an extensive expressway system has been constructed (and halted), an attempt has been made to control air pollution, a system of unified law enforcement has been implemented, and public transportation (particularly rapid transit) has been improved and extended. Naturally, the region-wide government has not been without its critics, who point especially to its lack of success with issues of health, welfare, housing, and urban renewal, to the problems of recent immigrants, and to a lack of resolution in the management of urban growth.

Radical Reforms

The preceding review of the various structural reforms of local government can be evaluated in the context of some more radical alternatives. Basically, those adopting a more radical view claim that the types of reforms just outlined involve mere structural tinkering, and that there is no hope for any real resolution of the fiscal and governmental dilemma until parallel administrative and political reforms are underway (Cox, 1984; Tabb, 1984). The types of parallel administrative and political reforms that are required vary, for just as there is a range of opinions among those advocating structural reforms, there is also an array of opinions among those promoting more radical solutions. Perhaps a brief outline of two of the more radical approaches might indicate the range of these views.

Increased Involvement of Higher Levels of Government   The first approach, which is probably best exemplified in the mixed capitalist–socialist systems of a number of countries in Western Europe (for example, Sweden, Denmark, the United Kingdom), involves a clear recognition that the problems of central cities and entire metropolitan areas cannot be resolved within their own borders, and that the close involvement of higher levels of government is required (Goldsmith and Villadsen, 1986; Newton and Karran, 1985). The highest level of government that should be involved is the national government, for it is at this level that various changes must be made in national priorities, fiscal redistribution, and control over investment decisions. These changes should be directed toward the creation of a national urban plan that would focus on the environment in which the bulk of the population resides. Let us now examine some of the elements of such a national plan.

If we accept that the basic cause of the problems facing metropolises lies in the decentralization of jobs and economic activities, and that this decentralization is the result of investment decisions made by the owners of capital, then it would seem logical for one element of the plan to involve a level of control over investment decisions. Thus, entrepreneurs and developers would be encouraged to invest their capital in locations that would help fulfill a national urban purpose. If the purpose is to maintain manufacturing jobs in central cities, then a range of schemes could be devised by government to achieve this goal, including tax breaks for those locating in inner cities.

Another element of such a plan would involve a reordering of national priorities to include recognition of the role of the state in ensuring equal access to health care, social services, welfare, housing, and education. This would result in a transfer of responsibilities to a higher level of government.

Centralization of Control   The second radical approach is rooted much more clearly in a class interpretation of North America (e.g., Levine, 1987). This view has been referred to previously as one that interprets society in the context of a perpetual struggle among different class interests. An example of this struggle occurs with fiscal zoning when a community endeavors to maintain certain elements of social and economic exclusivity. The fragmentation of political units plays into the hands of any interest group wishing to maintain certain sets of privileges.

Those adopting this second radical approach tend to advocate much greater centralization of control over urban functions and to eliminate political fragmentation as much as possible; they would also make the elimination of class interests a central objective of all levels of government. In this sense, all aspects of local government would be actively engaged in social engineering and social reconstruction.

Conclusion

From the preceding brief reviews of various strategies for fiscal and local government reform, it would appear that the two-tier approaches to metropolitan (and regional) government, especially federation, are most appealing. The two-tier approaches involve a workable compromise between the politically impossible supergovernments that control everything and the fragmented special districts that cannot operate beyond their single-function jurisdiction.

The main value of federated two-tier metropolitan governments is that they offer a new system that does not require complete dissolution of the old. Since they entail tax-sharing agreements and a shifting of responsibilities for health, welfare, and social service to higher levels of government, they offer hope of finding workable solutions to the problem of the proliferation of governments within metropolitan areas. As long as local governments are forced to balance their books within their own boundaries, it is unrealistic to expect them to endorse metropolitan-wide government. However, larger units of metropolitan government must become a more important part of our thinking because the organization of inhabited space is becoming more metropolitan. If we do not show a greater concern for, and make sacrifices to, the interests of the larger whole, the future of North American cities will continue to be fraught with fiscal and governmental problems.

Bibliography

ACIR (1984). *Fiscal Disparities: Central Cities and Suburbs, 1981.* Washington, D.C.: Advisory Commission on Intergovernmental Relations.

Abler, R., and J.S. Adams (1976). *A Comparative Atlas of America's Great Cities: Twenty Metropolitan Regions.* Minneapolis: Univ. of Minnesota Press.

Alonso, W. (1964). *Location and Land Use: Toward a General Theory of Land Rent.* Cambridge, Mass.: Harvard Univ. Press.

Anderson, J.E. (1985). "The Changing Structure of a City: Temporal Changes in Cubic Spline Urban Density Patterns." *Journal of Regional Science* 25 (3): 413–25.

Archer, J.C., and E.R. White (1985). "A Service Classification of American Metropolitan Areas." *Urban Geography* 6, 2: 122–51.

Armstrong, R.B. (1979). "National Trends in Office Construction, Employment and Headquarter Location in U.S. Metropolitan Areas." In *Spatial Patterns of Office Growth and Location,* edited by P.W. Daniels. New York: Wiley, pp. 61–94.

Baine, R.P., and A.L. McMurray (1977). *Toronto: An Urban Study.* Toronto: Clark, Irwin.

Barlowe, R. (1986). *Land Resource Economics: The Economics of Real Estate.* Englewood Cliffs, N.J.: Prentice-Hall.

Barresi, C. (1968). "The Role of the Real Estate Agent in Residential Location." *Sociological Forces* 1: 59–71.

Bateman, M. (1985). *Office Development: A Geographical Analysis.* London: Croom Helm; New York: St. Martin's Press.

Bell, D. (1976). *The Coming of Post-Industrial Society.* New York: Basic.

Bergman, E.M., and H.A. Goldstein (1983). "Dynamics and Structural Change in Metropolitan Economics." *Journal of the American Planning Association* 49 (3): 263–79.

Berry, B.J.L. (1965). "Internal Structure of the City." *Law and Contemporary Problems* 30: 111–19.

—— (1967). *Geography of Market Centers and Retail Distribution.* Englewood Cliffs, N.J.: Prentice-Hall.

—— (1973). *The Human Consequences of Urbanization.* London: Macmillan.

—— (1976). "The Counterurbanization Process: Urban America Since 1970." In *Urbanization and Counterurbanization,* edited by B.J.L. Berry. London: Sage.

—— (1981). *The Human Consequences of Urbanization.* rev. ed. London: Macmillan.

—— (1986). " 'The Nature of Cities' and Beyond" In *World Patterns of Modern Urban Change,* edited by M.P. Conzen. Chicago: Department of Geography, University of Chicago. Research Paper 217 and 218.

Berry, B.J.L., and W.L. Garrison (1958a). "Functional Bases of the Central Place Hierarchy." *Economic Geography* 34: 145–54.

—— and —— (1958b). "A Note on Central Place Theory and the Range of a Good." *Economic Geography* 34: 304–11.

—— and —— (1958c). "Recent Developments in Central Place Theory." *Papers of the Regional Science Association* 4: 107–20.

Berry, B.J.L., C.A. Goodwin, R.W. Lake, and K.B. Smith (1976). "Attitudes Toward Integration: The Role of Status in Community Response to Social Change." In *The Changing Face of the Suburbs,* edited by B. Schwartz. Chicago: Univ. of Chicago Press, pp. 221–64.

Berry, B.J.L., R.J. Tennant, B.J. Garner, and J.W. Simmons (1963). *Commercial Structure and Commercial Blight.* Chicago: Department of Geography, University of Chicago, Research Paper No. 85.

Bettison, D.G. (1975). *The Politics of Canadian Urban Development.* Edmonton: Univ. of Alberta Press.

Birch, E.L. (ed.) (1985). *The Unsheltered Woman: Woman and Housing in the 80's.* New Brunswick, N.J.: The Center for Urban Policy Research, Rutgers University.

Bird, R.M., and N.E. Slack (1983). *Urban Public Finance in Canada.* Toronto: Butterworths.

Blackley, P.R., and D. Greytak (1986). "Comparative Advantage and Industrial Location: An Intrametropolitan Evaluation." *Urban Studies* 23: 221–30.

Blowers, A. (1980). *The Limits of Power: The Politics of Local Planning Policy.* Oxford: Pergamon.

Bluestone, B., and B. Harrison (1982). *The Deindustrialization of America: Plant Closings, Community Abandonment, and the Dismantling of Basic Industry.* New York: Basic.

Boddy, M.J., and F. Gray (1979). "Filtering Theory, Housing Policy and the Legitimation of Inequality." *Policy and Politics* 7: 39–54.

Bogardus, E.S. (1926). "Social Distance in the City." In *The Urban Community,* edited by E.W. Bogardus. Chicago: Univ. of Chicago Press, pp. 48–54.

Borchert, J.R. (1967). "American Metropolitan Evolution." *Geographical Review* 57 (3): 301–32.

———— (1972). "America's Changing Metropolitan Regions." *Annals of the Association of American Geographers* 62: 352–73.

Borchert, J.R., and R.B. Adams (1963). *Trade Centers and Trade Areas of the Upper Midwest.* Minneapolis: Upper Midwest Economic Study, Univ. of Minnesota.

Bourne, L.S. (1981). *The Geography of Housing.* London: Arnold.

———— (1984). "Urbanization in Canada: Recent Trends and Research Questions." In *China in Canada: A Dialogue on Resources and Development,* edited by L. Gentlecore. Hamilton, Ontario: Department of Geography, McMaster University, pp. 152–65.

Bourne, L.S., A.M. Baker, W. Kalbach, R. Cressman, and D. Green (1986). *Canada's Ethnic Mosaic: Characteristics and Patterns of Ethnic Origin Groups in Urban Areas.* Toronto: Centre for Urban and Community Studies, University of Toronto.

Bourne, L.S., and J.W. Simmons (eds.) (1978). *Systems of Cities: Readings on Structure, Growth and Policy.* Toronto: Oxford Univ. Press.

Bradbury, J.H. (1984). "The Impact of Industrial Cycles in the Mining Sector: The Case of the Quebec–Labrador Region in Canada." *International Journal of Urban and Regional Research* 8 (3): 311–31.

———— (1985). "International Movements and Crises in Resource Oriented Companies: The Case of Inco in the Nickel Sector." *Economic Geography* 61 (2): 129–43.

Brown, L.A., and E. Moore (1970). "The Intra-Urban Migration Process: A Perspective." *Geografiska Annaler* 52B: 1–13.

Brown, M.A. (1981). "A Typology of Suburbs and Its Public Policy Implications." *Urban Geography* 2 (4): 288–310.

Brown, M.A., and R.K. Oldakowski (1986). "The Changing Morphology of Suburban Crime." *Urban Geography* 7 (1): 46–62.

Brunet, Y. (1980). "L'exode urbain. Essai de classification de la population exurbaine des Cantons de l'Est." *The Canadian Geographer* 24 (4): 385–405.

Bureau of the Census (1975). *Historical Statistics of the United States: Colonial Times to 1970.* Washington, D.C.: U.S. Department of Commerce.

———— (1984b). *Geographic Areas Handbook.* Washington, D.C.: U.S. Department of Commerce.

———— (1986). *We, the Black Americans.* Washington, D.C.: U.S. Department of Commerce.

Cadwallader, M. (1985). *Analytical Urban Geography.* Englewood Cliffs, N.J.: Prentice-Hall.

Cameron, G.C. (1973). "Intraurban Location and the New Plant." *Papers of the Regional Science Association* 31: 125–43.

Carey, G.W. (1976). "The New York–New Jersey Metropolitan Region." In *Contemporary Metropolitan America, vol. 1,* edited by J.S. Adams. Cambridge, Mass.: Ballinger, pp. 139–216.

Carlino, G.A. (1982). "Manufacturing Agglomeration Economies as Returns to Scale: A Production Function Approach." *Papers of the Regional Science Association* 50: 95–108.

Carter, J.R. (1984). *Computer Mapping: Progress in the '80s.* Washington, D.C.: Association of American Geographers.

Casetti, E. (1984). "Manufacturing Productivity and Snowbelt–Sunbelt Shifts." *Economic Geography* 60 (4): 313–24.

Castells, M. (1977). *The Urban Question.* London: Edward Arnold.

—— (1983). *The City and the Grassroots.* Berkeley: Univ. of California Press.

Cenzatti, M. (1985). "Book Review Essay: A Problematic Shift." *The Canadian Journal of Regional Science* 8 (3): 439–452.

Chandler Jr., A.D. (1977). *The Visible Hand: The Managerial Revolution in American Business.* Cambridge, Mass.: Harvard Univ. Press.

Chapman, K. (1985). "Control of Resources and the Recent Development of the Petrochemical Industry in Alberta." *The Canadian Geographer* 29 (4): 310–326.

Checkoway, B. (1984). "Large Builders, Federal Housing Programs and Postwar Suburbanization." In *Marxism and the Metropolis,* edited by W.K. Tabb and L. Sawers. New York: Oxford Univ. Press, pp. 152–73.

Chinitz, B. (1960). *Freight and the Metropolis.* Cambridge, Mass.: Harvard Univ. Press.

Chressanthis, G.A. (1986). "The Impact of Zoning Changes on Housing Prices: A Time Series Analysis." *Growth and Change* 17 (3): 49–70.

Christaller, W. (1933). *Central Places in Southern Germany.* Translated by C.W. Baskin (1966). Englewood Cliffs, N.J.: Prentice-Hall.

Christopherson, S., and M. Storper (1986). "The City as Studio, the World As Back Lot." *Society and Space* 4: 305–320.

Clapp, J.M. (1980). "The Intrametropolitan Location of Office Activities." *Journal of Regional Science* 20 (3): 387–399.

Clapp, J.M., and H.W. Richardson (1984). "Technological Change in Information Processing Industries and Regional Income Differentials in Developing Countries." *International Regional Science Review* 9 (3): 241–256.

Clark, C. (1951). "Urban Population Densities." *Journal of the Royal Statistical Society* A (114): 490–496.

Clark, G.L. (1984a). "The Changing Composition of Regional Employment." *Economic Geography* 60 (2): 175–193.

—— (1984b). "Who's to Blame for Racial Segregation." *Urban Geography* 5 (3): 193–209.

Clark, T.A. (1985). "The Interdependence among Gentrifying Neighborhoods: Central Denver Since 1970." *Urban Geography* 6 (3): 246–273.

Clark, W.A.V. (1982). "Recent Research on Migration and Mobility: A Review and Interpretation." *Progress in Planning* 18 (1): 1–56.

Clark, W.A.V., and P.L. Hosking (1986). *Statistical Methods for Geographers.* New York: Wiley.

Clark, W.A.V., and E.G. Moore (1982). "Residential Mobility and Public Programs: Current Gaps between Theory and Practice." *Journal of Social Issues* 38 (3): 35–50.

Clay, P.L. (1979). *Neighborhood Renewal: Middle-Class Resettlement and Incumbent Upgrading in American Neighborhoods.* Lexington, Mass.: Lexington.

Code, W.R. (1985). "The Decentralization of Office Space in Metropolitan Toronto." In *The Service Industries,* edited by P.W. Daniels. London: Methuen.

Conzen, M.P. (1983). "American Cities in Profound Transition: The New Geography of the 1980's." *Journal of Geography* 82: 94–102.

Conzen, M.P., and G.K. Lewis (1976). "Boston: A Geographical Portrait." In *Contemporary Metropolitan America: Cities of the Nation's Historic Metropolitan Core,* edited by J.S. Adams. Cambridge, Mass.: Ballinger.

Cooke, P. (1984). "Region, Class and Gender: A European Comparison." *Progress in Planning* 22 (1): 85–146.

Cox, K.R. (1984). "Social Change, Turf Politics, and Concepts of Turf Politics." In *Public Service Provision and Urban Development,* edited by A.M. Kirby *et al.* London: Croom Helm.

——— (1986). "Urban Social Movements and Neighborhood Conflicts: Questions of Space." *Urban Geography* 7 (6): 536–546.

Cox, K.R., and R.J. Johnston (eds.) (1982). *Conflict, Politics and the Urban Scene.* London: Longman.

Cutler, I. (1976). *Chicago Metropolis of the Mid-Continent.* Dubuque, Iowa: Kendall-Hunt.

Cutter, S. (1982). "Residential Satisfaction and the Suburban Homeowner." *Urban Geography* 3 (4): 315–327.

DREE (1979). *Single-Sector Communities.* Ottawa: Department of Regional Economic Expansion, Ministry of Supply and Services.

Dahmann, D.C. (1982). "Housing Opportunities for Black and White Households: Three Decades of Change in the Supply of Housing." *Special Demographic Analyses.* CDS 80–6. Washington, D.C.: Bureau of the Census.

Daniels, P.W. (1986). "The Geography of Services." *Progress in Human Geography* 10 (3): 436–444.

Davies, C.S. (1986). "Life at the Edge: Urban and Industrial Evolution of Texas, Frontier Wilderness—Frontier Space 1836–1986" *Southwestern Historical Quarterly* 89 (4): 443–554.

Davies, R.B., and A.R. Pickles (1985). "A Panel Study of Life-Cycle Effects on Residential Mobility." *Geographical Analysis* 17 (3): 199–216.

Davies, W.K.D. (1984). *Factorial Ecology.* Brookfield, Vt.: Gower.

Dawson, J.A. (1983). *Shopping Centre Development.* London: Longman.

Dear, M.J. (1976). "Abandoned Housing." In *Urban Policy-Making and Metropolitan Dynamics: A Comparative Geographical Analysis,* edited by J.S. Adams. Cambridge, Mass.: Ballinger.

Dear, M., and A.J. Scott (1981). *Urbanization and Urban Planning in Capitalist Society.* Andover, Mass.: Methuen.

Dembart, L. (1981). "L.A. Now a Minority City, 1980 Census Data Shows." *Los Angeles Times,* April 6, pp. 1, 3.

Dicken, P. (1986). *Global Shift.* London: Harper & Row.

Dingemans, D. (1979). "Redlining and Mortgage Lending in Sacramento." *Annals of the Association of American Geographers* 69: 225–239.

Eaton, B.C., and R.G. Lipsey (1982). "An Economic Theory of Central Places." *Economic Journal* 92: 56–72.

Edel, M. (1976). "Marx's Theory of Rent: Urban Applications." In *Housing and Class in Britain.* London: Conference of Socialist Economists, Political Economy of Housing Workshop, pp. 7–23.

Edel, M., and E. Sclar (1975). "The Distribution of Real Estate Value Changes: Metropolitan Boston, 1870–1970." *Journal of Urban Economics* 2: 366–387.

Edel, M., E. Sclar, and D. Lauria (1984). *Shaky Palaces: Homeownership and Social Mobility in Boston's Suburbanization.* New York: Columbia Univ. Press.

Edmonston, B., M.A. Goldberg, and J. Mercer (1985). "Urban Form in Canada and the United States: An Examination of Urban Density Gradients." *Urban Studies* 22: 209–217.

Erickson, R.A. (1974). "The Regional Impact of Growth Firms: The Case of Boeing, 1963–1968." *Land Economics* 50: 127–136.

—————— (1986). "Multinucleation in Metropolitan Economies." *Annals of the Association of American Geographers* 76 (3): 331–346.

Fabbro, I. (1986). "The Social Geography of Metropolitan Toronto: A Factorial Ecology Approach." Unpublished research paper. Toronto: Department of Geography, York University.

Fainstein, S.S., and N.I. Fainstein (1985). "Economic Restructuring and the Rise of Urban Social Movements." *Urban Affairs Quarterly* 21 (2): 187–206.

Fainstein, S.S., N.I. Fainstein, R.C. Hill, D.R. Judd, and M.P. Smith (1983). *Restructuring the City: The Political Economy of Urban Redevelopment.* New York: Longman.

Fairchild, H.H., and M.B. Tucker (1982). "Black Residential Mobility: Trends and Characteristics." *Journal of Social Issues* 38 (3): 51–74.

Farley, J.E. (1986). "Segregated City, Segregated Suburbs: To What Extent Are They the Products of Black–White Socio-Economic Differentials." *Urban Geography* 7 (2): 165–171.

Firey, W. (1945). "Sentiment and Symbolism as Ecological Variables." *American Sociological Review* 10: 140–148.

Foggin, P., and M. Polese (1976). *The Social Geography of Montreal.* Translated by the Centre for Urban and Community Studies. Toronto: Centre for Urban and Community Studies, University of Toronto, Research Paper No. 88.

Fotheringham, A.S. (1985). "Spatial Competition and Agglomeration in Urban Modeling." *Environment and Planning A* 17 (2): 213–230.

Fox, K. (1986). *Metropolitan America: Urban Life and Urban Policy in the United States, 1940–1980.* London: Macmillan.

Fox, M. (1983). "Working Women and Travel: The Access of Women to Work and Community Facilities." *Journal of the American Planning Association* 49 (2): 156–170.

Friedmann, J. (1973a). "The Urban Field as Human Habitat." In *The Place of Planning,* edited by S.P. Snow. Auburn, Ala.: Auburn Univ. Press.

—— (1973b). *Urbanization, Planning and National Development.* Beverly Hills: Sage.

Friedmann, J., and G. Wolff (1982). "World City Formation: An Agenda for Research and Action." *International Journal of Urban and Regional Research* 6 (2): 309–343.

Fuguitt, G.V. (1985). "The Nonmetropolitan Population Turnaround." *Annual Review of Sociology* 11: 259–280.

Fulton, P.N. (1983). "Public Transportation: Solving the Commuting Problem?" Washington, D.C.: Journey-to-Work and Migration Statistics, Bureau of the Census.

Furuseth, O.J., and J.T. Pierce (1982). *Agricultural Land in an Urban Society.* Washington, D.C.: A.A.G.

Gad, G.H.K. (1979). "Face-to-Face Linkages and Office Decentralization Potential: A Study of Toronto." In *Spatial Patterns of Office Growth and Location,* edited by P.W. Daniels. New York: Wiley, pp. 277–324.

Gaile, G.L., and C.J. Willmott (1984). *Spatial Statistics and Models.* Boston: Reidel.

Gans, H.J. (1962). "Urbanism and Suburbanism as Ways of Life: A Re-evaluation of Definitions." In *Human Behavior and Social Processes,* edited by A. Rose. Boston: Houghton Mifflin, pp. 625–648.

Garcia, P. (1985). "Immigration Issues in Urban Ecology: The Case of Los Angeles." In *Urban Ethnicity in the United States: New Immigrants and Old Minorities,* edited by L. Maldonado and J. Moore. Beverly Hills: Sage; Urban Affairs Annual Reviews 29: 73–100.

Garnick, D.H. (1984). "Shifting Balances in U.S. Metropolitan and Nonmetropolitan Area Growth." *International Regional Science Review* 9 (3): 257–273.

Gertler, M.C. (1985). "Industrialism, Deindustrialism and Regional Development in Central Canada." *The Canadian Journal of Regional Science* 8 (3): 353–376.

Getis, A. (1986). "The Economic Health of Municipalities Within a Metropolitan Region: The Case of Chicago." *Economic Geography* 62 (1): 52–73.

Gibson, E.M. (1976). *The Urbanization of the Strait of Georgia Region.* Ottawa: Environment Canada, Geographical Paper No. 57.

Gibson, L.J., and M.A. Worden (1981). "Estimating the Economic Base Multiplier: A Test of Alternative Procedures." *Economic Geography* 57: 146–159.

Giersch, H. (1984). "The Age of Schumpeter." *American Economic Review* 74: 103–109.

Glass, R. (ed.) (1964). *London: Aspects of Change.* London: MacGibbon and Kee; Centre for Urban Studies.

Gober, P. (1986). "How and Why Phoenix Households Changed: 1970–1980." *Annals of the Association of American Geographers* 76 (4): 536–549.

Goddard, J.B. (1975). *Office Location in Urban and Regional Development.* London: Oxford Univ. Press.

Goddard, J.B., and R. Pye (1977). "Telecommunications and Office Location." *Regional Studies* 11: 19–30.

Golant, S.M. (1984). *A Place to Grow Old: The Meaning of Environment in Old Age.* New York: Columbia Univ. Press.

Goldberg, M.A., and J. Mercer (1986). *The Myth of the North American City: Continentalism Challenged.* Vancouver: Univ. of British Columbia Press.

Goldsmith, M., and S. Villadsen (eds.) (1986). *Urban Political Theory and the Management of Fiscal Stress.* Aldershot, Eng.: Gower.

Golledge, R.G., and G. Rushton (1976). *Spatial Choice and Spatial Behavior.* Columbus: Ohio State Univ. Press.

Gordon, D.M. (1984). "Capitalist Development and the History of American Cities." In *Marxism and the Metropolis,* edited by W.K. Tabb and L. Sawers. New York: Oxford Univ. Press.

Gordon, P., H.W. Richardson, and H.L. Wong (1986). "The Distribution of Population and Employment in a Polycentric City: The Case of Los Angeles." *Environment and Planning A,* 18, 161–173.

Gottman, J. (1961). *Megalopolis.* New York: Twentieth Century Fund.

Graff, C.L. (1982). "Employment of Women, Suburbanization and House Styles." *Housing and Society* 9 (2): 111–117.

Greer-Wootten, B. (1972). "The Urban Model." In *Montreal Field Guide,* edited by L. Beauregard. Montreal: Les Presses de l'Universite de Montreal.

Gresch, P., and B. Smith (1985). "Managing Spatial Conflict: The Planning System in Switzerland." *Progress in Planning* 23 (1): 155–251.

Griffith, D.A. (1981). Evaluating the Transformation from a Monocentric to a Polycentric City." *The Professional Geographer* 33 (2): 189–196.

Gruen, N.J. (1984). "Sociological and Cultural Variables in Housing Theory." *Annals of Regional Science* 18: 1–10.

Haberler, G. (1963). *Prosperity and Depression: A Theoretical Analysis of Cyclical Movements.* New York: Atheneum.

Hall, P. (1985). "The Geography of the Fifth Kondratieff." In *Silicon Landscapes,* edited by P. Hall and A. Markusen. Boston: Allen and Unwin, pp. 1–19.

——— (ed.) (1966). *Von Thunen's Isolated State.* Oxford: Pergamon.

Hallman, H.W. (1977). *Small and Large Together: Governing the Metropolis.* Beverly Hills: Sage.

Hanson, S., and I. Johnston (1985). "Gender Differences in Work-Trip Length: Explanations and Implications." *Urban Geography* 6 (3): 193–219.

Harries, K.D. (1980). *Crime and the Environment.* Springfield, Ill.: Charles C. Thomas.

Harris, C. D., and E.L. Ullman (1945). "The Nature of Cities." *Annals of the American Academy of Political Science* 242: 7–17.

Harris, R. (1986). "Home Ownership and Class in Modern Canada." *International Journal of Urban and Regional Research* 10 (1): 67–86.

Harvey, D. (1973). *Social Justice and the City.* London: Edward Arnold.

——— (1982). *The Limits to Capital.* Oxford: Basil Blackwell.

——— (1985). *The Urbanization of Capital: Studies in the History and Theory of Capitalist Urbanization.* Baltimore, Md.: Johns Hopkins Univ. Press.

Harvey, D., and L. Chatterjee (1974). "Absolute Rent and the Structuring of Space by Governmental and Financial Institutions." *Antipode* 6: 22–36.

Hason, N. (1977). "The Emergence and Development of Zoning Controls in North American Municipalities: A Critical Analysis." Toronto: Dept. of Urban and Regional Planning, Univ. of Toronto. Papers on Planning and Development, No. 14.

Haynes, K.E., and S. Fotheringham (1984). *Gravity and Spatial Interaction Models.* Beverly Hills: Sage.

Hewings, G. (1986). *Regional Input–Output Analysis.* Beverly Hills: Sage.

Hirsch, A.R. (1983). "Making the Second Ghetto: Race and Housing in Chicago, 1940–1960." Cambridge: Cambridge Univ. Press.

Holcomb, B. (1984a). "Women in the City." *Urban Geography* 5, 3, 247–254.

———— (1984b). "Women in the Rebuilt Urban Environment: The United States Experience." *Built Environment* 10, 1, 18–24.

Holcomb, H.B., and R.A. Beauregard (1981). *Revitalizing Cities.* Washington, D.C.: Association of American Geographers.

Holmes, J. (1983). "Industrial Reorganization, Capital Restructuring and Locational Change: An Analysis of the Canadian Automobile Industry in the 1960's." *Economic Geography* 59 (3): 251–271.

———— (1986). "The Organization and Locational Structure of Production Subcontracting." In *Production, Work, Territory,* edited by A.J. Scott and M. Storper. Boston: Allen and Unwin, pp. 80–106.

———— (1987). "The Impact of Technical Change on the Organization and Locational Structure of Automobile Production in Canada." In *Technical Change and Industrial Policy,* edited by K. Chapman and G. Humphrys. Oxford: Basil Blackwell.

Hoover, E.M., and R. Vernon (1959). *Anatomy of a Metropolis.* New York: Doubleday.

Hoyt, H. (1939). *The Structure and Growth of Residential Neighborhoods in American Cities.* Washington, D.C.: Federal Housing Administration.

Huff, D.L. (1960). "A Topological Model of Consumer Space Preferences." *Papers and Proceedings of the Regional Science Association* 6: 159–173.

Huff, J.O. (1986). "Geographic Regularities in Residential Search Behavior." *Annals of the Association of American Geographers* 76 (2): 208–227.

Humphrys, G. (1982). "Power and Industrial Structure." In *The UK Space: Resources, Environment and the Future,* edited by J.W. House. London: Weidenfeld and Nicholson, pp. 282–355.

Isserman, A.M. (1980). "Estimating Export Activity in a Regional Economy: A Theoretical and Empirical Analysis of Alternative Methods." *International Regional Science Review* 5: 155–184.

Jackson, K.T. (1985). *Crabgrass Frontier: The Suburbanization of the United States.* New York: Oxford Univ. Press.

Jakubs, J.F. (1986). "Recent Racial Segregation in U.S. S.M.S.A.s." *Urban Geography* 7 (2): 146–163.

James, F. (1977). *Back to the City: An Appraisal of Housing Reinvestment and Population Change in Urban America.* Washington, D.C.: Urban Institute.

Janelle, D., and H.A. Millward (1976). "Locational Conflict Patterns and Urban Ecological Structure." *Tijdschrift voor Economische en Sociale Geographie* 67: 102–112.

Johnson, M.L. (1985). "Postwar Industrial Development in the Southeast and the Pioneer Role of Labor-Intensive Industry." *Economic Geography* 61 (1): 46–65.

Johnston, R.J. (1982). *The American Urban System: A Geographical Perspective.* New York: St. Martin's.

——— (1984). *Residential Segregation, the State, and Constitutional Conflict in American Urban Areas.* London: Academic Press.

Jones, H., and J.W. Simmons (1987). *Location, Location, Location: Analysing the Retail Environment.* Toronto: Methuen.

Jud, G.D., and J. Frew (1986). "Real Estate Brokers, Housing Prices, and the Demand for Housing." *Urban Studies* 23: 21–31.

Kaldor, N. (1966). *Causes of the Slow Rate of Economic Growth in the United Kingdom.* Cambridge: Cambridge Univ. Press.

Kantor, A.C., and J.D. Nystuen (1982). "De Facto Redlining: A Geographic View." *Economic Geography* 58 (4): 309–328.

Keinath Jr., W.F. (1985). "The Spatial Component of the Post-Industrial Society." *Economic Geography* 61 (3): 223–240.

Kellerman, A. (1985). "The Suburbanization of Retail Trade: A U.S. Nationwide View." *Geoforum* 16: 15–23.

Kemp, K.A. (1986). "Race, Ethnicity, Class and Urban Spatial Conflict: Chicago as a Crucial Test Case." *Urban Studies* 23: 197–208.

King, L.J. (1984). *Central Place Theory.* Beverly Hills: Sage.

Knox, P. (1982). *Urban Social Geography: An Introduction.* London: Longman.

Kondratieff, N.D. (1935). "The Long Wave in Economic Life." *Review of Economics and Statistics* 17: 105–115.

Krueger, R.R. (1982). "The Struggle to Preserve Specialty Crop Land in the Rural–Urban Fringe of the Niagara Peninsula of Ontario." *Environments* 14 (3): 1–10.

Kuznets, S. (1961). *Capital in the American Economy.* Princeton, N.J.: National Bureau of Economic Research.

Lake, R.W. (1981). *The New Suburbanites: Race and Housing in the Suburbs.* New Brunswick, N.J.: Rutgers University, Center for Urban Policy Research.

Lauria, M., and L. Knopp (1985). "Toward an Analysis of the Role of Gay Communities in the Urban Renaissance." *Urban Geography* 6 (2): 152–169.

Lawson, M. (1985). "The Flow of Federal Funds." *Intergovernmental Perspective* 11 (2/3): 18–19.

Leacy, F.H. (ed.) (1983). *Historical Statistics of Canada.* Ottawa: Statistics Canada and Social Science Federation of Canada.

Le Bourdais, C., and M. Beaudry (1988). "The Changing Residential Structure of Montreal." *The Canadian Geographer* 32 (2): 88–113.

Lee, Y., and M. McCracken (1982). "Spatial Adjustment of Retail Activity: A Spatial Analysis of Supermarkets in Metropolitan Denver, 1960–1980." *Regional Science Perspectives* 12 (2): 62–76.

Lefebvre, H. (1972). *La Pensée Marxiste et la Ville.* Paris: Casterman.

Lemon, J. (1985). *Toronto Since 1918: An Illustrated History.* Toronto: Lorimer.

Levin, C.L. (1978). "Growth and Nongrowth in Metropolitan Areas and the Emergence of Polycentric Metropolitan Form." *Papers of the Regional Science Association* 41: 101–112.

Levine, G.J. (1987). "To Tax or Not to Tax? Political Struggle Over Personal Property Taxation in Montreal and Toronto, 1870–1920." *International Journal of Urban and Regional Research* 11 (4): 543–566.

Lewis, P. (1983). "The Galactic Metropolis." In *Beyond the Urban Fringe,* edited by R. Platt and G. Macinko. Minneapolis: Univ. of Minnesota Press, pp. 23–49.

Ley, D. (1983). *A Social Geography of the City.* New York: Harper & Row.

——— (1986). "Alternative Explanations for Inner-City Gentrification: A Canadian Assessment." *Annals of the Association of American Geographers* 76 (4): 521–535.

Ley, D., and M.S. Samuels (1978). *Humanistic Geography.* Chicago: Maaroufa Press.

Lichtenberg, R.M. (1960). *One-Tenth of a Nation.* Cambridge, Mass.: Harvard Univ. Press.

London, B., B.A. Lee, and S.G. Lipton (1986). "The Determinants of Gentrification in the United States: A City-Level Analysis." *Urban Affairs Quarterly* 27 (3): 369–387.

Long, J.B., and C.I. Plosser (1983). "Real Business Cycles." *Journal of Political Economy* 91 (1): 39–69.

Long, L.H. (1983). "Population Redistribution in the U.S.: Issues for the 1980's." Washington, D.C.: Population Reference Bureau, Population Trends and Public Policy, No. 3.

Long, L.H., and C.G. Boertlein (1977). *The Geographical Mobility of Americans: An International Comparison.* Special Studies P-23, No. 64. Washington, D.C.: Bureau of the Census, Current Population Reports.

Long, L.H., and D.C. Dahmann (1980). "The City–Suburb Income Gap: Is it Being Narrowed by a Back-to-the-City Movement?" *Special Demographic Analyses.* CDS 80–1. Washington, D.C.: Bureau of the Census.

Long, L.H., and D. DeAre (1981). "The Suburbanization of Blacks." *American Demographics Magazine,* September 1981.

Lorimer, J. (1972). *A Citizen's Guide to City Politics.* Toronto: James Lewis and Samuel.

——— (1978). *The Developers.* Toronto: James Lorimer.

Lowry, I.S. (1964). *Model of a Metropolis.* RM-4035-RC. Santa Monica, Calif.: Rand Corporation.

Lupri, E. (1983). "The Changing Positions of Women and Men in Comparative Perspective." In *The Changing Position of Women in Family and Society,* edited by E. Lupri. Leiden: Brill, 3–39.

Maher, C.A. (1974). "Spatial Patterns in Urban Housing Markets: Filtering in Toronto." *The Canadian Geographer* 18: 108–124.

Maldonado, L., and J. Moore (eds.) (1985). *Urban Ethnicity in the United States: New Immigrants and Old Minorities.* Beverly Hills: Sage.

Malecki, E.J. (1981). "Product Cycles, Innovation Cycles and Regional Economic Change." *Technological Forecasting and Social Change* 19: 291–306.

——— (1985). "Industrial Location and Corporate Organization in High Technology Industries." *Economic Geography* 61 (4): 345–369.

Manson, G., and R. Groop (1986). "Nonemployment Income in the United States." Paper delivered at the 1986 American Association of Geographers Annual Meeting, Minneapolis–St. Paul.

Marchand, B. (1986). *The Emergence of Los Angeles.* London: Pion.

Massey, D. (1984a). *Spatial Divisions of Labor: Social Structures and the Geography of Production.* New York: Methuen.

——— (1984b). "Introduction: Geography Matters." In *Geography Matters!: A Reader,* edited by D. Massey and J. Allen. Cambridge: Cambridge Univ. Press, pp. 1–11.

Massey, D. *et al.* (1976). "A Strategy for Urban and Regional Research." *Regional Studies* 10: 381–387.

Mazey, M.E., and D. Lee (1983). *Her Space, Her Place: A Geography of Women.* Washington, D.C.: Association of American Geographers.

McCarthy, K.F. (1976). "The Household Life-Cycle and Housing Coices." *Papers of the Regional Science Association* 37: 55–80.

McClain, P.D. (1984) "Urban Neighborhoods, Black Residents, and Homicide Risks." *Urban Geography* 5, 3, 210–222.

McDermott, P., and M. Taylor (1982). *Industrial Organization and Location.* Cambridge: Cambridge Univ. Press.

McDonald, J. (1981). "Spatial Patterns of Business Land Values in Chicago." *Urban Geography* 2 (3): 201–215.

McDowell, L. (1983). "Toward an Understanding of the Gender Division of Urban Space." *Environment and Planning D: Society and Space* 1 (1): 59–72.

Miller, R.E., and P.D. Blair (1985). *Input–Output Analysis: Foundations and Extensions.* Englewood Cliffs, N.J.: Prentice-Hall.

Monden, Y. (1983). *Toyota Production System.* Norcross, Georgia: Industrial Engineering and Management Press.

Mooman, R.L. (1986). "Have Changes in Localization Economics Been Responsible for Declining Productivity Advantages in Large Cities?" *Journal of Regional Science* 26 (1): 19–32.

Moore, C.L., and M. Jacobsen (1984). "Minimum Requirements and Regional Economics, 1980." *Economic Geography* 60 (3): 217–224.

Moore, E. (1986). "Mobility Intention and Subsequent Relocation." *Urban Geography* 7 (6): 497–514.

Moore, E.G., and W.A.V. Clark (1986). "Stable Structure and Local Variation: A Comparison of Household Flows in Four Metropolitan Areas." *Urban Studies* 23: 185–196.

Morgan, K., and A. Sayer (1985). "The 'Modern' Industry in a 'Mature' Region: The Re-making of Management–Labour Relations." *International Journal of Urban and Regional Research* 9 (3): 383–404.

Morrill, R. L. (1982). "A Note: Continuing Deconcentrating Trends in Trade." *Growth and Change* 13 (1): 46–48.

——— (1987) "The Structure of Shopping in a Metropolis." *Urban Geography* 8 (2): 97–128.

Morrow-Jones, H.A. (1986). "The Geography of Housing: Elderly and Female Households." *Urban Geography* 7 (3): 263–269.

Moses, L.N., and H.F. Williamson (1967). "The Location of Economic Activity in Cities." *American Economic Review* 57: 211–222.

Muller, P.O. (1981). *Contemporary Suburban American.* Englewood Cliffs, N.J.: Prentice-Hall.

Mulligan, G.F. (1980). "The Effects of Multiplier Shifts in a Hierarchical City Size Model." *Regional Science and Urban Economics* 10: 53–76.

Murdie, R. (1969). *Factorial Ecology of Metropolitan Toronto, 1951–1961.* Chicago: Univ. of Chicago Press, Department of Geography, Research Paper No. 116.

Murdie, R.A. (1986). "Residential Mortgage Lending in Metropolitan Toronto: A Case Study of the Resale Market." *The Canadian Geographer* 30 (2): 98–110.

———— (1987). "Residential Structure of Metropolitan Toronto, 1951–1981." Paper presented at the 11th Annual Meeting of the Canadian Regional Science Association, May 29–30, 1987.

Muth, R.F. (1961). "The Spatial Structure of the Housing Market." *Papers of the Regional Science Association* 7: 207–220.

———— (1978). "The Allocation of Households to Dwellings." *Journal of Regional Science* 18: 159–178.

Myers, D. (1975). "Housing Allowances, Submarket Relationships, and the Filtering Process." *Urban Affairs Quarterly* 11: 215–240.

NAS/NRC (1982). *The Competitive State of the U.S. Auto Industry.* Washington: National Academy Press.

Nader, G.A. (1975). *Cities of Canada* (vols. 1 and 2). Toronto: Macmillan of Canada.

———— (1984). "The Rank-Size Model: A Non-Logarithmic Calibration." *The Professional Geographer* 36 (2): 221–227.

Nelson, H.J. (1983). *The Los Angeles Metropolis.* Dubuque, Iowa: Kendall/Hunt.

Nelson, K. (1986). "Labor Demand, Labor Supply and the Suburbanization of Low Wage Office Work." In *Production, Work, Territory: The Geographical Anatomy of Industrial Capitalism,* edited by A.J. Scott and M. Storper. Boston: Allen and Unwin.

Netzer, D. (1974). *Economics and Urban Problems* New York: Basic.

Newling, B.E. (1966). "Urban Growth and Spatial Structure: Mathematical Models and Empirical Evidence." *Geographical Review* 56: 213–225.

Newton K., and T.J. Karran (1985). *The Politics of Local Expenditure.* London: Macmillan.

Nilles, J.M., R. Carlson, P. Grey, and G. Heineman (1976). *Telecommunications–Transportation Trade-offs: Options for Tomorrow.* New York: Wiley.

Norcliffe, G.B. (1975). "A Theory of Manufacturing Places." In *Locational Dynamics of Manufacturing,* edited by L. Collins and D.F. Walker. New York: Wiley.

Norcliffe, G.B., and J.H. Stevens (1979). "The Heckscher–Ohlin Hypothesis and Structural Divergence in Quebec and Ontario, 1961–1969." *Canadian Geographer* 23 (3): 239–254.

Norton, R.D., and J. Rees (1979). "The Product Cycle and the Spatial Decentralization of American Manufacturing." *Regional Studies* 13: 141–151.

Oakey, R. (1985). "High-Technology Industries and Agglomeration Economics." In *Silicon Landscapes,* edited by P. Hall and A. Markusen. Boston: Allen and Unwin, pp. 94–117.

Ohta, H. (1984). "Agglomeration and Competition." *Regional Science and Urban Economics* 14 (1): 1–18.

OhUallachain, B. (1984). "Linkages and Direct Foreign Investment in the United States." *Economic Geography* 60 (3): 238–253.

O'Loughlin, J., and D.C. Munski (1979). "Housing Rehabilitation in the Inner City: A Comparison of Two Neighborhoods in New Orleans." *Economic Geography* 55: 52–70.

O'Leary, B. (1987). "Why Was the GLC Abolished?" *International Journal of Urban and Regional Research* 11 (2): 193–217.

Olson, S.H. (1979). "Baltimore Imitates the Spider." *Annals of the Association of American Geographers* 69 (4): 557–574.

Owen, W. (1966). *The Metropolitan Transportation Problem.* Washington, D.C.: The Brookings Institute.

Palen, J.J., and B. London (eds.) (1984). *Gentrification, Displacement and Neighborhood Revitalization.* Albany: State Univ. of New York Press.

Palm, R. (1976). "The Role of Real Estate Agents as Information Mediators in Two American Cities." *Geografiska Annaler,* 58B: 28–41.

——— (1985). "Ethnic Segmentation of Real Estate Agent Practice in the Urban Housing Market." *Annals of the Association of American Geographers* 75 (1): 58–68.

Park, R.E., E.W. Burgess, and R.D. McKenzie (1925). *The City.* Chicago: Chicago Univ. Press.

Parr, J.B., and C. Jones (1983). "City Size Distributions and Urban Density Functions: Some Interrelationships." *Journal of Regional Science* 23 (3): 283–308.

Pearce, D. (1983). "The Feminization of Ghetto Poverty." *Society.* Nov.–Dec.: 70–74.

Platt, R.H. (1985). "The Farmland Conversion Debate: NALS and Beyond." *The Professional Geographer* 37 (4): 433–442.

Popp, H. (1976). "The Residential Location Decision Process: Some Theoretical and Empirical Considerations." *Tijdschrift voor Economische en Social Geografie* 67: 300–306.

Potter, R.B. (1982). *The Urban Retailing System.* Aldershot, Eng.: Gower.

Pratt, E.E. (1911). *Industrial Causes of Congestion of Population in New York City.* New York: Columbia Univ. Press.

Pratt, G. (1986). "Housing Tenure and Social Cleavages in Urban Canada." *Annals of the Association of American Geographers* 76 (3): 366–380.

Pred, A. (1965). "Industrialization, Initial Advantage, and American Metropolitan Growth." *Geographical Review* 55 (2): 158–185.

——— (1985). "Interpenetrating Processes: Human Agency and the Becoming of Regional Spatial and Social Structures." *Papers of the Regional Science Association* 57: 7–17.

Quigley, J.M. (1978). "Housing Markets and Housing Demand: Analytical Approaches." In *Urban Housing Markets,* edited by L.S. Bourne and J.R. Hitchcock. Toronto: Univ. of Toronto Press, pp. 23–44.

Rees, P. (1968). "The Factorial Ecology of Metropolitan Chicago, 1960." Unpublished Ph.D. dissertation, University of Chicago.

———— (1970). "Concepts of Social Space: Toward an Urban Social Geography." In *Geographical Perspectives on Urban Systems,* edited by B.J.L. Berry and F. Horton. Englewood Cliffs, N.J.: Prentice-Hall.

Rose, H.M. (1971). *The Black Ghetto: A Spatial Behavioral Perspective.* New York: McGraw-Hill.

———— (1976). *Black Suburbanization: Access to Improved Quality of Life or Maintenance of the Status Quo.* Cambridge, Mass.: Ballinger.

Rose, H.M., and D.R. Deskins, Jr. (1980). "Felony Murder: The Case of Detroit." *Urban Geography* 1 (1): 1–22.

Rose, H.M., and P.D. McClain (1981). *Black Homicide and the Urban Environment.* Washington, D.C.: National Institutes of Health.

Roseman, C. (1980). "Exurban Areas and Exurban Migration." In *The American Metropolitan System,* edited by S.D. Brunn and J.O. Wheeler. New York: Halsted.

Rossi, P.H. (1980). *Why Families Move.* 2nd ed. Beverly Hills: Sage. Originally published in 1955.

Rossi, P.H., and A.B. Shlay (1982). "Residential Mobility and Public Policy Issues: Why Families Move Revisited." *Journal of Social Issues* 38 (3): 21–34.

Rostow, W.W. (1975). "Kondratieff, Schumpeter, and Kuznets." *Journal of Economic History* 35 (4): 719–733.

Rothwell, R. (1982). "The Role of Technology in Industrial Change: Implications for Regional Policy." *Regional Studies* 16 (5): 361–369.

Rowles, G.D. (1978). *Prisoners of Space?* Boulder, Colo.: Westview.

Russwurm, L.H., and C.R. Bryant (1984). "Changing Population Distribution and Rural/Urban Relationships in Canadian Urban Fields, 1941–1976." In *The Pressure of Change in Rural Canada,* edited by M.F. Bunce and M.J. Troughton. Toronto: York Univ. Press; Geographical Monographs, No. 14.

Sancton, A. (1985). *Governing the Island of Montreal: Language Differences and Metropolitan Politics.* Berkeley: Univ. of California Press.

Sands, G. (1982). *Land Office Business, Land and Housing Prices in Rapidly Growing Metropolitan Areas.* Lexington, Mass.: Heath.

Sawers, L., and W.K. Tabb (1984). *Sunbelt/Snowbelt: Urban Development and Regional Restructuring.* New York: Oxford Univ. Press.

Saxenian, A. (1984). "The Urban Contradictions of Silicon Valley: Regional Growth and the Restructuring of the Semiconductor Industry." In *Sunbelt/Snowbelt: Urban Development and Regional Restructuring,* edited by L. Sawers and W.K. Tabb. New York: Oxford Univ. Press.

Schaffer, R., and N. Smith (1986). "The Gentrification of Harlem?" *Annals of the Association of American Geographers* 76 (3): 347–365.

Schill, M.H., and R.P. Nathan (1983). *Revitalizing America's Cities: Neighborhood Reinvestment and Displacement.* Albany, N.Y.: SUNY Press.

Schoenberger, E. (1985). "Foreign Manufacturing Investment in the United States: Competitive Strategies and International Location." *Economic Geography* 61 (3): 241–259.

Schwartz, G.G. (1979). "The Office Pattern in New York City, 1960–79." In *Spatial Patterns of Office Growth and Location,* edited by P.W. Daniels. New York: Wiley, pp. 215–238.

Scott, A.J. (1980). *The Urban Land Nexus and the State.* London: Pion.

———— (1981). "The Spatial Structure of Metropolitan Labor Markets and the Theory of Intra-Urban Plant Location." *Urban Geography* 2: 1–30.

———— (1982a). "Locational Patterns and Dynamics of Industrial Activity in the Modern Metropolis." *Urban Studies* 19: 111–142.

———— (1982b). "Production System Dynamics and Metropolitan Development." *Annals of the Association of American Geographers* 72 (2): 185–200.

———— (1983a). "Industrial Organization and the Logic of Intra-Metropolitan Location: Theoretical Considerations." *Economic Geography* 59 (3): 233–250.

———— (1983b). "Industrial Organization and the Logic of Intra-Metropolitan Location: A Case Study of the Printed Circuits Industry in the Greater Los Angeles Region." *Economic Geography* 59 (4): 343–367.

———— (1983c). "Location and Linkage Systems: A Survey and Reassessment." *Annals of Regional Science* 17: 1–39.

———— (1984). "Industrial Organization and the Logic of Intra-Metropolitan Location: A Case Study of the Women's Dress Industry in the Greater Los Angeles Region." *Economic Geography* 60 (1): 3–27.

———— (1986a). "High Technology Industry and Territorial Development: The Rise of the Orange County Complex, 1955–1984." *Urban Geography* 7 (1): 3–45.

———— (1986b). "Industrial Organization and Location: Division of Labor, the Firm, and Spatial Process." *Economic Geography* 62 (3): 215–231.

———— (1988). *Metropolis: From Division of Labor to Urban Form.* Berkeley: Univ. of California Press.

Semple, R.K., and M.B. Green (1983). "Intraurban Corporate Headquarters Relocation in Canada." *Cahiers de Geographie du Quebec* 27 (72): 389–406.

Semple, R.K., and A.G. Phipps (1982). "The Spatial Evolution of Corporate Headquarters within an Urban System." *Urban Geography* 3 (3): 258–279.

Shearer, D. (1982). "How Progressives Won in Santa Monica." *Social Policy* 12 (Winter): 7–14.

Shevky, E., and W. Bell (1955). *Social Area Analysis: Theory, Illustrative Applications and Computational Procedures.* Stanford, Calif.: Stanford Univ. Press.

Shevky, E., and M. Williams (1949). *The Social Areas of Los Angeles: Analysis and Typology.* Los Angeles: Univ. of California Press.

Sidel, R. (1986). *Women and Children Last: The Plight of Poor Women in Affluent America.* New York: Viking.

Simmons, J.W. (1978). "The Organization of the Urban System." In *Systems of Cities: Readings on Structure, Growth and Policy,* edited by L.S. Bourne and J.W. Simmons. New York: Oxford Univ. Press.

———— (1984). "Government and the Canadian Urban System: Income Tax, Transfer Payments, and Employment." *The Canadian Geographer* 28 (1): 18–45.

Simmons, J.W., and L. Bourne (1982). "Urban/Regional Systems and the State." *Progress In Human Geography* 6 (3): 431–440.

Sinclair, V. (1906). *The Jungle.* New York: Doubleday, Page.

Slack, B. (1988). "The Evolution of Montreal's Post-service Industry." *The Canadian Geographer* 32 (2): 124–132.

Smith, N. (1979). "Gentrification and Capital: Theory, Practice, and Ideology in Society Hill." *Antipode* 11 (3): 24–35.

Smith, N., and M. LeFaivre (1984). "A Class Analysis of Gentrification." In *Gentrification, Displacement and Neighborhood Revitalization,* edited by J.J. Palen and B. London. Albany, N.Y.: SUNY Press.

Smith, P.J., and D.B. Johnson (1978). *The Edmonton–Calgary Corridor.* Edmonton: Department of Geography, University of Alberta.

Smith, P.J., and L.D. McCann (1981). "Residential Land Use Change in Inner Edmonton." *Annals of the Association of American Geographers* 71 (4): 536–551.

Smith, W.R. (1982). *Aspects of Growth in a Regional System: Southern Ontario, 1851–1921.* Toronto: York Univ. Press; Geographical Monographs No. 12.

Snow, D.A., and P.J. Leahy (1980). "The Making of a Black Slum Ghetto: A Case Study of Neighborhood Transition." *The Journal of Applied Behavioral Science* 16 (4): 459–481.

Spain, D., and Long, L.H. (1981). "Black Movers to the Suburbs: Are They Moving to Predominantly White Neighborhoods?" *Special Demographic Analyses.* CDS 80–4. Washington, D.C.: Bureau of the Census.

Stabler, J.C. (1987). "Trade Center Evolution in the Great Plains." *Journal of Regional Science* 27 (2): 225–244.

Statistics Canada (1984a). *Canada Yearbook, 1984.* Ottawa: Supply and Services.

——— (1984b). *Metropolitan Atlas Series.* Cat. 99-927. Ottawa: Supply and Services, Geography Division.

——— (1984c). *System of National Accounts, National Income and Expenditure Accounts: The Annual Estimates.* Cat. No. 13-201. Ottawa: Supply and Services.

Steed, G.P.F. (1973). "Intrametropolitan Manufacturing: Spatial Distribution and Locational Dynamics in Greater Vancouver." *The Canadian Geographer* 17: 235–258.

——— (1976). "Standardization, Scale, Incubation and Inertia: Montreal and Toronto Clothing Industries." *The Canadian Geographer* 20: 298–309.

Stephens, J.D., and B.P. Holly (1981). "City Systems Behavior and Corporate Influence: The Headquarters Location of U.S. Industrial Firms, 1955–1975." *Urban Studies* 18: 285–300.

Stone, M.E. (1978). "Housing, Mortgage Lending and the Contradictions of Capitalism." In *Marxism and the Metropolis,* edited by W.K. Tabb and L. Sawers. New York: Oxford Univ. Press, pp. 179–207.

Storper, M., and S. Christopherson (1987). "Flexible Specialization and Regional Industrial Agglomeration: The Case of the U.S. Motion Picture Industry." *Annals of the Association of American Geographers* 77 (1): 104–117.

Suarez-Villa, L. (1984). "The Manufacturing Process Cycle and the Industrialization of the United States–Mexico Borderlands." *Annals of Regional Science* 18 (1): 1–23.

Tabb, W.K. (1984). "The New York City Fiscal Crisis." In *Marxism and the Metropolis,* edited by W.K. Tabb and L. Sawers. New York: Oxford Univ. Press, pp. 323–345.

Taub, R.P., D.G. Taylor, and J.D. Durham (1984). *Paths of Neighborhood Change: Race and Crime in Urban America.* Chicago: Univ. of Chicago Press.

Thirwall, A.P. (1983). "A Plain Man's Guide to Kaldor's Growth Laws." *Journal of Post-Keynesian Economics* 5 (3): 345–358.

Trachte, K., and R. Ross (1985). "The Crisis of Detroit and the Emergence of Global Capitalism." *International Journal of Urban and Regional Research* 9 (2): 186–217.

United Nations (1983). *Industry in a Changing World.* Vienna: United Nations Industrial Development Organization.

Vance Jr., J.E. (1977). *This Scene of Man.* New York: Harper & Row.

van Duijn, J.J. (1983). *The Long Wave in Economic Life.* London: Allen and Unwin.

Varaiya, P., and M. Wiseman (1981). "Investment and Employment in Manufacturing in U.S. Metropolitan Areas 1960–1976." *Regional Science and Urban Economics* 11 (4): 431–469.

Vining Jr., D.R., Dobronyi, J.B., M.A. Otness, and J.E. Schwinn (1982). "A Principal Axis Shift in the American Spatial Economy?" *The Professional Geographer* 34 (3): 270–278.

Wacquant, L.J.D., and W.J. Wilson (1988). "Beyond Welfare Reform: Poverty, Joblessness, and the Social Transformation of the Inner City." Paper presented at the Rockefeller Foundation Conference on Welfare Reform, Williamsburg, Virginia, February, 1988.

Walker, R.A. (1981). "A Theory of Suburbanization: Capitalism and the Construction of Urban Space in the United States." In *Urbanization and Urban Planning in Capitalist Society,* edited by M. Dear and A. Scott. New York: Methuen, pp. 383–422.

———— (1985). "Class, Division of Labour and Employment in Space." In *Social Relations and Spatial Structures,* edited by D. Gregory and J. Urry. London: Macmillan, pp. 164–189.

Walker, R., and M. Storper (1981). "Capital and Industrial Location." *Progress in Human Geography* 5 (4): 473–511.

Wallace, I. (1985). "Towards a Geography of Agribusiness." *Progress in Human Geography* 9 (4): 491–514.

Ward, D. (1971). *Cities and Immigrants: A Geography of Change in Nineteenth Century America.* New York: Oxford Univ. Press.

Warner, B.J. (1962). *Streetcar Suburbs: The Process of Growth in Boston.* Cambridge, MA: Harvard Univ. Press.

Weaver, C.L., and R.F. Babcock (1979). *City Zoning: The Past and Future Frontier.* Chicago: American Planning Association.

Webber, M.J. (1984). *Industrial Location.* Beverly Hills: Sage.

Weber, A. (1929). *Theory of the Location of Industries.* Chicago: Univ. of Chicago Press. Originally published in 1909.

Weber, A.F. (1899). *The Growth of Cities in the Nineteenth Century.* New York: Macmillan. Reprinted by Cornell Univ. Press, 1965.

Webster, D. (1985). "Canadian Regional Decentralization in the New Global Context: Myth or Reality." *The Canadian Journal of Regional Science* 8 (3): 377–394.

Wheaton, W.C. (1983). "Theories of Urban Growth and Metropolitan Spatial Development." In *Research in Urban Economics,* edited by J. Henderson. Greenwich, Conn.: JAI Press Inc., pp. 3–36.

Wheeler, J.O., and C.L. Brown (1985). "The Metropolitan Corporate Hierarchy in the U.S. South, 1960–1980." *Economic Geography* 61 (1): 66–78.

Whitt, J.A., and G. Yago (1985). "Corporate Strategies and the Decline of Transit in U.S. Cities." *Urban Affairs Quarterly* 21 (September): 37–65.

Wilder, M.G. (1985). "Site and Situation Determinants of Land Use Change: An Empirical Example." *Economic Geography* 61 (4): 332–344.

Wilson, A.G. (1986). "Store and Shopping Centre Location and Size: A Review of British Research and Practice." *Working Paper 455.* Leeds: School of Geography, The University of Leeds, UK.

Wilson, F.D. (1979). *Residential Consumption, Economic Opportunity, and Race.* New York: Academic Press.

Winsberg, M.D. (1986). "Ethnic Segregation and Concentration in Chicago Suburbs." *Urban Geography* 7 (2): 135–145.

Winsborough, H., K.E. Taeuber, and A. Sorensen (1975). "Models of Change in Residential Segregation." Madison: Univ. of Wisconsin, Center for Demography and Ecology. Paper 75–26.

Wirth, L. (1938). "Urbanism as a Way of Life." *American Journal of Sociology* 44: 3–24.

Wolch, J.R., and R.K. Geiger (1986). "Urban Restructuring and the Not-for-Profit Sector." *Economic Geography* 62 (1): 3–18.

Yeates, M. (1965). "Some Factors Affecting the Spatial Distribution of Chicago Land Values." *Economic Geography* 41: 55–70.

——— (1975a). *Main Street: Windsor to Quebec City.* Toronto: Macmillan of Canada.

——— (1975b). *An Introduction to Quantitative Analysis in Human Geography.* New York: McGraw-Hill.

——— (1980). *North American Urban Patterns.* London: Edward Arnold.

——— (1984). "Urbanization in the Windsor–Quebec City Axis, 1921–1981." *Urban Geography* 5 (1): 2–24.

——— (1985a). *Land in Canada's Urban Heartland.* Ottawa: Environment Canada; Lands Directorate.

——— (1985b). "The Core/Periphery Model and Urban Development in Central Canada." *Urban Geography* 6 (2): 101–121.

——— (1986). "The Industrial Heartland: Its Changing Role and Internal Structure." In *Heartland and Hinterland: A Geography of Canada,* edited by L.D. McCann. Toronto: Prentice-Hall.

Young, M., and P. Willmot (1975). *The Symmetrical Family.* Middlesex, Eng.: Penguin.

Index

Abandoned farmland, 131, 208, 220
Abandoned housing, 215–218
  causes of, 216
  clusters of, 215
  cycle of, 217
  policy approaches, 218
Abandonment watch, 218
Absentee landlords, 176
Accessibility, 241
Accumulation of urban infrastructure, 126
Adult life cycle and residential location, 165
Aerospace industries, 52
Affordable housing, 219
Agglomeration, economies of, 86–87, 237
Aggregate transportation costs, 130
Aging population, 54
Agribusiness, 64
Agricultural revolution, 29
Aircraft manufacturing, 35, 52, 86–87
Air pollution, 285
Air transportation, 51
Akron, Ohio, 22
Albany, New York, 22
Albuquerque, New Mexico, 22, 264
Alienation, 151, 152
Allentown, Pennsylvania, 22
Amenities and land values, 133
Amenity factors, 87, 163
Amenity locations, 178
Anchorage–Greater Anchorage Borough, Alaska, 284

Ann Arbor, Michigan, 208
Arterial roads, 241
Aspatial processes, 2, 3
Assembly-type factory production, 93, 96
Assessed property values, 133, 145
Assimilation, 110
Atlanta, Georgia, 22, 23, 58, 251, 252, 254, 256, 264
  census, metropolitan area, 15
  Central Business District (CBD), 14, 104, 113, 114
  city of, 14
  daily urban system, 15
  journey to work, 15
  Metropolitan Atlanta Regional Transit Authority (MARTA), 14
  Standard Metropolitan Statistical Area (SMSA), 14
  urban field of 15
Austin, Texas, 22
Auto Pact, 64
Automobile, 115, 116
  industry, 34, 117
  ownership, 116
  and public transit, 115, 120
  rows, 242–243
Automotive Trade Agreement, 5, 64

Baby boom, 35, 122, 166
Bakersfield, California, 22
Baltimore, Maryland, 22–23, 37, 45, 101–103, 215, 223, 252, 270, 273
  ethnic areas, 213

major housing submarkets by source of finance, 210–212
  residential mobility rate, 163
Bay Area Rapid Transit System (BART), 109
Behavioral approaches, 6–8
Bellevue, Washington, 247–248
Belt-line freeways, 253
Belt-line railroads, 228
Belt Railroad Company, The (BRC), 229
Beverly Hills, California, 124
Biotechnology, 35
Birmingham, Alabama, 22, 252, 264
Birth rates, 4, 107
Black population, 120, 171, 250, 260
  community, 246
  core area, 171
  fringe area, 171
  ghettos, 171, 177
  spatial concentration of, 2
  suburbanization of, 147, 174
  zone in transition, 171
Blue-collar workers, 97, 176
Boise, Idaho, 252
Boston, Massachusetts, 22–23, 45, 59, 102, 106–107, 112, 134, 169, 175, 215, 226, 264, 269, 273, 284
  abondoned housing in, 217
  residential mobility rate, 163
Branch plant production, 63
Break-of-bulk sites, 84, 94
Bridgeport, Connecticut, 23
Brooklyn, New York, 39, 215, 252

Brown–Moore model, 196
Buffalo, New York, 22, 23, 51, 264
  residential mobility rate, 163
Building codes, 263, 279
Building industry sector, 205
Burgess's concentric zone model, 110
Burnaby, B.C., 231
Burrough, Kentucky, 84
Business cycles, 32, 43

Calgary, Alberta, 4, 22, 61–62, 64, 66, 100, 156, 269
  census metropolitan area (CMA), 155
  the elderly in, 156
  social area of, 157
Calgary–Edmonton corridor, 3, 66, 109, 110
Canada, constitutional framework in, 263
  urbanization in, 29
Canadian
  urban development, 66
  urban system, 30, 60
Canton, Ohio, 22, 23
Capital-to-capital relations, 89–90
Capital investments, 8, 68
Capitalism, 8, 47, 89
Capital-to-labor ratios, 70
Capital-labor relations, 90–91
Capital/labor substitution, 236
Capital-to-state relations, 91–92
Careerism, formal social arrangements in, 167
  lifestyle value, 167
Carrying charges, 187
Census tract, 149, 153, 158, 194, 212
Central business district (CBD), 106–108, 110, 131–132, 178, 237, 240–241, 246, 251, 259
  fringe of, 110, 119, 121, 133, 190; central Canada, 63
  manufacturing heartland of, 4
Central cities, 3, 49, 53, 120, 123, 143, 161, 181, 223, 227, 251, 262, 270, 274, 275
  indices of disparity with suburbs, 262–264
Central clusters, 233
  incubation function of, 237
  plants in, 233
Central density, 137
  change in, 138
  and city size, 138–139

Centrality, 131, 245
Central Mortgage and Housing Corporation (CMHC), 118, 189, 208
Central place theory, 19, 240
Chambers of commerce, 178
Charleston, 22
Charlotte, North Carolina, 22
Chattanooga, Tennessee, 22
Chicago, Illinois, 20, 22–24, 40, 45, 51, 58–59, 103, 105, 108, 111, 123, 133–134, 163, 173, 175, 207, 215, 226–229, 243, 252, 254, 264, 273
  black and white population in, 150
  residential mobility rate, 163
Chicago school of human ecology, 149
Chicoutimi–Jonquiere, Quebec, 4
Child care, 183, 184
Chinatown (San Francisco), 243
Chinese-Americans, 155
Cincinnati, Ohio, 22–23, 38, 40, 103, 239, 252
  residential mobility rate, 163
City, the, social structure of, 7, 153, 198
City-county consolidation, 284
  Baton Rouge-East Baton Rouge, 284
  problem with, 284
City government, 223
Cities, hierarchy of, 20
  fringe of, 177
City serving sector, 16
City supporting sector, 16
Clark model, 136, 137
Class, 106
  and conflict, 177, 182
  distinctions and control, 175
  divisions, 52, 105
  or racial bias, 207
  and social space, 175
Classical political economy, 8
Classic industrial city, 101, 102
Classification yards, 103
Clearing Industrial District, 229
Cleveland, Ohio, 22–23, 45, 51, 58, 144, 161, 199, 215, 226, 227–228, 252, 273, 279
  residential mobility rate, 163
Clinton Coalition of Concern (CCC), 178
Clothing industries, 86
Clustering, 241, 244
  centralized, 233
  decentralized, 233
Cognitive images, 249

Collective agreements, 91
Columbia, South Carolina, 22, 112
Columbus, Ohio, 22, 264
Columbus–Muscogee County, Ohio, 284
Commercial areas, 240
Commercial land uses, 98
Common law of nuisances, 143
Communications, 47
  technologies, 256
Communities, 149, 205
Community level nucleations, 246
Community space, 193
Commuter railroads, 103, 113, 115
Commuters' zone, 111
Commuting, 136, 190, 270
  behavior, 140
  cross-town, 115, 119, 126, 140
  fields, 51
Complete shopping service centers, 21
Components of costs to the firm, 80–81
Computer mapping, 6
Computers, 259
Concentration, 55
  of capital, 206
  diseconomies, 88
  economies, 88, 123, 231, 237
  of women, 180
Concentric zones, 129
  zone model, 149
Conditional grants, 272
Condominiums, 186
Conduits of capital, 93
Congestion, 106
Conservation, 279
Construction, companies, 206
  unions, 206
Consumer behavior and cognition, 240–248
Consumer
  durables, 235
  households, 8
  services, 239–240
  society, 35
Contact intensity, 255
  principles of, 255
Contacts, 153
Contact variety, 255
  the principle of, 255
Containers, 85
Contract rent, 129
Convenience goods and services, 244
Conversion of land use, 145
Core/periphery, 53, 77
  model, 47, 54

Corporate headquarters, 53, 66, 258
Corpus Christi, Texas, 264
Cosmopolitanism, lifestyle value, 167
Cost-sharing schemes, 272
Costs of delivery of goods, 81
Counterurbanization, 55, 58
County governments, 272
Crime, 196, 275
Crow Rate (Canada), 83
Cultural and ethnic groups, 152

Dallas, Texas, 52, 112, 123, 161, 215, 252, 264
    residential mobility rate, 163
Dallas–Fort Worth, Texas, 22–23, 58–59, 253, 273
Day care, 35, 183
    facilities, 166, 181
Dayton, Ohio, 22
Decentralization, 51, 117, 126, 140, 227, 230, 239, 250, 254, 256, 261, 275
    and developers and financial institutions, 119, 120
    and government, 117
Decentralized clusters, 237, 259
    plants in, 233
Declining death rates, 29
Deconcentration, 49, 55, 77, 93, 113, 147
Decongestion, 106
Decreasing heterogeneity, 58
Deindustrialization, 75, 188
Demand-side housing subsidies, 188, 189, 192
Demographic changes, 67
Demographic structure of the population, 186
Density gradient, 137, 141, 152
    change in, 138
    and city size, 138
    by population size, 139
Denver, Colorado, 22, 58, 199, 214, 235, 252, 253, 264
Denver–Boulder, Colorado, 23
Department of Housing and Urban Development (HUD), 188
Deregulation, 92
Des Moines, Iowa, 22, 112, 252
Detroit, Michigan, 20–24, 45, 51, 58, 138, 163, 215, 218, 226–227, 251, 264, 273
    residential mobility rate, 163
    SMSA, house prices and month rent values, 169
Developers, 145, 187, 205, 206, 210

Development companies, 120
Development process, 119
Differential rent, 134
Differential urban growth, 59
Differentiation of groups by social class, 151–153
Diffusion, 2, 20
Direct transfers, 268, 271
Disadvantaged, 178
Discount stores, 243
Discrimination, 142
Disinvesting, 222
Dispersed employment opportunities, 140
Diversified economies, 54
Division of labor, 52
Downtown area, 94, 123, 156, 165, 254, 255
    and cosmopolitan lifestyles, 167
Durable goods, 69, 70

Early industrial capitalism, 33, 38
Early industrial revolution era, 228
East Vancouver, B.C., 231
Ecological fallacy, 156
Ecological perspective and residential location, 192
Economic
    base approach, 16, 68
    computational difficulties, 17
    multiplier, 16
Economic cycles, 32
Economic differentiation, 152
Economic growth, 68, 69
Economic processes, 3
Economic rent, 127–129
    changing patterns of, 133
    curve for manufacturing, 131
    definition of, 128
    sources of, 134
Economies of concentration, 87
Economies of scale, 281
Edmonton, Alberta, 4, 22, 61, 62, 64, 66, 100
    light rail lines, 109
    West Edmonton Mall, 247
Elderly, 178, 192, 195, 262
Elderly poor, 189, 195, 210
Electric streetcar (trolley), 106
Elevated lines (El), 108
Elevated rapid transit systems, 109
Elizabeth, New Jersey, 123
El Paso, Texas, 22
Employee accessibility, 255
Employment, 198
    location of, 226
    opportunities, 53, 166, 183

Enabling technologies, 67, 89
Entertainment districts, 241, 242
Environmental impact studies, 107
Equalization payments, 5
Era of Industrial Capitalism, 64
Erie Canal, 38, 40
Ethnic, 250
    groups, 153, 198
    status factors, 152, 161
Ethnicity, 161, 184
    and race and locational decisions, 168
European Economic Community, 89
Evanston, Illinois, 151
Everett, Washington, 247
Exclusionary zoning, 145
Existing buildings sector, 205
Exotic markets, 242
Expansion, 32
Experiential information, 249
Expressways, 119, 241
External economies, 234, 237, 238, 241
Externalities, 144, 177, 276
Exurban fringe, 205
Exurbanization, 57
Exurbs, 103, 207, 222

Fabricated products, 81, 93
    integration of, 95
Fabricating activities, 77
Fabricating plants, 94
Face-to-face contact, 88, 93–94, 233, 255, 258–259
Factor analysis, 158, 160, 194
Factorial urban ecology, 156, 158, 159, 176, 192
Factors in rural/urban migration, 29
Factory system, 38
Familism, and the suburbs, 167
Family households, 186, 194
Family status, 153, 195
    construct, 161, 166
    factors, 159, 161
Federal expenditures, 49
Federal fair housing laws, 174
Federal Housing Act (1949), 117, 188
Federation, 284
Female labor participation, 156
Female participation rates, 257
Female workers, 240
FHA and VA programs, 211
FHA loan program, 187, 188
FHA mortgage guarantees, 213
Field work, 6

Fifth Kondratieff, 57, 64, 66, 179
    long waves, 122
Filtering, 200
    and public policy, 200
    rates of, 201
Financial institutions, 94, 115, 176
Firms, organizational structure of, 92
Fiscal responsibility, 274–277
Fiscal squeeze, 275
Fiscal zoning, 277
Flint, Michigan, 208
    black population in 1980, 209
    mortgage loan applications, 209
Flows of federal funds, 50, 56
Foreign immigration, 29
Foreign investment, 73
Fort MacMurray, Alberta, 66
Forward-and-backward linkages, 87
Fourth Kondtratieff long wave, 48
Freeway intersections, 131
Freeway, 119
    systems, 126, 241, 256
Freight charge, 44, 83
Fresno, California, 22
Friction of distance, 39
Fringe, 143
    zone, 116
Frontier–mercantile, 33–38, 60
Frontier–mercantile city, 102
Frontier–staples era, 60, 61
Full convenience service centers, 21
Furniture districts, 242
Furniture industries, 52

Galactic city, 101, 122, 126
Garden suburbs, 108
Gateway cities, 38, 41, 60–61, 102
Gateway ports, 84
Gay communities and redevelopment, 167
Gender discrimination, 179, 219
Gender roles, explanations of, 181–182
Gender theory, 181
General and spatial factors in location theory, 80
General zoning, 144
Gentrification, 218, 221–245
    benefits and costs, 223
    demographic explanation of, 222
    economic base explanations of, 222

economic causes of, 222
    the impact of, 222
    political economy explanations of, 222
    sociocultural explanation, 222
    theoretical explanations of, 221
Ghetto, definition of, 170
Glendale, California, 125, 235
Global capitalism, 58–59, 66, 96, 178
Government and housing supply, 188
Government area reform, 281
Government expenditures, 49
Government intervention, 178, 188
Government policies, 2, 211
Government spending, 48
Gravity model, 13
Great Depression, 47, 266
Great Lakes megalopolis, 51
Greenbelts, 145
Greenfield location, 232
Gross domestic product (GDP), 66, 69
Gross national product (GNP), 30, 48, 49, 63
    per capita, 31

Halifax, N.S., 4, 60–61, 221
Hamilton, Ontario, 4, 22, 61–62, 66, 95
Hamlet service centers, 21
Harris–Ullman multiple-nuclei model, 110, 113
Harrisburg, Pennsylvania, 22
Hartford, Connecticut, 22, 23
Headquarter offices, 64, 92, 96, 259
    location of, 23
Heartland, 49
Heavy manufacturing, 85, 113
Heterogeneity, 150–152, 168
Hierarchical zoning, 144
Hierarchy, 19, 42, 240–241, 245, 248
    changes in, 24
High and low income group trade-offs, 191
High-class residential areas, 111–113
Higher-order functions, 246
"Highest" and "best" land use, 129, 143
High family status, 154
High-income households, 190–191
High-revenue low service-cost land uses, 277
High-rise apartments, 194

High value-added, 72
    industries, 70
Highway facilities, 235
Highway improvements, 177
Highway-oriented ribbons, 243
Historical materialism, 10
Hobby-farm, 205
Home, value of, 153
Home financing, 212
Homeowners, 196, 218
Homeownership, 176, 187, 188, 208
Homicide rate, 172
Homogeneity, 150
Honolulu, Hawaii, 251–252
Horse car, 103
Horse-drawn omnibus, 103
Hourly earnings, 86
Household, 35
    and children, 262
    indifference curves, 190
    one-person, 156
    savings, 80
    size, 122
    type, 205
    units, 161
    wealth, 263
Houses, filtering of, 216
Housing, 187
    attributes, 185
    bylaws, 222
    choice and location, 189
    as a complex good, 185
    construction, 188
    costs and transportation costs trade-off, 190
    demand and supply for, 185, 186
    discrimination, 215
    lack of choice in, 200
    markets, 192, 198, 205, 217
    policies, 117
    starts, 101
    stock, 187, 203, 204
    subdivisions, 118
    submarket approach, 8
    submarkets, 201, 202, 203, 204
    submarkets and financial institutions, 209
    submarkets and real estate agents, 213
    supply of, 187, 188, 200
    tenure and politics, 204
    type, 204
Houston, Texas, 11, 22, 23, 52, 135, 215, 220, 252, 273
    residential mobility rate, 163
    ship canal, 52
Hoyt's sector model, 110
Human ecology approach, 203
Humanistic approach, 7

Huntington, West Virginia, 84
Hydropower sites, 37

Immigrants, 34
Immigration, 59, 107, 110, 151, 187
Impact zoning, 145
Improved capital value (ICV), 146, 147
Incipient cores, 53, 59
Income-differentiated communities, 122
Income gap, 223
Income-redistribution activities, 275
Incubator function, 235, 237
Incumbent upgrading, 218, 223, 224
    compared with gentrification, 223
    compared with redevelopment, 223
Indianapolis, Indiana, 22, 112, 252
Indifference curves, 190–191
Industrial
    activity in outer suburban ring, 232
    capitalism, 7
    districts, 105
    era, home and work in, 182
    heartland, 75
    innovation, 77
    land, 125–126
    land uses, 98
    park, 121, 234, 237
    restructuring, 88
    revolution, 29
    suburb, 113
Industrialization, 106
    full-scale, 43
Industry
    decentralization of, 231
    and property, 213
    spatial groups of, 231
Infant mortality in black areas, 172
Information technologies, 35, 66
In-migration, 171, 216, 275
Inner city, 88, 120, 121, 123, 174, 188, 207–208, 212, 215, 221, 260–262
Inner suburban ring, 121
Innovation, 152
Innovation diffusion, 46
Input/output approach, 17
Input/output multiplier, 16, 18, 19
Inputs, cost of, 81
Institutional investors, 187
Insurance agents, 205, 206

Integrated assembly plants, 95
Integration, 73, 93, 95, 151, 170
Interaction, 13, 20, 151
Intercity migration, 59
Interest groups, 178
Intergovernmental grants, 280
Intergovernmental transfers, 271
Interindustry linkages, 93, 95
Interpersonal contacts, 151
Interstate Highway Act (1956), 119
Interstate highway system, 41
Interurban analysis, 24
Interurban flows, 46
Intraurban issues, 24
Intraurban retail location, 240
Intraurban transportation, 102, 103, 106
Invasion–succession–dominance model, 149, 150
Inventory cycles, 32
Isodemographic map, 11
Italian/French dimension, 159

Jackson, Mississippi, 112
Jacksonville, Florida, 22
Jobs, decentralization of, 285
Journey to work, 115, 116, 122, 181, 257
    costs of, 190

Kansas City, Missouri, 22, 23
Keynesian multiplier, 16
Kingston, Ontario, 61
Kitchener, Ontario, 4
Knoxville, Tennessee, 20
Kondratieff
    long waves, 33, 67, 100
    swings, 33, 105, 119, 123, 215
Kuznet, or building, cycles, 100

Labor, 8
Labor costs, 80, 96
    and supplies, 95
    variations in, 86
Labor-intensive, 97
Labor-intensive industries, 77
Labor market areas, 257
Labor markets, 92, 93
Land, 8
    banks, 120
    consumption rates (LCR) and city size, 99
    development, 108
    market, 143
    owners, 8
    prices, 100, 147
    sales, 107
    use, 127
    use change, 179

use planning, 279
use zones, 129
use zones in a monocentric city, 132
use zones in a multicentered city, 132
value maps, 133
values, 127, 133, 241, 245
value surfaces for the city of Chicago, 134
Land developers, 108
Landlords and housing submarkets, 214
Large-lot zoning, 277
Large suburban nucleations, employment in, 227
Late adulthood, stage in life cycle, 165
Late capitalism, 7
Least-cost locations, 82
Least-cost theory, 78, 80, 96
Lender-insurance scheme, 189
Leverage, 214
Levittown, New York, 119
Lexington, Kentucky, 85
Lexington–Fayette County, 284
Life cycle, 198, 249, 250
    locational considerations, 164, 167
    major product, 33
    model, age and income, 166
    model, criticism of, 166
    model and household size, 166
    moves, 165, 166
    and social space, 164
    stages in, 192, 193, 219
Lifestyle, 194
    amenities, 215
Lifetime moves, interurban, 163
Light rail transit, 85, 109–110
Limited-access freeways, 119
Living conditions in nineteenth-century cities, 44
Loan defaults, 187
Local government, 86, 145, 205–206, 222, 235, 261, 263
    between 1910 and 1935, 266
    changing role of, 265
    at the end of the nineteenth century, 265
    finance, 263
    financial position of, 266
    fiscal problems, 274
    fiscal reform in, 280
    fragmentation, 272
    functions and city size, 282
    organizational problems, 274, 276

Local government (*Continued*)
   problems, radical reform to,
      285
   public awareness of, 279
   radical solutions to, 280
   range of responsibilities, 267
   reform, 264
   revenue, 267
   since World War II, 267
   structural reforms in, 280
   transfer of responsibilities
      from, 281
   two-tier structure of, 282
   unification of, 283
Localism and working-class
   neighborhoods, 167
Localization economies, 87
Locational flexibility, 89
Location decision, 80, 192
Location of an individual
   house, 190
Location or physical space, 193,
   195
Location theory, 78
Logical positivism, 6
London, Ontario, 4, 22, 61–62
Long Beach, California, 124
Long waves, 33
Los Angeles, California, 20, 22,
   45, 52, 58, 59, 109, 119,
   124, 140, 169, 207, 235,
   238, 246, 252, 254, 264,
   269
   housing stock in, 118
   printed circuit industry in,
      239
   SMSA, 118
Los Angeles–Long Beach, 23,
   227, 273
   residential mobility rate, 163
Los Angeles–San Diego,
   125–126
Louisville, Kentucky, 22, 252
Low-class residential, 113
Lower Great Lakes area, 11,
   39, 45, 53, 124
Low family status, 154
Low-income families, 169, 189
Low-income groups, 105
Low-income households, 191
Low-income housing, 179, 190,
   200
Low-rent areas, 112
Low-revenue high-cost uses,
   277
Lowry model, 13
Low value-added industries,
   70
Low value-added industries in
   central Canada, 72
Lynn, Massachusetts, 45

Machine-tool industry, 78
Madison, Wisconsin, 22
Major regional nucleations, 246
Major regional shopping center,
   121
Male/female wage-rate
   differentials, 182
Managers and professionals,
   176
Manhattan (New York City), 39,
   123, 178, 230, 254
Manufacturing, 62, 63
   belt, 69, 75, 77, 78, 84
   central clusters of, 231
   components of, 69
   employment, location of,
      227
   heartland, 46, 75
   intraurban location of, 236,
      237
   land use, 132
   location of, 10, 68, 78
   plant, 84
Maps, 10
Margin of production, 129
Marketing, 89
Market-oriented economies,
   178
Market potential, 24
Market system, 206
Marxist perspectives, 6
Material input, 81
Mathematical models, 13
Mature industrial capitalism,
   35, 47, 49, 89
Maximum place utility, 190
Meat-packing industry, 104
Medicaid, 275
Medical centers, 242–243
Medicare, 91
Medium-class residential, 113
Megalopolis, 49, 51
Memphis, Tennessee, 22
Mercantile, 36
   capitalism, 7
   city, 101–102
   frontier era, 41
Metropolitan, 126
   areas, 57
   era, 101
   finance, 263
   fringe, 200
   governments, two-tier, 286
   nonmetropolitan moves,
      reasons for, 198, 199
   regions, 122
   wholesale-retail service
      centers, 21
Metropolitanism, 106
Miami, Florida, 22, 23, 58, 59,
   251, 252, 264, 284

Middle industrial revolution
   railway era, 228
Middle suburban ring, 121
Migration, 2, 4, 46, 47, 110
Millage (mill.) rate, 146
Milwaukee, Wisconsin, 22, 23,
   51, 252, 279
   black ghetto in, 171
   city of, 172
   residential mobility rate, 163
   SMSA, 172
Minimum aggregate travel
   costs, 133
Minimum convenience service
   centers, 21, 24
Minimum requirements
   approach, 17–18
Minneapolis, Minnesota, 264
Minneapolis–St. Paul, 20,
   22–23, 123, 180, 252, 284
   residential mobility rate, 163
Minority groups, 208
   mobility of, 163
Minority women, 252
Mismatch hypothesis, 260
Mobile, Alabama, 22
Mobility, 154
Mobility and life cycle/lifestyle,
   163
Monocentric (or single-
   centered) city, 130, 190,
   246
   metropolises, 238
   patterns, 140
   population densities in, 136
Monopolistic control of land,
   177–178
Monopoly capitalism, 89
Monopoly consumer, 135
Monopoly power, 129
Monopoly producer, 135
Monopoly rent, 135
Montreal, Quebec, 4, 19, 20, 22,
   37, 38, 60, 61, 62, 64, 66,
   109, 158, 251, 252, 264, 284
   French/English dimension in,
      158
   residential structure of, 159
   urban community, 285
Mortgage, 166, 207, 209
   companies, 188
   debt, 187
   lenders, 205, 206
   lending, discrimination in,
      208
Motion-picture industry, 90
Motor vehicles, 235
Motor bus, 116
Multicentered city
   (polynucleated), 131, 139,
   191, 226

Multinational corporations, 35, 88
Multiple car ownership, 24
Multiple-family housing, 200, 215
Multiple-function districts, 278
Multiple nuclei model, 112
Multiple-plant corporations, 92–94, 96
Multiplier, 16
Multiplier and city size, 17
Municipal income tax, 281
Municipalities, 272
    expenditures by, 268
    sources of revenue, 269
Municipal payroll, 270
Murder rates in black areas, 172

NASA, 52
Nashville, Tennesee, 22
Nashville–Davidson County, 284
Nassau County, New York, 284
Nassau–Suffolk, 23
National corporations, 34
National housing programs, 186
National industrial capitalism, 34, 43, 112
National policy (in Canada), 61
Natural drainage areas, 278
Natural gas industry, 64
Neighborhood, 110, 177, 204, 205, 240, 245
    centers, 246
    deterioration, 199
    nucleations, 245
    preservation committees, 178
    tipping, 196
Neoclasssical economic approach, 189
Neoclassical economics, 6–7
Neoclassical view, 8
Net natural population increase, 29, 123, 227
Newark, New Jersey, 22, 23, 103, 215, 226, 227, 251, 252, 264, 273
    black population in, 123
    residential mobility rate, 163
New Haven, Connecticut, 22
New housing starts, 101, 187
New office space, 254
New Orleans, Louisiana, 22, 37, 39, 75, 102–103, 215, 223, 252
New Stanton, Pennsylvania, 73
New York, New York, 10, 22, 23, 24, 37, 38, 39, 58, 59, 70, 102, 103, 106, 119, 123, 163, 207, 215, 227, 230,

252, 254, 264, 265, 269, 270, 273, 275
New York metropolitan area, 20, 44–45, 117, 123
    residential mobility rate, 163
New York–New Jersey metropolitan area, 123
New York–New Jersey Port Authority, 279
New York State Urban Development Corporation, 179
Nodal region, 20
Nondurable goods, 69, 70
Nonfamily households, 186, 194
Nonlabor costs, 86
Nonmetropolitan, 57
    counties, 55, 57
    growth, 55, 122
    to metropolitan moves, 198
Non-white ghettos and residential location, 169
Norfolk, Virginia, 22, 45
North Vancouver, B.C., 231
Not-for-profit sector, 18
Nuclear energy, 47
Nucleations, 242, 245
Number of households by sex and race, 183

Oakland, California, 22, 39, 59, 215, 251, 284
Obsolescence, rate of, 187
Occupational status, 153
Office, 178
    employment, 240
    employment, location of, 254
    location and new technologies in, 256
    space, 254–256
    suburbanization of, 256
    theory of location, 255
Oklahoma City, Oklahoma, 22
Omaha, Nebraska, 22
Orlando, Florida, 22
Oshawa, 4, 66
Ottawa, Ontario, 22, 61, 62
Ottawa–Hull, 4, 61, 64
Outer city, 174, 262
Outer suburban ring, 121, 122, 123
Outlying business district, 113, 131, 133, 243
Outmigration, 64, 66
Overspeculation, 100
Oxnard, California, 124, 125

Parkways, 119
Partial shopping service centers, 21
Pasadena, California, 124

Paterson, New Jersey, 228
Paterson–Clifton–Passaic, residential mobility rate, 163
Patterns, 6
Pay equity, 182
Peak densities, 141
Peak-value intersection (PVI), 133
Peoria, Illinois, 22
Percentage zoning, 145
Peripheral areas, 188, 259
    locations in, 235
    plants located in, 235
Petroleum, 64
Pharmaceutical drug industry, 95
Phenomenological approach, 6
Philadelphia, Pennsylvania, 22, 23, 37, 45, 58, 102, 105, 109, 163, 215, 221, 223, 226, 227, 252, 264, 270, 273
    residential mobility rate, 163
Philosophical perspective, 5–6
Phoenix, Arizona, 22, 23, 58, 100, 264
Physically handicapped, 189
Pittsburgh, Pennsylvania, 22, 23, 45, 46, 51, 95, 103, 161, 163, 227, 252, 273, 284
    residential locations, 191
    residential mobility rate, 163
Place utility, 191, 197
Planned industrial parks, 121, 123
Planned shopping centers, 240
Planning, 178
Plant immigration, 231
Plants, out-migration of, 231
Plants in a random spread, 235
Policy making, 93
Political economy and social space, 174–175
Pollution control, 276
Polycentric, 123, 126, 131, 190, 235
    city, 246, 247
    galactic metropolis, 140
    metropolises, 238
    patterns, 140
    structure, 259
Poor, 192, 275
    housing, 53
    non-whites, 189
Population, 151
    density, 24, 137, 151
    density curves, 138
    growth, 49, 115
    growth rates, 55
    models, 127
    size, 153

Port cities, 37
Portland, Oregon, 22, 23, 251, 252
Positivist, 5
Postindustrial society, 64
Postwar suburbs, 120
Poverty, 218, 275
    feminization of, 181, 183
    and homicide risk in black ghettos, 172
    rate, 180
Prefabricated buildings, 120
Primary industries, 62
Primary wholesale-retail service centers, 21, 24
Primate rank-size distribution, 41
Printed circuits industry, 238
Printing districts, 241
Private property rights, 265
Private-sector financial institutions, 117
Privatization of public housing, 189
Probability models, 13
Processed products, 93
Processing, 73, 93
    cost of, 81
    plants, 84, 94
Producer services, 239
Product and process development, 93
Product and process innovation, 88, 92
Product cycle, length of, 236–237
Product differentiation, 89
Production, 78
    costs, 81, 86
    facilities, 94
    and living costs, 128
    of motor vehicles, 75
    process, stages of, 69
    workers, 44, 75, 86
    workers, changing geographical distribution of, 230
Productivity, 38, 78, 91
Profit maximizing, 80
Profits, 8
Property industry, 189, 223
    model of, 205–206
Property insurance companies, 205–206
Property investors, 205–206
Property owners, 144
Property rentals, rate of return on, 214
Property tax, 123, 133, 145, 187, 256, 268, 269

Property values, 208
Prourban, 222
Providence, Rhode Island, 22
Public and private transportation, 184
Public and quasi-public land uses, 98
Public enterprise, 78
Public health, 218
Publicly induced rent, 135
Public-private partnership in development, 120, 122, 220
Public-sector housing, 188, 204
Public transportation, 52, 117, 133, 181, 241, 255, 271, 285
    facilities, 133
    systems, 276
Public utilities, 205
Public water and sewer systems, 100
Puget Sound urban region, 19, 52, 67
Pure public goods, 271
Push and pull hypothesis, 29
Putting out, 182

Quantitative techniques, 12
Quebec City, Quebec, 22, 37, 60, 61, 62
Quebec–Hull, 4

Race, 140, 153
Racial composition, 142
Racial discrimination, 219
Racial minorities, 192
Racial transition, 199
Radial growth, 107–108
Railroad companies, 103, 228
    belt-line, 228
Railroad line, 103
Railroad network, 61, 228
Railroad tracks, 39, 104
Rail transport, 51
Raleigh–Durham, North Carolina, 279
Rank-size distribution, 40–42, 46, 53, 60
Rapid transit, 106, 108, 115, 285
    stations, 121
    system, 109
Rate of aging, 186
Rate of construction, 187
Rate of family formation, 115, 186
Raw-material locations, 84, 85, 94

Raw materials, 81, 93
Re-agglomeration, 90
Real estate agents, 198–199, 205–206, 213
    and black communities, 172
    contact network of, 214
    roles of, 213
Real estate boards, 178
Real estate industry, 144–145
Recession, 32
Recombinant DNA technology, 89
Recreational and social amenities, 165
Red Deer, Alberta, 66
Redevelopement, 120, 179, 218–219, 223–224, 245
    costs and benefits, 221
    evolutionary model of, 219
Redlining, 207, 224
    characteristics of, 207
    notion of risk, 207
Rees model, 195
Regina, Saskatchewan, 4
Regional centers, 246
Regional factors in location theory, 80
Regional input-output analysis, 13
Regional multiplier, 16
Regional nucleations, 246
Regional shopping centers, 119–121
Regression analysis, 13
Renovating, 118
Rental housing, 189
Rent differentiation, 112
Renters, 176, 218
Replacement demand, 186
Research and development, 88, 92, 94
Research-oriented universities, 78, 94
Residential, 107, 111, 113, 152
    land use, 98, 132
    mobility and public policy, 161, 164
Residential location, 164, 184, 195–196
    behavioral approach to, 195–199
    decision process, 196
    decision to move, 196, 197
    "empty-nest" syndrome, 196
    external stress, 196
    internal stress, 196
    life-cycle changes, 196
    lifestyle changes, 196
    market-oriented perspectives on, 201

model, 189, 191
model, criticism of, 192
relocation decision, 196–198
Resource development, 60, 62
Resource-owning households, 8
Resource-processing industries, 77
Restructuring the city, 115
Retail activities, 227, 240–241
clustering of, 241
employment opportunities, 252
establishments, 248
geographic range of, 250
nucleations, 248
spatial aspects of, 240
Retail sales, percent change in, 251
Retail structure, 249
geography of, 240
mental maps of, 249
suburbanization of, 250
Retirement stage in life cycle, 165
Revenue productivity, 270
Ribbons, 242, 243
Richmond, Virginia, 22, 23, 106
Riverside, California, 125
Road and highway land uses, 98
Rochester, New York, 22, 23
Rooming houses, 114, 179
Row housing, 120
Rural areas, 24
Rural/urban fringe, 99, 123, 131, 138, 147
Rural/urban shift, 151
Rust belt, 52

Sacramento, California, 22
St. Catharines–Niagara, 4, 61
Saint John, N.B., 4
St. John's, Newfoundland, 4, 60, 61
St. Louis, Missouri, 22, 23, 39, 58, 103, 142, 207, 215, 264, 270, 273
Sales tax, 270
Salt Lake City, Utah, 22
San Antonio, Texas, 22, 58, 251–252
planned shopping centers in, 253
San Bernardino, California, 124
San Diego, California, 22, 23, 52, 58, 125, 279
San Francisco, California, 22, 39, 59, 109, 123, 155, 243, 246, 252, 256, 264, 269

San Francisco–Oakland, 23, 226–227, 273
residential mobility rate, 163
San Jose, California, 23, 59, 251, 252
Santa Ana, California, 124, 252
Santa Barbara, California, 52, 124
Santa Monica, California, 124
tenants' movement in, 178
Saskatoon, Saskatchewan, 4
Savings-and-loan associations, 210, 213
Scale and interdependence, 16
Scale economies, 90
Scales of analysis, 13
School districts, 265, 272
Scientific method, 6
Scranton–Wilkes-Barre, 22
Seattle, Washington, 22, 52, 112, 248, 251, 264
hierarchy of retail nucleations, 247
Seattle–Everett, 23
Secondary wholesale-retail service centers, 21
Second-generation immigrants, 111
Sectoral growth, 108
Sector model, the, 111
Sector pattern, 106
Segregated patterns and self-interested behavior, 168
Segregation, 142, 145, 153
mechanistic definition, 154
as a process, 154
Semiconductor industry, 87
Sentiment and symbolism, 222
and residential location, 169
Service charges, 270, 276
Service sector, 182
Service society, 35
Settlement pattern, 47
Shopping behavior, 24
Shopping centers, 259, 277
sales volumes of, 252
Shreveport, Louisiana, 22
Silicon Valley, 59, 87
Single-family homes, 154, 159, 194, 213
Single-function districts, 278
Single-industry, 62
Single-parent households, 108, 122, 166
and residential development, 35, 219
Single women, 123

Site value, 146
taxation, 147, 281
Size of households, 122
Skid row, 245
Slum clearance, 188
Slumlords, 207
Snow belt, 52–54
Snow belt–sun belt shifts, 55, 75
Social area analysis, 149–151, 158, 192
application, 154
Social/cultural processes, 3
Social disorientation, 152
Social distance, 150
in higher-income suburbs, 151
and the probability of interaction, 150
Social engineering, 285
Social fixed-overhead capital, 88
Social human ecology, 6
Social justice, 218
Social (or class) rent, 136
Social safety net, 91
Social space, 192–193, 204
patterns of, 159
Social status, 161, 219
Socioeconomic inequalities, 53, 148
Space costs/transportation costs trade-off, 136
Spatial conflicts, 177
Spatial differentiation within the metropolis, 110
Spatial division of labor, 24, 92
Spatially distributed data, 13
Spatial patterns, 2, 5, 126
lagged nature of, 3
Spatial segregation, 200
Spatial separation of economic activities, 103
Spatial separation of social classes, 102, 105
Spatial structure, 2–3
and communication technology, 258
Special districts, 272, 273, 277
Specialization, 24, 151
Specialized areas, 241, 242, 243
Specific zoning, 144
Speculation, 107
Sphere of exchange, 8
Sphere of production, 8
Spillover hypothesis and black suburbanization, 174
Spillovers, 276
Spokane, Washington, 22, 252
Springfield, Massachusetts, 22
S-shaped curve, 27

Stamford, Connecticut, 23
Staple products, 36, 60
Strategic raw materials, 92–93
Streetcar, 113, 116
    network, 108
    suburbs, 108, 121
Structuralist, 6–7
Subcontracting, 90, 182
Suburban, 4, 94, 101, 121–123,
        126, 176, 226–227, 240, 246
    to-central city journeys to
        work, 119
    circumferential highway
        pattern, 134
    communities, 277
    housing, 184
    labor pool, 256
    malls, 250
    planned regional shopping
        malls, 123, 248, 251
    research parks, 94
    tract new-home sales,
        118–120
Suburbanization, 52, 53, 105,
        108, 118, 136, 151, 189,
        216, 247, 255
    of blacks, 142
    of offices, 257
    of population, 117
Suburbs, 119, 142, 222, 243,
        251, 254, 261, 274
    indices of disparity in, 264
Subways, 108, 184
Sudbury, Ontario, 4, 84
Sun belt, 52, 53, 87
Supermarkets, location of,
        252–254
Superregional malls, 247, 253
Supply-driven renewal stage of
        development, 220
Supply-side subsidies, 188, 189
Surgical and medical
        instruments industry, 95
Surplus product, 27
Symmetrical family, 182
Syracuse, New York, 22
Systems of cities, 24

Tampa, Florida, 22
Tax base, 218
Tax-free bonds, 100
Techniques for analysis, 6
Technological change, 34–35,
        49, 78, 115
Technological control, 93–95
Telecommunications
        technology, 259
Tenants' associations, 178
Tenements, 106, 179
Terminal charges, 54, 81, 84
Tertiary activities, 49, 62

Textile industries, 52, 86
Thompson, Manitoba, 84
Threshold of business activity,
        246
Thunder Bay, Ontario, 4
Times Square, redevelopment
        of, 178
Toronto, Ontario, 3, 4, 20, 22,
        24, 52, 61–62, 64, 66, 105,
        109, 113–114, 123, 230, 234,
        243, 244, 246, 269, 274
    incumbent upgrading in, 224
Total transportation costs, 82
Trade union movement, 44, 90
Traditional shopping street,
        242–244
Transaction center, 178
Transfer zoning, 145
Transit companies, 108
Transportation, modes of, 81
Transportation cost, 80–81, 83,
        85, 96, 128
    curve for finished products,
        83
    and distance, 81
Transportation networks, 117
Transport corridors, 59
Transport innovations, 103
Transshipment points, 84
Trenton, New Jersey, 22
Trois-Rivières, Quebec, 4
Trolley coach, 116
Truck transport, 81, 117
Tucson, Arizona, 22
Tulsa, Oklahoma, 22, 23, 123,
        264
Turnover costs, 255

Undoubling, 186
Unemployment, 43, 123, 178,
        219
    gang wars and drugs, 174
Unimproved capital value
        (UCV), 146
United States
    constitutional frameworks in,
        263
    durable goods manufacturing
        in, 71
    manufacturing in, 75
    nondurable goods
        manufacturing in, 71
    preindustrial, 228
    urbanization in, 29
    urban system, 36
Upper-income groups, 105
Upper-income white suburbs,
        123
Upward mobility, 110
Urban, 3, 7, 35, 44, 59, 69
    arterial ribbons, 244

conflict analysis, 177
decay, 69, 216
development and economic
    cycles, 32, 103
encroachment on prime
    fruitlands, 99
functions, economy of scale
    for, 283
infrastructure, 31, 122
land-use models, 127
population, models of, 136
renewal, 188
retail location, 240
retail pattern, major
    components of, 242
revitalization, 202, 203, 218
rural fringe, 145
social space, 149
social movements, 10
Urban analysis, components of,
    5, 6
Urban areas, 14
    creativity in, 153
    as productive units, 29
Urban arterial, 242
Urbanization, 27, 153
    causes of, 27
    economies/diseconomies,
        87–88
    and social relationships, 151
User fees, 100, 268
Utica, New York, 22
Utility districts, 100

Vacancy rate, 163, 186, 187
VA loan program, 118, 187–188
Value, labor theory of, 10
Value added, 69, 70
Value-added per
    production-worker hour, 75
Value and quality of housing
    unit, 193
Vancouver, B.C., 4, 22, 62, 66,
    204, 230, 231
    light rail line, 109
Vancouver–Victoria, 66
Vandalism, 208, 217
Victoria, B.C., 4
Von Thünen's concept of
    economic rent, 128, 130

Walnut Creek–Concord, 256
Waltham, Massachusetts, 228
War on poverty, 120
Washington, D.C., 20, 22, 23,
    70, 77, 180, 207, 215, 252,
    254, 264, 266, 273
    residential mobility rate,
        163
Waterfront locations, 177, 228
Water transport, 81, 104

Waves of accumulation, 30
Weight loss, 82, 93, 94, 96
    in manufacturing, 83
    variations in, 83
White-collar occupations, 153
White-collar workers, 176
White population, 250, 260
White exurbanization, 142
Wichita, Kansas, 22, 23, 264
Williamsburg Bridge, 276
Wilmington, Delaware, 22
Windsor, Ontario, 4, 61, 64, 66

Windsor–Quebec City axis,
    1971, 65
Winnipeg, Manitoba, 4, 22, 62,
    64, 66
    unicity, 285
Women, 180, 183
    in central cities, 180
    in the labor force, 122, 150
    office workers, 256
    and public transportation,
        181
    and social space, 179

Young adulthood, stage in life
    cycle, 165
Youngstown, Ohio, 22

Zonation of land uses, 130
Zone in transition, 111
Zoning, 143, 178, 222, 275
    appeals of, 144
    ordinances, 263
    and performance standards,
        144, 145
    and planning, 144, 145